THE QUESTION OF GOD

This important new text by a well-known author provides a lively and approachable introduction to the six great arguments for the existence of God. Requiring no specialist knowledge of philosophy, an important feature of *The Question of God* is the inclusion of a wealth of primary sources drawn from both classic and contemporary texts. With its combination of critical analysis and extensive extracts, this book will be particularly attractive to students and teachers of philosophy, religious studies and theology, at school or university level, who are looking for a text that offers a detailed and authoritative account of these famous arguments.

- **The Ontological Argument** (sources: Anselm, Haight, Descartes, Kant, Findlay, Malcolm, Hick)

- **The Cosmological Argument** (sources: Aquinas, Taylor, Hume, Kant)

- **The Argument from Design** (sources: Paley, Hume, Darwin, Dawkins, Ward)

- **The Argument from Miracles** (sources: Hume, Hambourger, Coleman, Flew, Swinburne, Diamond)

- **The Moral Argument** (sources: Plato, Lewis, Kant, Rachels, Martin, Nielsen)

- **The Pragmatic Argument** (sources: Pascal, Gracely, Stich, Penelhum, James, Moore).

This user-friendly books also offers: • Revision questions to aid comprehension • Key reading for each chapter and an extensive bibliography • Illustrated biographies of key thinkers and their works • Marginal notes and summaries of arguments.

Dr Michael Palmer was formerly a Teaching Fellow at McMaster University and Humboldt Fellow at Marburg University. He has also taught at Marlborough College and Bristol University, and was for many years Head of the Department of Religion and Philosophy at The Manchester Grammar School. A widely read author, his *Moral Problems* (1991) has already established itself as a core text in schools and colleges. Other publications include *Paul Tillich's Philosophy of Art* (1984), the six-volume *Paul Tillich: Hauptwerke/Main Works* (ed., 1990), *Freud and Jung on Religion* (Routledge, 1997) and *Moral Problems in Medicine* (1999).

THE QUESTION OF GOD
An introduction and sourcebook

Michael Palmer

London and New York

First published 2001 by Routledge
11 New Fetter Lane, London EC4P 4EE

Simultaneously published in the USA and Canada
by Routledge
29 West 35th Street, New York, NY 10001

Reprinted 2002

Routledge is an imprint of the Taylor & Francis Group

Designed and Typeset in Garamond and Sabon
by Keystroke, Jacaranda Lodge, Wolverhampton
Printed and bound in Great Britain
by TJ International Ltd, Padstow, Cornwall

British Library Cataloguing in Publication Data
A catalogue record for this book is available from the British Library

Library of Congress Cataloging in Publication Data
Palmer, Michael F., 1945–
    The question of God : an introduction and sourcebook / Michael Palmer.
        p. cm.
    Includes bibliographical references and index.
    1. God—Proof. I. Title.

BT103 .P35 2001
212′.1—dc21   00–065304

ISBN 0–415–22386–5 hbk
        0–415–22387–3 pbk

For
John Heywood Thomas

CONTENTS

PLATES

PREFACE

There are many arguments for and against the existence of God, and this book is not intended to be a compendium of them. Rather it offers a critical assessment of what are, beyond dispute, six of the most important arguments for God within the Western theological tradition, and couples that analysis with an anthology of some of the primary texts associated with them. There are, however, two classes of reader for whom this work is specifically designed. First, there are those who have just started a programme of study in this area, either at school or university level; and second, there are those more general readers who, lacking professional support, wish by themselves to gain some idea of the momentous debates and great literature that this area covers. To this second group I should add that this book requires no initial knowledge of philosophy, that technical terms are kept to an absolute minimum, and that I have tried, in line with some other books of mine, to make this one as 'user-friendly' as possible.

To this end I have employed a somewhat unusual format, which I should explain here. Each chapter is split into five sections: (1) Commentary; (2) Questions; (3) Sources; (4) Key Texts; and (5) Bibliography. These are, I hope, self-explanatory, with the first and third sections being the most important. The Commentary is my own summary and appraisal of the argument under discussion, liberally peppered with exercises and short biographies to assist the reader. The Sources are the primary texts to which I sometimes refer during the course of my analysis. So, for example, when examining Anselm's ontological argument in Chapter 1, I cite Anselm's original *Proslogium*, which may then be read in the appropriate section.

If the inclusion of primary sources turns this book into a rather unusual hybrid – part textbook and part anthology – it also and inevitably raises the question posed by any sourcebook: what to select? This is always a difficult problem, and I am reconciled to the fact that my choices will not be to everybody's taste. To highlight its location, an arrow is positioned in the margin opposite every source reference. Some of the sources, of course, select themselves: Aquinas' 'Five Ways', Paley on design, Hume on miracles, Pascal's Wager, and so on. To these I have added passages which, although sometimes unfamiliar, advance the argument in an interesting direction, even though perhaps running counter to my own in the Commentary. But that, I think, is all to the good. At any event, I believe that there is no substitute for reading primary sources, and that it is always better to let authors speak for themselves than to meet them solely through the writings of others.

For the most part this book incorporates a series of lectures first given at the University of Bristol some years ago as part of an introductory course on the Philosophy of Religion, which makes this the second set of my Bristol lectures that Routledge has published. As with *Freud and Jung on Religion* (1997), the experience of publication has been a problem-free pleasure, and for that I have to thank four people: my commissioning editor Roger Thorp, my production editor Ruth Bourne, and my copy editor Pauline Marsh. I owe a particular debt of gratitude, however, to Moira Taylor, my development editor, who with limitless patience and good humour has been a constant source of constructive ideas and enthusiastic support.

This book has been read in its entirety by Professor John Heywood Thomas, and I have deeply valued his many criticisms and suggestions. It is affectionately dedicated to him as my friend and teacher for over thirty years.

Michael Palmer

USING THE INTERNET

One of the extracts used in this book – Martin's 'Atheism, Christian Theism and Rape' – comes from the Internet. The Internet is now an indispensable resource for academic study, providing students with a wealth of material, including primary sources, lectures, book reviews, and much else besides. The easiest introduction is to use one of the many search engines available, and to type in your request, whether it be a specific philosopher (for example, Anselm) or a specific area of interest (for example, Existentialism). In all probability there will then follow an almost limitless list of web-sites for you to surf. There are, however, some specific web-sites, which are worth mentioning here and which I have found particularly useful.

1. There are three on-line encyclopedias of philosophy: the *Routledge Encylopedia of Philosophy* (www.rep.routledge.com), *The Stanford Encyclopedia of Philosophy* (www.plato.standford.edu) and the *Internet Encyclopedia of Philosophy* (www.utm.edu:80/research/iep/. Equally useful is *The Dictionary of Philosophical Terms and Names* (www.people.delphi.com/gkemerling/dy/) and the research facility at erraticimpact.com. (See Appendix on page 348 for instructions on searching the *Routledge Encyclopedia of Philosophy* for information relating to *The Question of God.*)

2. Some web-sites are excellent for providing links to other sites. *EpistemeLincs.com* includes thousands of sorted links to other philosophy resources, as does *About.com Guide to Philosophy* and *Philosophy in Cyberspace.* The Philosophy Department at Glasgow University (www.gla.ac.uk/Acad/Philosophy/links.html) is a model of its kind, and includes information about other philosophy departments, primary texts, and the job market.

3. Most interesting of all are the dedicated web-sites, providing information on individual philosophers. Again, the various search engines will help here. I have found the following to be particularly intriguing: the sites on Aquinas (www.aquinasonline.com), Hume (www.utm.edu/research/hume/hume.html) and Kant (www.hkbu.edu.hk/~ppp/Kant.html).

chapter 1   THE ONTOLOGICAL ARGUMENT

INTRODUCTION: A PRIORI AND A POSTERIORI ARGUMENTS

The ontological argument has had a long but chequered career. Most famously presented in the eleventh century by St Anselm, abbot of Bec and later Archbishop of Canterbury, it was later rejected by St Thomas Aquinas in the twelfth century, then revived in the sixteenth and seventeenth centuries by Descartes, Spinoza and Leibniz. In the eighteenth century, however, the criticisms made by Kant proved almost fatal, and as a result it was largely ignored for over a century and a half. In our own time, however, interest has been rekindled by the work of philosophers and theologians such as Karl Barth (1931), Charles Hartshorne (1941), Norman Malcolm (1960), Alvin Plantinga (1974) and Carl Kordig (1981).[1]

Certainly it is not difficult to see its fascination. Marked by an extreme formal elegance, it is unique among the arguments for God's existence. This is so because it alone may be classified as an a priori argument, with all other arguments for God's existence being classified as a posteriori arguments. What do these terms mean?

A priori propositions

The terms 'a priori' and 'a posteriori' distinguish between two types of proposition: a proposition that is not dependent on experience and a proposition that is dependent on experience. So the statement 'I cannot be simultaneously in the room and out of it' is an a priori true proposition, whereas the statement 'This ball is square and round' is an a priori false proposition. They are what philosophers call *necessarily true* and *necessarily false*, and no amount of experience or observation will render them otherwise. In one sense, of course, to say that a priori propositions make no appeal to experience is misleading. After all, how can we say this of the two statements just cited when they include words like 'room' and 'ball'? Surely without some experience of, say, being in rooms and playing with balls, these terms would have no meaning at all. The point is that, once we know what these terms mean, no experiential evidence is then required to determine the truth or falsity of the a priori statements in which they appear. Take the proposition 'All bachelors are unmarried men'. While it is certainly true that one requires some experience

---

1. See Barth, *Fides Quaerens Intellectum*, Munich, Chr. Kaiser, 1931. English translation by Ian Robertson, London, SCM Press, and Richmond, Va., John Knox Press, 1960; Hartshorne, *Man's Vision of God* (1941), reprinted Hamden, Conn., Archon Books, 1964; Anselm's *Discovery*, La Salle, Ill., Open Court, 1965, and *The Logic of Perfection*, La Salle, Ill., Open Court, 1962; Plantinga, *The Nature of Necessity*, Oxford, Clarendon Press, 1974, and *God, Freedom, and Evil*, New York, Harper & Row, 1974; and Carl Kordig, 'A Deontic Argument for God's Existence', *Noûs*, 15, 1981, pp. 207–228. According to Graham Oppy's taxonomy there are no fewer than seven major types of ontological argument. See Oppy, *Ontological Arguments and Belief in God*, New York, Cambridge University Press, 1995.

of the world to talk of bachelors in the first place, the truth of this proposition does not depend on this experience but on the *definition of the term*: being a bachelor simply *means* being an unmarried man. In this sense it is a priori true: it provides its own verification and may be regarded as true in itself.

The same, however, cannot be said of a posteriori propositions, like 'The sun is shining' or 'My cat is brown'. Whether these statements are true or false can only be decided by observation, by direct confrontation with the evidence. They are what we call *contingently true* or *contingently false* because their truth or falsity is dependent (or contingent) on the circumstances, on what the world happens to be like. Unlike a priori propositions, therefore, a posteriori propositions are not universally and unconditionally true or false, nor do they provide their own corroboration, but are justified only to the extent that they are verified or falsified by our experience. So we must distinguish between the statement 'A bachelor is an unmarried man' and the statement 'Mr Jones is a bachelor'. The first is a necessarily true proposition, proceeding from the definition of the term; and the second is a contingent proposition, which subsequent evidence may show to be either true or false.

A posteriori propositions

Which of the following statements are a priori true or false or a posteriori true or false?

Triangles have three sides.

The sun will rise tomorrow.

Reagan was President of the United States.

If A knows B, and if B knows C, then A knows C.

If A precedes B, and if B precedes C, then A precedes C.

No object can be completely red and green all over.

A man cannot walk on water.

Every man has a mother.

I am reading this sentence.

A straight line is the shortest distance between two points.

EXERCISE 1.1

With this distinction between a priori and a posteriori behind us, we can now appreciate why the ontological argument for God's existence is unique. All the other arguments we shall look at – for example, the causal argument, the argument from design, the argument from miracles, and so on – base their case on what is the most plausible explanation for various experiences we have of the world. They do not argue that a particular explanation is by definition the only possible explanation but rather that, on the evidence before them, it is the only likely explanation. To this extent they have the form of a posteriori arguments. The ontological argument, on the other hand, is alone in maintaining that God's existence can be established without recourse to *empirical* evidence – that is, evidence drawn from experience – and thus solely on the basis of an analysis of the concept of God. It is not, then, that our

Why the ontological argument is unique

experience justifies the conclusion that God exists. It is rather that the very idea of God implies that God exists, in much the same way as, say, the idea of a triangle implies a three-sided figure of 180 degrees. The proof of God lies, as it were, in the logic of 'God', in the logical implications of what we must say about him. To speak of God and to deny his existence is, as we shall now see, a contradiction in terms.

St Anselm (*c.* 1033–1109) (left), Our lady of Bec (centre), Lanfranc (right)

Born in Aosta, Italy, Anselm entered the monastery at Bec in Normandy as a novice in 1060, succeeding Lanfranc as prior in 1063, and becoming abbot in 1078. Under his direction Bec became a great intellectual centre, celebrated throughout Europe. It was during this period that Anselm wrote his *Monologium* (1076) and *Proslogium* (1077–1078), the latter containing his famous ontological argument. Anselm continued his ecclesiastical career in England; it culminated in his appointment as the second Norman Archbishop of Canterbury in 1093. Generally recognized as the greatest theologian of his day, he emphasized the priority of faith over reason, maintaining that truth was obtained only through *fides quaerens intellectum* or 'faith seeking understanding'. Anselm's tomb at Canterbury became an object of veneration and pilgrimage and he was canonized in 1494.

ANSELM'S ARGUMENT: STAGE I

⇒

The ontological argument was first presented by St Anselm in his *Proslogium* (chs 2–4) and in his *Responsio* to a contemporary critic, the monk Gaunilo (SOURCE 1: PP. 31–33).[2] Many present-day commentators argue that *Proslogium* 2 and 4 present a different argument from *Proslogium* 3 and the *Responsio*. Whether this is so is a matter of some debate. What we can say, however, is that the second phase is structurally dependent on the first, and that in the first phase Anselm is concerned to establish the *fact* of God's existence and in the second the *nature* of that existence.

Anselm's definition of God

Anselm's *Proslogium* 2 begins with a famous definition of God: 'God is something than which nothing greater can be conceived' ('aliquid quo nihil maius cogitari possit'). The word 'greater' is admittedly ambiguous; but it soon becomes clear that Anselm does not mean greater in size but greater in value – indeed, in the *Proslogium, maius* ('greater') is sometimes replaced by *melius* ('better'). Nor does Anselm make any attempt to fill in the details of God's greatness or superiority. Nothing is said, for instance, of the attributes traditionally ascribed to him: his omnipotence, omniscience, immutability,

2. Extracts are taken from *Anselm: Basic Writings* (*Proslogium, Monologium*, Gaunilo's *On Behalf of the Fool, Cur Deus Homo?*) trans by S. N. Deane, with an Introduction by Charles Hartshorne, La Salle, Ill., Open Court, 1962.

impassibility, etc. Such descriptions of God's qualities are rendered irrelevant by the very generality of Anselm's definition. For whatever the qualities attributed to God (love, mercy), this definition means that God must possess them to an absolute and ultimate degree (the most loving, the most merciful). Hence it is not just that God is the greatest conceivable being but rather that, being this being, he must possess all conceivable qualities to the greatest conceivable extent.

Having set up this definition, Anselm proceeds to the second phase of his argument. Some people, of course, will deny that God exists. Such a one is 'the fool' of Psalm 14:1, who 'hath said in his heart: "There is no God."' But what are we to make of this fool? The first thing to say is that, though he may deny God's actual existence in reality (*in re*), he does not, and cannot, deny God's existence in his mind or understanding (*in intellectu*). This is so because to deny the existence of anything must presuppose the existence of that thing as an idea, i.e., as a thing existing in the mind. For example, if I deny that unicorns exist, I must have an idea in my mind of what a unicorn is like (i.e., a horse with a horn in its forehead). If I did not have this prior concept of what a unicorn is, I could not then deny that such a thing exists. I would indeed have no idea of what I am denying. Now Anselm argues that the same holds for atheists. To deny God's existence must presuppose a concept of God in the mind. If they have no such concept, no such denial can be made.

Anselm next asks an apparently innocuous question. Which is greater, something that exists in the mind or something that also exists in reality? First consider the following:

Of the following choices, which would you prefer? Are they all appropriate examples of Anselm's argument? What conclusions do you draw from your answers?

EXERCISE 1.2

1 To be shot by an imaginary bullet or by a real one?

2 To be given an imaginary million dollars or a real million dollars?

3 To fight an actual war or an imaginary one?

4 To fall in love with a real person or a fictional person?

5 To combat a real threat or an imaginary threat?

Anselm's conclusion is that a thing is more valuable or more terrible, or indeed more anything, if it exists in reality than if it exists in the mind only. And from this he draws another conclusion: that the notion of the greatest conceivable being cannot be conceived in thought alone but must actually exist; that, in other words, any being that exists in reality will be greater than any being that is merely conceived of; and that consequently the greatest conceivable being, God, must exist.

In order to clarify this, let us formulate Anselm's argument in a slightly different way. In differentiating between two kinds of existence – existence-in-the-mind and existence-in-reality – Anselm is presupposing an important distinction between what later philosophers have called *intentional* and *formal* existence. Briefly put, intentional existence refers to the content of my idea (for example, my idea of a baseball bat), and formal existence refers to the real thing in the world to which that idea refers (for example, the actual baseball bat in the locker-room). Anselm's own example is between the ideas a painter has before painting (intentional) and the finished product, the actual painting (formal).

Now, to repeat, Anselm has claimed that the concept of God *is* the concept of the greatest conceivable being. He has also argued that even the atheist, in denying the existence of God, is denying the existence of this particular being. In other words, *both* the believer and the unbeliever, in affirming and denying God, have an idea of this being in their minds to begin with: they are both thinking of the *intentional* existence of God. But, Anselm asks, can the idea of God, as the greatest conceivable being, be merely the idea of an intentional existence? It cannot, he says. Why? Because if God's existence is solely intentional, then it will be possible to conceive of a greater God, a God who is not only an idea but who actually exists, who also has formal existence. *For something is greater if it is both conceived of and exists than if it is merely conceived of.* Thus it follows that the being which exists only intentionally cannot be the greatest conceivable being: it lacks the extra attribute of real, formal existence. We may put this another way. Which is greater (i.e., which contains the greater number of attributes), the 'idea of X' or the 'idea of an X that actually exists'? Clearly the latter because, unlike the former, it has the extra attribute of actual existence: it alone exists apart from the mind's conception of it. Thus the thing that is the greatest conceivable being must exist. For if it did not exist I could conceive of a greater thing by simply adding to it the extra quality of existence.

> Therefore, if that, than which nothing greater can be conceived, exists in the understanding alone, the very being, than which nothing greater can be conceived, is one, than which a greater can be conceived. But obviously this is impossible. Hence, there is no doubt that there exists a being, than which nothing greater can be conceived, and it exists both in the understanding and in reality.[3]

We can now see why Anselm considers atheists fools. If they accept the idea of God but deny his actual existence, they are involved in a blatant contradiction, a contradiction as obvious as the denial that triangles are three-sided figures. They are denying what is *implied* in the idea of the greatest conceivable being – namely, that this being must exist, must possess the additional attribute of formal existence. What they are saying, in effect, is that

---

3. *Ibid.*, p. 11.

they reject the existence of a being whose being implies existence: 'that a being that must exist does not exist'. Thus their foolishness is exposed in the meaningless of their claim.

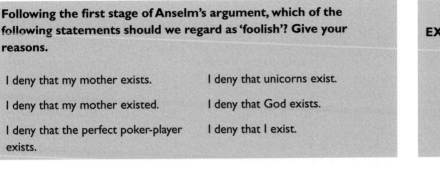

Following the first stage of Anselm's argument, which of the following statements should we regard as 'foolish'? Give your reasons.

I deny that my mother exists.   I deny that unicorns exist.

I deny that my mother existed.   I deny that God exists.

I deny that the perfect poker-player   I deny that I exist.
exists.

EXERCISE 1.3

ANSELM'S ARGUMENT: STAGE 2

The second stage of Anselm's ontological argument is contained in his reply to his fellow Benedictine, the monk Gaunilo of Marmoutier, near Tours in France. Gaunilo's criticisms are important for two reasons: first, they foreshadow many later objections to the argument; and second, they allow Anselm, in his *Responsio*, to strengthen his case in a way which, many believe, makes it much more persuasive.[4]

Gaunilo's criticism appears, fittingly enough, under the title *On Behalf of the Fool* (*Liber pro Insipiente*). Gaunilo employs a *reductio ad absurdum* argument to reveal what he considers the basic flaw in Anselm's proof – that is, he argues that the argument must be false because of the absurdities that result if it is accepted. The absurdity that Gaunilo presents is an ontological argument for the existence of a perfect island.

> Now, if someone should tell me that there is such an island, I should easily understand his words, in which there is no difficulty, but suppose that he went on to say, as if by a logical inference: 'You can no longer doubt that this island which is more excellent than all lands exists somewhere, since you have no doubt that it is in your understanding. And since it is more excellent not to be in the understanding alone, but to exist both in the understanding and in reality, for this reason it

Gaunilo's criticism of Anselm's argument

---

4. From early on the *Proslogium* appeared with Gaunilo's criticisms attached. This was Anselm's own suggestion. His first biographer and contemporary, Eadmer, writes: 'A friend sent this [Gaunilo's refutation] to Anselm who read it with pleasure, expressed his thanks to his critic and wrote his reply to the criticism. He had this reply attached to the treatise which had been sent to him, and returned it to the friend from whom it had come, desiring him and others who might deign to have his little book to write out at the end of it the criticism of his argument and his own reply to the criticism.' Eadmer, *The Life of St Anselm*, ed. and trans. R. W. Southern, Oxford, Clarendon Press, 1972, p. 31.

must exist. For if it does not exist, any land which really exists will be more excellent than it; and so the island already understood by you to be more excellent will not be more excellent.[5]

Gaunilo's analogy of the perfect island

For Gaunilo, therefore, the fact that you can define the greatest conceivable being does not mean that such a being exists. This can be shown by applying the ontological argument to the notion of a perfect island. The definition of a perfect island would be an island 'than which nothing greater can be conceived'. If we follow Anselm, having the *idea* of this all-perfect island (intentional existence) must imply that this island also exists (formal existence). But this is quite absurd. For if it is not absurd, you could prove, simply by defining not only the perfect island but anything else for that matter, that all these things actually exist – for example, the perfect razor blade, the perfect car, or, more sensationally, as the Haights have suggested, a perfectly evil being (SOURCE 2: PP. 33–34). Gaunilo continues:

⇒

> If a man should try to prove to me by such reasoning that this island truly exists, and that its existence should no longer be doubted, either I should believe that he was jesting, or I know not which I ought to regard as the greater fool: myself, supposing that I should allow this proof; or him, if he should suppose that he had established with any certainty the existence of this island. For he ought to show first that the hypothetical excellence of this island exists as a real and indubitable fact, and in no wise as any unreal object, or one whose existence is uncertain, in my understanding.[6]

Gaunilo's criticism is directed against Anselm's argument in *Proslogium* 2. Anselm's *Responsio*, however, draws on the argument already presented in *Proslogium* 3. The ontological argument has so far tried to show that the notion of the greatest conceivable being must include actual existence. But what type of existence? Existence that can fail to be (i.e., contingent existence) or existence that cannot fail to be (i.e., necessary existence)? Anselm maintains that it must include the latter. For it is self-evident, he argues, that that which *cannot* be conceived not to exist (necessary being) is greater than that which *can* be conceived not to exist (contingent being). It follows, therefore, that only necessary being is adequate to the notion of the greatest conceivable.

> And it assuredly exists so truly, that it cannot be conceived not to exist. For, it is possible to conceive of a being which cannot be conceived not to exist; and this is greater than one which can be conceived not to exist. Hence, if that, than which nothing greater can be conceived, can be conceived not to exist, it is not that, than which nothing greater can be conceived. But this is an irreconcilable contradiction. There is, then, so

---

5. *Appendix to St. Anselm*, trans. S. N. Deane, Chicago, Open Court, 1963, p. 158.
6. *Ibid.*, p. 159.

truly a being than which nothing greater can be conceived to exist, that it cannot even be conceived not to exist; and this being thou art, O Lord, our God.[7]

A man is reading the obituary columns of *The Times*. Suddenly he shouts out, 'Good gracious! A catastrophe! Elvis has died!' He reads on, and then shouts again. 'Oh no, another catastrophe, even worse! God has died!'

Do you consider this likely/unlikely or possible/impossible? What distinctions would you draw between Elvis' death and God's? What relevance has your answer for Anselm's argument?

EXERCISE 1.4

In his *Responsio* Anselm exploits the difference between contingent existence and necessary existence to great effect. It is of course true that an island can always be thought of as not existing. Islands, even the most excellent, are, like razor blades and cars, contingent things, and a contingent thing is by definition something that can either exist or not exist. Gaunilo's mistake, however, is to suppose that contingent existence also applies to God, whereas in fact God, as the greatest conceivable being, must belong to a different order of being, necessary being. To repeat, a necessary being is one that *cannot not exist*: it *must* exist. God is therefore the greatest conceivable being precisely because in him alone is existence a constitutive property rather like a triangle which cannot be thought of without its three intersecting sides. Gaunilo, in other words, has made an illegitimate jump from one order of being to another – from contingent being to necessary being – and has thus missed the whole point of the ontological argument. For as that argument demonstrated, God is the only being that cannot be thought of as not existing; or, to put the same point another way, *God is the only being to which the ontological argument can apply because he is the only being whose non-existence is inconceivable.*

Anselm: the necessity of God's existence

DESCARTES' ONTOLOGICAL ARGUMENT

As we noted at the beginning of this chapter, Anselm's ontological argument lay neglected for over five centuries. In the seventeenth century, however, it was revived by René Descartes. As we shall see, Descartes' version provides an important support for Anselm's argument in his *Responsio*.

Descartes' argument appears in the fifth of his *Meditations* (SOURCE 3: PP. 35–36).[8] He begins with the notion of the supremely *perfect* being and not with Anselm's negative formulation of a being than which no greater can be *conceived*. As the supremely perfect being, God must possess all possible

Descartes' definition of God

⇐

---

7. *Op. cit.*, p. 11.
8. In *Philosophical Writings*, translated and edited by Elizabeth Anscombe and Peter Geach, with an Introduction by Alexandre Koyré, London, Thomas Nelson & Sons, 1954, pp. 101–108.

René Descartes
(1596–1650)

One of the most influential of all philosophers, Descartes was born at La Haye in Touraine, France, finally settling in Holland in 1628. His first major book, *Discourses* (1637), is a set of three short essays on physical and mathematical topics, and is generally regarded as the first great philosophical work in French, having as its Preface the famous *Discourse on the Method*. Here Descartes introduces his procedure known as 'methodical doubt', which leads in turn to the famous formula *cogito, ergo sum* ('I think, therefore I am'). Descartes' ontological argument appears in the fifth of his *Meditations on First Philosophy* (1641) and is strikingly similar to St Anselm's. He later set out a more systematic exposition of his philosophy in *Principles of Philosophy* (1644). In 1649 Descartes was persuaded, much against his better judgment, to become private tutor in philosophy to Queen Christina of Sweden. However, his heavy workload – tutorials began at 5 a.m. – and the dreadful climate took their toll, and on 11 February 1650 he died of pneumonia.

perfections, amongst which we must include the perfection of existence. Here Descartes' argument dovetails with Anselm's in *Proslogium* 2. Any being that ever failed to exist, or could ever fail to exist, would be less perfect than any being for which this would be an impossibility. Existence must therefore be a *necessary attribute* of the perfect being.

This conclusion Descartes clarifies with an example. Consider, he says, the idea of a triangle. Having this idea clearly does not require that this idea exists – it remains the product of my imagination – but what it does require is that what I am thinking about must have the property of having the sum of its three angles equal to two right angles, and so on. Now, it is in this sense, Descartes continues, that we must understand existence as a necessary attribute of the perfect being. Just as the sum of its angles equalling 180 degrees is entailed in the very idea of a triangle, so existence is entailed in the very idea of a perfect being. Consequently it would be just as contradictory to think of this supremely perfect being without existence as it would be, to use another example, to conceive of a mountain without a valley.

Here Descartes considers a possible objection. The fact that I cannot conceive of a mountain without a valley does not mean that there are such things, actual mountains and actual valleys. All that is entailed is that *if* there is a mountain there is also a valley. Cannot the same be said of God? Cannot it also be said here that, while I certainly may be able to conceive of God as existing, this does not mean that he actually exists? Descartes' reply recalls Anselm's reply to Gaunilo. This is like saying 'God, who must exist, does not exist.' Whereas the notion of a mountain or valley does not include the attribute of existence, the idea of a perfect being does. It is therefore self-contradictory to deny the existence of the supremely perfect being when the attribute of existence is a necessary component of his perfection. In God alone, therefore, we are entitled to infer his existence from the notion of him as the supremely perfect being.

THE TWO STAGES OF THE ARGUMENT: A SUMMARY

The two stages of the ontological argument may be summarized briefly as follows:

FIRST STAGE: EXISTENCE IS A PERFECTION

Anything that exists will be greater or more perfect than anything that does not exist. Put otherwise, anything that has both intentional and formal existence will be greater or more perfect than anything that has only intentional existence. Thus, whether we define God as the greatest conceivable being (Anselm) or as the being possessing every perfection (Descartes), this being must exist.

SECOND STAGE: NECESSARY EXISTENCE IS A PERFECTION

Anything that cannot fail to exist will be greater or more perfect than anything that can fail to exist. Put otherwise, anything that has necessary existence will be greater or more perfect than anything that has contingent existence. Thus, whether we define God as the greatest conceivable being (Anselm) or as the being possessing every perfection (Descartes), this being must necessarily exist.

> **SUMMARY:**
> THE TWO STAGES OF THE ONTOLOGICAL ARGUMENT

KANT'S CRITICISM OF THE ONTOLOGICAL ARGUMENT (FIRST STAGE)

Of the many criticisms levelled against the ontological argument, the most famous is that made by Immanuel Kant in his *Critique of Pure Reason* of 1781 (SOURCE 4: PP. 36–38).[9] Although Kant's objections are directed at Descartes' version, his criticisms are generally held to be equally applicable to Anselm's.

Kant's criticism of the first form concentrates on Descartes' claim that 'Existence is a perfection'. For in saying this Descartes is suggesting that existence is a *property* or *characteristic*, the presence or absence of which will determine whether some things are perfect and others are not. Much the same idea occurs in Anselm's *Proslogium* 2. He too proposed that something is greater if it is both conceived of and exists (i.e., has intentional and formal existence) than if it is merely conceived of (i.e., has only intentional existence). Here, then, it is the extra *attribute* of existence that is required for the greatest being to be the greatest conceivable being. However, it is Kant's contention that existence is not a property, characteristic or attribute at all, and that accordingly the ontological argument is impossible. This he summarizes in his famous, but admittedly rather obscure, remark that 'Existence is not a predicate'.

---

9. Trans. Norman Kemp Smith, London, Macmillan, 1929.

**Immanuel Kant
(1724–1804)**

A dominant figure in the Western philosophical tradition, Kant was one of the last philosophers to construct a complete philosophical 'system', comprehensive in scope and covering most of the major issues of philosophy. This is all the more remarkable because Kant, on the face of it, was a man of limited experience, living the uneventful life of a scholarly bachelor in his provincial birthplace of Königsberg, East Prussia – prompting the German poet Heinrich Heine to speak of the contrast between Kant's outward life and 'his world-destroying thought'. In common with other philosophers of the Enlightenment, Kant attaches particular importance to man's rational faculty – his capacity to think objectively and apart from his own circumstances or preferences – a view developed in perhaps his greatest work, the *Critique of Pure Reason* (1781), which also contains his celebrated attack on the main theistic arguments, including the ontological argument. A less technical exposition of his views is found in his *Prolegomena to any Future Metaphysic* (1783). His criticism of all metaphysical speculation did not, however, prevent him from developing an argument for God, as a 'postulate' of morality, in his *Critique of Practical Reason* (1788).

Kant: 'existence' is not a predicate

What is a predicate? Predicates are words that refer to the properties of things. For example, in the statement 'Mary is blonde', 'Mary' is the subject and 'is blonde' is the predicate. Other predicates might be 'is a musician', 'is a midget', 'has a toothache', and so on. The question now is: Is 'existence' a predicate? Does this word refer to the property or quality of a thing? Kant's reply is that, since when we say that something exists we are *not* ascribing to it any particular attribute, the word 'existence' cannot be considered a real predicate. His point here is that, if 'existence' is not a predicate, then there can be no quality of existence to which that word refers. And if there is no quality of existence, then Descartes and Anselm cannot claim that existence is something that God must possess (as a quality) to be God.

He illustrates this point with an example. What is the difference between a real hundred pounds and an imaginary hundred pounds? Obviously considerable. I can purchase something with the former but not with the latter – this, after all, was the point originally made by Anselm. But what is the difference between them in the *concept* 'a hundred pounds'? None whatever. The concept is the same in both cases. Indeed, I could add any number of characteristics (or predicates) to the concept. I could talk about the colour of the notes, the watermark, and the picture of the Queen. But however many we may cite, these predicates would not provide extra evidence that the money exists. All they do is offer additional information so that, when anyone seeks the hundred pounds, they know what to look for. When they find anything that has these characteristics, they can say that the hundred pounds actually exists.

Let us take another – and true – example. A sociology student is taking his final university exam. He has done no revision but is blessed with an active imagination. In his essays he cites the work of the 'distinguished Polish sociologist Poniatowski, whose work has unfortunately not been translated into English'. He provides graphs and figures to illustrate Poniatowski's theories. The examiners are impressed by the student's erudition and he obtains his degree. But Poniatowski does not exist, and the examiners have been duped into believing that he does by the attributes heaped upon him. But no matter how many predicates are thus ascribed to the fictional Pole, he remains a fiction: nothing in the world corresponds to the concept and its predicates. Thus existence is not part of the concept but something which must be independently validated.

Answer the question at the end of this dialogue. How does your reply relate to Kant's argument?

EXERCISE 1.5

Wizard: I can create anything that you can imagine.
Boy: I am imagining a unicorn.
Wizard: Describe it to me.
Boy: Well, basically it's a white horse with a golden horn in the middle of its forehead. And it has a brown patch on its left flank. And it answers to the name of 'Rupert'.
Wizard (waving his wand): Now, open the door.
Boy: Gracious, it's my unicorn! Hello, Rupert.
Wizard: So how does your description of your imagined unicorn differ from your description of this real unicorn? Are they the same or not?

Interestingly enough, much the same point Kant has just made about predicates reappears in Bertrand Russell's famous theory of descriptions. This theory, first outlined in his article 'On Denoting' (1905), is generally held to be Russell's most original contribution to philosophy.[10]

Like Kant before him, Russell is concerned to distinguish between propositions about properties or characteristics (predicative propositions) and propositions about the objects, if any, possessing these properties (existential propositions); or, to put it another way, between the *is* of predication ('The so-and-so is such-and-such') and the *is* of existence ('There is a so-and-so'). The failure to distinguish between these two types of proposition results in the kind of confusion apparent in the ontological argument. 'Existence', he repeats, is not a predicate.

Russell's theory begins with a perplexity. It appears possible not only to talk intelligibly about things that do not exist but also to create the impression that, because we can talk about them, they must in fact exist, that there must be

Russell: the theory of descriptions

---

10. 'On Denoting', *Mind*, 56, October 1905, pp. 479–493. Also available in Russell, *Logic and Knowledge: Essays 1901–1950*, ed. R. C. Marsh, London, Allen & Unwin, 1956, pp. 39ff. Russell summarizes his theory of descriptions in his *History of Western Philosophy*, London, George Allen & Unwin, 1946, pp. 859–860. A useful discussion of the theory is to be found in *Modern British Philosophy*, ed. Bryan Magee, London, Secker & Warburg, 1971, pp. 24–27, 145–149.

Bertrand Russell
(1872–1970)

The grandson of the British Prime Minister, Lord John Russell, and godson of John Stuart Mill, Russell is the most famous representative of twentieth-century British empiricism. His early work was in mathematics, culminating in his *Principia Mathematica* (1910–1913), co-authored with A. N. Whitehead. Applying similar analytical methods to philosophical questions, Russell, influenced also by his pupil Wittgenstein, developed the doctrine of Logical Atomism, from which he believed one could construct a complete description of the world. Throughout his long life, Russell was prominently engaged in matters of social and political concern. Jailed for his pacifism during the First World War, he was active on behalf of women's suffrage and nuclear disarmament. He was also an outspoken critic of religion, regarding it 'as a disease born of fear and as a source of untold misery to the human race'. His agnostic alternative and its vision of a universe of blind matter first appear in *The Free Man's Worship* (1903), and he is particularly dismissive of the theistic proofs in his seminal essay 'Why I am Not a Christian' (1927). He was awarded the Order of Merit in 1949 and the Nobel Prize for literature in 1950.

some object being referred to. For example, suppose I say, 'The present King of France does not exist', and suppose you then ask, 'What is it that does not exist?' When I reply, 'It is the present King of France', I am attributing some kind of existence to this King, even though no present King of France actually exists. Let us take another example. If I say, 'The President of the United States is over 50 years old', then this statement is true if the person denoted by the description 'The President of the United States' is over 50 years old, and false if he is not. But what if I now change the country referred to and speak of 'Great Britain' instead? It is evidently untrue to say that 'The President of Great Britain is over 50 years old' because there isn't such a person; but if it is then *false* to say 'The President of Great Britain is over 50 years old', this seems to imply that 'The President of Great Britain is not over 50 years old' is *true* – which again suggests that there is such a being, that there must be a President of Great Britain for us to be able to deny that he is over 50 years old.

Russell's way round this difficulty is as follows. When I ask a question like 'Do cows exist?' I am in fact asking: 'Is there an object which satisfies those properties associated with the *description* "cow"?' If there is not, I may justifiably conclude that such animals do not exist. In other words, a statement that affirms the existence of X is affirming that there is an object answering to the description 'X'; and a statement that denies the existence of X is denying that there is any such object answering to such a description. Thus 'Cows exist' means 'There are X's such that "X is a cow" is true'. Similarly, to say 'Fairies do not exist' is the same as saying 'There are no X's such that "X is a fairy" is true'. Now, in each case we are not talking about the existence or non-existence of certain objects, but rather about *whether or not there are actual instances of certain descriptions*. Thus neither statement is a statement about cows or fairies. Rather, the first is a statement asserting that there are actual instances of the description 'cow'; and the second is a statement asserting that there are no such instances of the description 'fairy'.

How does this affect the ontological argument? These examples tell us how deceptive the word 'exists' can be. While grammatically a predicate, it is not a real predicate because its logical function is entirely different: its role is not to ascribe a quality or property to a particular thing, but rather to assert that there is an actual instance of a particular description. Now, if this is the case, then the question before Anselm and Descartes is not whether 'existence' must be predicated of God (as the perfect being), but rather whether the concept of the greatest conceivable and most perfect being is instantiated anywhere in existence – whether the description of God as this being is anywhere fulfilled in reality. The ontological argument is, in other words, based on 'bad grammar': it confuses a grammatical predicate with a real one, hypothetical existence with actual existence. For if, as Kant claims, 'existence' is not a real predicate, then it is not enough for Anselm and Descartes to tell us what is required for God to be God or what constitutes an accurate description of his attributes. For what we must then discover is whether there is anything in the real world that meets these requirements or fulfils this description – and here it is an open question whether we shall be successful or not. It is accordingly no proof of God's existence to say that nothing can be *called* God unless it really exists, because it does not follow from saying this that there is anything that *is* God. Nothing, in other words, can be defined into existence. From the definition of X, it does not follow that X exists.

Application of Russell's theory of descriptions to the ontological argument

What, according to Kant and Russell, is the error contained in the following dialogue?

President: I need a new Secretary of State.
Adviser 1: Well, there's Smith, Mr President. He speaks eight languages, is very rich, and thinks you're wonderful.
Adviser 2: And then there's Jones, Mr President. He also speaks eight languages, is very rich, and thinks you're the best President we've ever had.
President: What sensible men! But how can I choose between them? They seem identical.
Adviser 1: Oh, Smith's the better choice, Mr President. He has one quality that Jones lacks.
President: What's that?
Adviser 1: He exists.

EXERCISE 1.6

In Descartes' version of the ontological argument, but no less in Anselm's, existence is a property an object must have to be perfect. Thus, in determining whether A is more perfect than B, where A is otherwise identical to B, A's quality of existence and B's lack of existence will be decisive: A will be more perfect. But what, we may ask, is the comparison between? It is between an object that exists and an object that does not exist. How then can a comparison be made?

For what one is in fact deciding between is a something and a nothing. Thus to compare, as in the example above, an existing Smith with a non-existent Jones is to compare a real candidate with something that *could not be a candidate because of its non-existence.* To repeat: when we say, for example, that candidates A and B are equally loyal and good with money, we are attributing certain *properties* to them; but if we then say that A is a better candidate than B because A exists and B does not exist, we are not conceding to A an *additional* property but rather asserting that the thing we have described as having these qualities *also exists*; that, indeed, in the matter of which person the President should appoint, there is only one choice. Accordingly, to exist is not more perfect than not to exist. For, if it were, it would suppose that existence is itself a quality which makes for perfection. But it isn't. For to say that something exists is not to introduce an additional quality but to say that there is in the world an X in which the qualities already specified are actually exhibited.

KANT'S CRITICISM OF THE ONTOLOGICAL ARGUMENT (SECOND STAGE)

Kant: 'necessary existence' is not a predicate

Kant, who has already attacked the notion that 'existence' is a real predicate, now attacks the notion that 'necessary existence' can be a predicate. He begins, however, by agreeing with Descartes that certain concepts require certain essential and necessary features. So having three angles is an essential and necessary feature of triangles, and to state otherwise would be self-contradictory. But to be logically consistent about triangles does not mean that triangles exist; or, to give another example, while it is necessary that bachelors be unmarried, it is not necessary that bachelors exist. And the same, Kant concludes, can be said of the concept of God as a necessary being. So all that the ontological argument can claim is that 'If anything is God, then it exists necessarily' – that this subject and this predicate are logically conjoined – but not that there is anything existing that is God.

> To posit a triangle, and yet to reject its three angles, is self-contradictory: but there is no contradiction in rejecting the triangle together with its three angles. The same holds true of the concept of an absolutely necessary being. If its existence is rejected, we reject the thing itself with all its predicates; and no question of contradiction can then arise.[11]

Descartes, of course, has already rejected this conclusion. While it may be true, he says, that the definition of X does not entail the existence of X, this is not the case with God. For here the definition of God as the perfect being *does* require the impossibility of his non-existence. In all other cases, therefore, it is true that subject and predicate may be rejected together as referring to nothing that exists; but in the case of God we have a unique predicate – the predicate

11. *Ibid.*, p. 502.

of not-capable-of-not-existing – which is necessary to this unique subject. Thus to deny the existence of this subject – and this subject alone – involves a contradiction. For necessary existence, as Anselm pointed out to Gaunilo, is a unique attribute of the greatest conceivable being.

In the following statements, what are the criteria for using the word 'exist'?

EXERCISE 1.7

Mountains exist.	Unicorns exist.
Toothaches exist.	Squares exist.
Gravity exists.	I exist.
Ghosts exist.	God exists.
Delusions exist.	

In order to demolish Descartes' position, Kant produces a remarkable, and highly influential, argument. The reason why, he contends, God cannot be an exception to the rule – why, in other words, the predicate of necessary being cannot be attributed even to this subject – is that *the predicate itself is meaningless and self-contradictory*. This damning conclusion derives from Kant's distinction between *analytic* and *synthetic* propositions. He defines them as follows:

> *Analytic proposition*: a proposition in which the predicate term is contained within the subject term (for example, A triangle is a three-sided figure).

> *Synthetic proposition*: a proposition in which the predicate term is not contained within the subject term (for example, This ball is red).

Kant's distinction between analytic and synthetic propositions

Without going into all the philosophical ramifications of this distinction, it is sufficient for our purposes to note that the difference between analytic and synthetic propositions corresponds to the difference between necessary and contingent propositions already mentioned at the beginning of this chapter. An analytic proposition, in other words, is a logically necessary proposition (known a priori), and a synthetic proposition is an empirical and contingent proposition (known a posteriori). The first, we may say, gives no information about the world and our experience of it; and the second does give such information about the world and is based on our experience of it. Accordingly, the validity of an analytic proposition, unlike a synthetic one, depends solely on the terms or symbols it employs, and is therefore impossible to deny without contradiction.

Kant now exploits this difference to the full. To argue that there is a necessary being is to say that it would be self-contradictory to deny its existence; and this in turn would mean that at least one existential statement (i.e., a statement that refers to existence) has the status of a necessary truth. But this cannot be allowed. *For it is logically impossible for any existential proposition to be logically necessary.*

What does Kant mean by this? To clarify his argument, let us retrace our steps. As we have seen already, the distinguishing feature of an existential statement is that its truth or falsity is established on the basis of our observations of the world. This means in turn that the possibility of this statement's being either true or false is a *permanent* possibility. In other words, it is not logic that decides here (a priori) but fallible experience (a posteriori). This, of course, does not mean that we can never be *certain* about the truth or falsity of our empirical judgments. For example, the statements 'The sun cannot stand still in the heavens' and 'All men die' we regard as empirically certain because our experience is so overwhelmingly against the opposite happening. The point is, however, that no matter how great our certainty, we cannot exclude the *possibility* of such events, namely, that the sun could stand still (as reported in the Old Testament following a command of Joshua) and that one man might not die (as is claimed of the prophet Elijah). To repeat, such things would be factually extraordinary but not logically impossible. That there is this alternative is, accordingly, part and parcel of an existential statement being an existential statement. All existential propositions can therefore be denied without self-contradiction.

But what of necessary propositions? To deny the truth of a necessary proposition like 'A bachelor is an unmarried man' is not just false but self-contradictory because here the word 'bachelor' implies 'unmarried man': the truth of the proposition follows logically from the definitions we have employed. All that is being stated here is what it means to be a bachelor or, more exactly, what the correct verbal usage is when we use this particular word. But whether there are such things as bachelors, or whether any particular man is a bachelor, is another matter and can only be decided by appeal to experience. To say, then, that 'This bachelor is not unmarried' is absurd: it can be shown to be false by appealing to nothing more than logic and the meaning of terms. But to say 'My brother is not unmarried' is not absurd, and whether it is true or not will depend on the evidence gathered.

We thus arrive at the following important conclusion. The truth of a synthetic (and existential) statement contains the possibility of its being otherwise (for example, no matter how certain I am that this ball is red, it might not be); and the truth of an analytic (and non-existential) statement does not contain the possibility of its being otherwise (for example, for me to deny that this triangle is a three-sided figure is absurd and self-contradictory).

The predicate of 'necessary existence' is meaningless and self-contradictory

This conclusion enables Kant to reject the second stage of the ontological argument. To assert, with Anselm and Descartes, that God exists necessarily – and thus to assert that the possibility of God's non-existence is impossible – is to be profoundly confused about the nature of those statements that can and cannot refer to existence. They are saying in effect that a synthetic proposition has here attained the status of an analytic proposition; or rather that here we have an assertion which, although requiring the possibility of being false, now excludes it. Indeed, we may go further and say that any attempt to establish a *proof* of the existence of *anything* must be radically misconceived. For proof, which excludes doubt, cannot apply to anything whose existence is being discussed, and where therefore the possibility of its non-existence must be entertained. The ontological argument, of course, denies this; but it does so, says Kant, only by first building the notion of existence into the concept of the thing it is seeking to prove exists, that is, by producing what he calls a 'miserable tautology'. This, then, is Kant's final condemnation of the ontological argument: the argument succeeds only to the extent that it proves what it has already assumed.

> The attempt to establish the existence of a supreme being by the famous ontological argument of Descartes is therefore merely so much labour and effort lost; we can no more extend our stock of [theoretical] insight by mere ideas, than a merchant can better his position by adding a few noughts to his cash account.[12]

THE ONTOLOGICAL ARGUMENT REVISITED: FINDLAY AND MALCOLM

Although Kant was not the first philosopher to employ the argument just mentioned – we find much the same in Hume[13] – the general thrust of his argument is duplicated by many critics, not least in our own day: Bertrand Russell, for example, uses it in his famous conversation with Frederick Copleston.[14] It is also employed to great effect by J. N. Findlay in his much-discussed article of 1948, entitled 'Can God's Existence be Disproved?' (SOURCE 5: PP. 38–40).[15] In this remarkable essay Findlay, by considerably tightening Kant's argument, presents not merely a criticism of Anselm but an ontological argument in reverse: a formal *disproof* of divine existence. Anselm, he argues, was right to say that only a being that exists necessarily can be the proper focus of religious belief: one could hardly be expected to worship a being whose existence is merely contingent. This requirement is, however, impossible because, following Kant, nothing can be conceived to exist that cannot also be conceived not to exist. We thus arrive at what Charles Hartshorne has called 'Findlay's paradox':[16]

Findlay's disproof of God

⇐

12. Ibid., p. 507.
13. So: 'I shall begin with observing that there is an evident absurdity in pretending to demonstrate a matter of fact, or to prove it by any arguments *a priori*. Nothing is demonstrable, unless the contrary implies a contradiction. Nothing, that is distinctly conceivable, implies a contradiction. Whatever we conceive as existent, we can also conceive as non-existent. There is no Being, therefore, whose non-existence implies a contradiction. Consequently there is no Being, whose existence is demonstrable. I propose this argument as entirely decisive, and am willing to rest the whole controversy upon it.' *Dialogues Concerning Natural Religion* (1779), edited with an Introduction by Norman Kemp Smith, London, Thomas Nelson, 1947, p. 189.
14. 'The Existence of God – A Debate' (BBC, 1948). Reprinted in Russell, *Why I am Not a Christian*, London, George Allen & Unwin, 1967, pp. 133–136.
15. *Mind*, April 1948. Reprinted in *New Essays in Philosophical Theology*, ed. Antony Flew and Alasdair MacIntyre, London, Macmillan, 1955, pp. 47–67.
16. *Anselm's Discovery*, Lasalle, Ill., Open Court, 1965, p. 37. Hartshorne assesses Findlay's argument on pp. 255–261.

Findlay's paradox

(a) A contingent being would not deserve worship.

(b) A necessary being is a logical absurdity.

Or to express it another way:

(a) Only necessary being can be the object of religious devotion.

(b) Necessary being cannot be attributed to an actually existing God.

What religion requires is thus denied by logic. Findlay, while admitting his debt to Kant, finds it strange that Kant should not have seen that this is not just a criticism of Anselm but rather an inversion of the ontological argument itself, not a proof but a dis-proof of the existence of God. For if it is (a) logically possible that God does not exist (i.e., if we conceive God as contingent), then God's existence is not merely doubtful but *impossible*, since by definition nothing capable of non-existence could be God at all. But if we say (b) that God is therefore not capable of non-existence (i.e., that his existence is necessary), we are repeating that his existence is not merely doubtful but *impossible*, since nothing incapable of non-existence can exist. Thus Findlay concludes:

> It was indeed an ill day for Anselm when he hit upon his famous proof. For on that day he not only laid bare something that is of the essence of an adequate religious object, but also something that entails its necessary nonexistence.[17]

Malcolm's reply to Findlay

Not surprisingly, Findlay's argument has also been challenged. Charles Hartshorne has pointed out that, if it makes sense to speak, as Findlay has just done, of God's 'necessary non-existence', then it is difficult to see why it does not make sense to speak of its alternative, God's 'necessary existence' – the one implies the other's negation. Findlay has accepted this as a valid criticism.[18] Hartshorne, however, is joined by his fellow American, Norman Malcolm, in a second criticism.[19] The view that all existential propositions are contingent propositions represents a particular tradition in philosophy, extending back to Hume and Kant, but it is not the only one. Malcolm points to the work of his own teacher, Ludwig Wittgenstein (1889–1951), as a case in point. For our purposes, it is sufficient here to note that Wittgenstein in his later period challenges the assumption that all meaningful statements are either analytic or synthetic, and argues instead that the meaning of terms may also be derived from their actual *use* in ordinary contexts, from their function in a particular

---

17. *Op. cit.*, p. 55.

18. 'Some Reflections on Necessary Existence', in *Process and Divinity: The Hartshorne Festschrift*, ed. William L. Reese and Eugene Freeman, La Salle, Ill., Open Court, 1964, pp. 515–527.

19. For what follows, see Malcolm, 'Anselm's Ontological Arguments', *Philosophical Review*, 69(1) January 1960, pp. 41–62. Reprinted in: John Hick and Arthur C. McGill (eds), *The Many-Faced Argument*, London, Macmillan, 1968, pp. 301–320; and (edition used) Alvin Plantinga (ed.), The *Ontological Argument*, London, Macmillan, 1968, pp. 136–159.

'language-game'. Malcolm now applies this principle to Findlay's argument (SOURCE 6: PP. 40–42). Rather than simply dismissing the idea of a 'necessary being' as a meaningless concept, what we must do is to look at the *religious context* in which it is set. What was the original reason for Anselm's introducing this idea in *Proslogium* 3? It was designed to show, says Malcolm, that *God exists in the greatest conceivable manner, the ordinary and contingent way of existing being defective.* The concept of necessary being, in other words, is designed to exclude the possibility of non-existence – which implies a precarious existence or an existence by chance from the concept of the perfect being. And this, Malcolm contends, is not a nonsensical thing to do. For it is not nonsensical to reject the idea of God as a limited being, who either was caused to come into existence or merely happened to come into existence. And neither is it an error of logic to say, in common with the main tradition of theistic belief, that God, if so limited, cannot be the proper object of religious devotion. Here he agrees with Findlay. To be capable of non-existence is to be unworthy of worship.

True to his method, Malcolm clarifies his position by looking to see how the contrast between contingent and necessary being operates in everyday usage. This he does by comparing it to the contrast between *dependence* and *independence.* He maintains that in common language we regard the notions of dependence and independence as respectively inferior and superior. For example, if two sets of dishes are alike in all respects except that one is fragile and the other is not, we regard the fragile set as inferior since it depends on gentle handling for its continued existence. The same is true of the contrast *limited* and *unlimited.* An engine that requires fuel is limited because dependent on its fuel supply, and is thus regarded as inferior to one that is the same in all respects except that it requires no fuel. Similarly, *contingent* beings are limited because dependent on other things (parents, food) both for their coming into existence and for their continued existence. This, however, establishes their inferiority to that which cannot be thought of as being either brought into existence by anything or as depending for its existence on anything; and this can only be what Anselm means when he calls God a *necessary* being, i.e., a being whose non-existence is inconceivable and who thus exists independently of anything whatsoever.

Malcolm now replies to Kant. That God is a necessary being is part of the logic of God's innate superiority. If we deny this and say, with Kant, that necessary existence cannot be a property of God, then we are conceiving of a lesser God than the perfect being. For if anything lacks logically necessary being – that is, if its existence can be denied without contradiction – then it must logically depend for its existence on something else and so be inferior. Far from being meaningless, therefore, the concept of necessary being renders intelligible the idea of God as the greatest conceivable and most perfect being.

This conclusion allows Malcolm to turn the tables on Kant. According to Kant, we remember, all that the ontological argument has established is the logical truth of the conditional proposition '*If* such a being (God) exists, then it necessarily exists'. This proposition, to repeat, like the proposition about triangles, does not entail the existence of anything. But what, asks Malcolm, is

Kant really saying here? He is surely saying that the non-existence of God is in fact conceivable; that despite the logical requirement of necessary existence *if* God exists, he may not actually exist. But this, says Malcolm, involves Kant in a blatant contradiction. At one moment he is saying that he cannot conceive of the non-existence of God and at the next moment that he can. On the one hand, he has accepted that necessary existence is a logical requirement of the concept of God (i.e., cannot be thought of as not existing), and, on the other, denied that it is (i.e., can be thought of as not existing). The result, Malcolm concludes, is a combination of two incompatible propositions: 'God (who must exist) might not exist.' This, it is claimed, resolves Findlay's paradox:

(a) Only necessary being can be the object of religious devotion.
(b) It is self-contradictory to claim that necessary being cannot be attributed to God.

Malcolm's ontological argument

With this argument behind him, Malcolm now proceeds to his own restatement of the ontological proof:

Let me summarize the proof. If God, a being a greater than which cannot be conceived, does not exist then he cannot *come* into existence. For if He did He would either have been caused to come into existence or have *happened* to come into existence, and in either case He would be a limited being, which by our conception of Him He is not. Since he cannot come into existence, if He does not exist His existence is impossible. If He does exist He cannot have come into existence (for the reasons given), nor can He cease to exist, for nothing could cause Him to cease to exist nor could it just happen that He ceased to exist. So if God exists His existence is necessary. Thus God's existence is either impossible or necessary. It can be the former only if the concept of such a being is self-contradictory or in some way logically absurd. Assuming that this is not so, it follows that He necessarily exists.[20]

Much of Malcolm's argument has been already discussed in his reply to Kant; but for clarity's sake it may be unpacked into the following eight stages:

SUMMARY: MALCOLM'S ONTOLOGICAL ARGUMENT

1 God, as the greatest conceivable being, cannot be a limited being.

2 Therefore, if God doesn't exist, he can neither be caused to come into existence nor merely happen to come into existence. Both cases would impose a limitation on God and contradict 1.

3 Similarly, if God does exist, he cannot merely come into existence or cease to exist. Both cases would also impose a limitation on God and so contradict 1.

20. *Ibid.*, p. 146.

SUMMARY:
CONTINUED

4 The implication of 2 is that, if God does not exist, his existence is impossible; and the implication of 3 is that, if he does exist, his existence is necessary.

5 Either God does not exist or he does exist.

6 Therefore God's existence is either impossible or necessary.

7 God's existence is not impossible (i.e., the notion of his existence is not self-contradictory).

8 Therefore God necessarily exists.

John Hick

Hick's reply to Malcolm: the distinction between factually necessary being and logically necessary being

It perhaps goes without saying that Malcolm's argument has also been attacked. The principal objection, voiced most notably by John Hick,[21] is that it confuses two different concepts of necessary being, namely, *factually* necessary being and *logically* necessary being (SOURCE 7: PP. 42–45).

Factually necessary being is the form of existence which is described by Malcolm in premiss 1 and which played such a part in his reply to Kant. It is existence *independent* of any other existence, involving a being which is thus intrinsically superior to any other kind of being. As Malcolm pointed out, it was this sort of existence – an existence without beginning or end and incapable of decay or decomposition – that Anselm meant by 'a being which cannot be

21. John Hick, 'Necessary Being', *Scottish Journal of Theology*, 14, December 1961, pp. 353–369; and 'God as Necessary Being', *Journal of Philosophy*, 57, October 1960, pp. 725–734.

conceived not to exist'. This, indeed, is the scholastic notion of *aseity* (existence *a se*, 'self-existence'), which Anselm describes in his *Monologium*:

> The supreme Substance, then, does not exist through any efficient agent, and does not derive existence from any matter, and was not aided in being brought into existence by any external causes. Nevertheless, it by no means exists through nothing, or derives existence from nothing; since, through itself and from itself, it is whatever it is.[22]

Now it is true that, from premiss 1, we can validly infer 4, that God's existence is either factually necessary or impossible. For if such an eternal and incorruptible being exists, he evidently cannot cease to exist (i.e., his existence is necessary); and if this being does not exist, he cannot, if conceived as eternal, come into existence (i.e., his existence is impossible).

The question now is: Can the existence of God as a factually necessary being be denied? Or rather, can we adopt Kant's tactic and say that, even though we may accept the logical coherence of the concept (i.e., Malcolm's propositions 1–4), we may yet deny that it refers to anything that exists? Malcolm, of course, in his criticism of Kant, has already denied that we can. To reject the existence of a being who is a necessary being (i.e., one that cannot not exist) is a contradiction in terms. This same point now reappears in his own version of the proof. For if, as we have just seen in 4, the choice before us is between God's necessary existence or his impossibility, and if it is not the *assertion* of God's necessary existence that is impossible (and self-contradictory) but its denial, then we may legitimately infer that God necessarily exists (propositions 6–8).

The point is, however, that Malcolm is now talking about *logically* necessary being, that is, about the kind of existence that Descartes was referring to when he likened it to the necessity of a triangle having three sides, i.e., the kind of existence that it would be contradictory to deny. In other words, in propositions 1–4 'necessary existence' means 'factually necessary existence', and in propositions 6–8 it means 'logically necessary existence'. If, therefore, Malcolm's proof is to be consistent, proposition 6, which is the turning-point of his argument, should read 'God's existence is either impossible or *eternal*'. Once translated in these terms, Malcolm's reworking of the ontological proof becomes untenable. For although eternal existence or factually necessary existence cannot be conceived to have a beginning and an end – that would involve a contradiction in linguistic usage – *it can be denied without self-contradiction*. For, as we have noted already, the key to the notion of factual necessity is the idea of aseity, which is causal, and not the idea of contradiction, which is logical. Thus the denial that a being exists *a se* is not self-contradictory. It is not an error of reasoning to reject the idea that there exists a being which nothing could cause to be or cause to cease to be – indeed, to suppose that it is would be contrary to the main biblical tradition, in which atheism, although

---

22. Anselm, *Basic Writings*, pp. 48–49.

considered false and sinful, is not considered self-contradictory. From this it follows that Malcolm cannot infer the logical necessity of 8.

From the necessity of a divine attribute (eternality, aseity) one cannot therefore derive the existence of a being having that attribute. Even if we grant that there is a concept of 'a being which cannot be conceived not to exist', it still remains an open question whether there is an actual instance of this particular concept anywhere in reality. Again, we are not contradicting ourselves if we say that there is no such instance. *The assertion that the concept is logically coherent does not mean that the denial of its existence is logically incoherent.* Thus it is legitimate to conceive that there is not a being which cannot be conceived not to exist. This conclusion does no more than recall Kant's final remark: 'Whatever, therefore, and however much, our concept of an object may contain, we must go outside it, if we are to ascribe existence to the object.'[23]

KARL BARTH: A THEOLOGICAL INTERPRETATION

There remains one last interpretation of the ontological argument which I should like briefly to consider. This is offered by arguably the most influential Protestant theologian of the twentieth century, Karl Barth. Barth's account is highly original and unlike any we have discussed so far.

Born in Basle, Switzerland, Barth was educated in the so-called 'liberal Protestant' wing of the Reformed church. He became, however, increasingly discontented with liberalism and what he saw as its alarming dilution of the Christian message through its accommodation with modern culture. In his *The Epistle to the Romans* (1919) he deplored this rapprochement, emphasizing the radical qualitative distinction between the Christian gospel and the world: God is the 'wholly other', known only through revelation, a view which impinges directly on his own highly distinctive interpretation of the ontological argument (1931). With the advent of Hitler, Barth emerged as the leader of church opposition, expressed in the Barmen Declaration of 1934. Deprived of his professorship at Bonn, he returned to Basle in 1935 and there continued work on his gigantic *Church Dogmatics*, unfinished but of enormous theological influence.

Karl Barth
(1886–1968)

The title of Barth's monograph on Anselm is *Fides Quaerens Intellectum* (*Faith Seeking Understanding*)[24] – which was indeed the original title of Anselm's *Proslogium*. 'I believe in order to understand' (*credo ut intelligam*) was a statement first enunciated by St Augustine (354–430) and later employed by Anselm to clarify the relation between faith and reason. Thus in Chapter 1 of

23. *Op. cit.*, p. 506.
24. *Op. cit.*

the *Proslogium* we read: 'For I do not seek to understand that I may believe (*intelligere ut credam*) but I believe in order to understand (*credo ut intelligam*). For this also I believe, – that unless I believed, I should not understand.'[25]

This gives the key to Barth's interpretation of the ontological argument. Anselm is not here providing an argument whose logic must convince us that God exists but rather one which is an *expression of faith*, in which the existence of God is presupposed. It is hardly surprising, therefore, that the argument should fail as a proof because to provide a proof for the man outside faith was never Anselm's intention. His intention was not to deduce the existence of God from the definition of his being as the greatest conceivable perfection, so that the Fool is a fool precisely because he denies what is already implied, but rather to provide a meditation on the supremacy of God as an *article of faith*, in which the role of the Fool is to confirm the view that it is the believer alone who is in a position to understand. To support this interpretation Barth points to the setting of the proofs, namely, that they begin and end with *prayer*, with an address to God. Given that Anselm's critics, beginning with Gaunilo, ignore this fact, it is not surprising, Barth argues, that they have ignored the theological presupposition of the proofs and accordingly misinterpreted them as a priori philosophical deductions. Anselm's proof is therefore entirely different from Descartes', and so it is 'so much nonsense' to suppose that 'it is even remotely affected by what Kant put forward against these doctrines'.[26]

This interpretation of the ontological argument as an expression of faith is reinforced in Barth's discussion of the specific arguments of the *Proslogium*. Take, for example, the famous definition of *Proslogium* 2: that God is 'something than which nothing greater can be conceived'. This does not present, as is commonly supposed by commentators, a philosophical platform upon which to construct a logical and irrefutable proof of God's existence, but rather provides a theological description, negatively expressed, of *who God is*. In this sense, therefore, the description stands as a 'revealed Name' of God, revealed by God to Anselm in a moment of prophetic insight, and by which he came to recognize the impossibility for faith of denying the existence or the perfect nature of the God designated by that Name. What is revealed, in other words, has less to do with the specific character of God's nature and more to do with the limits imposed on human thought when thinking of him, namely, that it cannot conceive of anything greater. This, Barth maintains, is the absolute rule of thought (*Denkregel*) which the Christian derives from revelation and which provides the norm of all theological thinking: it is an acknowledgement of the complete Christian dependence on God's prior communication of himself to believers. To suppose, therefore, that God could somehow be 'proved' would mean that men need no longer wait upon God's self-revelation for their knowledge of his existence and that they had therefore a degree of independence from him. Neither view, however, is supported by the creator–creature relationship to which holy scripture bears witness.

---

25. *Ibid.*, p. 7.
26. *Op. cit.*, p. 171.

Manuscript page from Barth's *fides quaerens intellectum*

Like Malcolm and Hartshorne, Barth detects a subtle shift in the argument of *Proslogium* 3, with Anselm moving from the demonstration that God exists to an account of the uniqueness of that existence. And here too Barth provides a novel treatment. In the assertion of God's necessary existence – that God is the only being who cannot be thought not to exist – we do not find a logical proof of the impossibility of atheism but a theological statement of the utter dependence of creature upon creator, such that to conceive of the non-existence of God is to conceive also of the non-existence of existence itself. This, too, is an article of faith. For the man of belief the existence of God is the presupposition of his own existence.

> The reason why there is such a thing as existence is that God exists. With his Existence stands or falls the existence of all beings that are distinct from him. . . . Thus, with the prohibition against conceiving anything greater than him and with this prohibition ruling out the thought of his nonexistence – thus does God alone confront man. Thus he and he alone is objective reality.[27]

---

27. *Ibid.*, p. 155.

According to Barth, therefore, the arguments of the *Proslogium* are primarily reflections upon the meaning of the Christian creed, with Anselm always working as a theologian, always reasoning from faith to faith, from what is given in revelation to an explanation of it for those who, while yet believing, do not fully understand. The purpose of the proofs is therefore neither to sustain faith in the believer nor to induce faith in the unbeliever – faith in either case remains the free gift of God – but rather, in the one, to bring joy to faith by increasing understanding, and, in the other, to indicate the limits of understanding without faith.

Criticism of Barth

The most persistent criticism of Barth is that he has here infused Anselm's theology with his own. Without going into this point in any detail, it is worth mentioning, as many others have done, that the book on Anselm is a turning-point in Barth's own theological development, particularly in his growing conviction that no genuine knowledge of God is possible apart from the Christian revelation.[28] For Barth the ideas drawn from secular thought and philosophy are intrinsically different from those of the biblical text, about which only the Holy Spirit can enlighten us, so that the task of the theologian is to present and describe the word of God, and not to indulge in the apologetic task of convincing the unbeliever of his folly.

But is Barth right about Anselm? Does Anselm show an equal lack of apologetic concern, and does he agree that philosophical reasoning can have no bearing upon faith? If we look at Anselm's own account of his intentions, this view is hard to sustain. In the first chapter of the *Monologium*, written a year before the *Proslogium*, he clarifies his position:

> If any man, either from ignorance or unbelief, has no knowledge of one Nature which is the highest of all existing beings . . . and if he has no knowledge of many other things, which we necessarily believe regarding God and his creatures, he still believes that he can at least convince himself of these truths in great part, even if his mental powers are very ordinary, by the force of reason alone (*sola ratione*).[29]

Similarly, in the Preface to the *Proslogium*, Anselm explains that he wants to find a completely independent argument which 'would require no other for its proof than itself alone; and alone would suffice to demonstrate that God truly exists'.[30] Nor, fourteen years later, does Anselm hesitate in grouping the two works together:

> I have written two small works, the *Monologion* and the *Proslogion*, which are intended particularly to show that it is possible to prove by necessary means, apart from Scriptural authority, those things which we hold by faith concerning the divine nature.[31]

---

28. See, for example, Heinz Zahrnt, *The Question of God*, trans. R. A. Wilson, London, Collins, 1969, pp. 88–89.
29. Anselm, *Basic Writings*, pp. 37–38.
30. *Ibid.*, p. 1.
31. *Epistola de Incarnatione Verbi* (*On the Incarnation of the Word*), n.p., n.d., 6, S II, 20, pp. 16–19.

On the evidence of these extracts at least, Anselm seems to be saying that the truth of God's existence can indeed be established through the arguments of reason alone, through arguments that are rationally compelling and without recourse to the authority of the Bible or the church. Thus the contradiction that Anselm believes the Fool has perpetrated, when he denies that God exists after having accepted Anselm's famous definition, should be construed as an error in *logical reasoning*. It is not a contradiction which, in some roundabout way, contrasts the states of belief and unbelief, but one which quite precisely establishes why the Fool is a fool. Here was a man who did not understand 'what was evident to any rational mind', namely, that his own atheism was rendered self-contradictory by the logic of the definition accepted by him.

In support of this view, Charlesworth makes a telling point. If Barth is right, then Gaunilo's attack on Anselm is not simply invalid but irrelevant: he would be criticizing the ontological argument as a rational argument, which Anselm did not intend it to be.

> But this is evidently not how Anselm sees it. Anselm never complains that Gaunilo's criticisms are irrelevant but confronts Gaunilo's objections on Gaunilo's own grounds and attempts to show that they are invalid. In other words, what is obvious in Anselm's reply is that he agrees with Gaunilo's reading of the *Proslogion* argument as a rational proof of the existence of God.[32]

Other critics have pointed out that Barth, in stressing the dependence of belief on God's self-revelation, has correspondingly neglected the account Anselm gives of the role played by reason in the way faith comes to an understanding of what it believes. Barth, of course, is right to underline the difference between the intellectual assent *that* God exists and the commitment of belief *in* the God who exists; but for Anselm the rational justification of the one still remains the necessary precondition of the other, showing that faith is not without logical foundation. Clearly the arguments adduced by Anselm are not designed to show how an appeal to the intellect must lead to faith; but they are designed to show that faith may be reassured by such an appeal, that so cogent are the arguments presented that the believer can, with full confidence, proclaim the intelligibility of his faith. This, after all, explains the role of the Fool. In addressing himself to the man who says there is no God, Anselm is concerned to prove that God does exist; and the foolishness of the Fool consists precisely in failing to see what faith sees, in not appreciating the sheer force of the logic which undergirds faith.

> For although they (the infidels) appeal to reason because they do not believe, but we, on the other hand, because we do believe; nevertheless, the thing sought is one and the same.[33]

---

32. M. J. Charlesworth, *St Anselm's Proslogion*, translated and with an Introduction and philosophical commentary by Charlesworth, Oxford, Clarendon Press, 1965, p. 43. Charlesworth makes the additional point that Anselm's immediate disciples, Rodulfus and Gilbert Crispin, did not interpret Anselm on 'Barthian' lines but themselves adopted a 'rational apologetic', pp. 44–45.
33. *Cur Deus Homo?*, in Anselm, *Basic Writings*, p. 182.

The argument, in other words, remains the same for both, and is not, as Barth supposes, appreciable only within the framework of faith. This, indeed, constitutes the peculiar apologetic strength of the ontological argument: the argument which enlightens believers in their faith is also that which, once accepted, will remove the unbeliever's intellectual doubt *that* God exists and so prepare him, through God's grace, for the full commitment of belief *in* God. Thus one argument simultaneously defends the rationality of God's existence for both belief and unbelief. Whether, of course, Anselm is justified in this is another matter.

CONCLUSION

Aquinas rejects the ontological argument

The ontological argument, while philosophically fascinating, does not resolve the question whether or not God exists a priori. Indeed, even if further refinements should be made to the argument – even if it should be shown that it is a formally valid argument – we would be no nearer to claiming that the argument therefore *proves* that God exists – for the simple reason that we cannot *know* that these premises are true. This is the reason why St Thomas Aquinas (1225–1275) rejects the proof. To move from a definition of God to a demonstration of his existence requires a direct awareness of the divine nature or 'essence' of God that no human being can immediately or naturally have. This is, in effect, the same as saying that the ontological argument is workable only for God himself, and that all we can say is that Anselm's proof is a provisional hypothesis to the effect that, *if* God is the greatest conceivable being, *then* he necessarily exists. In this sense, God himself could know whether the argument works, but we cannot. This is not to say, of course, that no knowledge of God can be obtained. For if all our natural knowledge – as opposed to the knowledge that comes through revelation – comes from the information gained by our senses, it must be possible, if God exists, to demonstrate his existence by a similar procedure, that is, from the most familiar and ordinary facts of our experience. Thus the failure of the a priori proof leaves us with the question of whether God's existence can be established a posteriori.

QUESTIONS

1 In what respects is the ontological proof a unique argument for the existence of God?

2 Carefully explain and distinguish between Anselm's two stages of the ontological argument.

3 How does Gaunilo criticize the ontological argument? Assess Anselm's reply.

4 Analyse the argument presented by the statement 'Existence is not a predicate'.

5 How does Kant employ the distinction between analytic and synthetic propositions in his criticism of the ontological argument?

QUESTIONS
continued

6 Critically analyse Findlay's disproof of the existence of God.

7 Analyse and critically discuss Norman Malcolm's version of the ontological argument.

8 What is the difference between factual and necessary existence? What relevance does this difference have for the ontological argument?

9 Assess the ontological argument for the existence of the Devil. What relevance does this alternative have for Anselm's argument?

10 'The ontological argument is no more than a play on words.' Discuss.

SOURCES: THE ONTOLOGICAL ARGUMENT

1 ANSELM: THE ONTOLOGICAL ARGUMENT[1]

PROSLOGIUM: CHAPTER II

Truly there is a God, although the fool hath said in his heart, There is no God.

And so, Lord, do thou, who dost give understanding to faith, give me, so far as thou knowest it to be profitable, to understand that thou art as we believe; and that thou art that which we believe. And indeed, we believe that thou art a being than which nothing greater can be conceived. Or is there no such nature, since the fool hath said in his heart, there is no God? (Psalm xiv. 1). But, at any rate, this very fool. when he hears of this being of which I speak – a being than which nothing greater can be conceived – understands what he hears, and what he understands is in his understanding; although he does not understand it to exist.

For, it is one thing for an object to be in the understanding, and another to understand that the object exists. When a painter first conceives of what he will afterwards perform, he has it in his understanding, but he does not yet understand it to be, because he has not yet performed it. But after he has made the painting, he both has it in his understanding, and he understands that it exists, because he has made it.

Hence, even the fool is convinced that something exists in the understanding, at least, than which nothing greater can be conceived. For, when he hears of this, he understands it. And whatever is understood, exists in the understanding. And assuredly that, than which nothing greater can be conceived, cannot exist in the understanding alone. For, suppose it exists in the understanding alone: then it can be conceived to exist in reality; which is greater.

---

1. Extracted from *Anselm's Basic Writings*, trans. by S. N. Deane, with an Introduction by Charles Hartshorne, La Salle, Ill., Open Court, 1962, pp. 1–11, 158–159.

Therefore, if that, than which nothing greater can be conceived, exists in the understanding alone, the very being, than which nothing greater can be conceived, is one, than which a greater can be conceived. But obviously this is impossible. Hence, there is no doubt that there exists a being, than which nothing greater can be conceived, and it exists both in the understanding and in reality.

PROSLOGIUM: CHAPTER III

God cannot be conceived not to exist. – God is that, than which nothing greater can be conceived. – That which can be conceived not to exist is not God.

And it assuredly exists so truly, that it cannot be conceived not to exist. For, it is possible to conceive of a being which cannot be conceived not to exist; and this is greater than one which can be conceived not to exist. Hence, if that, than which nothing greater can be conceived, can be conceived not to exist, it is not that, than which nothing greater can be conceived. But this is an irreconcilable contradiction. There is, then, so truly a being than which nothing greater can be conceived to exist, that it cannot even be conceived not to exist; and this being thou art, O Lord, our God.

So truly, therefore, dost thou exist, O Lord, my God, that thou canst not be conceived not to exist; and rightly. For, if a mind could conceive of a being better than thee, the creature would rise above the Creator; and this is most absurd. And, indeed, whatever else there is, except thee alone, can be conceived not to exist. To thee alone, therefore, it belongs to exist more truly than all other beings, and hence in a higher degree than all others. For, whatever else exists does not exist so truly, and hence in a less degree it belongs to it to exist. Why, then, has the fool said in his heart, there is no God (Psalm xiv.1), since it is so evident, to a rational mind, that thou dost exist in the highest degree of all? Why, except that he is dull and a fool?

LIBER APOLOGETICUS CONTRA GUANILONEM (CHAPTER III)

A criticism of Gaunilo's example, in which he tries to show that in this way the existence of a lost island might be inferred from the fact of its being conceived.

But, you say, it is as if one should suppose an island in the ocean, which surpasses all lands in its fertility, and which, because of the difficulty, or rather the impossibility, of discovering what does not exist, is called a lost island; and should say that there can be no doubt that this island truly exists in reality, for this reason, that one who hears it described easily understands what he hears.

Now I promise confidently that if any man shall devise anything existing either in reality or in concept alone (except that than which a greater cannot be conceived) to which he can adapt the sequence of my reasoning, I will discover that thing, and will give him his lost island, not to be lost again.

But it now appears that this being than which a greater is inconceivable cannot be conceived not to be, because it exists on so assured a ground of truth; for otherwise it would not exist at all.

Hence, if any one says that he conceives this being not to exist, I say that at the time when he conceives of this either he conceives of a being than which a greater is inconceivable, or he does not conceive at all. If he does not conceive, he does not conceive of the non-existence of that of which he does not conceive. But if he does conceive, he certainly conceives of a being which cannot be even conceived not to exist. For if it could be conceived not to exist, it could be conceived to have a beginning and an end. But this is impossible.

He, then, who conceives of this being conceives of a being which cannot be even conceived not to exist; but he who conceives of this being does not conceive that it does not exist; else he conceives what is inconceivable. The non-existence, then, of that than which a greater cannot be conceived is inconceivable.

2 D. AND M. HAIGHT: AN ONTOLOGICAL ARGUMENT FOR THE DEVIL[2]

After so many centuries of debate, much of it even quite recent, as to the credibility of Anselm's and others' ontological arguments for the existence of God, it seems only fair to the opposition that some such argument be proposed for Satan's existence. It must be noted, however, that in advocating the Devil's existence, we may be no more than playing the Devil's advocate.

We intend to argue that if Anselm's first ontological argument successfully proves that God indeed exists, then, by parity of reasoning, Satan, or the devil, exists as well. Or, to put it conversely, we shall claim that if Satan does not exist, then neither can God, at least in terms of what the Anselmian argument asserts. Finally, we shall claim that if Satan does not exist, it will not be because of the possible fact that the ontological argument establishes God's existence, but rather it will be because of something that the Anselmian argument *presupposes*, which may not be provable in any argument. Anselm's first argument, roughly, is as follows:

(1) I have a concept of something 'than which nothing greater can be conceived.'
(2) If that 'something' did not actually, or in fact, exist, it would not be 'that than which nothing greater can be conceived,' for something could always be conceived to be greater, viz., something that actually exists.
(3) This 'greatest something' is, by logical equivalence, or definition, 'God.'
(∴) God exists.

An ontological argument for the devil, by analogue of reason, goes as follows:

(1) I have a concept of something than which nothing worse can be conceived.
(2) If that 'something' did not actually, or in fact, exist, it would not be 'that than which nothing *worse* could be conceived,' because something could always be conceived to be much worse, viz., something that actually exists.

---

2. *The Monist*, 54, (1970), pp. 218–200.

(3)   This 'greatest something' we shall call the Devil.

(∴) The Devil exists.

This second ontological argument, by parity of reasoning with the first, seems sound, if indeed, the first is. Is it not conceivable that not only do we have an idea of something that is the worst possible thing, but that it would *have* to exist if it truly *were* the worst possible thing? Hence, the very possibility of the Devil implies his actuality, just as the very possibility of God implies his existence. The logic is the same, in both cases: a devil would not be the Devil unless he existed and was therefore the most awful thing, just as a god would not be God unless he existed and was therefore the greatest thing.

This ontological argument for Satan seems shocking enough, at least at first reading, but something even more startling might be suggested: the two arguments are not only analogous – they are identical. Might it not be suggested that they both establish the existence of the *one* thing – call it God or Satan – namely, a supreme Being who is the 'greatest' and the 'worst' possible being. This suggestion, however, can be made good *only if* it can be plausibly argued that the word 'greater' in the first argument does *not* imply the word 'better'. For it is surely the case that if Anselm means 'better' when he uses the word 'greater', there would be an overt contradiction between the two ontological arguments, viz., the conflict between a 'best being' and a 'worst being.' But does Anselm, in fact, mean 'better' by 'greater'? It has definitely been claimed, subsequent to Anselm, that his argument assumes 'existence to be a perfection,' or that it is *better* to be than not to be, and with this supplementation, it certainly seems to be the case that Anselm equated the two terms or at least implied the one by the other.

But is this really explicit in Anselm's argument? Is he saying that existence is a perfection? If he is, then his argument seems question-begging, because the argument seems to assume what it purports to prove, viz., that it is better for God to exist than not to exist. Presumably, too, if existence is good, God must be good, but one may not be able to assume that existence is good without, first, proving that God exists and is good. Hence, one cannot, or must not, reverse the order of argument such as Anselm seems to do – one must not assume that existence is good or a perfection unless one has *already* proved God's existence. But, actually, the plausibility of Anselm's proof, at least as it has been here paraphrased, is partly contingent upon the word 'greater'. The 'greatest' possible being must be God. Or, it might be the Devil, for it does not follow from Anselm's argument that God is good, only that he exists. And if the word 'greater' does not involve 'perfection,' then both ontological arguments establish the existence of one and only one being. It is then a matter of faith as to whether one calls it God or Satan, a benign *daemon* or a malicious demon. And this faith may, after all, be simply cause of itself.

3 DESCARTES: THE SUPREMELY PERFECT BEING[3]

Now if it follows, from my mere ability to elicit the idea of some object from my consciousness (*cogitatione*), that all the properties that I clearly and distinctly perceive the object to have do really belong to it; could not this give rise to an argument by which the existence of God might be proved? I assuredly find in myself the idea of God – of a supremely perfect being – no less than the idea of a figure or a number; and I clearly and distinctly understand that everlasting existence belongs to his nature, no less than I can see that what I prove of some figure, or number, belongs to the nature of that figure, or number. So, even if my meditations on previous days were not entirely true, yet I ought to hold the existence of God with at least the same degree of certainty as I have so far held mathematical truths.

At first sight, indeed, this is not quite clear; it bears a certain appearance of being a fallacy. For, since I am accustomed to the distinction of existence and essence in all other objects, I am readily convinced that existence can be disjoined even from the divine essence, and that thus God can be conceived (*cogitari*) as non-existent. But on more careful consideration it becomes obvious that existence can no more be taken away from the divine essence than the magnitude of its three angles together (that is, their being equal to two right angles) can be taken away from the essence of a triangle; or than the idea of a valley can be taken away from the idea of a hill. So it is not less absurd to think of God (that is, a supremely perfect being) lacking existence (that is, lacking a certain perfection), than to think of a hill without a valley.

'Perhaps I cannot think of (*cogitare*) God except as existing, just as I cannot think of a hill without a valley. But from my thinking of a hill without a valley, it does not follow that there is any hill in the world; similarly, it appears not to follow, from my thinking of God as existent, that God does exist. For my thought (*cogitatio*) imposes no necessity on things; and just as I can imagine a winged horse, although no horse has wings, so, it may be, I can feign the conjunction of God and existence even though no God should exist.'

There is a lurking fallacy here. What follows from my inability to think of a mountain apart from a valley is not that a mountain and a valley exist somewhere, but only that mountain and valley, whether they exist or not, are mutually inseparable. But from my inability to think of God as non-existent, it follows that existence is inseparable from God and thus that he really does exist. It is not that my thought makes this so, or imposes any necessity on anything; on the contrary, the necessity of the fact itself, that is, of God's existence, is what determines me to think this way. I am not free to think of God apart from existence (that is, of a supremely perfect apart from the supreme perfection) in the way that I can freely imagine a horse either with or without wings.

Moreover, I must not say at this point: 'After supposing God to have all perfections, I must certainly suppose him to be existent, since existence is one

---

3. Extracted from *Descartes: Philosophical Writings*, a selection translated and edited by Elizabeth Anscombe and Peter Geach, with an Introduction by Alexandre Koyré, London, Nelson's University Paperbacks, 1975, pp. 103–105.

among perfections; but the initial supposition was not necessary. In the same way, there is no necessity for me to think all quadrilaterals can be inscribed in a circle; but given that I do think so, I shall necessarily have to admit that a rhombus can be inscribed in a circle; this, however, is obviously false.' For there is indeed no necessity for me ever to happen upon any thought of (*cogitationem de*) God; but whenever I choose to think of (*cogitare de*) the First and Supreme Being, and as it were bring out the idea of him from the treasury of my mind, I must necessarily ascribe to him all perfections, even if I do not at the moment enumerate them all, or attend to each. This necessity clearly ensures that, when later on I observe that existence is a perfection, I am justified in concluding that the First and Supreme Being exists. In the same way, it is not necessary that I should ever imagine any triangle; but whenever I choose to consider a rectilinear figure that has just three angles, I must ascribe to it properties from which it is rightly inferred that its three angles are not greater than two right angles; even if I do not notice this at the time. When, on the other hand, I examine what figures can be inscribed in circles, it is in no way necessary for me to think all quadrilaterals belong to this class; indeed, I cannot even imagine this, so long as I will admit only what I clearly and distinctly understand. Thus there is a great difference between such false suppositions and my genuine innate ideas, among which the first and chief is my idea of God. In many ways, I can see that this idea is no fiction depending on my way of thinking (*cogitatione*), but an image of a real and immutable nature. First, I can frame no other concept of anything to whose essence existence belongs, except God alone; again, I cannot conceive of two or more such Gods; and given that one God exists, I clearly see that necessarily he has existed from all eternity, and will exist to all eternity; and I perceive many other Divine attributes, which I can in no wise diminish or alter.

4 KANT: THE IMPOSSIBILITY OF AN ONTOLOGICAL PROOF[4]

If, in an identical proposition, I reject the predicate while retaining the subject, contradiction results; and I therefore say that the former belongs necessarily to the latter. But if we reject subject and predicate alike, there is no contradiction; for nothing is then left that can be contradicted. To posit a triangle, and yet to reject its three angles, is self-contradictory; but there is no contradiction in rejecting the triangle together with its three angles. The same holds true of the concept of an absolutely necessary being. If its existence is rejected, we reject the thing itself with all its predicates; and no question of contradiction can then arise. There is nothing outside it that would then be contradicted, since the necessity of the thing is not supposed to be derived from anything external; nor is there anything internal that would be contradicted, since in rejecting the thing itself we have at the same time rejected all its internal properties. 'God is omnipotent' is a necessary judgment. The omnipotence cannot be rejected if we posit a Deity, that is, an

4. Immanuel Kant, *Critique of Pure Reason*, trans. Norman Kemp Smith, London, Macmillan, 1929, pp. 502–506.

infinite being; for the two concepts are identical. But if we say, 'There is no God', neither the omnipotence nor any other of its predicates is given; they are one and all rejected together with the subject, and there is therefore not the least contradiction in such a judgment . . .

Notwithstanding all these general considerations, in which every one must concur, we may be challenged with a case which is brought forward as proof that in actual fact the contrary holds, namely, that there is one concept, and indeed only one, in reference to which the not-being or rejection of its object is in itself contradictory, namely, the concept of the *ens realissimum*. It is declared that it possesses all reality, and that we are justified in assuming that such a being is possible (the fact that a concept does not contradict itself by no means proves the possibility of its object: but the contrary assertion I am for the moment willing to allow). Now [the argument proceeds] 'all reality' includes existence; existence is therefore contained in the concept of a thing that is possible. If, then, this thing is rejected, the internal possibility of the thing is rejected – which is self-contradictory.

My answer is as follows. There is already a contradiction in introducing the concept of existence – no matter under what title it may be disguised – into the concept of a thing which we profess to be thinking solely in reference to its possibility. If that be allowed as legitimate, a seeming victory has been won; but in actual fact nothing at all is said: the assertion is a mere tautology. We must ask: Is the proposition that *this or that thing* (which, whatever it may be, is allowed as possible) exists, an analytic or a synthetic proposition? If it is analytic, the assertion of the existence of the thing adds nothing to the thought of the thing; but in that case either the thought, which is in us, is the thing itself, or we have presupposed an existence as belonging to the realm of the possible, and have then, on that pretext, inferred its existence from its internal possibility – which is nothing but a miserable tautology. The word 'reality', which is in the concept of the thing sounds other than the word 'existence' in the concept of the predicate, is of no avail in meeting this objection. For if all positing (no matter what it may be that is posited) is entitled reality, the thing with all its predicates is already posited in the concept of the subject, and is assumed as actual; and in the predicate this is merely repeated. But if, on the other hand, we admit, as every reasonable person must, that all existential propositions are synthetic, how can we profess to maintain that the predicate of existence cannot be rejected without contradiction? This is a feature which is found only in analytic propositions, and is indeed precisely what constitutes their analytic character . . .

'*Being*' is obviously not a real predicate; that is, it is not a concept of something which could be added to the concept of a thing. It is merely the positing of a thing, or of certain determinations, as existing in themselves. Logically, it is merely the copula of a judgment. The proposition, 'God is omnipotent', contains two concepts, each of which has its object – God and omnipotence. The small word 'is' adds no new predicate, but only serves to posit the predicate *in its relation* to the subject. If, now, we take the subject (God) with all its predicates (among which is omnipotence), and say 'God is', or 'There is a God', we attach no new predicate to the concept of God, but only posit the subject itself with all its predicates, and indeed posit it as being an *object* that stands in relation to my *concept*. The content of both must be one and the same; nothing can have been added to the concept, which expressess merely what is possible, by my thinking its object (through the expression 'it is') as given absolutely. Otherwise stated, the real contains no more than the merely possible. A hundred real thalers do not contain the least coin more than a hundred possible thalers. For as the latter signify the concept, and the former the object and the positing of the object, should the former contain more than the latter, my concept would not, in that case, express the whole object, and would not therefore be an adequate concept of it. My financial position is, however, affected very differently by a hundred real thalers than it is by the mere concept of them (that is, of their possibility). For the object, as it actually exists, is not analytically contained in my concept but is added to my concept (which is a determination of my state) synthetically; and yet the conceived hundred thalers are not themselves in the least increased through thus acquiring existence outside my concept.

By whatever and by however many predicates we may think a thing – even if we completely determine it – we do not make the least addition to the thing when we further declare that this thing is. Otherwise, it would not be exactly the same thing that exists, but something more than we had thought in the concept; and we could not, therefore, say that the exact object of my concept exists. If we think in a thing every feature of reality except one, the missing reality is not added by my saying that this defective thing exists. On the contrary, it exists with the same defect with which I have thought it, since otherwise what exists would be something different from what I thought. When, therefore, I think a being as the supreme reality, without any defect, the question still remains whether it exists or not.

5 FINDLAY: DISPROOF OF GOD'S EXISTENCE[5]

But we are also led on irresistibly to a yet more stringent demand, which raises difficulties which make the difficulties we have mentioned seem wholly inconsiderable: we can't help feeling that the worthy object of our worship can never be a thing that merely *happens* to exist, nor one on which all other objects merely *happen* to depend. The true object of religious reverence must not be one, merely, to which no *actual* independent realities stand opposed: it must be one to which such opposition is totally *inconceivable*. God mustn't merely cover the territory of the actual, but also, with equal comprehensiveness, the territory of the possible. And not only must the existence of *other* things be unthinkable without him, but his own non-existence must be wholly unthinkable in any circumstances. There must, in short, be no conceivable alternative to an existence properly termed 'divine': God must be wholly inescapable, as we remarked previously, whether for thought or reality. And so we are led on insensibly to the barely intelligible notion of a Being in whom Essence and Existence lose their separateness. And all that the great medieval thinkers really did was to carry such a development to its logical limit.

---

5. J. N. Findlay, 'Can God's Existence be Disproved?', in *New Essays in Philosophical Theology*, ed. Antony Flew and Alasdair MacIntyre, London, Macmillan, 1955, pp. 52–55.

We may, however, approach the matter from a slightly different angle. Not only is it contrary to the demands and claims inherent in religious attitudes that their object should *exist* 'accidentally': it is also contrary to those demands that it should *possess its various excellences* in some merely adventitious or contingent manner. It would be quite unsatisfactory from the religious standpoint, if an object merely *happened* to be wise, good, powerful and so forth, even to a superlative degree, and if other beings had, *as a mere matter of fact*, derived their excellences from this single source. An object of this sort would doubtless deserve respect and admiration, and other quasi-religious attitudes, but it would not deserve the utter self-abandonment peculiar to the religious frame of mind. . . . And so we are led on irresistibly, by the demands inherent in religious reverence, to hold that an adequate object of our worship must possess its various qualities *in some necessary manner*. These qualities must be intrinsically incapable of belonging to anything except in so far as they belong primarily to the object of our worship. Again we are led on to a queer and barely intelligible Scholastic doctrine, that God isn't merely good, but is in some manner indistinguishable from his own (and anything else's) goodness.

What, however, are the consequences of these requirements upon the possibility of God's existence? Plainly, (for all who share a contemporary outlook), they entail not only that there isn't a God, but that the Divine Existence is either senseless or impossible. The modern mind feels not the faintest axiomatic force in principles which trace contingent things back to some necessarily existent source, nor does it find it hard to conceive that things should display various excellent qualities without deriving them from a source which manifests them supremely. Those who believe in necessary truths which aren't merely tautological, think that such truths merely connect the *possible* instances of various characteristics with each other: they don't expect such truths to tell them whether there *will* be instances of any characteristics. This is the outcome of the whole medieval and Kantian criticism of the Ontological Proof. And, on a yet more modern view of the matter, necessity in propositions merely reflects our use of words, the arbitrary conventions of our language. On such a view the Divine Existence could only be a necessary matter if we had made up our minds to speak theistically *whatever the empirical circumstances might turn out to be*. This, doubtless, would suffice for some, who speak theistically, much as Spinoza spoke monistically, merely to give expression to a particular way of looking at things, or of feeling about them. And it would also suffice for those who make use of the term 'God' to cover whatever tendencies towards righteousness and beauty are actually included in the make-up of our world. But it wouldn't suffice for the full-blooded worshipper, who can't help finding our actual world anything but edifying, and its half-formed tendencies towards righteousness and beauty very far from adorable. The religious frame of mind seems, in fact, to be in a quandary; it seems invincibly determined both to eat its cake and have it. It desires the Divine Existence both to have that inescapable character which can, on modern views, only be found where truth reflects an arbitrary convention, and also the character of 'making a real difference' which is only possible where truth doesn't have this merely linguistic basis. We may accordingly deny that modern approaches allow us to remain agnostically poised in regard to God: they force us to come down on the atheistic side. For if

God is to satisfy religious claims and needs, he must be a being in every way inescapable, One whose existence and whose possession of certain excellences we cannot possibly conceive away. And modern views make it self-evidently absurd (if they don't make it ungrammatical) to speak of such a Being and attribute existence to him. It was indeed an ill day for Anselm when he hit upon his famous proof. For on that day he not only laid bare something that is of the essence of an adequate religious object, but also something that entails its necessary non-existence.

6 MALCOLM: ANSELM'S SECOND ONTOLOGICAL PROOF[6]

Anselm is maintaining (in his second ontological proof) . . . not that existence is a perfection, but that *the logical impossibility of nonexistence is a perfection*. In other words, *necessary existence is a perfection*. His first ontological proof uses the principle that a thing is greater if it exists than if it does not exist. His second proof employs the different principle that a thing is greater if it necessarily exists than if it does not necessarily exist.

Some remarks about the notion of *dependence* may help to make this latter principle intelligible. Many things depend for their existence on other things and events. My house was built by a carpenter: its coming into existence was dependent on a certain creative activity. Its continued existence is dependent on many things: that a tree does not crush it, that it is not consumed by fire, and so on. If we reflect on the common meaning of the word 'God' (no matter how vague and confused this is), we realize that it is incompatible with this meaning that God's existence should *depend* on anything. Whether we believe in Him or not we must admit that the 'almighty and everlasting God' (as several ancient prayers begin), the 'Maker of heaven and earth, and of all things visible and invisible' (as is said in the Nicene Creed), cannot be thought of as being brought into existence by anything or as depending for His continued existence on anything. To conceive of anything as dependent upon something else for its existence is to conceive of it as a lesser being than God.

If a housewife has a set of extremely fragile dishes, then as dishes they are *inferior* to those of another set like them in all respects except that they are *not* fragile. Those of the first set are *dependent* for their continued existence on gentle handling; those of the second set are not. There is a definite connection in common language between the notions of dependency and inferiority, and independence and superiority. To say that something which was dependent on nothing whatever was superior to ('greater than') anything that was dependent in any way upon anything is quite in keeping with the everyday use of the terms 'superior' and 'greater'. Correlative with the notions of dependence and independence are the notions of *limited* and *unlimited*. An engine requires fuel and this is a limitation.

6. Norman Malcolm, *Knowledge and Certainty*, Englewood Cliffs, Prentice-Hall, 1963. Extracted from *The Ontological Argument*, ed. Alvin Plantinga, with an Introduction by Richard Taylor, London, Macmillan, 1968, pp. 142–145.

It is the same thing to say that an engine's operation is *dependent* on as that it is *limited* by its fuel supply. An engine that could accomplish the same work in the same time and was in other respects satisfactory, but did not require fuel, would be a *superior* engine.

God is usually conceived of as an *unlimited* being. He is conceived of as a being who could not be limited, that is, as an absolutely unlimited being. This is no less than to conceive of Him as *something a greater than which cannot be conceived*. If God is conceived to be an absolutely unlimited being He must be conceived to be unlimited in regard to His existence as well as His operation. In this conception it will not make sense to say that He depends on anything for coming into or continuing in existence. Nor, as Spinoza observed, will it make sense to say that something could *prevent* Him from existing. Lack of moisture can prevent trees from existing in a certain region of the earth. But it would be contrary to the concept of God as an unlimited being to suppose that anything other than God Himself could prevent Him from existing, and it would be self-contradictory to suppose that He Himself could do it.

Some may be inclined to object that although nothing could prevent God's existence, still it might just *happen* that He did not exist. And if He did exist that too could be by chance. I think, however, that from the supposition that it could happen that God did not exist it would follow that, if He existed, He would have mere duration and not eternity. It would make sense to ask, 'How long has He existed?', 'Will He still exist next week?', 'He was in existence yesterday but how about today?', and so on. It seems absurd to make God the subject of such questions. According to our ordinary conception of Him, He is an eternal being. And eternity does not mean endless duration, as Spinoza noted. To ascribe eternity to something is to exclude as senseless all sentences that imply that it has duration. If a thing has duration then it would be merely a *contingent* fact, if it was a fact, that its duration was endless. The moon could have endless duration but not eternity. If something has endless duration it will make sense (although it will be false) to say that it will cease to exist, and it will make sense (although it will be false) to say that something will *cause* it to cease to exist. A being with endless duration is not, therefore, an absolutely unlimited being. That God is conceived to be eternal follows from the fact that He is conceived to be an absolutely unlimited being.

I have been trying to expand the argument of *Proslogion 3*. In *Responsio 1* Anselm adds the following acute point: if you can conceive of a certain thing and this thing does not exist then if it *were* to exist its nonexistence would be *possible*. If follows, I believe, that if the thing were to exist it would depend on other things both for coming into and continuing in existence, and also that it would have duration and not eternity. Therefore it would not be, either in reality or in conception, an unlimited being, *aliquid quo nihil maius cogitari possit . . . .* What Anselm has proved is that the notion of contingent existence or of contingent nonexistence cannot have any application to God. His existence must either be logically necessary or logically impossible. The only intelligible way of rejecting Anselm's claim that God's existence is necessary is to maintain that the concept of God, as a being greater than which cannot be conceived, is self-contradictory and nonsensical. Supposing that this is false, Anselm is right to deduce God's necessary existence from his characterization of Him as a being a greater than which cannot be conceived.

Let me summarize the proof. If God, a being a greater than which cannot be conceived, does not exist then He cannot *come* into existence. For if He did He would either have been *caused* to come into existence or have *happened* to come into existence, and in either case He would be a limited being, which by our conception of Him He is not. Since He cannot come into existence, if He does not exist His existence is impossible. If He does exist He cannot have come into existence (for the reasons given), nor can He cease to exist, for nothing could cause Him to cease to exist nor could it just happen that He ceased to exist. So if God exists His existence is necessary. Thus God's existence is either impossible or necessary. It can be the former only if the concept of such a being is self-contradictory or in some way logically absurd. Assuming that this is not so, it follows that He necessarily exists.

It may be helpful to express ourselves in the following way: to say, not that *omnipotence* is a property of God, but rather that *necessary omnipotence* is; and to say, not that omniscience is a property of God, but rather that *necessary omniscience* is. We have criteria for determining that a man knows this and that and can do this and that, and for determining that one man has greater knowledge and abilities in a certain subject than another. We could think of various tests to give them. But there is nothing we should wish to describe, seriously and literally, as "testing" God's knowledge and powers. That God is omniscient and omnipotent has not been determined by the application of criteria: rather these are requirements of our conception of Him. They are internal properties of the concept, although they are also rightly said to be properties of God. *Necessary existence* is a property of God in the *same sense* that *necessary omnipotence* and *necessary omniscience* are His properties. And we are not to think that "necessarily exists" means that it follows necessarily from something that God exists *contingently*. The a priori proposition "God necessarily exists" entails the proposition "God exists", if and only if the latter also is understood as an a priori proposition: in which case the two propositions are equivalent. In this sense Anselm's proof is a proof of God's existence.

7 HICK: NECESSARY BEING[7]

We may distinguish in Findlay's argument a philosophical premise to the effect that no existential propositions can be necessary truths, and a theological premise to the effect that an adequate object of religious worship must be such that it is logically necessary that he exists. Of these two premises I wish to accept the former and reject the latter. I deny, that is to say, the theological doctrine that God must be conceived, if at all, in such a way that 'God exists' is a logically necessary truth. I deny this for precisely the same reason as Findlay, namely that the demand that 'God exists' should be a necessary truth is, like the demand that a circle should be

7. John Hick, 'Necessary Being', *Scottish Journal of Theology*, 14, December 1961, pp. 353–369.

square, not a proper demand at all, but a misuse of langauge. Only, whereas Findlay concludes that the notion of an adequate object of religious attitude is an absurdity, I conclude that that of which the idea is an absurdity cannot be an adequate object of religious attitudes; it would on the contrary be an unqualified *in*adequate object of worship.

Let us then ask the question, which seems highly appropriate at this point, as to how religious persons actually think of the Being whom they regard as the adequate object of their worship. What aspect of the Christian experience of God lies behind the idea of necessary being?

The concept of God held by the biblical writers was based upon their experience of God as awesome power and holy will confronting them and drawing them into the sphere of His ongoing purpose. God was known as a dynamic will interacting with their own wills; a sheer given reality, as inescapably to be reckoned with as destructive storm or lifegiving sunshine . . . God was not for them an inferred reality; He was an experienced reality. . . . They thought of this holy presence as unique – as the maker and ruler of the Universe, the sole rightful sovereign of men and angels, as eternal and infinite, and as the ultimate reality and determining power, in relation to whom His creatures have no standing except as the objects of His grace. But nowhere in the biblical thought about God is use made of the idea of logical necessity. The notion is quite foreign to the characteristically Hebraic and concrete utterances found in the Bible, and forms no part of the biblical concept or concepts of God.

But, it might be said, was it not to the biblical writers inconceivable that God should *not* exist, or that he should cease to exist, or should lose His divine powers and virtues? Would it not be inconceivable to them that God might one day go out of existence, or cease to be good and become evil? And does not this attitude involve an implicit belief that God exists necessarily, and possesses His divine characteristics in some necessary manner? The answer, I think, is that it was to the biblical writers psychologically inconceivable – as we say colloquially, unthinkable – that God might not exist, or that His nature might undergo change. . . . They would have allowed as a verbal concession only that there might possibly be no God; for they were convinced that they were at many times directly aware of His presence and of His dealings with them. But the question whether the non-existence of God is *logically* inconceivable, or *logically* impossible, is a purely philosophical puzzle which could not be answered by the prophets and apostles out of their own first-hand religious experience. This does not of course represent any special limitation of the biblical figures. The logical concept of necessary being cannot be given in religious experience. It is an object of philosophical thought and not of religious experience. It is a product – as Findlay argues, a malformed product – of reflection. A religious person's reply to the question, Is God's existence logically necessary? will be determined by his view of the nature of logical necessity; and this is not part of his religion but of his system of logic. The biblical writers in point of fact display no view of the nature of logical necessity, and would doubtless have regarded the topic as of no religious significance. It cannot reasonably be claimed then, that necessary existence was part of their conception of the adequate object of human worship.

What, we must therefore ask, has led Findlay to hold so confidently that logically necessary existence is an essential element in the religious man's concept of God? His process of thought is revealed in these words: 'We can't help feeling that the worthy object of our worship can never be a thing that merely *happens* to exist, nor one on which all other objects merely *happen* to depend.' The reasoning here is that if a being does not exist by logical necessity, He merely happens to exist; and in this case He ought not to be worshipped as God. But in presenting the dilemma, either God exists necessarily, or He merely happens to exist, Findlay makes the very mistake for which he has criticised the theologians. Findlay should be the last person to use this dichotomy, since he has himself rendered it inoperative by pointing out that one half of the dichotomy is meaningless. And to remove half a dichotomy is to remove the dichotomy. If for example it is said that all human beings are either witches or non-witches, and it is then discovered that there is no such thing as a witch, it becomes pointless, and indeed misleading, to describe everyone as a non-witch. Likewise, having concluded that the notion of necessary existence has no meaning, to continue to speak of things merely *happening* to exist, as though this stood in contrast to some other mode of existing, no longer has any validity. From an empiricist standpoint, there are not two different ways of existing, existing by logical necessity and merely happening to exist. A thing either exists or does not exist; or to be more exact a description either has or does not have a referent. But Findlay, after ruling out the notion of necessary existence, in relation to which alone the contrasting idea of 'merely happening to exist' has any meaning, continues to use the latter category, and what is more, to use it as a term of reproach! This is a very advanced form of the method of having it both ways.

Our conclusion must be that Findlay has only disproved the existence of God if we mean by God a being whose existence is a matter of logical necessity. Since, however, we do not mean this, we may take Findlay's argument instead as emphasising that we must either abandon the traditional phrase 'necessary being', or else be very clear that the necessary being of God is not to be construed a *logically* necessary being.

We have arrived thus far at an identification of the necessary being of the Godhead with incorruptible and indestructible being without beginning or end. These characteristics, however, can properly be regarded as different aspects of the more fundamental characteristic which the Scholastics termed aseity, or being *a se*. The usual English translation, 'self-existence', is strictly a meaningless phrase, but for the lack of a better we must continue to use it. The core of the notion of aseity is independent being. That God exists *a se* means that He is not dependent upon anything for His existence. In contrast to this the created Universe and everything in it exist *ab alio*. For it is true of each distinguishable item composing the Universe that Its existence depends upon some factors beyond itself. Only God exists in total non-dependence; He alone exists absolutely as sheer unconditioned, self-existent being . . .

Finally, to refer back to Findlay's discussion, it is meaningless to say of the self-existent being that He might not have existed or that He merely happens to exist. For what could it mean to say of the eternal, uncreated Creator of everything other than Himself that He merely happens to exist? When we assert of a dependent and temporally finite being, such as myself, that I only happen to exist, we mean that if such-and-such an event had occurred in the past, or if such-and-such another event had failed to occur, I should not now exist. But no such meaning can be given to the statement, 'A self-existent being only happens to exist', or 'might not have existed.' There is no conceivable event such that if it had occurred, or failed to occur, a self-existent being would not have existed; for the concept of aseity is precisely the exclusion of such dependence. There is and could be nothing that would have prevented a self-existent being from coming to exist, for it is meaningless to speak of a self-existent being as *coming* to exist.

What may properly be meant, then, by the statement that God is, or has, necessary as distinguished from contingent being is that God *is*, without beginning or end, and without origin, cause or ground of any kind whatsoever. He *is*, as the ultimate, unconditioned, absolute, unlimited being.

KEY TEXTS

Anselm. *Basic Writings* (*Proslogium, Monologium,* Gaunilo's *On Behalf of the Fool, Cur Deus Homo?*), translated by S. N. Deane, with an Introduction by Charles Hartshorne, La Salle, Ill., Open Court, 1962.

Barnes, Jonathan. *The Ontological Argument*, London, Macmillan, 1972.

Charlesworth, M. J. *St Anselm's Proslogion*, translated and with an Introduction and philosophical commentary by Charlesworth, Oxford, Clarendon Press, 1965.

Hick, John (ed., with Arthur C. McGill). *The Many-Faced Argument*, London, Macmillan, 1968.

Kant, Immanuel. *Critique of Pure Reason*, trans. Norman Kemp Smith, London, Macmillan, 1929, pp. 500–507.

Plantinga, Alvin. *The Ontological Argument*, London, Macmillan, 1968.

BIBLIOGRAPHY

Adams, R. 'The Logical Structure of Anselm's Argument', *Philosophical Review*, 80, 1971, pp. 28–54.

—— 'Presumption and the Necessary Existence of God', *Nous*, 22, 1988, pp. 19–34.

Alston, W. 'The Ontological Argument Revisited', *Philosophical Review*, 69, 1960, pp. 452–474.

Anselm. *Appendix to Anselm*, trans. S. N. Deane, Chicago, Open Court, 1963.

—— *Basic Writings* (*Proslogium, Monologium,* Gaunilo's *On Behalf of the Fool, Cur Deus Homo?*), translated by S. N. Deane, with an Introduction by Charles Hartshorne, La Salle, Ill., Open Court, 1962.

Barnes, Jonathan. *The Ontological Argument*, London, Macmillan, 1972.

Barth, Karl. *Fides Quaerens Intellectum*, Munich, Chr. Kaiser, 1931. English translation by Ian Robertson, *Anselm: Fides Quaerens Intellectum*, London, SCM Press and Richmond, Va., John Knox Press, 1960.

Brecher, Robert. *Anselm's Argument*, Aldershot, Gower, 1985.

Chandler, H. 'Some Ontological Arguments', *Faith and Philosophy*, 10, 1993, pp. 18–32.

Charlesworth, M. J. *St. Anselm's Proslogion*, translated and with an Introduction and philosophical commentary by Charlesworth, Oxford, Clarendon Press, 1965.

Davies, Brian. *An Introduction to the Philosophy of Religion*, Oxford, Oxford University Press, 1982, pp. 26–37.

Descartes, René. *Philosophical Writings*, translated and edited by Elizabeth Anscombe and Peter Geach, with an Introduction by Alexandre Koyré, London, Thomas Nelson & Sons, 1954.

Eadmer. *The Life of St Anselm*, edited with an Introduction, notes and translation by R. W. Southern, Oxford, Clarendon Press, 1972.

Findlay, J. N. 'Can God's Existence be Disproved?', *Mind*, 57, 1948. Reprinted in *New Essays in Philosophical Theology*, ed. Antony Flew and Alasdair MacIntyre, London, SCM Press, 1955, pp. 47–56.

—— 'Some Reflections on Necessary Existence', in *Process and Divinity: The Hartshorn Festschrift*, ed. William L. Reese and Eugene Freeman, La Salle, Ill., Open Court, 1964, pp. 515–527.

Grim, Patrick. 'In Behalf of "In Behalf of the Fool"', *International Journal for the Philosophy of Religion*, 13, 1982, pp. 33–42.

Haight, David and Marjorie. 'An Ontological Argument for the Devil', *The Monist*, 54, 1970, pp. 218–220.

Hartshorne, Charles. *Anselm's Discovery*, La Salle, Ill., Open Court, 1965.

—— *The Logic of Perfection*, La Salle, Ill., Open Court, 1962.

Hick, John. 'God as Necessary Being', *Journal of Philosophy*, 57, October 1960, pp. 725–734.

—— 'Necessary Being', *Scottish Journal of Theology*, 14, December 1961, pp. 353–369.

Hick, John and Arthur C. McGill (eds). *The Many-Faced Argument*, London, Macmillan, 1968.

Hopkins, Jasper. *A Companion to the Study of St. Anselm*, Minneapolis, University of Minnesota Press, 1972.

Hume, David. *Dialogues Concerning Natural Religion* (1779), edited with an Introduction by Norman Kemp Smith, Thomas Nelson & Sons, 1947.

Inwagen, P. van. 'Ontological Arguments', *Noûs*, 11, 1977, pp. 375–395.

Kant, Immanuel. *Critique of Pure Reason*, trans. Norman Kemp Smith, London, Macmillan, 1929, pp. 500–507.

Kordig, Carl R. 'A Deontic Argument for God's Existence', *Noûs*, 15, 1981, pp. 207–228.

Lewis, D. 'Anselm and Actuality', *Noûs*, 4, 1970, pp. 175–188.

Mackie, J. L. *The Miracle of Theism*, Oxford, Clarendon Press, 1982, pp. 41–63.

Malcolm, Norman. 'Anselm's Ontological Arguments', *Philosophical Review*, 69(1), January 1960, pp. 41–62. Reprinted in John Hick and Arthur C. McGill (eds), *The Many-Faced Argument*, London, Macmillan, 1968, pp. 301–320; and in Alvin Plantinga (ed.), *The Ontological Argument*, London, Macmillan, 1968, pp. 136–159.

Oppenheimer, P. (with E. Zalta). 'On the Logic of the Ontological Argument', in J. Tomberlin (ed.), *Philosophical Perspectives 5: The Philosophy of Religion*, Atascadero, Calif., Ridgeview, 1991, pp. 509–529.

Oppy, Graham. *Ontological Arguments and Belief in God*, New York, Cambridge University Press, 1995.

Plantinga, Alvin. *God, Freedom, and Evil*, New York, Harper & Row, 1974.

—— *The Nature of Necessity*, Oxford, Oxford University Press, 1974.

—— *The Ontological Argument*, London, Macmillan, 1968.

Rowe, William. 'The Ontological Argument', in Joel Feinberg (ed.), *Reason and Responsibility: Readings in Some Basic Problems of Philosophy*, 3rd edn, Encino, Calif., Dickenson Publishing Co., 1973, pp. 8–17.

Russell, Bertrand. 'On Denoting' (1905), in *Readings in Philosophical Analysis*, ed. Herbert Feigl and Wilfrid Sellars, New York, 1949, pp. 103–115.

Salmon, N. 'Existence', in J. Tomberlin (ed.), *Philosophical Perspectives 1: Metaphysics*, Atascadero, Calif., Ridgeview, 1987, pp. 47–108.

chapter 2   THE COSMOLOGICAL ARGUMENT

INTRODUCTION: THE ARGUMENT AS AN
A POSTERIORI PROOF

The cosmological argument is, as its name suggests (from the Greek *cosmos*, meaning 'universe' or 'world'), an a posteriori argument for the existence of God. This means that, unlike the ontological argument, it does not seek to prove God's existence from a definition of the concept of God but rather from an analysis of our experiences of the world about us. This reference to the world, we should add, gives the cosmological argument, and indeed all other a posteriori arguments, its distinctive form as a *proof*. It is not a proof in that it seeks to demonstrate, following Anselm and Descartes, that the denial of God's existence is self-contradictory, but a proof in that it seeks to show how unreasonable that denial is, given the weight of evidence against it. It bases its case, in other words, on what is the most plausible explanation for the various experiences we have of the world. It does not argue, therefore, that the explanation it offers is the only logically possible one but rather that, on the evidence gathered, it is the only likely explanation that can be presented beyond rational doubt.

The cosmological argument has had a long and distinguished history. Among its advocates may be numbered Plato, Aristotle, the Arabic philosopher Averroes, the Jewish philosopher Maimonides, Descartes, Spinoza, Locke, and many contemporary theologians, most notably E. L. Mascall (1943), Austin Farrer (1943), Frederick Copleston (1955) and, more recently, Richard Taylor (1963). Three other modern versions are worth mentioning. Bruce Reichenbach (1972) and William Craig (1979) have presented *deductive* defences of the argument, the latter resurrecting the so-called Kalam cosmological argument – a version originating with the sixth-century Christian philosopher Joannes Philoponos, and deployed to great effect by medieval Islamic theologians of the Kalam school. Richard Swinburne's presentation (1979) is equally unconventional but *inductive* in form, employing conclusions drawn from confirmation and probability theory.[1] Among the argument's critics we may count Hume, Kant and John Stuart Mill, the last-named being a particular influence on two more recent critics, Bertrand Russell and C. D. Broad. Kant himself testified to the argument's importance when he conceded that it was 'the most convincing not only for common sense but even for speculative understanding'.[2]

---

1. See Mascall, *He Who Is*, London, Longmans, 1943; Farrer, *Finite and Infinite*, London, Dacre Press, 1943; Copleston, *Thomas Aquinas*, London, Search Press, 1955; Taylor, *Metaphysics*, Englewood Cliffs, N.J., Prentice-Hall, 1963; Reichenbach, *The Cosmological Argument: A Reassessment*, Springfield, Ill., Charles C. Thomas, 1972; William Lane Craig, *The Kalam Cosmological Argument*, New York, Barnes & Noble, 1979; and Richard Swinburne, *The Existence of God*, Oxford, Clarendon Press, 1979. A powerful critique of the last three is given by Michael Martin in *Atheism: A Philosophical Justification*, Philadelphia, Temple University Press, 1990, pp. 101–124.
2. *Critique of Pure Reason*, trans. Norman Kemp Smith, London, Macmillan, 1929, p. 508.

ST THOMAS AQUINAS: THE ARGUMENTS FROM MOTION AND CAUSE

⇒ The most famous version of the cosmological argument is that presented by St Thomas Aquinas (1225–1274) in his *Summa Theologiae* (SOURCE 1: PP. 75–76). Here Aquinas sets out his famous 'Five Ways' (*quinque viae*) by which the existence of God can be established.

St Thomas Aquinas
(c. 1225–1274)

An aristocrat by birth, Aquinas joined the Dominican order in 1244, much to the disapproval of his family, and rapidly established himself as a student of extraordinary intellectual talent. From 1245 to 1252 he studied at Cologne under Albert the Great, where he encountered the work of Aristotle, and subsequently taught at Paris and Rome, where he acted as adviser and lecturer to the papal court. His enormous philosophical output culminated in his unfinished *Summa Theologiae* (also known as *Summa Theologicae*, *The Sum of Theology*. Later editions and translations also use the title *Summa Theologica* or *The Theological Sum*). Begun in 1256, the *Summa* presents the most complete statement of his philosophical system, and includes his 'Five Ways' to prove God's existence. Aquinas was canonized in 1323 and proclaimed Doctor of the Church (Angelicus Doctor) in 1567. His philosophy was recognized by Pope Leo XIII in the encyclical *Aeterni Patris* (1879) as the official theology of the church and so made mandatory in all Roman Catholic education.

Aquinas: the Five Ways

Aquinas' 'Five Ways' are: (1) the argument from motion; (2) the argument from cause; (3) the argument from contingency; (4) the argument from perfection; (5) the argument from design. The cosmological argument is generally regarded as covering the first three of these arguments. In them Aquinas claims that the evidence we require for God's existence is furnished by the most familiar and commonplace facts of our experience. Thus he begins with two indisputable empirical phenomena: the fact that things move and the fact that things are caused. These two arguments are so similar in form that they may be conveniently treated together.

SUMMARY:
THE ARGUMENTS FROM MOTION AND CAUSE

It is an a posteriori truth that some things are in motion and others at rest. A thing that moves must be caused to move by something else, that is, it cannot move unless its potentiality is actualized by something already in a state of actuality. Since, however, nothing can be simultaneously in a state of potentiality and actuality, nothing can move itself. Hence whatever moves must be caused to move by something else, and so on. There cannot, however, be an infinite series of things causing movement to take place. For if there were no first mover there would be no subsequent movers and thus no present motion, which is contrary to our experience. Thus the series of 'moved movers' implies an 'unmoved mover', a mover that is not itself moved by something else, and this is God.

THE ARGUMENT FROM CAUSE

It is an a posteriori truth that everything that occurs has an efficient cause or active agent, and that this efficient cause also has a cause. There cannot, however, be an infinite regress of causes. For if there were no first cause there would be no subsequent causes and thus no present effects, which is contrary to our experience. Thus the series of 'caused causes' implies a 'first cause', a cause that is not caused by anything else, and this is God.

SUMMARY:
Continued

Neither of these arguments is original, as Aquinas is ready to admit. Both are indebted to the work of Plato's most celebrated pupil, Aristotle (384–322 BC), and to the famous distinction he draws between *actuality* (*actus*) and *potentiality* (*potentia*).[3]

Motion or change (Latin, *motus*) is the process by which an object acquires a new form. An object, that is, has the potentiality to become something different, and change is thus the actualization of the potential of one form of matter to become another form of matter. Aristotle's favourite example is the potential of a block of marble to become the actual statue. The capacity of the marble to become the statue is, as it were, latent within the marble, a particular disposition that it possesses; but it cannot possess this disposition to become a statue and actually be this statue simultaneously. In this respect, therefore, potency and act are utterly distinct. So, to use Aquinas' example, wood, which is potentially hot, can by the agency of fire become actually hot; but it would be absurd to suppose that wood can possess both the quality of becoming hot and being hot at the same time and in the same respect (*in potentia* and *in actu*). Change is therefore the movement between two opposing states: A's capacity to become B, and the realization of that capacity when A becomes B.

The next question is: If nothing can be simultaneously in a state of potency and act, how is the transition from one state to the other brought about? It is

Aristotle

Aristotle: the distinction between actuality and potentiality

---

3. *Actus* and *potentia* being the scholastic translations of Aristotle's *energeia* or *entelecheia*, and *dynamis*.

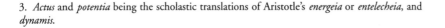

achieved through the agency of what Aristotle calls the 'efficient cause', which must itself be in a state of actuality. Why so? Because if the efficient cause were not actual it would not exist to be the cause of anything, let alone the cause of the transition from potency to act in any other being. To give an example: An acorn has the potential to become an oak. What therefore is the efficient cause of the movement from acorn to oak? Let us say, water. Potential or actual water? Obviously actual water, replies Aristotle, because the state of potential water is in fact no state of real water at all. Thus we conclude that for change to occur there must be an additional entity, the efficient cause, which is itself in a state of actuality, and which, being actual, can provoke the transition from potency to act.

Describe the following in terms of Aristotle's distinction between potency and actuality, specifying the efficient causes:

Water	Bankruptcy
Fear	Tuberculosis
Fairies	Yeti
Squares	Olympic runner
Crop growth	Wealth

The final question is: If every transition from potency to act requires an actual and efficient cause to initiate it, and if every state of actuality presupposes a prior state of potency, is the chain of potency–act one which stretches back through infinity, or is it inaugurated at a specific point? Aquinas' arguments from motion and cause answer this. An infinite series of movers and causes must be rejected in favour of an unmoved mover and an uncaused cause. His reasoning now becomes plain. For unless we presume the existence of a being that is pure act (*actus purus*) – a being, that is, that lacks the prior state of potency and whose actuality does not therefore depend on the existence of any other actual thing – we must presume the existence of a being in potential only, namely, one that cannot, in the absence of any prior actuality, inaugurate anything, and which cannot therefore account for the immediate evidence we have before us of motion and change. It is, accordingly, only by presupposing the actual existence of a first mover or first cause that we can make sense of our present experience that things do move and are caused.

A PROBLEM OF INTERPRETATION: TEMPORAL OR ONTOLOGICAL CAUSE?

Although Aquinas' argument appears straightforward enough, there is a problem of interpretation here that is often overlooked. What exactly is Aquinas rejecting when he denies the possibility of a causal chain of infinite length? The most obvious answer is that he is rejecting an *infinite temporal succession* of movers or causes: that because everything must be moved or have a cause, and because this series of movers or causes cannot stretch back indefinitely into the past, there must have been a first mover or first cause 'in the beginning'. On this interpretation, Aquinas' argument would go something like this: Suppose I observe a chain of upright dominoes stretching beyond the horizon and out of sight. When I later observe each domino falling and causing its neighbour to fall, I must conclude that this chain has a beginning in a domino that was not itself caused to fall. Why so? Because a chain of dominoes reaching back over an infinite duration of time would presumably take an infinite length of time to reach those dominoes I now observe falling, and would thus not reach those dominoes. It is accordingly only by presuming a first domino that I can account for the immediate and indisputable experience I have of dominoes being caused to fall.

God as temporal first cause

Commentators as diverse as Copleston, Kenny and Flew reject this inter-pretation – Flew, indeed, goes so far as to call it a 'peculiarly gross howler'.[4] Certainly there are difficulties with the idea of God as the temporal first cause. The first is that the argument now appears self-contradictory: the conclusion, which says that there is an unmoved mover or first cause, con-tradicts the premiss that everything must be moved and have a cause. Thus either the premiss is true and the conclusion untrue or the conclusion is true and the premiss untrue. The second difficulty is that, even if consistent, the argument gives no reason for concluding that what causes change 'in the beginning' should now exist at all. There is, accordingly, nothing against the suggestion that, having initiated the fall of dominoes, the Great Domino should cease to be. That God is the first cause does not therefore imply that God now exists.

F. C. Copleston avoids these difficulties by making an important amend-ment. Aquinas, he argues, is not speaking of a temporal first cause but of an *ontologically ultimate cause*; of a cause which is not part of a series stretching back into the past but of a 'hierarchy of efficient cause, a subordinate cause being dependent on the cause above it in the hierarchy'.

> What he [Aquinas] is thinking of can be illustrated in this way. A son is dependent on his father, in the sense that he would not have existed except for the causal activity of his father. But when the son acts for himself, he is not dependent here and now on his father. But he is dependent here and now on other factors. Without the activity of the air, for instance, he could not himself act, and the life-preserving activity of the air is itself dependent here and now on other factors, and they in turn on other factors. I do not say that this illustration is in all respects adequate for the purpose; but it at least illustrates the fact that when

God as ontologically ultimate cause

---

4. *An Introduction to Western Philosophy*, London, Thames & Hudson, 1971, p. 192. Flew makes the same point in his *God and Philosophy*, London, Hutchinson, 1966, pp. 85–87.

Aquinas talks about an 'order' of efficient causes he is not thinking of a series stretching back into the past, but of a hierarchy of causes, in which a subordinate member is here and now dependent on the causal activity of a higher member. If I wind up my watch at night, it then proceeds to work without further interference on my part. But the activity of the pen tracing these words on the page is here and now dependent on the activity of my hand, which in turn is here and now dependent on other factors.[5]

Causes *in fieri* and causes *in esse*

Frederick Copleston, SJ (1907–94)

Copleston is here drawing attention to two types of causes: a cause *in fieri* and a cause *in esse*.[6] A cause *in fieri* is one which causes an effect *becoming* what it is, and a cause *in esse* is one which sustains the *being* of that effect. Thus the relation of father and son is an example of a cause *in fieri*. Here the continued existence of the effect (son) does not require the continued existence of the cause (father) which first produced it. On the other hand, the relation of the pen to my hand is an example of a cause *in esse*. The activity of the pen (effect) could not persist once the action of my hand (cause) had ceased. The difference that Copleston is drawing attention to is therefore between a God whose continued existence is not necessary to the process initiated by him and a God whose

existence is necessary. This latter is the *ontologically ultimate cause*, the God whose permanent existence sustains the existence of everything else. In this sense, to use another analogy, God is like a candle which produces light in a room and whose continued presence is necessary if the illumination is to continue. Once the candle is removed, the light forthwith ceases.

This distinction clarifies Aquinas' argument. He is not concerned with causes *in fieri* but with causes *in esse* – not with a lineal or horizontal series but with a vertical hierarchy – and an infinite regression of these causes is impossible. For without the first member, a mover which is not itself moved or a cause which does not itself depend on the causal activity of a higher cause, it is impossible to explain why there is motion or change *here and now* amongst the lower members. Self-evidently a thing cannot cause itself. Thus, if it is not uncaused or its own cause, its present existence must be caused by another, whose own existence sustains it. Since, therefore, no member of any

5. *Thomas Aquinas*, London, Search Press, 1955, p. 122.
6. For a discussion of this distinction, see G. H. Joyce, *Principles of Natural Theology*, London, Longmans, Green & Co., 1923, pp. 58ff.

causal series can exist except through the present operation of a first cause, no dependent causes could operate without this superior cause. Thus we are led to conclude that there must be a first efficient and completely non-dependent cause, an actual cause now operating to preserve the being of all existing things and without which the whole universe would immediately cease to be.

Using the distinction between causes *in fieri* and causes *in esse*, can you decide what causal relationship is being expressed in the following?

EXERCISE 2.2

I am the author of this book.

Standing in front of a mirror causes a reflection.

I am wet because it has been raining.

His death was due to natural causes.

He died when the doctor switched off the respirator.

I am overweight because I eat too much.

Electric current causes a deflection of the magnetic needle.

Kissing causes babies.

A bolt of lightning struck him dead.

Friction causes heat.

ST THOMAS AQUINAS: THE ARGUMENT FROM CONTINGENCY

Copleston's interpretation of Aquinas is justified by the fact that it conforms to the third argument Aquinas presents in his cosmological proof, the argument from contingency. This argument deals specifically with the theme already detected by Copleston, that is, with the notion of God as the ontological ground of being, sustaining all that is.

Aquinas' argument proceeds as follows. It is an a posteriori fact of our experience not just that things exist but that they exist *contingently*: that they have the possibility of either existing or not existing, 'of being generated and corrupted'. A contingent being, in other words, does not have existence as a constitutive property because its existence is precarious: it is part of its make-up that at one time it did not exist and that at some future time it might not exist. But this, Aquinas continues, is not all that can be said of our experience of the contingency of things. For what, we should ask, are the consequences that follow from the statement that 'Everything that exists exists contingently?' It is this: if *all* objects in the world could fail to exist, then at some time each object was or would become non-existent. To make this clear, let us assume an infinite amount of time. Now, in infinite time the capacity of all things not to exist will inevitably be realized. If we assume, in other words, that the world

Existent things exist contingently

has been going on for an indefinite period, there must be a time when every contingent object actualizes its capacity *not to be*, when therefore no objects existed at all. However, if, following the hypothesis of infinite time, the possibility of nothing existing must be fulfilled, then it is equally impossible for anything now to exist – nothing, after all, can come from nothing. And, again, this conclusion contradicts the immediate evidence of our senses.

Perhaps another example will make this rather ungainly argument clearer. Imagine a roulette wheel without numbers and with only the two colours, red and black. Red stands for existence and black stands for non-existence. While one spin of one wheel will have a fifty–fifty chance of black, the introduction of more wheels will greatly diminish the chance of *all* wheels selecting black *at the same time*. But if we now introduce the notion of infinite time, Aquinas argues that, however many wheels may be spinning, it is absolutely certain that eventually all wheels will select black simultaneously. Thus we may conclude that the contingency of existing things requires the prior existence of nothing at all.

We thus arrive at the following dilemma. If at one time no contingent objects existed, how are we to account for the certain fact that objects do now exist? This can only be done by rejecting the view that everything that exists is contingent and by supposing that there does exist something that is *incapable* of existing or not existing. We are thus led inexorably to the conclusion that there exists a *necessary being*, a being who, in the words of Anthony Kenny, 'always will be and always was; and cannot nor could not nor will not be able not to be'.[7] The existence of contingent beings can therefore be explained only by the presupposition of a necessary being, which bestows and sustains existence through its inexhaustible power to be. However, this necessary being, for the same reasons outlined by Copleston in the arguments from motion and cause, cannot itself be part of an infinite series or hierarchy of contingent beings. Otherwise we could not explain the existence here and now of beings capable of not existing. Thus we have to affirm the existence of a being which is the cause of its own necessity, which depends on nothing outside itself for its own existence; and this thing 'all humans speak of as God'.

Compared with Aquinas' arguments from motion and cause, the argument from contingency is somewhat tortuous. Let us therefore reduce it to the following eight steps:

God exists necessarily

SUMMARY: THE ARGUMENT FROM CONTINGENCY

1 We observe things that exist.
2 Things that exist exist contingently (i.e., they may or may not exist).
3 If all things that exist may not exist, then at some time previously nothing existed.
4 If at some time previously nothing existed, then nothing exists now.
5 It is false to say that nothing exists now.

7. 'Necessary Being', *Sophia*, 1(8), 1962, p. 284.

6 It is therefore false to say that the only things that exist exist contingently.

7 There is therefore a necessary being (i.e., a being who cannot not exist).

8 This necessary being is God.

SUMMARY:
continued

It will be noted that the conclusion reached here that God is a necessary being is identical to that reached in the second form of the ontological argument. Not, of course, that the method employed is the same. The ontological remains an *a priori* proof, proceeding from the definition of God's perfection, whereas the argument from contingency is an *a posteriori* proof, based on our experience of observable phenomena. But the fact that each arrives at a common end underlines their common purpose. This is to assert *the unique ontological status of God's existence*. Malcolm, in his defence of the ontological argument, has already interpreted 'necessary being' in terms of independent being: unlike that of contingent beings, God's existence does not depend on, nor is it sustained by, the existence of any other being. This, we remember, was the meaning of 'factual necessity'.[8] And precisely the same idea operates in the argument from contingency. Although scholars agree that Aquinas in his earlier writings conceives God as a logically necessary being – i.e., in the sense that to deny God's existence is self-contradictory – they also agree that, in his later writings, and particularly in the *Summa Theologiae* – where the contingency argument appears – he has moved to the view that God is a factually necessary being. Here too Aquinas asserts that God is an eternal and imperishable being, whose unique ontological status is realized in his independent and non-derivative existence.

All three cosmological arguments converge at this point. Nothing can move or cause God to come into existence, nothing can move or cause God to pass out of existence, and nothing that moves or is caused can be ultimately accounted for without presupposing God's existence. Although cumbersome, the argument from contingency achieves its pre-eminence as a cosmological proof by its graphic concentration upon these themes. A contingent cosmos cannot account for its own existence: it must depend on another reality to bring it about. To suppose, however, that this reality is also contingent offers no satisfactory explanation, because this reality must similarly be accounted for. We must therefore acknowledge the reality of a necessary being, an unmoved mover, an uncaused cause. Without such a being the cosmos remains unintelligible. For without such a being there would be nothing at all.

---

8. See above, pp. 23–24.

EXERCISE 2.3

Which of the following express a *causal* or *logical* relation?

Being a girl:	Not being a boy
Stone hits man:	Man injured
Friction:	Heat
Smoking:	Cancer
Having three sides:	Being a triangle
My existing now:	My father exists
My existing now:	God exists
Wishing to win the lottery:	Winning the lottery
The stone moved:	Something moved the stone
Something moved:	There is an 'efficient' mover
There is an efficient mover	God is the first mover

CRITICISM (1): THE PRINCIPLE OF SUFFICIENT REASON

The cosmological argument raises a whole host of major philosophical problems, problems to do with motion, causality, infinity, necessity, and many others. To simplify matters, I shall concentrate in my criticisms on what I take to be the three major areas of debate. These are: (1) the principle of sufficient reason; (2) the argument from cause; and (3) the concept of necessary being.

The principle defined

The principle of sufficient reason states that nothing occurs without a sufficient reason for why it is and not otherwise; it assumes, in other words, that any fact, X, divorced from an account of how it came about will be unintelligible: it is not enough to know *that* X is one must also presume that there is a reason *why* X is. In its simplest form, then, the principle is a technical way of saying that, whenever we ask the question 'Why?' of something, we always presume that there must be some explanation for it, even though we may not know it at the time. So doctors will admit that there are diseases with unknown causes; but they are less likely to accept that there are diseases without causes.

Aquinas adopts much the same procedure in his cosmological argument. Questions about movement, cause and existence presuppose not only that there must be some explanation for them, whether known or unknown, but also that, without such an explanation, these common features of our experience would be meaningless. But where do we look for this explanation? Evidently not in the world of contingent things because these are dependent on the actual conditions that prevail: they are themselves causally determined by other things and would not have occurred if these conditions had been different. It is for this reason that Aquinas argues that the sufficient condition for the world must lie beyond or apart from the world; and this, he concludes, must be a necessary being, the first efficient and non-dependent cause of all that is.

It is worth beginning our analysis of this argument with an important general point. It is that the requirement to find an explanation for our world is not a *logical requirement*. It may of course be true to say that the principle of sufficient reason, whereby we seek such explanation, and indeed derive intellectual and emotional satisfaction from it, is part of our rational make-up – what Richard Taylor, in his own imaginative account of the cosmological argument (SOURCE 2: PP. 76–83), has called a 'presupposition of reason itself';[9] and few would deny that the success achieved in the study of, say, physics and the behavioural sciences has meant that it is reasonable to suppose that such explanations will usually be found. But this is not the same as saying that it is a matter of *logical necessity* either that such explanations will be found or, more importantly, that such explanations exist to be found. As Mackie remarks, the principles we establish about the symmetries, continuities and regularities of nature are justified a posteriori, that is, by their success in helping us to interpret our world; but they are not justified a priori, that is, by asserting that it is part of the *definition* of a particular thing that it can be explained.[10] To this extent, then, the principle of sufficient reason is an assumption that many feel obliged to make in order to avoid the conclusion that the world is pointless; but to conclude that the world is pointless is not in itself contradictory. When, therefore, the cosmological argument presents us with the dilemma 'Either there is a God or the universe is ultimately inexplicable', it is not an error of logic to conclude that the universe is inexplicable and that accordingly there is no God.

Let me begin by recalling a celebrated conversation between Frederick Copleston and Bertrand Russell:

> **RUSSELL:**   It all turns on this question of sufficient reason, and I must say you haven't defined 'sufficient reason' in any way that I can under-stand – what do you mean by sufficient reason? You don't mean cause?
>
> **COPLESTON:**   Not necessarily. Cause is a kind of sufficient reason. Only contingent being can have a cause. God is his own sufficient reason; and he is not the cause of himself. By sufficient reason in the full sense I mean an explanation adequate to the existence of some particular being.
>
> **RUSSELL:**   But when is an explanation adequate? Suppose I am about to make a flame with a match. You may say that the adequate explanation of that is that I rub it on the box.
>
> **COPLESTON:**   Well for practical purposes – but theoretically, that is only a partial explanation. An adequate explanation must ultimately be a total explanation, to which nothing further can be added.

Sufficient reason not a logical requirement

⇐

Debate between Copleston and Russell

---

9. *Metaphysics*, 4th edn, Englewood Cliffs, N.J., Prentice-Hall, 1992, p. 101.
10. *The Miracle of Theism*, Oxford, Clarendon Press, 1982, pp. 34–35.

RUSSELL: Then I can only say that you're looking for something which can't be got, and which one ought not to expect to get.

COPLESTON: To say that one has not found it is one thing; to say that one should not look for it seems to me rather dogmatic.

RUSSELL: Well, I don't know. I mean, the explanation of one thing is another thing which makes the other thing dependent on yet another, and you have to grasp this sorry scheme of things entire to do what you want, and that we can't do.[11]

Russell is here challenging the assumption that a thing becomes intelligible only when completely explained. For Russell it is not merely that it is practically impossible to provide the kind of explanation Copleston requires – where everything referred to in the explanation is itself explained – but more precisely that such comprehensiveness is not required for a thing to be made intelligible. For example, suppose I am asked to explain why Mrs Thatcher remained Prime Minister of Great Britain for so long. I might reply that this was due to the weakness of successive Labour oppositions. If this were thought insufficient, I could go on to explain her success in terms of her reform of the trade unions, her conduct of the Falklands War, and so on. If this too were not sufficiently enlightening, I might then include facets of her character, of her dominance over colleagues and her appeal to certain sections of the public. But if it should then be argued that even this explanation is incomplete and that what is finally required is some account of why Mrs Thatcher exists – which in turn calls for a history of her family back to the amoeba and the existence of a necessary being – we might justifiably reply with Russell that this requirement is now an unreasonable one, given that the explanations already offered *have satisfactorily answered the original question.*

From this we may conclude that, even if an explanation is not ultimately comprehensive, and even if the explanation offered is expressed solely in terms of the relation between one contingent item and another, this does not mean that the explanation offered is unsatisfactory or that the initial question remains somehow obscure because it cannot be answered to the point of completeness. For what matters here is whether the particular answer being given satisfies the particular question being asked. When therefore cosmologists insist that the only sufficient reason for the existence of any particular contingent being is an ultimate explanation which assumes the necessary existence of God, they are employing, so the criticism runs, a totally misguided conception of what an explanation can and cannot do. Not only is it difficult to see how any explanation could ever satisfy the demand for absolute comprehensiveness, but even *not* satisfying it does not render that explanation inadequate. For as we have seen, a thing can be explained, and thus rendered intelligible, in a more limited way, namely, in terms of its causal

---

11. 'The Existence of God – A Debate' (BBC, 1948). Reprinted in Russell, *Why I am Not a Christian*, London, George Allen & Unwin, 1967, p. 138.

connection with other contingent things, and without recourse to a regressive series of explanations.

This reply, however, does not satisfy Copleston and other advocates of the cosmological argument. Even if an item within the world could be explained by reference to other contingent items, we have not broken out of the circle of contingency: we have still not provided a sufficient reason why *the world as a whole exists.*

> What we call the world is intrinsically unintelligible apart from the existence of God. The infinity of the series of events, if such an infinity could be proved, would not be in the slightest degree relevant to the situation. If you add up chocolates, you get chocolates after all, and not a sheep. If you add up chocolates to infinity, you presumably get an infinite number of chocolates. So, if you add up contingent beings to infinity, you still get contingent beings, not a necessary being.[12]

It would seem that we are back where we started. Even if we can explain why any particular thing exists by reference to other contingent things, this does not explain why the *totality* of contingent things exists, why there should be a world at all. Since, therefore, the sufficient reason for the existence of *all* contingent things cannot be found within the world, it must lie outside the world, namely, in some non-contingent existence upon which all contingent and relative being depends. All contingent existences, and all contingent explanations, must consequently depend in the end on an absolute existence, on a necessary being which alone contains the reason for its own existence.

This line of reasoning, however, falls foul of an argument urged by many critics, most notably by David Hume (1711–1776) in his posthumous *Dialogues Concerning Natural Religion* (1779), a book to which I shall refer many times in this and subsequent chapters (SOURCE 3: PP. 83–84). $\Leftarrow$

> But the WHOLE you say, wants a Cause. I answer, that the uniting of these Parts into a whole, like the uniting of several distinct counties into one kingdom, or several distinct members into one body, is performed merely by an arbitrary act of the mind, and has no influence on the nature of things. Did I show you the particular causes of each individual in a collection of twenty particles of matter, I should think it very unreasonable, should you afterwards ask me, what was the cause of the whole twenty. That is sufficiently explained in explaining the cause of the parts.[13]

The weakness that Hume is exposing here is called by logicians the 'fallacy of composition'. This fallacy consists in claiming that, since every member of

Hume and the fallacy of composition

---

12. *Ibid.*, p. 139.
13. *Dialogues Concerning Natural Religion*, edited with an Introduction by Norman Kemp Smith, London, Thomas Nelson & Sons, 1947, pp. 190–191. A biographical note on Hume appears below, pp. 64–65.

a class has a certain property, the class as a whole has the same property. Russell makes the same point in his reply to Copleston.

> I can illustrate what seems to me your fallacy. Every man who exists has a mother and it seems to me your argument is that therefore the human race must have a mother, but obviously the human race hasn't a mother – that's a different logical sphere.[14]

This example does not, however, settle the issue, since other examples could be given in which the fallacy of composition does not apply. For instance, if every member of a parliamentary constituency votes Labour, then it is correct to say that this is a Labour constituency. Here there is no error of reasoning when the characteristics of each member of the group are applied to the group as a whole. But examples like this do not reduce the force of the objection being voiced by Hume and Russell. For their point is that the fallacy of composition is committed when we move from the *existence* of the members of a group to the *existence* of the group itself; when we assume with the cosmological argument that, because there must be a causal explanation for the existence of the contingent things within the group, there must be a causal explanation for the *totality* of contingent things (i.e., the world). In other words, advocates of the cosmological argument have been seduced by their own language. Because collective nouns like 'group', 'class', 'world' and 'universe' do often function in sentences as if they refer to specific objects, it is tempting to suppose that we can ask for a causal explanation of a group or class in the same way that we can ask for the causal explanation of a particular thing, like a tree or a house. But that is not the case, the reason being that the group is not something distinct from its membership; and that accordingly to explain the activity of the individual members is the same as to explain the activities of the group.

EXERCISE 2.4

Does the fallacy of composition apply in these cases?

1 A: 'Three friends of mine are in Washington: Michael to see his lawyer, George to see his girlfriend, and John to go to a concert.'
   B: 'Fine. But what I want to know is why this whole group of friends is in Washington.'

2 The immoral behaviour of the President just goes to show how immoral the government is.

3 All my relations are rich; therefore my family is rich.

4 Iraq is a militant country. Thus every Iraqi is militant.

5 Everything must have a cause; therefore there must be something that is the cause of everything.

---

14. *Op. cit.*, p. 140.

The difficulty in asking for the sufficient reason of the universe as a whole can be explained from a slightly different angle. It has been suggested that all explanations fall into one of two kinds – mechanical and purposive – and that in each case the explanation is given in terms of *something other* than the thing being explained, be it an event or process, intention or desire.[15] Why won't the car start? Because the fuel tank is empty (mechanical). Why did he kill his mother? Because he wanted her money (purposive). Sometimes these two types combine. Why has Smith a broken jaw? Because (a) a brick hit him (mechanical) and because (b) the neighbour he insulted threw it at him (purposive). Now, it makes sense to ask why-questions of this sort – questions, that is, directed at things within the world – because in each case there is *something else*, apart from the thing to be explained, which can provide the answer. So, in the previous exercise, the explanation was given by reference to what brought each person to Washington. But what can this other thing be when we ask why-questions of the world as a whole? What can be said to exist apart from the totality of all existing things? How, then, can the question of the world as a whole be a meaningful one if there is nothing else in terms of which an explanation can be provided? We have here, in other words, exhausted the normal usage of 'explanation'. It makes sense to ask why-questions of A when there exists a B to which reference may be made; but it does not make sense to ask such questions of A + B when together they constitute the world as a whole, because where then is the answer to come from?

Mechanical and purposive explanations

According to the cosmological argument, of course, the answer comes from God, whose necessary existence does distinguish him quite precisely from the contingent existence of everything else. But in that case, so the criticism runs, the argument is guilty of a blatant contradiction. The argument's conclusion – that the why-question of the world as a whole is answered by the necessary existence of God – is reached by the insistence that the principle of sufficient reason is all-inclusive, that it applies to *all that is*. This, however, the argument then contradicts by insisting that the principle does *not* apply to the existence of God; that God is the exception to the rule that the principle has established – in other words, the cosmological answer 'The cause is God' does not admit the question 'What, then, caused God?' This question is ruled out because to seek the cause of a necessary being – a being which by definition excludes questions of its cause – is meaningless. Yet no reason is given why the necessary being thus presented should be the exception or why we should accept it as an explanation even when it flouts the rule that holds for explanations, namely, that an explanation requires a reference to something else.

This is the same as saying that the conclusion of the cosmological argument contradicts the a posteriori character of the argument generally. To recall Mackie's remarks, the principle of sufficient reason is not known a priori but is subject to the test of empirical observation: its justification lies in the degree to which it helps us make sense of things within the world. But when we ask

A priori character of the argument

---

15. See Wallace Matson, *The Existence of God*, Ithaca, N.Y., Cornell University Press, 1965, pp. 62–65.

for the sufficient reason for the world as a whole, we have moved outside the framework within which empirical observations operate. The answer to this question can therefore be provided only on the assumption that there *must be* such an answer; that, in other words, the principle of sufficient reason is a *logical* truth, and that accordingly a necessary relation must hold between the world as a whole and its ultimate cause. But to suppose this is really no more than what Hume calls an 'arbitrary act of the mind', an understandable assumption on our part, made to render our world intelligible. But however emotionally or intellectually reassuring this assumption may be, the world does not have to comply with it. To this extent the cosmological argument has, thus far, failed as a proof. It may be highly plausible to claim that the objects of our experience have explanations, whether we know them or not; but no justification has yet been given for the supposition that all such objects, taken together, remain unintelligible without the ultimate explanation of necessary being.

CRITICISM (2): THE ARGUMENT FROM CAUSALITY

The causal argument proceeds in three stages, each of which is open to dispute.

SUMMARY:
THE ARGUMENT
FROM CAUSALITY

1   Experiential evidence confirms that every event must have a cause. Thus for any event (C) that exists there must be a prior event (B) that brings C into existence, and a prior event (A) that brings B into existence, and so on.

2   This chain of causes and effects cannot, however, be traced back *ad infinitum*. For an unlimited succession of causes means that there is no beginning to the series; and having no beginning means that there can be no subsequent succession of causes, which is contrary to our experience.

3   Therefore there must be a first cause, called God.

FIRST STAGE

The first stage of the causal argument is governed by the claim, supposedly accepted by all rational people as self-evident, that *every event must have a cause*. This belief has, however, been classically challenged by David Hume.

Scottish philosopher, historian and essayist, Hume is arguably the most influential naturalist philosopher of the eighteenth century. The son of a minor Scottish landowner, he briefly attended Edinburgh University, then studied for a legal career, but left Scotland in 1734 to continue his education privately at La Flèche in Anjou. Here he wrote *A Treatise of Human Nature*, which was published, without success, on Hume's return to London, in 1739–1740. He had more success with two volumes of *Essays: Moral and Political* (1741–1742), but after failing to secure a professorship in Moral Philosophy at Edinburgh, largely because of the opposition of the local clergy, Hume turned to less literary pursuits, including diplomatic duties in Vienna and Turin. In 1748 he published his *Enquiry Concerning Human Understanding*, a more accessible version of the first part of his *Treatise*, but including as new material his famous essay 'Of Miracles', which brought him further notoriety. His appointment as librarian at the Advocates' Library in Edinburgh provided him with sufficient financial security to produce his highly successful six-volume *History of England* (1754–1762), which brought him wealth and fame. During this period Hume also wrote his two major works on religion: *The Dialogues Concerning Natural Religion*, which on advice was not published until after his death,[16] and *The Natural History of Religion* (1757). Further diplomatic service followed in Paris, and Hume returned to England in 1766 accompanied by Rousseau, with whom he quarrelled. He settled finally in Edinburgh in 1769. His cheerful dignity before a painful death on 25 August 1776 established him as something of a secular saint, his continued irreligious attitudes discomforting Boswell but provoking unpleasant remarks from Dr Johnson.

David Hume
(1711–1776)

Hume's argument is set out in Book 1 of his *Treatise of Human Nature* (1739–1740) and in Sections 4 and 7 of his *An Enquiry Concerning Human Understanding* of 1748 (SOURCE 4: PP. 84–86).

In one sense it is strikingly similar to the argument just presented against the principle of sufficient reason. For Hume, to repeat, while it may be intellectually satisfying to suppose that the world requires an explanation, this still remains an assumption on our part – 'an arbitrary act of the mind' – and is not accordingly a matter of logical necessity. And the same, Hume now claims, can be said of the relation between cause and effect. That every event must have a cause is taken for granted *not* because this causal principle is either intuitively obvious or demonstrable but because, once again, there is a 'determination of the mind', a psychological disposition on our part, that there must be an actual link between one event and another.

⇐

Hume and the relation between cause and effect

John Passmore has given a helpful illustration of how Hume's argument proceeds.[17] A baby boy is given a rubber ball by his uncle. Because he has only played with soft toys, the boy cannot know beforehand that this toy will not drop softly to the ground but bounce. But what does the uncle expect to see? He does expect the ball to bounce. Why? He will reply: because my nephew *caused* the ball to bounce by dropping it; or because rubber balls have the *power* or characteristic of bouncing when dropped; or because rubber balls must

16. For more on the *Dialogues*, see below, p. 104.
17. *The Great Philosophers*, ed. Bryan Magee, London, BBC Books, 1987, pp. 147–148.

drop, because there is a *necessary connection* between rubber balls dropping and bouncing. But why exactly does the uncle employ concepts like 'cause', 'power' and 'necessary connection'? Presumably, says Hume, it is because the uncle, unlike his nephew, has observed a great many instances of balls dropping and bouncing, and because indeed he has *never* come across an example in which this has not occurred. To use Hume's terminology, within the uncle's experience there has therefore been a *constant conjunction* between a ball's falling and bouncing.

Hume's next question is decisive. What exactly is it about the uncle's experience that generates concepts like 'cause', 'power' and 'necessary connection'? The uncle has seen a ball dropping many times and his nephew only once. But this is the same as saying that the uncle has seen *the same event repeated but has not seen anything new*. The uncle has not therefore seen anything that his nephew has not seen, but has rather had the same experience *more often*. Where, then, does the idea of a causal link – the 'necessary connection' – come from if it has never been directly observed?

> Hume's answer is that although experiencing the same sequence of events on innumerable occasions does not reveal something we did not notice on the first occasion – a causal link – it does affect the workings of our mind in a special kind of way. It *forms the habit in us* of expecting a rubber ball to bounce when it drops. To believe that A causes B, or that there is a necessary connection between A and B, or that A *makes* B happen, amounts, then, to nothing more than this: our minds are so constituted that when, having in our experience found A and B to be constantly conjoined, we meet with an A we expect it to be followed by a B; and when we meet with a B we presume it to have been preceded by an A. Our experience generates in us a habit of expecting; our consciousness of this habit is our idea of necessary connection. However, we mistakenly project it into the world around us, wrongly supposing that we perceive necessary connection there rather than simply feel impelled to make particular inferences.[18]

It is beyond the scope of this book to offer an analysis of Hume's argument.[19] For our purposes it is sufficient to note that the first premiss of Aquinas' argument incorporates a theory of causation that can be, and has been, disputed. The causal argument begins with the statement that the relation of cause and effect belongs to what Aquinas calls 'the world of sense', and this classification is duplicated in the argument from motion where the relation

---

18. *Ibid.*, p. 148.
19. A clear exposition of Hume's argument is given by Bertrand Russell in his *History of Western Philosophy*, London, George Allen & Unwin, 1946, pp. 685–700, and by Antony Flew in two books: *David Hume*, Oxford, Basil Blackwell, 1986; and *Hume's Philosophy of Belief*, London, Routledge & Kegan Paul, 1961. See also Edward Craig, 'Hume on Thought and Belief', in *Philosophers Ancient and Modern*, ed. Godfrey Vesey, Cambridge, Cambridge University Press, 1986, pp. 93–110.

between mover and thing moved is described as 'certain, and evident to our senses'. So, at the heart of our idea of the world, and of our idea of our own experience, we find this indispensable notion of causality, which, Aquinas maintains, can be validated a posteriori, by experience and observation. Hume does not challenge the centrality of the notion, but he does challenge the process by which it is established. This he does because there is no valid logical justification for saying 'that instances, of which we have had no experience, must resemble those, of which we have had experience, and that the course of nature continues always the same'.[20]

In the light of Hume's criticisms of causality, consider the following:

EXERCISE 2.5

1 The sun will rise tomorrow.

2 Jumping from skyscrapers is foolish.

3 Every man has a mother.

4 Since, as a 95-year-old, I have survived more nights than a 25-year-old girl, I have a better chance than she of surviving this night.

5 Two aborigines see water-skiing for the first time. 'Why is that boat going so fast?' asks one. 'Because it's being chased by that idiot on a string', replies the other.[21]

Hume's conclusion is, then, that the expectation that future experiences will somehow conform to past experiences is justified on the assumption that *nature is uniform*; that what has been the case will be the case. But the principle that nature is uniform cannot be established. The repetition of instances, which leads us to the belief that A causes B, in turn reinforces our expectation – or what Hume calls a 'habit' or 'custom' – that the same will occur in the future. But the expectation that the relation between A and B will persist does not establish that it will. What we mean therefore by the 'uniformity of nature' is no more than a determination of the mind to think about events *in a causal way*, to organize our experience of events by establishing necessary connections between them. But these connections are not logical, since in this instance we cannot say that A implies B or that there is something about A which must produce B. It is therefore only the constant conjunction of A and B in past experience that induces the belief that they are necessarily connected; but the actual connection between them is a psychological one.

---

20. *A Treatise of Human Nature* (1739), Book 1, Part III, Section VI, ed. L. A. Selby-Bigge, London, Oxford University Press, reprint 1965, p. 89.
21. Given by John Allen Paulos, *I Think, therefore I Laugh*, New York, Columbia University Press, 1985, p. 67.

In this way, then, Hume challenges the first premiss of the causal argument. He has shown that the accepted maxim that every event must have a cause is neither self-evident nor demonstrable. But more than that, he has shown the extent to which Aquinas, by explaining causal connections in terms of the uniformity of nature, has assumed the point he is seeking to prove. For to say that nature is uniform is the same as saying that there is a necessary connection between cause and effect, and this is precisely the point at issue. From the outset, therefore, Aquinas has postulated that the universe is ultimately rational but has provided no evidence that it is, only the assumption that it is.

SECOND STAGE

Criticism of Aquinas on infinite regression

The second stage of the causal argument maintains that *an infinite series of regressive causes is inconceivable.* For Aquinas this claim has immediate empirical support. To suppose that there is an infinite series of causes logically requires that we deny that there was a beginning to the series and thus no subsequent effects, i.e., that nothing exists now. Since, therefore, something evidently does exist now, we may reject the idea of an infinite series as manifestly absurd. Both the arguments from motion and cause follow this reasoning, but it is best expressed in the argument from contingency. Here the capacity of anything 'not to be' would be realized in infinite time. Hence there would be a time in the past when nothing existed, and thus nothing existing now. And once again it is the manifest absurdity of this conclusion which forces Aquinas to reject the notion of infinite regression.

This argument is also vulnerable. The first thing to say is that it is logically possible to conceive of a series which has no first member. Mathematicians do just this. Hans Reichenbach explains:

> There need not have been a first event; we can imagine that every event was preceded by an earlier event, and that time has no beginning. The infinity of time, in both directions, offers no difficulties to the understanding. We know that the series of numbers has no end, that for every number there is a larger number. If we include the negative numbers, the number series has no beginning either; for every number there is a smaller number. Infinite series without a beginning and an end have been successfully treated in mathematics; there is nothing paradoxical in them. To object that there must have been a first event, a beginning of time, is the attitude of an untrained mind. Logic does not tell us anything about the structure of time. Logic offers the means of dealing with infinite series without a beginning as well as with series that have a beginning. If scientific evidence is in favour of an infinite time, coming from infinity and going to infinity, logic has no objection.[22]

---

22. *The Rise of Scientific Philosophy,* Berkeley, University of California Press, 1951, pp. 207–208.

But to this, as we have seen, Aquinas has a ready reply. There is an obvious difference between admitting the logical possibility of an infinite series of integers and admitting the logical possibility of an infinite series of events. In the first case, any number can be increased or decreased by simply adding or subtracting 1; but in the second, to postulate *no beginning* to a causal series produces the absurd conclusion that there are no events *now occurring*. For to suppose that the history of events is infinite is to suppose a causal chain without a first member; and to take away the first member is to take away the primary cause of all subsequent members, and thus to imply their non-existence. So without A, Z could not exist. But Z exists. Therefore A exists.

The notion that Aquinas wishes to bring out here is of a finite and conditioned existence being *dependent* on an infinite and unconditioned existence; that because every member of the causal chain exists by virtue of God's existence, the denial of his existence results in the absurdity that nothing exists. Again, the contingency argument makes this very clear, making much of the ancient axiom that 'out of nothing nothing can come' (*ex nihilo nihil fit*). The choice, it appears, is between accepting (1) the empirical untruth that even now there is nothing existing, which follows from postulating an infinite series in which everything has the capacity of not being; and (2) the empirical truth that something exists, which follows from postulating that not everything is capable of not being, that indeed there must be something that is necessary. This choice serves to highlight the fact that it is God's *sustaining* existence which provides the support for all existing things, and that this support would be lacking if there were an infinite regression.

Aquinas' reply has been much criticized.[23] That the history of events is infinite does not imply that at some time in the past there was nothing existing but rather that within that series there was nothing uncaused, nothing that did not have a beginning, nothing in fact that can lay claim to the exalted position of first cause within the chain of causal events. Is this a plausible alternative? I think it is. On the presumption that there is infinite past time, and that everything has the possibility of not being, the conclusion is not that at some time there was nothing – i.e., that at some time *everything* was not – but rather that at some time *each* thing was not. In other words, Aquinas' conclusion will not do because he is here assuming the *simultaneous* actualization of everything's capacity not to be. But the time when A was not could (logically) be different from the time that B was not, and so on. We can, for example, imagine a series, each item of which is finite but whose period of existence was not identical but overlapped: there would then be no time when there was nothing. Or we could imagine a contingent thing whose existence has lasted through all past time but which is to perish at some future time. In either case, it is an error of reasoning to suppose that 'each thing at some time is not' entails 'a time when everything was not'. This being the case, Aquinas is wrong to suppose that an infinite series entails the absurdity that nothing exists now; and thus he is wrong

23. For a defence, see Stephen T. Davis, *God, Reason and Theistic Proofs*, Edinburgh, Edinburgh University Press, 1997, pp. 60–77.

to suppose that what exists now cannot be the result of an infinite causal regression. The existence of a necessary being is not therefore required to explain the empirical truth that things exist.

Nor does Copleston's suggestion that Aquinas is here talking of causes *in esse*, and not causes *in fieri*, avoid these difficulties. While it may be true that Aquinas is speaking of an ontological cause rather than a temporal cause – of a primary supporting existence, upon which everything now existing depends – this cause remains a cause. Why, then, may we not suppose an infinite regression of this vertical hierarchy? For if the series were infinite, or if the finite items within that series overlapped, or if something within that series had not as yet ceased to be, there would still be something existing, and so still something which could provide the ontological support to account for the existence of things here and now.

THIRD STAGE

Hume and the notion of God as first cause

Let us now set aside these objections and assume that Aquinas has successfully established that there is a first cause. The question now arises: why is God identified as this first cause? The answer, as we have seen, is that, while everything else must have a cause, God does not require one because his existence is self-caused. In this sense God is the only candidate for the job of first cause. But is this the case? For if God can be self-caused, why cannot the universe itself be self-caused? Hume writes:

> But if we stop, and go no further; why go so far? Why not stop at the material world? How can we satisfy ourselves without going on *in infinitum*? And after all, what satisfaction is there in that infinite progression? Let us remember the story of the *Indian* Philosopher and his Elephant. It was never more applicable than to the present subject. If the material world rests upon a similar ideal world, this ideal world must rest upon some other; and so on, without end. It were better, therefore, never to look beyond the present material world. By supposing it to contain the principle of its order within itself, we really assert it to be God; and the sooner we arrive at that divine Being so much the better. When you go one step beyond the mundane system, you only excite an inquisitive humour, which it is impossible ever to satisfy.[24]

In referring to the Indian and the Elephant, Hume is repeating a story already told by the English philosopher John Locke (1632–1704) in another context. An Indian asserts that the world is supported by a great elephant, who in turn rests upon the back of a great tortoise; but when asked what the tortoise stands on, the Indian replies, 'something, he knows not what'.[25] Aquinas,

---

24. *Dialogues Concerning Natural Religion*, pp. 161–162.
25. *An Essay Concerning Human Understanding*, ed. A. C. Fraser, Oxford, Clarendon Press, 1894, II.xxiii, pp. 1–5.

however, does know. This kind of causal regression must terminate with the identification of God as first cause. But for Hume this conclusion is entirely arbitrary since we are still faced with another alternative: that the first cause is not God but *the universe itself*. This possibility, which for Hume is more consistent with what we already know of the world, requires no supernatural agent or divine author: the world, evolving from a primordial supply of matter, actualizes itself. And we may note, following earlier remarks, that this is possible even if the universe consists entirely of things which individually have the possibility of not existing. Thus there is nothing contradictory in the claim that the universe came into being without a cause, or that it always existed, and that accordingly it had no beginning.

Critique of Pure Reason, title page, first edition

Hume's remarks drew from Immanuel Kant, in his *Critique of Pure Reason*, more general conclusions about why the causal argument fails (SOURCE 5: PP. 86–89).[26] The argument has an empirical starting-point – our immediate experience of causality – and from thence it seeks to establish the existence of an uncaused cause. But this transition is wholly unjustified. The principle of causality, Kant contends, must remain within the realm in which it operates, i.e., within the world of sense-experience; and it cannot be employed to convey us beyond this world to another in which it does not operate.

The principle of causality has no meaning and no criterion for its application save only in the sensible world. But in the cosmological proof it is precisely in order to enable us to advance beyond the sensible world that it is employed.[27]

Kant's criticism of the cosmological argument

⇐

More generally, then, the cosmological argument fails because it attempts to reason beyond the scope of experience and thus beyond the point at which we have any guarantee that our conclusions are justified. Whether it be the

26. *Op. cit.*, pp. 507–514.
27. *Ibid.*, p. 511.

experience of causality or of the precarious and contingent nature of our existence, these experiences, while they may lead us to the hypothesis of an uncaused and necessary being, do not allow us to conclude that there actually exists such a being, that the reality of this being can be inferred from these experiences. For both Hume and Kant, therefore, any proof of the existence of God founded on the limits of sense information is an exercise in futility. It is not that God does not exist, but rather that we have, within these limits, no means of assessing the validity of an argument that says he exists. As an a posteriori proof, the cosmological argument thus begins in the world of sense and ends, predictably enough for our two authors, in the world of pure speculation.

CRITICISM (3): THE CONCEPT OF NECESSARY BEING

The final criticism of the cosmological argument – or more exactly of the argument from contingency – focuses on the concept of God as a necessary being, the objection being that this concept is meaningless. We have already met this criticism in Kant's analysis of the second form of the ontological argument.[28] Kant now repeats his objection, claiming in justification that 'the so-called cosmological proof really owes any cogency which it may have to the ontological proof from mere concepts'.[29]

Kant's remark is not entirely accurate. The ontological argument maintains that we can move from the idea of a perfect being to its existence, from the definition of X to the reality of X. The contingency argument, on the other hand, moves in an opposite direction, from existence to idea, from the empirically given fact that *something* exists to the requirement of a necessary existence to explain this fact. Unlike Anselm, therefore, Aquinas is seeking to express a relation of *ontological dependence* and not a relation of *logical implication*. To this extent, at least, the cosmological argument is immune to the criticism that one cannot derive actual existence from an initial definition.

Kant's objection

But Kant's remark does carry weight if we concentrate not on the process but on the outcome, i.e., on whether by a priori or a posteriori argumentation it can be established that there exists a being *which cannot not exist*. This explains why, in the second form of the ontological argument, it is self-contradictory to deny the existence of this being; and why, in the contingency argument, it is illegitimate to ask the question 'What brought God into existence?' This reveals the connection between the two arguments. In both it is irrational to suppose that God might not have existed, and both attest to the fact that in God existence is not an accidental quality but something intrinsic to his nature; that God, to be God, must have the characteristic of necessity.

I have already dealt with Kant's objection at this point. Employing his distinction between *analytic* and *synthetic* propositions, Kant concludes that the predicate 'necessary being' cannot be attributed to God because

---

28. See above, pp. 16–19.
29. *Op. cit.*, p. 510.

Immanuel Kant: the Königsberg statue

this predicate is meaningless and self-contradictory. For whereas no necessary or analytic proposition can be denied without self-contradiction, all existential or synthetic propositions can be so denied. It is therefore logically impossible for *any* synthetic proposition to be logically necessary. This objection, which we find also in Hume, is taken up in our own day by several critics, most notably by J. N. Findlay, to whom I have already referred.[30]

We have also seen, however, that this criticism derives from a particular tendency in modern philosophical thought and ignores or is unaware of the way in which the concept of necessary being is used within the main biblical and theological tradition. For both Anselm and Aquinas necessary being does not imply, as Findlay assumes, a logically necessary existence but rather a kind of factual necessity, exemplified by the scholastic notion of *aseity* or self-existence, in which God's being, eternal and incorruptible, is causally independent of any other being. It is true that the existence of a logically necessary being cannot be denied without contradiction; but the existence of a factually necessary being can be so denied. And such denials are not, we recall, alien to the biblical tradition, although they may well be considered false and sinful by believers.

This interpretation of divine necessity as factual, rather than logical, necessity may well safeguard the contingency argument, and the ontological argument for that matter, from the kind of criticism offered by Kant and Findlay. There remains, however, one last point to notice. This is the way in which the concept of factual necessity has radically altered the character of the contingency argument. For if by factual necessity we mean a certain cosmological independence that cannot be rationally demonstrated but which can, and is, *experienced by belief,* then we are no longer dealing with a proof but with an argument that requires a particular psychological disposition on the part of its adherents. What we are now dealing with is faith's own expression of its dependence on God. This indeed is how the distinguished theologian Paul Tillich (1886–1965) interprets the cosmological argument. As a rational demonstration, the proof fails; but it succeeds inasmuch as it shows how the experience of contingency – what Tillich calls the experience of the threat of non-being – drives people 'to the question of being conquering non-being and

Tillich's interpretation of the cosmological argument

---

30. See above, p. 19.

of courage conquering anxiety. This question is the cosmological question of God.'[31] In this sense, then, the anxiety felt by human beings about their own annihilation provides the cosmological route to an awareness of divine reality.

This interpretation may indeed circumvent the logical problems we have noted in this chapter; but it does so only by rejecting Aquinas' original claim to provide a demonstration a posteriori, in which the existence of God is not assumed but is the outcome of rational inference. For Tillich it may be the case that people of faith require no theistic proofs; but this was evidently not the case with Aquinas. That God exists is, of course, an article of faith; but it is also, according to Aquinas, a proposition capable of proof by the natural light of reason. But in this, as I have tried to show, Aquinas was mistaken. The existence of a necessary being cannot be demonstrated, and thus the possibility that the universe is ultimately unintelligible remains.

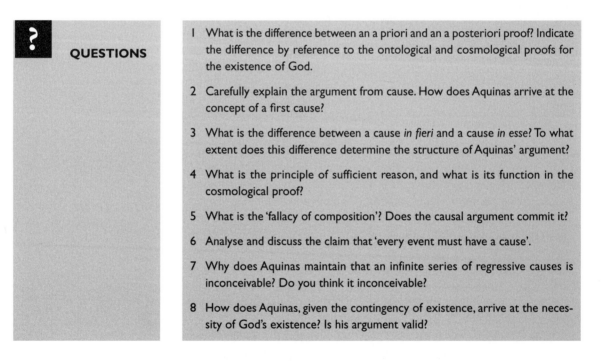

QUESTIONS

1   What is the difference between an a priori and an a posteriori proof? Indicate the difference by reference to the ontological and cosmological proofs for the existence of God.

2   Carefully explain the argument from cause. How does Aquinas arrive at the concept of a first cause?

3   What is the difference between a cause *in fieri* and a cause *in esse*? To what extent does this difference determine the structure of Aquinas' argument?

4   What is the principle of sufficient reason, and what is its function in the cosmological proof?

5   What is the 'fallacy of composition'? Does the causal argument commit it?

6   Analyse and discuss the claim that 'every event must have a cause'.

7   Why does Aquinas maintain that an infinite series of regressive causes is inconceivable? Do you think it inconceivable?

8   How does Aquinas, given the contingency of existence, arrive at the necessity of God's existence? Is his argument valid?

---

31. *Systematic Theology*, London, James Nisbet & Co., 1953, Vol. I, p. 231. I shall have more to say about Tillich's argument in Chapter 5. For biographical information about him, see below, p. 199.

SOURCES: THE COSMOLOGICAL
ARGUMENT

I AQUINAS: THE FIVE PROOFS OF GOD'S EXISTENCE[1]

The existence of God can be proved in five ways.

The first and more manifest way is the argument from motion. It is certain, and evident to our senses, that in the world some things are in motion. Now whatever is in motion is put in motion by another, for nothing can be in motion except it is in potentiality to that towards which it is in motion; whereas a thing moves inasmuch as it is in act. For motion is nothing else than the reduction of something from potentiality to actuality. But nothing can be reduced from potentiality to actuality, except by something in a state of actuality. Thus that which is actually hot, as fire, makes wood, which is potentially hot, to be actually hot, and thereby moves and changes it. Now it is not possible that the same thing should be at once in actuality and potentiality in the same respect, but only in different respects. For what is actually hot cannot simultaneously be potentially hot; but it is simultaneously potentially cold. It is therefore impossible that in the same respect and in the same way a thing should be both mover and moved, i.e., that it should move itself. Therefore, whatever is in motion must be put in motion by another. If that by which it is put in motion be itself put in motion, then this also must needs be put in motion by another, and that by another again. But this cannot go on to infinity, because then there would be no first mover, and, consequently, no other mover; seeing that subsequent movers move only inasmuch as they are put in motion by the first mover; as the staff moves only because it is put in motion by the hand. Therefore it is necessary to arrive at a first mover, put in motion by no other; and this everyone understands to be God.

The second way is from the nature of the efficient cause. In the world of sense we find there is an order of efficient causes. There is no case known (neither is it, indeed, possible) in which a thing is found to be the efficient cause of itself; for so it would be prior to itself which is impossible. Now in efficient causes it is not possible to go on to infinity, because in all efficient causes following in order, the first is the cause of the intermediate cause, and the intermediate is the cause of the ultimate cause, whether the intermediate cause be several or one only. Now to take away the cause is to take away the effect. Therefore, if there be no first cause among efficient causes, there will be no ultimate, nor any intermediate cause. But if in efficient causes it is possible to go on to infinity, there will be no first efficient cause, neither will there be an ultimate effect, nor any intermediate efficient causes; all of which is plainly false. Therefore it is necessary to admit a first efficient cause, to which everyone gives the name of God.

The third way is taken from possibility and necessity and runs thus. We find in nature things that are possible to be and not to be, since they are found to be generated, and to corrupt, and consequently, they are possible to be and not to

---

1. *Summa Theologiae*, Part a, 2, 3, London, Eyre & Spottiswoode, 1972.

be. But it is impossible for these always to exist, for that which is possible not to be at some time is not. Therefore, if everything is possible not to be, then at one time there could have been nothing in existence. Now if this were true, even now there would be nothing in existence, because that which does not exist only begins to exist by something already existing. Therefore, if at one time nothing was in existence, it would have been impossible for anything to have begun to exist; and thus even now nothing would be in existence – which is absurd. Therefore, not all beings are merely possible, but there must exist something the existence of which is necessary. But every necessary thing either has its necessity caused by another, or not. Now it is impossible to go on to infinity in necessary things which have their necessity caused by another, as has been already proved in regard to efficient causes. Therefore we cannot but postulate the existence of some being having of itself its own necessity, and not receiving it from another, but rather causing in others their necessity. This all men speak of as God.

The fourth way is taken from the gradation to be found in things. Among beings there are some more and some less good, true, noble, and the like. But 'more' and 'less' are predicated of different things, according as they resemble in their different ways something which is the maximum, as a thing is said to be hotter according as it more nearly resembles that which is hottest; so that there is something which is truest, something best, something noblest, and, consequently, something which is uttermost being; for those things that are greatest in truth are greatest in being, as it is written in Metaph. ii. Now the maximum in any genus is the cause of all in that genus; as fire, which is the maximum of heat, is the cause of all hot things. Therefore there must also be something which is to all beings the cause of their being, goodness, and every other perfection; and this we call God.

The fifth way is taken from the governance of the world. We see that things which lack intelligence, such as natural bodies, act for an end, and this is evident from their acting always, or nearly always, in the same way, so as to obtain the best result. Hence it is plain that not fortuitously, but designedly, do they achieve their end. Now whatever lacks intelligence cannot move towards an end, unless it be directed by some being endowed with knowledge and intelligence; as the arrow is shot to its mark by the archer. Therefore some intelligent being exists, by whom all natural things are directed to their end; and this being we call God.

2 TAYLOR: THE PRINCIPLE OF SUFFICIENT REASON[2]

Suppose you were strolling in the woods and, in addition to the sticks, stones, and other accustomed litter of the forest floor, you one day came upon some quite unaccustomed object, something not quite like what you had ever seen before and would never expect to find in such a place. Suppose, for example, that it is a large ball, about your own height, perfectly smooth and translucent. You would deem

---

Richard Taylor, *Metaphysics*, Englewood Cliffs, N.J., Prentice-Hall, 1963, pp. 91–97.

this puzzling and mysterious, certainly, but if one considers the matter, it is no more inherently mysterious that such a thing should exist than that anything else should exist. If you were quite accustomed to finding such objects of various sizes around you most of the time, but had never seen an ordinary rock, then upon finding a large rock in the woods one day you would be just as puzzled and mystified. This illustrates the fact that something that is mysterious ceases to seem so simply by its accustomed presence. It is strange indeed, for example, that a world such as ours should exist; yet few men are very often struck by this strangeness, but simply take it for granted.

Suppose, then, that you have found this translucent ball and are mystified by it. Now whatever else you might wonder about it, there is one thing you would hardly question; namely, that it did not appear there all by itself, that it owes its existence to something. You might not have the remotest idea whence and how it came to be there, but you would hardly doubt that there was an explanation. The idea that it might have come from nothing at all, that it might exist without there being any explanation of its existence, is one that few people would consider worthy of entertaining.

This illustrates a metaphysical belief that seems to be almost a part of reason itself, even though few men ever think upon it; the belief, namely, that there is some explanation for the existence of anything whatever, some reason why it should exist rather than not. The sheer nonexistence of anything, which is not to be confused with the passing out of existence of something, never requires a reason; but existence does. That there should never have been any such ball in the forest does not require any explanation or reason, but that there should ever be such a ball does. If one were to look upon a barren plain and ask why there is not and never has been any large translucent ball there, the natural response would be to ask why there should be; but if one finds such a ball, and wonders why it is there it is not quite so natural to ask why it should *not* be, as though existence should simply be taken for granted. That anything should not exist, then, and that, for instance, no such ball should exist in the forest, or that there should be no forest for it to occupy, or no continent containing a forest, or no earth, nor any world at all, do not seem to be things for which there needs to be any explanation or reason; but that such things should be, does seem to require a reason.

The principle involved here has been called the principle of sufficient reason. Actually, it is a very general principle, and is best expressed by saying that, in the case of any positive truth, there is some sufficient reason for it, something which, in this sense, makes it true – in short, that there is some sort of explanation, known or unknown, for everything.

Now some truths depend on something else, and are accordingly called *contingent*, while others depend only upon themselves, that is, are true by their very natures and are accordingly called *necessary*. There is, for example, a reason why the stone on my window sill is warm; namely, that the sun is shining upon it. This happens to be true, but not by its very nature. Hence, it is contingent, and depends upon something other than itself. It is also true that all the points of a circle are equidistant from the center, but this truth depends upon nothing but itself. No matter what happens, nothing can make it false. Similarly, it is a truth, and a necessary one, that if the stone on my window sill is a body, as it is, then it has a form, since this fact depends upon nothing but itself for its confirmation. Untruths are also, of course, either contingent or necessary, it being contingently false, for example, that the stone on my window sill is cold, and necessarily false that it is both a body and formless, since this is by its very nature impossible.

The principle of sufficient reason can be illustrated in various ways, as we have done, and if one thinks about it, he is apt to find that he presupposes it in his thinking about reality, but it cannot be proved. It does not appear to be itself a necessary truth, and at the same time it would be most odd to say it is contingent. If one were to try proving it, he would sooner or later have to appeal to considerations that are less plausible than the principle itself. Indeed, it is hard to see how one could even make an argument for it, without already assuming it. For this reason it might properly be called a presupposition of reason itself. One can deny that it is true, without embarrassment or fear of refutation, but one is then apt to find that what he is denying is not really what the principle asserts. We shall, then, treat it here as a datum – not something that is provably true, but as something which all men, whether they ever reflect upon it or not, seem more or less to presuppose.

It happens to be true that something exists, that there is, for example, a world, and while no one ever seriously supposes that this might not be so, that there might exist nothing at all, there still seems to be nothing the least necessary in this, considering it just by itself. That no world should ever exist at all is perfectly comprehensible and seems to express not the slightest absurdity. Considering any particular item in the world it seems not at all necessary in itself that it should ever have existed, nor does it appear any more necessary that the totality of these things, or any totality of things, should ever exist.

From the principle of sufficient reason it follows, of course, that there must be a reason, not only for the existence of everything in the world but for the world itself, meaning by "the world" simply everything that ever does exist, except God, in case there is a god. This principle does not imply that there must be some purpose or goal for everything, or for the totality of all things; for explanations need not, and in fact seldom are, teleological or purposeful. All the principle requires is that there be some sort of reason for everything. And it would certainly be odd to maintain that everything in the world owes its existence to something, that nothing in the world is either purely accidental, or such that it just bestows its own being upon itself, and then to deny this of the world itself. One can indeed *say* that the world is in some sense a pure accident, that there simply is no reason at all why this or any world should exist, and one can equally say that the world exists by its very nature, or is an inherently necessary being. But it is at least very odd and arbitrary to deny of this existing world the need for any sufficient reason, whether independent of itself or not, while presupposing that there is a reason for every other thing that ever exists.

Consider again the strange ball that we imagine has been found in the forest. Now we can hardly doubt that there must be an explanation for the existence of such a thing, though we may have no notion what that explanation is. It is not, moreover, the fact of its having been found in the forest rather than elsewhere that renders an explanation necessary. It matters not in the least where it happens to be, for our question is not how it happens to be *there* but how it happens to exist at all. If we in our imagination annihilate the forest, leaving only this ball in an open field, our conviction that it is a contingent thing and owes its existence to something other than itself is not reduced in the least. If we now imagine the field to be annihilated, and in fact everything else as well to vanish into nothingness, leaving only this ball to constitute the entire physical universe, then we cannot for a moment suppose that its existence has thereby been explained, or the need of any explanation eliminated, or that its existence is suddenly rendered self-explanatory. If we now carry this thought one step further and suppose that no other reality ever has existed or ever will exist, that this ball forever constitutes the entire physical universe, then we must still insist on there being some reason independent of itself why it should exist rather than not. If there must be a reason for the existence of any particular thing, then the necessity of such a reason is not eliminated by the mere supposition that certain other things do *not* exist. And again, it matters not at all what the thing in question is, whether it be large and complex, such as the world we actually find ourselves in, or whether it be something small, simple and insignificant, such as a ball, a bacterium, or the merest grain of sand. We do not avoid the necessity of a reason for the existence of something merely by describing it in this way or that. And it would, in any event, seem quite plainly absurd to say that if the world were comprised entirely of a single ball about six feet in diameter, or of a single grain of sand, then it would be contingent and there would have to be some explanation other than itself why such a thing exists, but that, since the actual world is vastly more complex than this, there is no need for an explanation of its existence, independent of itself.

It should now be noted that it is no answer to the question, why a thing exists, to state *how long* it has existed. A geologist does not suppose that he explained why there should be rivers and mountains merely by pointing out that they are old. Similarly, if one were to ask, concerning the ball of which we have spoken, for some sufficient reason for its being, he would not receive any answer upon being told that it had been there since yesterday. Nor would it be any better answer to say that it had existed since before anyone could remember, or even that it had always existed; for the question was not one concerning its age but its existence. If, to be sure, one were to ask where a given thing came from, or how it came into being, then upon learning that it had always existed he would learn that it never really *came* into being at all; but he could still reasonably wonder why it should exist at all. If, accordingly, the world – that is, the totality of all things excepting God, in case there is a god – had really no beginning at all, but has always existed in some form or other, then it is clearly no answer to the question, where it came from and when; it did not, on this supposition, *come* from anything at all, at any time. But still, it can be asked why there is a world, why indeed there is a beginningless world, why there should have perhaps always been something rather than nothing. And, if the principle of sufficient reason is a good principle, there must be an answer to that question, an answer that is by no means supplied by giving the world an age, or even an infinite age.

This brings out an important point with respect to the concept of creation that is often misunderstood, particularly by those whose thinking has been influenced by Christian ideas. People tend to think that creation – for example, the creation of the world by God – *means* creation *in time*, from which it of course logically follows that if the world had no beginning in time, then it cannot be the creation of God. This, however, is erroneous, for creation means essentially *dependence*, even in Christian theology. If one thing is the creation of another, then it depends for its existence on that other, and this is perfectly consistent with saying that both are eternal, that neither ever came into being, and hence, that neither was ever created at any point of time. Perhaps an analogy will help convey this point. Consider, then, a flame that is casting beams of light. Now there seems to be a clear sense in which the beams of light are dependent for their existence upon the flame, which is their source, while the flame, on the other hand, is not similarly dependent for its existence upon them. The beams of light arise from the flame, but the flame does not arise from them. In this sense, they are the creation of the flame; they derive their existence from it. And none of this has any reference to time; the relationship of dependence in such a case would not be altered in the slightest if we supposed that the flame, and with it the beams of light, had always existed, that neither had ever *come* into being.

Now if the world is the creation of God, its relationship to God should be thought of in this fashion; namely, that the world depends for its existence upon God, and could not exist independently of God. If God is eternal, as those who believe in God generally assume, then the world may (though it need not) be eternal too, without that altering in the least its dependence upon God for its existence, and hence without altering its being the creation of God. The supposition of God's eternality, on the other hand, does not by itself imply that the world is eternal too; for there is not the least reason why something of finite duration might not depend for its existence upon something of infinite duration – though the reverse is, of course, impossible.

If we think of God as 'the creator of heaven and earth', and if we consider heaven and earth to include everything that exists except God, then we appear to have, in the foregoing considerations, fairly strong reasons for asserting that God, as so conceived, exists. Now of course most people have much more in mind than this when they think of God, for religions have ascribed to God ever so many attributes that are not at all implied by describing him merely as the creator of the world; but this is not at all implied by describing him merely as the creator of the world; but that is not relevant here. Most religious persons do, in any case, think of God, as being at least the creator, as that being upon which everything ultimately depends, no matter what else they may say about him in addition. It is, in fact, the first item in the creeds of Christianity that God is the 'creator of heaven and earth'. And, it seems, there are good metaphysical reasons, as distinguished from the persuasions of faith, for thinking that such a creative being exists.

If, as seems clearly implied by the principle of sufficient reason, there must be a reason for the existence of heaven and earth – i.e., for the world – then that reason must be found either in the world itself or outside it, in something that is literally supranatural, or outside heaven and earth. Now if we suppose that the world – i.e., the totality of all things except God – contains within itself the reason for its existence, we are supposing that it exists by its very nature, that is, that it is a necessary being. In that case there would, of course, be no reason for saying that it must depend upon God or anything else for its existence; for if it exists by its very nature, then it depends upon nothing but itself, much as the sun depends upon nothing but itself for its heat. This, however, is implausible, for we find nothing about the world or anything in it to suggest that it exists by its own nature, and we do find, on the contrary, ever so many things to suggest that it does not. For in the first place, anything which exists by its very nature must necessarily be eternal and indestructible. It would be a self-contradiction to say of anything that it exists by its own nature, or is a necessarily existing thing, and at the same time to say that it comes into being or passes away, or that it ever could come into being or pass away. Nothing about the world seems at all like this, for concerning anything in the world, we can perfectly easily think of it as being annihilated, or as never having existed in the first place, without there being the slightest hint of any absurdity in such a supposition. Some of the things in the universe are, to be sure, very old; the moon, for example, or the stars and the planets. It is even possible to imagine that they have always existed. Yet it seems quite impossible to suppose that they owe their existence to nothing but themselves, that they bestow existence upon themselves by their very natures, or that they are in themselves things of such nature that it would be impossible for them not to exist. Even if we suppose that something, such as the sun, for instance, has existed forever, and will never cease, still we cannot conclude just from this that it exists by its own nature. If, as is of course very doubtful, the sun has existed forever and will never cease, then it is possible that its heat and light have also existed forever and will never cease; but that would not show that the heat and light of the sun exist by their own natures. They are obviously contingent and depend on the sun for their existence, whether they are beginningless and everlasting or not.

There seems to be nothing in the world, then, concerning which it is at all plausible to suppose that it exists by its own nature, or contains within itself the reason for its existence. In fact, everything in the world appears to be quite plainly the opposite, namely, something that not only need not exist, but at some time or other, past or future or both, does not in fact exist. Everything in the world seems to have a finite duration, whether long or short. Most things, such as ourselves, exist only for a short while; they come into being, then soon cease. Other things, like the heavenly bodies, last longer, but they are still corruptible, and from all that we can gather about them, they too seem destined eventually to perish. We arrive at the conclusion, then, that while the world may contain some things which have always existed and are destined never to perish, it is nevertheless doubtful that it contains any such thing and, in any case, everything in the world is capable of perishing, and nothing in it, however long it may already have existed and however long it may yet remain, exists by its own nature, but depends instead upon something else.

While this might be true of everything in the world, is it necessarily true of the world itself? That is, if we grant, as we seem forced to, that nothing in the world exists by its own nature, that everything in the world is contingent and perishable, must we also say that the world itself or the totality of all these perishable things, is also contingent and perishable? Logically, we are not forced to, for it is logically possible that the totality of all perishable things might itself be imperishable, and hence, that the world might exist by its own nature, even though it is comprised exclusively of things which are contingent. It is not logically necessary that a totality should share the defects of its members. For example, even though every man is mortal, it does not follow from this that the human race, or the totality of all men, is also mortal for it is possible that there will always be human beings, even though there are no human beings which will always exist. Similarly, it is possible that the world is in itself a necessary thing, even though it is comprised entirely of things that are contingent.

This is logically possible, but it is not plausible. For we find nothing whatever about the world, any more than in its parts, to suggest that it exists by its own nature. Concerning anything in the world, we have not the slightest difficulty in supposing that it should perish. or even, that it should never have existed in the first place. We have almost as little difficulty in supposing this of the world itself. It might be somewhat hard to think of everything as utterly perishing and leaving no trace whatever of its ever having been, but there seems to be not the slightest difficulty in imagining that the world should never have existed in the first place. We can, for instance, perfectly easily suppose that nothing in the world had ever existed except, let us suppose, a single grain of sand, and we can thus suppose that this grain of sand has forever constituted the whole universe. Now if we consider just this grain of sand, it is quite impossible for us to suppose that it exists by its very nature, and could never have failed to exist. It clearly depends for its existence upon something other than itself if it depends on anything at all. The same will be true if we consider the world to consist, not of one grain of sand, but of two, or of a million, or, as we in fact find, of a vast number of stars and planets and all their minuter parts.

It would seem, then, that the world, in case it happens to exist at all – and this is quite beyond doubt – is contingent and thus dependent upon something other than itself for its existence, if it depends upon anything at all. And it must depend upon something, for otherwise there could be no reason why it exists in the first place. Now that upon which the world depends must be something that either exists by its own nature or does not. If it does not exist by its own nature, then it, in turn, depends for its existence upon something else, and so on. Now then, we can say either of two things; namely, (1) that the world depends for its existence upon something else, which in turn depends on still another thing, this depending upon still another, *ad infinitum*; or (2) that the world derives its existence from something that exists by its own nature and which is accordingly eternal and imperishable, and is the creator of heaven and earth. The first of these alternatives, however, is impossible, for it does not render a sufficient reason why anything should exist in the first place. Instead of supplying a reason why any world should exist, it repeatedly begs off giving a reason. It explains what is dependent and perishable in terms of what is itself dependent and perishable, leaving us still without a reason why perishable things should exist at all, which is what we are seeking. Ultimately, then, it would seem that the world, or the totality of contingent or perishable things, in case it exists at all, must depend upon something that is necessary and imperishable, and which accordingly exists, not in dependence upon something else, but by its own nature.

3 HUME: OBJECTIONS TO THE COSMOLOGICAL ARGUMENT[3]

But farther; why may not the material universe be the necessarily existent Being, according to this pretended explication of necessity? We dare not affirm that we know all the qualities of matter; and for aught we can determine, it may contain some qualities, which, were they known, would make its non-existence appear as great a contradiction as that twice two is five. I find only one argument employed to prove, that the material world is not the necessarily existent Being; and this argument is derived from the contingency both of the matter and the form of the world. 'Any particle of matter,' it is said, 'may be *conceived* to be annihilated; and any form may be *conceived* to be altered. Such an annihilation or alteration, therefore, is not impossible.' But it seems a great partiality not to perceive, that the same argument extends equally to the Deity, so far as we have any conception of him; and that the mind can at least imagine him to be non-existent, or his attributes to be altered. It must be some unknown, inconceivable qualities, which can make his non-existence appear impossible, or his attributes unalterable: And no reason can be assigned, why these qualities may not belong to matter. As they are altogether unknown and inconceivable, they can never be proved incompatible with it.

Add to this, that in tracing an eternal succession of objects, it seems absurd to inquire for a general cause or first Author. How can any thing, that exists from eternity, have a cause, since that relation implies a priority in time and a beginning of existence?

In such a chain too, or succession of objects, each part is caused by that which preceded it, and causes that which succeeds it. Where then is the difficulty? But the WHOLE, you say, wants a cause. I answer, that the uniting of these parts into a whole, like the uniting of several distinct counties into one kingdom, or several distinct members into one body, is performed merely by an arbitrary act of the mind, and has no influence on the nature of things. Did I show you the particular causes of each individual in a collection of twenty particles of matter, I should think it very unreasonable, should you afterwards ask me, what was the cause of the whole twenty. This is sufficiently explained in explaining the cause of the parts.

Though the reasonings, which you have urged, CLEANTHES, may well excuse me, said PHILO, from starting any farther difficulties; yet I cannot forbear insisting still upon another topic. It is observed by arithmeticians, that the products of 9 compose always either 9 or some less product of 9; if you add together all the characters, of which any of the former products is composed. Thus, of 18, 27, 36, which are products of 9, you make 9 by adding 1 to 8, 2 to 7, 3 to 6. Thus 369 is a product also of 9; and if you add 3, 6, and 9, you make 18, a lesser product of 9. To a superficial observer, so wonderful a regularity may be admired as the effect either of chance or design; but a skilful algebraist immediately concludes it to be the work of necessity, and demonstrates, that it must for ever result from the nature of these numbers. Is it not probable, I ask, that the whole œconomy of the universe

---

3. David Hume, *Dialogues Concerning Natural Religion* (1779), edited with an Introduction by Norman Kemp Smith, Edinburgh, Thomas Nelson, 1947, pp. 190–191.

is conducted by a like necessity, though no human algebra can furnish a key which solves the difficulty? And instead of admiring the order of natural things, may it not happen, that, could we penetrate into the intimate nature of bodies, we should clearly see why it was absolutely impossible, they could ever admit any other disposition? So dangerous is it to introduce this idea of necessity into the present question! And so naturally does it afford an inference directly opposite to the religious hypothesis!

4 HUME: THE RELATION OF CAUSE AND EFFECT[4]

All reasonings concerning matter of fact seem to be founded on the relation of *cause* and *effect*. By means of that relation alone we can go beyond the evidence of our memory and senses. If you were to ask a man why he believes any matter of fact which is absent, for instance, that his friend is in the country or in France, he would give you a reason, and this reason would be some other fact: as a letter received from him or the knowledge of his former resolutions and promises. A man finding a watch or any other machine in a desert island would conclude that there had once been men in that island. All our reasonings concerning fact are of the same nature. And here it is constantly supposed that there is a connection between the present fact and that which is inferred from it. Were there nothing to bind them together, the inference would be entirely precarious. The hearing of an articulate voice and rational discourse in the dark assures us of the presence of some person. Why? Because these are the effects of the human make and fabric, and closely connected with it. If we anatomize all the other reasonings of this nature, we shall find that they are founded on the relation of cause and effect, and that this relation is either near or remote, direct or collateral. Heat and light are collateral effects of fire, and the one effect may justly be inferred from the other.

If we would satisfy ourselves, therefore, concerning the nature of that evidence which assures us of matters of fact, we must inquire how we arrive at the knowledge of cause and effect.

I shall venture to affirm, as a general proposition which admits of no exception, that the knowledge of this relation is not, in any instance, attained by reasonings *a priori*, but arises entirely from experience, when we find that any particular objects are constantly conjoined with each other. Let an object be presented to a man of ever so strong natural reason and abilities – if that object be entirely new to him, he will not be able, by the most accurate examination of its sensible qualities, to discover any of its causes or effects. Adam, though his rational faculties be supposed, at the very first, entirely perfect, could not have inferred from the fluidity and transparency of water that it would suffocate him, or from the light and warmth of fire that it would consume him. No object ever discovers, by the qualities which appear to the senses, either the causes which produced it or the

4. David Hume, *An Enquiry Concerning Human Understanding,* Section IV (1748), ed. L.A. Selby-Bigge; 3rd edn. revised by P.H. Nidditch, Oxford, Clarendon Press, 1975, pp. 26–31.

effects which will arise from it; nor can our reason, unassisted by experience, ever draw any inference concerning real existence and matter of fact.

This proposition, *that causes and effects are discoverable, not by reason, but by experience*, will readily be admitted with regard to such objects as we remember to have once been altogether unknown to us, since we must be conscious of the utter inability which we then lay under of foretelling what would arise from them. Present two smooth pieces of marble to a man who has no tincture of natural philosophy; he will never discover that they will adhere together in such a manner as to require great force to separate them in a direct line, while they make so small a resistance to a lateral pressure. Such events as bear little analogy to the common course of nature are also readily confessed to be known only by experience, nor does any man imagine that the explosion of gunpowder or the attraction of a loadstone could ever be discovered by arguments *a priori*. In like manner, when an effect is supposed to depend upon an intricate machinery or secret structure of parts, we make no difficulty in attributing all our knowledge of it to experience. Who will assert that he can give the ultimate reason why milk or bread is proper nourishment for a man, not for a lion or tiger?

But the same truth may not appear at first sight to have the same evidence with regard to events which have become familiar to us from our first appearance in the world, which bear a close analogy to the whole course of nature, and which are supposed to depend on the simple qualities of objects without any secret structure of parts. We are apt to imagine that we could discover these effects by the mere operation of our reason without experience. We fancy that, were we brought on a sudden into this world, we could at first have inferred that one billiard ball would communicate motion to another upon impulse, and that we needed not to have waited for the event in order to pronounce with certainty concerning it. Such is the influence of custom that where it is strongest it not only covers our natural ignorance but even conceals it, and seems not to take place, merely because it is found in the highest degree.

But to convince us that all the laws of nature and all the operations of bodies without exception are known only by experience, the following reflections may perhaps suffice. Were any object presented to us, and were we required to pronounce concerning the effect which will result from it without consulting past observation, after what manner, I beseech you, must the mind proceed in this operation? It must invent or imagine some event which it ascribes to the object as its effect; and it is plain that this invention must be entirely arbitrary. The mind can never possibly find the effect in the supposed cause by the most accurate scrutiny and examination. For the effect is totally different from the cause, and consequently can never be discovered in it. Motion in the second billiard ball is a quite distinct event from motion in the first, nor is there anything in the one to suggest the smallest hint of the other. A stone or piece of metal raised into the air and left without any support immediately falls. But to consider the matter *a priori*, is there anything we discover in this situation which can beget the idea of a downward rather than an upward or any other motion in the stone or metal?

And as the first imagination or invention of a particular effect in all natural operations is arbitrary where we consult not experience, so must we also esteem the supposed tie or connection between the cause and effect which binds them together and renders it impossible that any other effect could result from the operation of that cause. When I see, for instance, a billiard ball moving in a straight line toward another, even suppose motion in the second ball should by accident be suggested to me as the result of their contact or impulse, may I not conceive that a hundred different events might as well follow from that cause? May not both these balls remain at absolute rest? May not the first ball return in a straight line or leap off from the second in any line or direction? All these suppositions are consistent and conceivable. Why, then, should we give the preference to one which is no more consistent or conceivable than the rest? All our reasonings *a priori* will never be able to show us any foundation for this preference.

In a word, then, every effect is a distinct event from its cause. It could not, therefore, be discovered in the cause, and the first invention or conception of it, *a priori*, must be entirely arbitrary. And even after it is suggested, the conjunction of it with the cause must appear equally arbitrary, since there are always many other effects which, to reason, must seem fully as consistent and natural. In vain, therefore, should we pretend to determine any single event or infer any cause or effect without the assistance of observation and experience.

Hence we may discover the reason why no philosopher who is rational and modest has ever pretended to assign the ultimate cause of any natural operation, or to show distinctly the action of that power which produces any single effect in the universe. It is confessed that the utmost effort of human reason is to reduce the principles productive of natural phenomena to a greater simplicity, and to resolve the many particular effects into a few general causes, by means of reasonings from analogy, experience, and observation. But as to the causes of the general causes, we should in vain attempt their discovery, nor shall we ever be able to satisfy ourselves by any particular explication of them. These ultimate springs and principles are totally shut up from human curiosity and inquiry. Elasticity, gravity, cohesion of parts, communication of motion by impulse – these are probably the ultimate causes and principles which we shall ever discover in nature; and we may esteem ourselves sufficiently happy if, by accurate inquiry and reasoning, we can trace up the particular phenomena to, or near to, these general principles. The most perfect philosophy of the natural kind only staves off our ignorance a little longer, as perhaps the most perfect philosophy of the moral or metaphysical kind serves only to discover larger portions of it. Thus the observation of human blindness and weakness is the result of all philosophy, and meets us, at every turn, in spite of our endeavors to elude or avoid it.

5 KANT: THE IMPOSSIBILITY OF A COSMOLOGICAL PROOF[5]

The *cosmological proof* which we are now about to examine, retains the connection of absolute necessity with the highest reality, but instead of reasoning,

---

5. Immanuel Kant, *Critique of Pure Reason* (1781), trans. by Norman Kemp Smith, London, Macmillan, 1929, pp. 508–513.

like the former proof (the ontological), from the highest reality to necessity of existence, it reasons from the previously given unconditioned necessity of some being to the unlimited reality of that being. It thus enters upon a course of reasoning which, whether rational or only pseudo-rational, is at any rate natural, and the most convincing not only for common sense but even for speculative understanding. It also sketches the first outline of all the proofs in natural theology, an outline which has always been and always will be followed, however much embellished and disguised by superfluous additions. This proof, termed by Leibniz the proof a *contingentia mundi*, we shall now proceed to expound and examine. It runs thus: If anything exists, an absolutely necessary being must also exist. Now I, at least, exist. Therefore an absolutely necessary being exists. The minor premiss contains an experience, the major premiss the inference from there being any experience at all to the existence of the necessary. The proof therefore really begins with experience, and is not wholly *a priori* or ontological. For this reason, and because the object of all possible experience is called the world, it is entitled the *cosmological* proof. Since, in dealing with the objects of experience, the proof abstracts from all special properties through which this world may differ from any other possible world, the title also serves to distinguish it from the physico-theological proof, which is based upon observations of the particular properties of the world disclosed to us by our senses.

The proof then proceeds as follows: The necessary being can be determined in one way only, that is, by one out of each possible pair of opposed predicates. It must therefore be *completely* determined through its own concept. Now there is only one possible concept which determines a thing completely *a priori*, namely, the concept of the *ens realissimum*. The concept of the *ens realissimum* is therefore the only concept through which a necessary being can be thought. In other words, a supreme being necessarily exists.

. . . In order to lay a secure foundation for itself, this proof takes its stand on experience, and thereby makes profession of being distinct from the ontological proof, which puts its entire trust in pure *a priori* concepts. But the cosmological proof uses this experience only for a single step in the argument, namely, to conclude the existence of a necessary being. What properties this being may have, the empirical premiss cannot tell us. Reason therefore abandons experience altogether, and endeavours to discover from mere concepts what properties an absolutely necessary being must have, that is, which among all possible things contains in itself the conditions (*requisita*) essential to absolute necessity. Now these, it is supposed, are nowhere to be found save in the concept of an *ens realissimum*; and the conclusion is therefore drawn, that the *ens realissimum* is the absolutely necessary being. But it is evident that we are here presupposing that the concept of the highest reality is completely adequate to the concept of absolute necessity of existence: that is, that the latter can be inferred from the former. Now this is the presupposition maintained by the ontological proof, and indeed made the basis of the proof; and yet it is an assumption with which this latter proof has professed to dispense. For absolute necessity is an existence determined from mere concepts. If I say, the concept of the *ens realissimum* is a concept, and indeed the only concept, which is appropriate and adequate to necessary existence, I must also admit that necessary existence can be inferred from this concept. Thus the so-called cosmological proof really owes any cogency which it may have to the ontological proof from mere concepts. The appeal to experience is quite superfluous; experience may perhaps lead us to the concept of absolute necessity, but is unable to demonstrate this necessity as belonging to any determinate thing. For immediately we endeavour to do so, we must abandon all experience and search among pure concepts to discover whether any one of them contains the conditions of the possibility of an absolutely necessary being. If in this way we can determine the possibility of a necessary being, we likewise establish its existence. For what we are then saying is this: that of all possible beings there is one which carries with it absolute necessity, that is, that this being exists with absolute necessity . . .

I have stated that in this cosmological argument there lies hidden a whole nest of dialectical assumptions, which the transcendental critique can easily detect and destroy. These deceptive principles I shall merely enumerate, leaving to the reader, who by this time will be sufficiently expert in these matters, the task of investigating them further, and of refuting them.

We find, for instance, (1) the transcendental principle whereby from the contingent we infer a cause. This principle is applicable only in the sensible world; outside that world it has no meaning whatsoever. For the mere intellectual concept of the contingent cannot give rise to any synthetic proposition, such as that of causality. The principle of causality has no meaning and no criterion for its application save only in the sensible world. But in the cosmological proof it is precisely in order to enable us to advance beyond the sensible world that it is employed. (2) The inference to a first cause, from the impossibility of an infinite series of causes, given one after the other, in the sensible world. The principles of the employment of reason do not justify this conclusion even within the world of experience, still less beyond this world in a realm into which this series can never be extended. (3) The unjustified self-satisfaction of reason in respect of the completion of this series. The removal of all the conditions without which no concept of necessity is possible is taken by reason to be a completion of the concept of the series, on the ground that we can then conceive nothing further. (4) The confusion between the logical possibility of a concept of all reality united into one (without inner contradiction) and the transcendental possibility of such a reality. In the case of the latter there is needed a principle to establish the practicability of such a synthesis, a principle which itself, however, can apply only to the field of possible experiences – etc.

The procedure of the cosmological proof is artfully designed to enable us to escape having to prove the existence of a necessary being *a priori* through mere concepts. Such proof would require to be carried out in the ontological manner, and that is an enterprise for which we feel ourselves to be altogether incompetent. Accordingly, we take as the starting-point of our inference an actual existence (an experience in general), and advance, in such manner as we can, to some absolutely necessary condition of this existence. We have then no need to show the possibility of this condition. For if it has been proved to exist, the question as to its possibility is entirely superfluous. If now we want to determine more fully the nature of this necessary being, we do not endeavour to do so in the manner that would be really adequate, namely, by discovering from its concept the necessity of its existence.

For could we do that, we should be in no need of an empirical starting-point. No, all we seek is the negative condition (*conditio sine qua non*), without which a being would not be absolutely necessary. And in all other kinds of reasoning from a given consequence to its ground this would be legitimate; but in the present case it unfortunately happens that the condition which is needed for absolute necessity is only to be found in one single being. This being must therefore contain in its concept all that is required for absolute necessity, and consequently it enables me to infer this absolute necessity *a priori*. I must therefore be able also to reverse the inference, and to say: Anything to which this concept (of supreme reality) applies is absolutely necessary. If I cannot make this inference (as I must concede, if I am to avoid admitting the ontological proof), I have come to grief in the new way that I have been following, and am back again at my starting-point. The concept of the supreme being satisfies all questions *a priori* which can be raised regarding the inner determinations of a thing, and is therefore an ideal that is quite unique, in that the concept, while universal, also at the same time designates an individual as being among the things that are possible. But it does not give satisfaction concerning the question of its own existence – though this is the real purpose of our enquiries – and if anyone admitted the existence of a necessary being but wanted to know which among all [existing] things is to be identified with that being, we could not answer: "This, not that, is the necessary being."

We may indeed be allowed to *postulate* the existence of an all-sufficient being, as the cause of all possible effects, with a view to lightening the task of reason in its search for the unity of the grounds of explanation. But in presuming so far as to say that such a being *necessarily exists*, we are no longer giving modest expression to an admissible hypothesis, but are confidently laying claim to apodeictic certainty. For the knowledge of what we profess to know as absolutely necessary must itself carry with it absolute necessity.

The whole problem of the transcendental ideal amounts to this: either, given absolute necessity, to find a concept which possesses it, or, given the concept of something, to find that something to be absolutely necessary. If either task be possible, so must the other; for reason recognises that only as absolutely necessary which follows of necessity from its concept. But both tasks are quite beyond our utmost efforts to *satisfy* our understanding in this matter; and equally unavailing are all attempts to induce it to acquiesce in its capacity.

KEY TEXTS

Aquinas, Thomas. *Summa Theologiae*, Part 1a, 2, 3, London, Eyre & Spottiswoode, 1972.

Copleston, F. C. *Thomas Aquinas*, London, Search Press, 1955.

Hume, David. *An Enquiry Concerning Human Understanding*, Section IV (1748), ed. L. A. Selby-Bigge; 3rd edn revised by P. H. Nidditch, Oxford, Clarendon Press, 1975.

Mackie, J. L. *The Miracle of Theism*, Oxford, Clarendon Press, 1982, pp. 31–101.

Rowe, William L. *The Cosmological Argument*, Princeton, N. J., Princeton University Press, 1975.

Aquinas, Thomas. *Summa Theologiae*, Part 1a, 2, 3, London, Eyre & Spottiswoode, 1972.

Bartel, Timothy. 'The Cosmological Argument and the Uniqueness of God', *International Journal for the Philosophy of Religion*, 3, 1982, pp. 23–31.

Burrill, Donald R. *The Cosmological Arguments*, Garden City, N.Y., Anchor Books, 1967.

Conway, David A. '"It Would have Happened already": On One Argument for a First Cause', *Analysis*, 54, 1984, pp. 159–166.

Copleston, F. C. *Thomas Aquinas*, London, Search Press, 1955.

Craig, William. *The Cosmological Argument from Plato to Leibniz*, New York, Barnes & Noble, 1980.

—— *The Kalam Cosmological Argument*, New York, Barnes & Noble, 1979.

Davies, Brian. *An Introduction to the Philosophy of Religion*, Oxford, Oxford University Press, 1982, pp. 38-49.

Davis, Stephen T. *God, Reason and Theistic Proofs*, Edinburgh, Edinburgh University Press, 1997, pp. 60–77.

Edwards, Paul. *The Cosmological Argument*, New York, Doubleday, 1967.

Farrer, A. *Finite and Infinite*, London, Dacre Press, 1943.

Flew, Antony. *God and Philosophy*, London, Hutchinson, 1966, pp. 85–98.

—— *Hume's Philosophy of Belief*, London, Routledge & Kegan Paul, 1961.

Geach, Peter. 'Aquinas', in G. E. M. Anscombe and P. T. Geach, *Three Philosophers*, Oxford, Basil Blackwell, 1963.

Hepburn, R. W. 'From World to God', *Mind*, 72, 1963. Reprinted in *The Philosophy of Religion*, ed. Basil Mitchell, Oxford, Oxford University Press, 1971, pp. 168–178.

Hick, John. *Philosophy of Religion*, Englewood Cliffs, N.J., Prentice-Hall, 1990, pp. 20–23.

Hume, David. *Dialogues Concerning Natural Religion* (1779), edited with an Introduction by Norman Kemp Smith, London and Edinburgh, Thomas Nelson, 1935; 2nd edn, 1947.

—— *An Enquiry Concerning Human Understanding*, Section IV (1748), ed. L. A. Selby-Bigge; 3rd edn, revised by P. H. Nidditch, Oxford, Clarendon Press, 1975.

Kant, Immanuel. *Critique of Pure Reason* (1781), trans. Norman Kemp Smith, London, Macmillan, 1929, pp. 417–421, 507–518.

Kennick, W. E. 'A New Way with the Five Ways', *Australasian Journal of Philosophy*, 38, 1960, pp. 225–233.

Kenny, A. *The Five Ways*, London, Routledge & Kegan Paul, 1969.

Mackie, J. L. *The Miracle of Theism*, Oxford, Clarendon Press, 1982, pp. 31–101.

Malcolm, Norman. 'Anselm's Ontological Arguments', *Philosophical Review*, 69(1), January 1960, pp. 41–62.

Martin, Michael. *Atheism: A Philosophical Justification*, Philadelphia, Temple University Press, 1990.

Mascall, E. L. *Existence and Analogy*, London, Longmans, 1949.

—— *He Who is*, London, Longmans, 1943.

Matson, Wallace. *The Existence of God*, Ithaca, N.Y., Cornell University Press, 1965, pp. 56–86.

Reichenbach, Bruce. *The Cosmological Argument: A Reassessment*, Springfield, Ill., Charles C. Thomas, 1972.

Rowe, William L. *The Cosmological Argument*, Princeton, N.J., Princeton University Press, 1975.

Russell, Bertrand (with F. C. Copleston). 'The Existence of God – A Debate', BBC, 1948. Reprinted in Russell, *Why I am Not a Christian*, London, George Allen & Unwin, 1967, pp. 133–153.

Swinburne, Richard. *The Existence of God*, Oxford, Clarendon Press, 1979.

Taylor, Richard. *Metaphysics*, Englewood Cliffs, N.J., Prentice-Hall, 1963.

Tillich, Paul. 'Two Types of Philosophy of Religion', in *Theology of Culture*, ed. Robert C. Kimball, New York, Oxford University Press, 1964, pp. 10–29.

chapter 3 THE ARGUMENT FROM DESIGN

INTRODUCTION

The most popular of all the arguments for the existence of God is the argument from design, otherwise known as the teleological argument (from the Greek *telos*, meaning 'end' or 'goal').[1] As its name suggests, the design argument is another type of cosmological argument, basing its conclusions not so much on *that* the universe (*cosmos*) exists but rather on that it exists *in a particular way* – namely, that it exhibits order and design. From this it also follows that the design argument is a posteriori in character, which is to say that, unlike the ontological argument, it does not claim that its conclusions are logically true – true, that is, in the sense that to deny them would be self-contradictory. But here we should draw a distinction. The cosmological argument, as Aquinas presented it, began with certain empirical facts, which he claimed are so evident to our senses that they are undeniable, i.e., that things move, are caused, and exist. Aquinas drew out the logical implications of these facts, and concluded that they must depend on an absolutely necessary being. The design argument follows a different route. For although it begins with what it takes to be an empirical fact – the fact that the world exhibits order and design – it establishes the world's ontological dependence on God not by a series of deductive steps but by a *comparative study* between this world and other things that exhibit design. The evidence it presents, in other words, is derived primarily from a *study of parallel cases* of design; and these cases, so it claims, while not establishing God's existence conclusively, do confer upon it a high degree of probability.

Distinctive form as a cosmological proof

THE ARGUMENT STATED (I)

Like the ontological and cosmological arguments, the design argument has had a distinguished history. We find perhaps the earliest reference to it in the work of the Stoic philosopher Anaxagoras, and there are more extended discussions in Plato's dialogues *Timaeus* and *Philebus*. In medieval theology the argument won general acceptance – largely because of the pervasive influence of Aristotelian physics, according to which all natural objects act in a purposeful or teleological manner – and it figures as the fifth of Aquinas' 'Five Ways' in his *Summa Theologiae*. The argument was particularly popular in the eighteenth

---

1. I am here keeping to the convention of describing the argument as 'the argument *from* design'. In fact Antony Flew is right to object that this is misleading and that a more accurate alternative would be 'the argument *to* design'. For if the argument precedes from the presupposition of design, the inference that there is a designer immediately follows. Whether the universe is or is not designed is, however, precisely the point at issue. See Flew, *An Introduction to Western Philosophy*, London, Thames and Hudson, 1971, p. 206.

and nineteenth centuries, and here the most famous example is from William Paley's *Natural Theology* (1802). More recent formulations are presented by F. R. Tennant (1928–1930), A. E. Taylor (1945), Peter Bertocci (1951), Richard Taylor (1963), Alvin Plantinga (1967) and Richard Swinburne (1979).[2]

As might be expected from their earlier attacks on the cosmological argument, the two outstanding critics are Hume and Kant; and it is fair to say that contemporary criticism largely follows their arguments.[3] This is not to say, however, that Hume and Kant were unaware of the enormous appeal of this argument. Kant calls it the 'physico-theological proof' and always mentions it with respect, calling it 'the oldest, the clearest, and the best suited to ordinary human reason';[4] and Hume presents a classic account of it in his *Dialogues Concerning Natural Religion* (1779). Here one of Hume's main characters, Cleanthes, argues as follows:

Hume's summary of the argument

Look round the world: Contemplate the whole and every part of it: You will find it to be nothing but one great machine, subdivided into an infinite number of lesser machines, which again admit of subdivisions, to a degree beyond what human senses and faculties can trace and explain. All these various machines, and even their most minute parts, are adjusted to each other with an accuracy, which ravishes into admiration all men, who have ever contemplated them. The curious adapting of means to ends, throughout nature, resembles exactly, though it much exceeds, the productions of human contrivance; of human design, thought, wisdom, and intelligence. Since therefore the effects resemble each other, we are led to infer, by all the rules of analogy, that the causes also resemble; and that the Author of nature is somewhat similar to the mind of man; though possessed of much larger faculties, proportioned to the grandeur of the work, which he has executed. By this argument a posteriori, and by this argument alone, do we prove at once the existence of a Deity, and his similarity to human mind and intelligence.[5]

The simplicity of this argument is part of its appeal. Investigation of the physical, chemical and biological aspects of our world reveals a pattern or order in nature. We notice the regularity of the seasons, the movement of planets, the growth and regeneration of plant life, the mechanism of the human body,

2. See F. R. Tennant, *Philosophical Theology*, 2 vols, Cambridge: Cambridge University Press, 1928–1930; A. E. Taylor, *Does God Exist?*, New York, Macmillan, 1945; Peter Bertocci, *Introduction to the Philosophy of Religion*, Englewood Cliffs, N.J., Prentice-Hall, 1951; Richard Taylor, *Metaphysics*, Englewood Cliffs, N.J., Prentice-Hall, 1963; Alvin Plantinga, *God and Other Minds*, Ithaca, N.Y., Cornell University Press, 1967; and Richard Swinburne, *The Existence of God*, Oxford, Oxford University Press, 1979.
3. For a history of the argument, see Thomas McPherson, *The Argument from Design*, London, Macmillan, 1972.
4. *Critique of Pure Reason*, trans. Norman Kemp Smith, London, Macmillan, 1929, p. 520.
5. David Hume, *Dialogues Concerning Natural Religion*, edited with an Introduction by Norman Kemp Smith, London, Thomas Nelson & Sons, 1947, p. 143.

and so forth. But still more remarkably, this order or pattern is not merely seen in the general plan of the universe but reaches down to the more intricate and minute relationships within its parts. To quote Sir Isaac Newton (1642–1727):

> Whence is it that the eyes of all sorts of living creatures are transparent to the very bottom . . . with a crystalline lens in the middle and a pupil before the lens, all of them so finely shaped and fitted for vision that no artist can mend them? Did blind chance know that there was light, and what was its refraction, and fit the eyes of all creatures after the most curious manner to make use of it? These and suchlike considerations always have and ever will prevail with mankind to believe that there is a Being who made all things and has all things in his power, and who is therefore to be feared.[6]

Why the order observed in nature should point to the existence of a 'Being who made all things' has already been anticipated. This conclusion results from a *study of parallel cases of design*. The natural order bears a strong resemblance to what we see in the man-made world. Here, too, human artifacts, like the washing-machine or word-processor, do not merely act in an orderly fashion but act to achieve some goal; and here also the various individual parts of the mechanism are so harmoniously adjusted to each other that the intended result is achieved. We additionally know, however, that this 'curious adapting of means to ends', to use Hume's phrase, is the result of human intelligence and planning; that indeed it would be absurd to suppose that something as complex as, say, the motor-car could be due to some kind of cosmic accident. Since therefore the *effects* of human contrivance are so similar to the effects that we discover in the natural world, we may legitimately infer that the *causes* which produce these effects are similarly alike. So, just as in cases of human manufacture the cause is human intelligence, so in the cases of natural phenomena the cause must also be an intelligence of some kind; and since, moreover, the complexity of the universe vastly exceeds the complexity of anything man-made, we may further infer that this designer vastly exceeds in intelligence any human designer, that it is indeed a divine intelligence.

All these features of the design argument appear again in its most celebrated version, given by the former archdeacon of Carlisle, William Paley, in his *Natural Theology* of 1802 (**SOURCE 1: PP. 145–146**).[7]

Paley's account proceeds as follows. If, while walking across a barren wasteland, I saw a stone and wondered how it came to exist, I could legitimately account for it through chance factors like wind, heat and rain, etc. I would not, however, come to the same conclusion if I came across a watch. For such is its

Parallel cases of design

⇐

Paley's watch

---

6. Quoted from 'A Short Scheme of the True Religion', in D. Brewster, *Memoirs of the Life, Writings, and Discoveries of Sir Isaac Newton*, Edinburgh, T. Constable, 1850, Vol. I, pp. 347–348.
7. Such was its popularity that the book went through twenty editions in eighteen years. Paley's argument is still in use: see Robert Clark, *The Universe – Plan or Accident?*, Philadelphia, Muhlenburg Press, 1961.

William Paley
(1743–1805)

Educated at Christ's College, Cambridge, Paley was appointed fellow and tutor there in 1766, where he quickly established himself as skilled lecturer on metaphysics, morals and the Greek Testament. He was ordained as an Anglican priest in 1767 and subsequently became archdeacon of Carlisle in 1782. In his own day Paley became famous as a writer of influential textbooks on utilitarian moral philosophy and Christianity. His *A View of the Evidences of Christianity* (1794) went through many editions and was required reading for entrance to Cambridge until the twentieth century. An equally famous book, *Natural Theology* (1802), provided the standard exposition for many years of the design argument, including as it does his famous, some would say notorious, comparison between the universe and a watch. An unoriginal thinker – even the watch analogy is an alleged plagiarism – Paley excelled as an educator, and his unfussy way of presenting arguments had a substantial influence on many generations of students, including Charles Darwin.

manifest complexity – with all its wheels, cogs, gears and springs operating together to measure the passage of time – that it would be absurd to suppose that it too owed its existence to a set of chance occurrences. Thus we must postulate some intelligence at work in the watch's creation: a watchmaker. Paley further claims that this conclusion is not weakened (1) if we have never seen a watch being made and are incapable of making a watch ourselves; (2) if the watch can, and does, sometimes go wrong; and (3) if there are parts of the watch we do not understand.

Having established the connection between, on the one hand, the evidence of design in the watch and, on the other, the need for a designer to explain that design, Paley extends his argument to the universe generally and to particular natural objects within it. He details the many evidences of design in natural organisms and organs, notes the division between animals and vegetables and the further sub-division of each into genera and species, and, like Sir Isaac Newton, pays particular attention to that miracle of creation, the human eye, the examination of which is virtually a cure for atheism. 'Were there no example in the world of contrivance except the *eye*, it would be alone sufficient to support the conclusion which we draw from it, as to the necessity of an intelligent creator.'[8] Such wonderful intricacy, such subserviency of means to an end, surpassing anything that the human mind can create, implies the presence of mind and the activity of a rational being employing his intelligence not merely in the eye's construction but in the creation of all that is.

8. *Natural Theology*, abridged and edited by Frederick Ferré, Indianapolis, Bobbs-Merrill, 1963, p. 32.

In summary, then, the design argument moves through six stages:

1 Man-made machines act to achieve some end or goal.

2 The universe, although infinitely more complex, resembles a vast man-made machine.

3 Man-made machines are the products (effects) of intelligent design (cause).

4 Like effects have like causes.

Therefore

5 Probably the cause of the universe is an intelligent being.

6 This cause is God.

SUMMARY:
THE DESIGN
ARGUMENT

Construct a design argument on the basis of the following phenomena:

The eye

Venomous snakes

Rocks

Planetary motion

Snowflakes

EXERCISE 3.1

THE ARGUMENT (2): INDUCTION AND ANALOGY

Commentators frequently point to a further feature of the design argument, namely, that it is both *inductive* and *analogical*. I shall now explain these terms in some detail. As we shall see in a moment, it is a major criticism of the argument that it employs induction and analogy improperly.

INDUCTION

Induction is generally contrasted with *deduction*. Deduction is the process of reasoning applicable to the knowledge reached independently of our experience and observation (a priori) and thus generates propositions regarded as necessarily or analytically true or false, for example, the truths of logic and pure mathematics. Induction, on the other hand, is the process of reasoning applicable to the knowledge dependent on empirical knowledge (a posteriori) and thus generates propositions regarded as contingently or synthetically true or false. More technically, and to recall Kant's earlier examples,[9] in a deductive

Induction contrasted with deduction

9. See above, p. 17.

argument the conclusion is entailed in the premiss (for example, A triangle is a three-sided figure); and in an inductive argument the conclusion is not so entailed, although the premiss may justify our acceptance of the conclusion as highly probable (for example, This ball is red).

Consider, for example, the statement 'All men are mortal.' Why is this a proposition about which we have not the slightest doubt? The reason is that we have, unwittingly perhaps, applied an inductive procedure known as 'simple enumeration'. This involves no more than counting the instances and finding them all to have a certain property. So:

1　Matthew died.
2　Mark died.
3　John died.
4　Therefore all men die.

It is important to realize, however, that the conclusion that all men die is not conclusively certain, since indeed the appearance of a single exception would invalidate it. While the statements about Matthew, Mark and John may thus be true, this does not exclude the possibility (however remote) that there is someone now living, or someone yet unborn, who will live for ever, and that therefore the conclusion about the mortality of *all* men is false. All that can be hoped for in this case is that the more frequently we observe object O to have the property P, the more probable it is that another O-type will exhibit the same property. The reasoning we employ is, in this sense, *retrospective*: from our observations of what has happened in the past we draw probable conclusions about what will happen in the future; and the more evidence we can accumulate about the invariability of what has happened in the past, the more certain we can be about the likelihood of its future repetition.

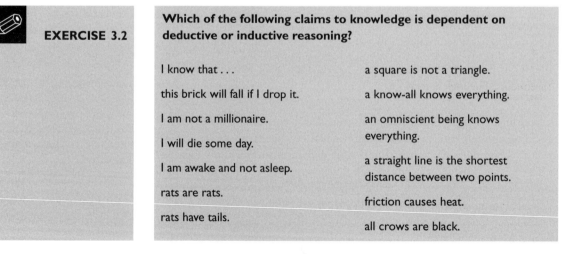

EXERCISE 3.2

Which of the following claims to knowledge is dependent on deductive or inductive reasoning?

I know that . . .

this brick will fall if I drop it.

I am not a millionaire.

I will die some day.

I am awake and not asleep.

rats are rats.

rats have tails.

a square is not a triangle.

a know-all knows everything.

an omniscient being knows everything.

a straight line is the shortest distance between two points.

friction causes heat.

all crows are black.

ANALOGY

Analogy is a form of induction, which makes it clear at once that an argument from analogy is never conclusive but is rather a matter of higher or lesser degrees of probability, and further that, as with all inductive procedures, the accuracy of its conclusions will depend largely on the amount of data available and how specifically relevant these data are to the conclusion being sought. In an analogical argument, however, the data used depend not so much on the accumulation of instances ('simple enumeration') as on the resemblances observed between these instances. An argument from analogy is, therefore, *an argument from resemblances*. These resemblances are then used to support additional claims that these instances further resemble each other in ways that are not immediately observable or testable.

Let us suppose, for example, that we want to discover whether object O has property P, where P cannot be known directly. If we compare O with other objects (Bs) that we know possess the property P, and if we find that O resembles these objects in other respects, we may legitimately conclude that O also resembles them in possessing the property P, even though we have not observed them to resemble each other in this respect. For example, let us assume that O is a particularly ferocious animal, recently discovered, called a Laycock. Let us further suppose that P is the property of having a brain. What we want to establish is whether it is reasonable or unreasonable to suppose that a Laycock has a brain. Since in form, behaviour, habitat and diet, the Laycock bears a striking *resemblance* to various members of the ape family (Bs) – it being a tailless monkey, like a gorilla, chimpanzee or gibbon (all of which do possess brains) – we may conclude that a Laycock has a brain as well. This conclusion is not reached by dissection of the Laycock, but by the process of analogy. Since the Laycock (O) and apes (Bs) are alike in various respects, it is fair to assume that they further resemble each other in another respect, that is, in possessing the property P (brains).

This assumption, to repeat, is not conclusive. That O resembles other objects (Bs) in various ways does not in itself prove that it resembles them in another way (that it has the property P). Indeed, to suppose that it does is to commit a well-known logical mistake, known as the fallacy of the 'affirmation of the consequent'. The logical form is:

> A implies B;
> B is true;
> Therefore A is true

or:

> When Max has had no food, he gets angry;
> Max is angry
> Therefore Max has had no food.

The fallacy displayed here seems fairly obvious. There may be a whole host of reasons, quite apart from his digestion, that account for Max's irritability: he

Analogy: an argument from resemblances

Fallacy of the affirmation of the consequent

may have had a row with his wife or received an unpleasant letter from his bank manager. There may therefore be a great number of causes which have the same effect, or, to put it more technically, there may be more than one antecedent which leads to a particular consequent. Therefore neither retrospective reasoning, which we found in the inductive procedure of 'simple enumeration', nor comparative reasoning, which we found in the resemblances of analogy, can exclude the possibility of error. Evidently a theory which conflicts with the facts cannot be true; but if there is more than one theory which can account for those facts, there is no logical necessity why one should prefer one theory over another merely because it agrees with the evidence. Thus, despite the resemblances of the Laycock (O) to apes (Bs) and the legitimate inference of the possession of a brain (P) it remains a permanent possibility that dissection might reveal no brain at all.

EXERCISE 3.3

Which of these statements commits the fallacy of the affirmation of the consequent?

Coffee keeps me awake; I had a bad night, so I drank coffee before bed.

If George didn't do it, he wouldn't be hiding; but he is hiding, so he did it.

The house is untidy, so young David's holiday must have started.

Charles I lost his head, so he died.

Cigarette-smoking causes cancer; she has cancer, so she smokes.

'I shot him through the heart.' 'No, you didn't: he's still standing.'

If Toots is a mother, Toots must be female. Toots is a female. Therefore Toots is a mother.

If I am in Edinburgh, then I am in Scotland. I am in Scotland. Therefore I am in Edinburgh.

Both light-bulbs and stars emit light; light-bulbs require electricity to do this; therefore stars require electricity to emit light.

THE ARGUMENT (3): ITS ANALOGICAL FORM

The rules of analogy

Let us now return to the design argument. We remember that, in Hume's account of it, Cleanthes appeals directly to the 'rules of analogy'; and certainly his presentation, like Paley's, falls neatly into the scheme of analogical reasoning we have just described. First, a comparison is made between two classes of objects – artifacts and organisms – and attention is then drawn to a remarkable resemblance between them, namely, the degree to which both adapt their means to ends. So the regular operation of the gears in a watch, which results in the accurate measurement of hours, can be compared to the regular movement of the earth round the sun, which accounts for the transition from night to day. Next, by treating both artifacts and organisms as *effects*, Cleanthes and Paley may inductively infer that, following this similarity in adaptation, their *causes* are also similar, i.e., that both artifacts and organisms are the products of intelligent design. Thus, because a watch has property P (for example, the property of functional adaptation), and because the universe is also observed to have property P, we may legitimately conclude, in the absence of specific evidence to the contrary, that the universe also resembles a watch *in another respect*: namely, in the all-important respect of possessing the additional property, the property of having an intelligent designer and creator. And finally, given that the degree of adaptation in organisms is far greater and more complex than anything we find among human artifacts, we may further conclude that the intelligence at work in the manufacture of organisms is infinitely greater than any human intelligence. And to this supremely intelligent creator we give the name 'God'.

It is worth stressing here that, like all inductive and analogical arguments, the design argument does not offer, nor does it seek to offer, conclusive proof – indeed, if it did so, it could no longer be counted an induction. That object O and object B resemble each other in possessing various properties is not in itself evidence that O must further resemble B in possessing an additional property to account for those properties. Here we may again invoke the fallacy of affirming the consequent. That the *effects* may be the same does not *prove* that the causes are the same. Thus the similarity in functional adaptation between artifact and organism or between watch and universe does not demonstrate conclusively that a controlling mind is at work in the creation of either. In the case of the watch, of course, this is unlikely because of the innumerable instances in which watches have been observed to be created by watchmakers. Here we may invoke the principle of simple enumeration: 'All observed Os have the property P. Therefore (probably) all Os have the property P.' But this is evidently not the case with a universe, where no such universe-maker has been or could be observed. Thus it has to be allowed that a multiplicity of theories could account for the phenomenon of order and design without supposing the existence of a designer.

It is worth reminding ourselves, however, that proponents of the design argument are willing to concede this point. To repeat, an inductive-analogical argument does not render an alternative explanation impossible, but it does render it unlikely. Again, it is the *degree of probability* involved which allows us to discount any other hypothesis. Thus you may confidently purchase a Cadillac on the grounds that it will have the same characteristics as the Cadillac you tested beforehand. You have to allow, of course, that your confidence *may* be misplaced – that by some fault in manufacture the car you buy will lack the qualities of the car you tested – but it is still a legitimate expectation that this will not be the case; and accordingly it is not an error of reasoning in this instance to buy with confidence. So too with the design argument. As an a posteriori argument for the existence of God it does not seek to exclude doubt but rather to render such doubt unreasonable. So this argument too may be bought with confidence. True, the existence of God cannot be conclusively verified by observation; nor can it, if the ontological argument is anything to go by, be demonstrated a priori. But this is not to say that the claim that God exists cannot be supported on the basis of certain inductive inferences. We may agree, then, that no deductive argument will be forthcoming to defend religious belief; but the inductive argument looks strong nonetheless, based as it is on the analogical principle of parallel cases, and may thus be regarded as sufficient to meet the needs of faith.

There is, however, one final feature of the design argument to mention. Advocates of this argument are well aware that their analogical thinking is concerned not with literal resemblances but with showing how the same inductive inference from design to designer can be discerned in different modes: on the one hand, the relation of watch to watchmaker, and, on the other, the relation of universe to God. The presupposition of this argument is clear enough. This inductive inference is so fundamental that it can be repeated in each mode, and can accordingly be formulated both in terms of the structure of the microcosm (the relation of artifact to artificer) and in terms of the structure of the macrocosm (the relation of God to the universe). This allows us to extend the inference from one dimension to another, and thereby to illustrate the relation of dependence which obtains between God and his creation by means of analogies drawn from our own immediate experience.

But what justifies this extension? What makes us so certain that the requirement of a watchmaker for a watch is duplicated in the relation of God to universe? What makes the existence of such a being, if not a matter of logical necessity, at least a matter of high probability for theists?

The answer lies in the final and most basic presupposition of the design argument. This is that there is a fundamental *order of things* to be discerned in every part of the universe, so that the structure of a certain part, such as belongs to organisms, can be inferred from the structure of another part, such as belongs to artifacts. This assumption of a *uniformity of nature* is similarly implied in every case of induction. We observe A followed by B not once, not twice, but a hundred times, and may thus safely predict that the next time we see A we shall also see B. In this sense we assume that nature is repetitious – that the sun will rise tomorrow because it rose today – and, on the basis of these recurring uniformities, we formulate certain laws regarding future states of affairs: that arsenic is poisonous, that fire warms, that all men die, and so on.

The same assumption is at work in all arguments from analogy, summarized in the notion, which forms the backbone of the design argument, that *like effects require like causes*. If we have variously observed a connection between the effect B (for example, machines) and the cause A (for example, mechanics), then by analogy when we meet a new instance of B we may infer that it must have had a cause A. Here the regularity of nature is presumed not merely in our observation that all machines require mechanics but also in our further assumption that, when we see a new machine, whose creation we cannot directly observe, we may by analogy infer that here too a mechanic has been at work. The design argument follows this same pattern and requires the same presumption of a uniformity in nature. It is saying that there is a resemblance between things

Design presupposes uniformity of nature

Like effects have like causes

like machines and the universe, and that, since we have observed all machines to have mechanics, we are entitled to infer by analogy that the universe also has a mechanic.

This, to repeat, is not a logical proof – no argument from analogy can be that. This explains why we must always allow that, however many machines we may have observed to have mechanics, and however convinced we may be that all future machines will have mechanics, the machine now under examination did not have a mechanic. All we can say is that it most probably had one. But the non-deductive character of this argument is not seen as a weakness by those who use it to demonstrate God's existence. Rather it is seen as a strength, placing the argument fully in line with the problematic character of all empirical observations. Here we are dealing with probabilities and not with logical certainties. Their claim is rather that the uniformity of nature observed within our world is such that it is as probable that the world has a designer as it is that any machine we come across has a mechanic. And the more instances we can call upon to reinforce this understanding of machines, the more likely becomes our interpretation of the world's origin. These instances are almost infinitely numerous. Thus to deny that the world has a designer is to deny the cumulative evidence of our senses.

Which of the following are examples of sound or unsound analogical reasoning?

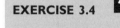

EXERCISE 3.4

345 is to 346 as 678 is to (a) 347 (b) 677 (c) 679

Dog is to bark as horse is to . . .?

There is life on earth; therefore there is life on Pluto.

There are buildings on Pluto; there therefore is or has been life on Pluto.

I have a right to life; therefore the foetus has a right to life.

Marriages are made in heaven, not on earth; therefore divorce is always immoral.

I understand Hamlet's distress: I had a girlfriend just like Ophelia.

I can imagine how angry she must have been when she missed her flight: the same thing's happened to me.

I don't steal and neither should you (even though you are a kleptomaniac).

The jury acquitted the battered wife of murdering her husband: they knew they'd have done the same.

HUME'S CRITIQUE OF THE DESIGN ARGUMENT

⇒ In his *Dialogues Concerning Natural Religion* (SOURCE 2: PP. 146–153) Hume
(in the guise of Cleanthes) presents one of the most celebrated summaries of
the design argument, followed by its most famous critique; and it is one of the
more piquant curiosities of philosophical history that his criticism was
presented some twenty-three years *before* Paley's presentation of the case. Not
that this provides Paley with much consolation. Being oblivious of Hume's
criticisms, Paley does not answer them. Hume, on the other hand, is at least
aware of the type of argument that Paley presents, even to the point of
considering the analogy of a watch. This analogy indeed was a fairly
commonplace one – to the extent that Paley was accused of plagiarism when
he introduced it – and can be traced as far back as Cicero's *De Natura Deorum*,
to which Hume also refers.[10]

> Hume's preliminary critique of the design argument appears in Section XI
> of Hume's *An Enquiry Concerning Human Understanding* (1748), and he
> gives a more general account of its importance for religious belief in his *The
> Natural History of Religion* (1757); but his most sustained attack is found
> in his posthumous *Dialogues Concerning Natural Religion* (1779), a book
> described (accurately, in my view) by Terence Penelhum as 'in all respects
> [Hume's] maturest work . . . beyond any question the greatest work on
> philosophy of religion in the English language'.[11] The *Dialogues* took
> over twenty-five years to write (from 1751 to 1776) and were finished only
> shortly before the author's death in 1776. It is a measure of its controversial
> character that both its original dedicatee, Professor Hugh Blair of Edinburgh
> University, and his literary executor, Adam Smith, advised against pub-
> lication, fearing that it would bring down on Hume, and probably on them
> as well, accusations of infidelity and atheism. It was thus left to Hume's 22-
> year-old nephew, young David Hume, to publish the book anonymously
> three years after his uncle's death.

The *Dialogues* constitute a dispute between three men, Demea, Cleanthes
and Philo. This presents some difficulties for scholars because it is unclear
which, if any, of the three expresses Hume's own position. I shall assume, in
line with most other commentators, that Hume is represented by Philo.
Certainly it is he who presents the crucial objections to the design argument.[12]
These criticisms concentrate on three main areas of debate:

---

10. For contemporary references to the analogy, see Leslie Stephen, *History of English Thought in the Eighteenth Century* (1881), London, Rupert Hart-Davis, 1962, p. 347.
11. In *Hume*, London, Macmillan, 1975, p. 171.
12. That Philo is Hume is convincingly maintained by N. Kemp Smith in his edition of the *Dialogues*, Oxford, Clarendon Press, 1935, Ch. V. A full account of the history of the book's publication is given by John Valdimir Price in his edition: Oxford, Clarendon Press, 1976, pp. 105–128.

1 The uniqueness of the universe
2 The diversity of causal explanation
3 The principle of proportionality.

Dialogues concerning natural Religion

Pamphilus to Hermippus.

It has been remark'd, my Hermippus, that, tho' the antient Philosophers convey'd most of their Instruction in the form of Dialogue, this Method of Composition has been little practis'd in later Ages, and has seldom succeeded in the hands of those, who have attempted it. Accurate and regular Argument, indeed, such as is now expected of philosophical Inquirers, naturally throws a man into the methodical & didactic manner; where he can immediately, without Preparation, explain the Point, at which he aims; and thence proceed without Interruption, to deduce the Proofs, on which it is establish'd. To deliver a System in Conversation scarcely appears natural; and while the Dialogue-Writer desires, by departing from the direct Style of Composition, to give a freer Air to his Performance, and avoid the Appearance of Author and Reader, he is apt to run into a worse Inconvenience, and convey the Image of Pedagogue and Pupil. Or if he carries on the Dispute in the natural Spirit of Good-company, by throwing in a Variety of Topics, and preserving a proper Ballance among the Speakers; he

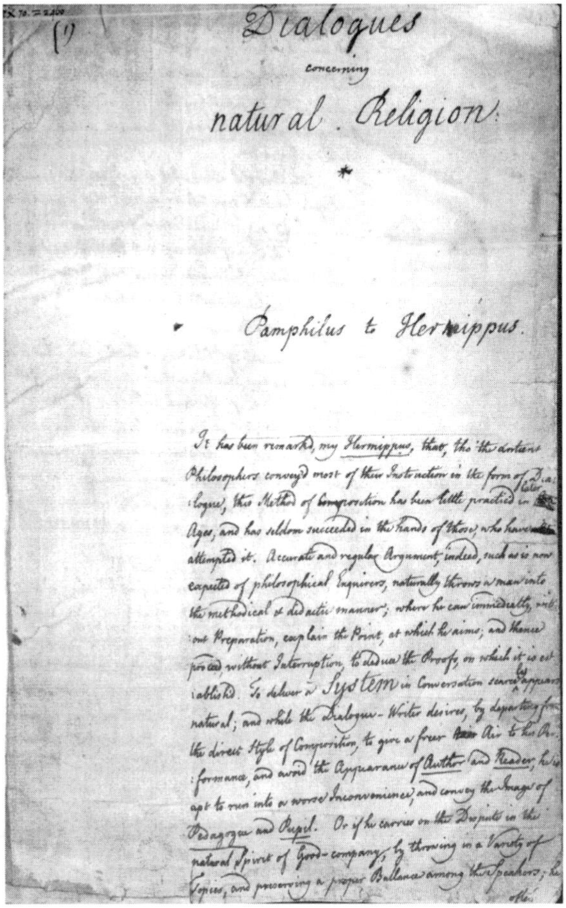

Manuscript page from Hume's *Dialogues Concerning Natural Religion*

The Uniqueness of the Universe

Hume's criticism of the argument's analogical structure

Here Hume attacks the analogical form of the design argument. Analogy, we remember, depends on a demonstration of *resemblances.* If an object (O) resembles B in possessing certain properties (Ps), then we may legitimately infer that O will also resemble B in possessing the additional property (Y). The greater the resemblance, the stronger the inference. But by the same token, the weaker the resemblance, the weaker the inference. For Hume, therefore, the supposition that the universe and human artifacts have property Y in common (i.e., the property of being designed) is not compelling because the more general resemblances (Ps) between the two are insufficient to support it. So, while it may be perfectly legitimate to infer that, if blood circulates in George, it will also circulate in Bob, it becomes less plausible on that account to assert that sap circulates in vegetables – the greater the difference in cases,

the more implausible is any analogical inference based on them. Take, for example, a comparison between a house and the universe:

> If we see a house, Cleanthes, we conclude, with the greatest certainty, that it had an architect or builder; because this is precisely that species of effect, which we have experienced to proceed from that species of cause. But surely you will not affirm, that the universe bears such a resemblance to a house, that we can with the same certainty infer a similar cause, or that the analogy is here entire and perfect. The dissimilitude is so striking, that the utmost you can here pretend to is a guess, a conjecture, a presumption concerning a similar cause; and how that pretension will be received in the world, I leave you to consider.[13]

In a later passage in the *Dialogues* Hume is still more precise about the fallacy of comparing the universe with human artifacts. While we are able to judge within our experience what causes houses to be built or watches to be made, we cannot do this with universes and thus cannot determine whether similar

Uniqueness precludes analogy

causes operate in universe-making as in watchmaking. An effective analogy, in other words, requires the examination of many instances of the objects being compared. The trouble with this is that the universe is neither an artifact like a watch nor an organ like an eye nor an organism like a monkey: *it is unique*. Therefore, since we have no experience of the origins of universes in general, we can say nothing about the origin of this universe.

> When two species of objects have always been observed to be conjoined together, I can infer, by custom, the existence of one, wherever I see the existence of the other. And this I call an argument from experience. But how this argument can have place, where the objects, as in the present case, are single, individual, without parallel, or specific resemblance, may be difficult to explain. And will any man tell me with a serious countenance, that an orderly universe must arise from some thought and art, like the human; because we have experience of it? To ascertain this reasoning, it were requisite, that we had experience of the origin of worlds; and it is not sufficient surely, that we have seen ships and cities arise from human art and contrivance.[14]

In his *Enquiry* Hume expands upon this point in one of his most elegant passages. First, and true to his method, he presents a formidable case for design:

> If you saw, for instance, a half-finished building surrounded with heaps of brick and stone and mortar and all the instruments of masonry; could you not *infer* from the effect, that it was the work of design and con-trivance? And could you not return again, from this inferred cause, to

---

13. *Dialogues*, ed. Smith, p. 144.
14. *Ibid.*, p. 150.

infer new additions to the effect, and conclude, that the building would soon be finished, and receive all further improvements which art could bestow upon it? If you saw upon the sea-shore the print of one human foot, you would conclude, that a man had passed that way, and that he had also left the traces of the other foot, though effaced by the rolling of the sands or inundation of the waters. Why then do you refuse to admit the same method of reasoning with regard to the order of nature?[15]

The question seems a fair one. Why not accept a parity of reasoning in this case, and admit that, if the inductive inference is legitimate in one case, it is legitimate in the other? As Hume puts it, 'Are not these methods of reasoning exactly similar? And under what pretence can you embrace the one, while you reject the other?'[16] But after having posed the question, Hume replies by pointing out that the inference employed in the design argument – what he here calls 'the religious hypothesis' – must fail, given that both the supposed cause (God) and its alleged effect (the universe) are unique by definition.

The Deity is known to us only by his productions, and is a single being in the universe, not comprehended under any species or genus, from whose experienced attributes or qualities, we can, by analogy, infer any attribute or quality in him. . . . The great source of our mistake in this subject . . . is, that we tacitly consider ourselves, as in the place of the Supreme Being. . . . But, besides that the ordinary course of nature may convince us, that almost everything is regulated by principles and maxims very different from ours . . . it must evidently appear contrary to all rules of analogy to reason from the intentions and projects of men, to those of a Being so different and so much superior. . . . But this method of reasoning can never have place with regard to a Being, so remote and incomprehensible, who bears much less analogy to any other being in the universe than the sun to a waxen taper, and who discovers himself only by some faint traces or outlines, beyond which we have no authority to ascribe to him any attribute or perfection. . . . In a word, I much doubt whether it is possible for a cause to be known only by its effect (as you have all along supposed) or to be of so singular and particular a nature as to have no parallel and no similarity with any other cause or object, that has ever fallen under our observation.[17]

Opinion is divided about this criticism. Antony Flew calls it Hume's 'killing blow',[18] arguing that 'we do not have, and we necessarily could not have, experience of other Universes to tell us that Universes, or Universes with these particular features, are always, or most likely, the work of Gods, or of Gods of

Some replies to Hume

15. *Enquiry Concerning Human Understanding*, ed. L. A. Selby-Bigge, 3rd edn revised by P. H. Nidditch, Oxford, Clarendon Press, 1975, pp. 147–148.
16. *Ibid.*, p. 143.
17. *Ibid.*, pp. 147–148.
18. *David Hume: Philosopher of Moral Science*, Oxford, Basil Blackwell, 1986, p. 64.

this or that particular sort'.[19] Here Flew also introduces a point that I have already made when discussing the cosmological argument, specifically in relation to the principle of sufficient reason.[20] Even if we accept the principle (which Flew regards as demonstrably false) that there has to be a sufficient reason why anything and everything is as it is, the explanation given must at least be offered in terms of *something other* than the thing being explained; or, as Flew puts it, 'every system of explanation must include at least some fundamentals which are not themselves explained'.[21] But what can this other thing be when we ask why-questions of the universe, when the universe constitutes the totality of existing things, thereby excluding any other element outside itself in terms of which it may be explained? Asking for a cause of the whole universe, as we have observed before, has a different logical status from asking for a cause of an individual object or event within that universe.

Others, however, are less taken with this criticism.[22] Hume's objection appears to be that it is impossible to form hypotheses about singular or unique objects, in which case, of course, any argument which employs the notion of a universe on one side of an analogy will be ruled out of court from the beginning. Richard Swinburne, to whom we shall return presently, argues that this assumption is false. After all, we know of only one human race, but that does not prevent anthropologists from speculating about the origins of man.[23] The important point to note here is that, while the universe may be unique, it is not for that reason *indescribable*; and having been described as a collection of parts – e.g., sun, stars and planets, down to the simplest microscopic organisms – it may be treated as the legitimate object of scientific study.

I am not sure, however, that this reply meets the full force of Hume's objection. Such talk of the universe contains the prior assumption that the universe has a predominant characteristic: i.e., that it *is* a whole, namely, a unified system of organized and mutually supportive functional adaptations, coordinated, moreover, if one is to take the comparison with artifacts seriously, for the realization of certain goals. But what, asks Hume, are the warrants for this assumption? For while it is clearly possible to establish that regularities do exist in the association of different parts within our world – it is possible, for example, to observe empirically whether certain conditions within it are regularly connected (for example, friction and heat) – it is quite impossible to stand, as it were, outside the universe and so observe whether such associations pertain to the universe generally. This explains why it is quite impossible to determine whether the extent of adaptiveness in the universe *as a whole* is

---

19. 'Hume's Philosophy of Religion', in *Philosophers Ancient and Modern*, ed. Godfrey Vesey, Cambridge, Cambridge University Press, 1986, p. 138.
20. See above, p. 63.
21. *Ibid.*, p. 139.
22. See, for example, Richard Swinburne, 'The Argument from Design', *Philosophy*, 43, 1968, pp. 199–212; Thomas McPherson, *Philosophy and Religious Belief*, London, Hutchinson University Library, 1974, pp. 65–67; Stephen Evans, *Philosophy of Religion*, Leicester, Inter-Varsity Press, 1982, p. 64; Brian Davies, *An Introduction to the Philosophy of Religion*, Oxford, Oxford University Press, 1982, p. 54.
23. *Op. cit.*, p. 208.

sufficient to warrant the analogy between it and an artifact, and thus to warrant the theistic conclusion.

The point to be stressed here is that Hume is not questioning the propriety of ever speaking about the origin of the universe – as we shall see in a moment, he is prepared to entertain often bizarre accounts of its creation – but he is doubting that there is, or could be, evidence to justify any analogical reference which includes the universe *as a whole*. What he is trying to establish, in other words, is not that the analogy between a universe and a watch is demonstrably false but that whether this analogy is true or false is not something which, in the particular and unique case of the universe, we shall ever be in a position to demonstrate. This is because we have nothing else comparable to the universe, and because we cannot force upon it general characteristics which may, for all we know, pertain only to a small part of it.

> Thought, design, intelligence, such as we discover in men and other animals, is no more than one of the springs and principles of the universe, as well as heat or cold, attraction or repulsion, and a hundred others, which fall under daily observation. It is an active cause, by which some particular parts of nature, we find, produce alterations on other parts. But can a conclusion, with any propriety, be transferred from parts to the whole? Does not the great disproportion bar all comparison and inference? From observing the growth of a hair, can we learn anything concerning the generation of a man? Would the manner of a leaf's blowing, even though perfectly known, afford us any instruction concerning the vegetation of a tree? [24]

It is not difficult to see, I think, that behind this first criticism lies Hume's general dissatisfaction with all cosmological arguments. Within our experience certain conditions are said to prevail, whether it be the relation of cause to effect or the phenomenon of functional adaptation. But this conclusion will not take us as far as theists want to go: they want also to say that these conditions pertain to the *world as a whole*, which thereby justifies further questions about the existence of a causal agent or designer to account for that world. But this point cannot be reached on the a posteriori certainty that these conditions do in fact apply – there being no possibility of this claim ever being justified – but only on the a priori certainty that these conditions *must* apply. We have thus returned to the undemonstrable assumption that *nature is uniform*: 'that instances, of which we have had no experience, must resemble those, of which we have had experience, and that the course of nature continues always the same'.[25] There is, however, no logical or empirical reason why this should be so, and therefore no logical or empirical reason why we should elevate one characteristic within the universe to the role of primary characteristic of the universe as a whole. But we can at least understand why this is done. It follows from a 'determination

Uniformity of nature: an undemonstrable assumption

---

24. *Dialogues*, ed. Smith, p. 147.
25. *A Treatise of Human Nature* (1739), Book I, Part III, Section VI, ed. L. A. Selby-Bigge, London, Oxford University Press, reprint 1965, p. 89.

of the mind' on our part to think that what applies to a *part* must also apply to the *whole*, and from our preference for a particular characteristic which lends support to the view that the universe is ultimately intelligible. The design argument therefore assumes what it is seeking to prove: not that *order* exists – this is not in dispute – but that order exists generally; that, in other words, nature is uniform. But this cannot be demonstrated. That the universe is alleged to have this *supposed* property in common with artifacts does not allow us to make the inductive inference that it has another property, namely, that it is the product of design.

EXERCISE 3.5

How would Hume argue against the following propositions? Do you agree with him?

The universe is like any other artifact: it is the product of design.

The universe is like my son: unique and brought into being by a creator.

The order I see in the universe points to an orderer of the universe.

THE DIVERSITY OF CAUSAL EXPLANATION

Even if the first part of Hume's argument is rejected – even if we accept for the moment that the analogy between world and artifact justifies the conclusion that the world has a designer – the next phase of his argument, which many regard as the more devastating, reduces this possibility still further. Given that there is order in the world, there may be other explanations besides the theistic one to account for it, explanations at least as probable as the design–designer hypothesis. To express the matter formally: the analogy between objects O and B may be denied if the effects they have in common can be accounted for by other means. Thus, if O resembles B in having various properties (Ps), this does not require that O further resembles B in having the same cause to account for those properties. To suppose otherwise, we remember, is to commit the fallacy of the 'affirmation of the consequent', since there may be a great variety of causes producing the same effects.

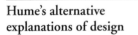

Hume's alternative
explanations of design

That various causes can produce the same effects is a point that Hume now exploits to the full. He proceeds, therefore, to offer two alternative explanations for the appearance of design. In the first he considers the possibility that order and design, while certainly resembling the effects of human activity, may yet more closely resemble the (equally perceptible) effects achieved by the biological activities of animals and plants. Here the principles of instinct, generation and vegetation operate to produce an ordered world without any external and intelligent agency. Why not, then, conceive of this planetary system as a 'great Vegetable' producing 'within itself certain seeds, which, being scattered into the surrounding chaos, vegetate into new worlds'? Why not see the world as an 'Animal', with a comet as its egg? Why not join with the Brahmins and assert that 'the world arose from an infinite spider, who spun this whole complicated mass from his bowels'?[26] Admittedly these alternatives are offered very much tongue in cheek, and Hume's Philo admits as much; but however fanciful, they cannot be dismissed, as Demea would have us do, simply on the grounds that there is no evidence to support them. That misses the point at issue. We are dealing here with rival theories concerning the causes of order in nature. On the one hand, we have the theory of a designing intelligence, drawn from our experience of human effects; on the other, we have the theory of natural self-regulation and growth, drawn from our experience of biological effects. But if one theory is rejected through lack of evidence, there is no reason why we cannot reject the other on the same grounds:

> I have still asserted [says Philo], that we have no data to establish any system of cosmogony. Our experience, so imperfect in itself, and so limited both in extent and duration, can afford us no probable conjecture concerning the whole of things. But if we must needs fix on some hypothesis; by what rule, pray, ought we to determine our choice? Is there any other rule than the greater similarity of the objects compared? And does not a plant or an animal, which springs from vegetation or generation, bear a stronger resemblance to the world, than does any artificial machine, which arises from reason and design? . . . To say that all this order in animals and vegetables proceeds ultimately from design is begging the question; nor can that great point be ascertained otherwise than by proving a priori, both that order is, from its nature, inseparably attached to thought, and that it can never, of itself, or from original unknown principles, belong to matter.[27]

The strength of this criticism is not lost on Cleanthes, who, while claiming that Philo's objections are contrary to sense and reason, retreats from the field, admitting that as yet he can find no satisfactory answer to them.

Hume admits that his second explanation for the appearance, if not the fact, of design is similarly fanciful; but its absurdity is again beside the point. What has to be established is whether it is any *less* absurd than the theistic alternative. So, simply going on the evidence before us, it is possible to offer a thoroughly materialistic and mechanistic interpretation of the world about us. For all we know, Philo argues, the order we observe could result from the chance collisions of particles of matter, without any guiding intelligence. This is the so-called 'Epicurean hypothesis' suggested by the Greek philosopher Epicurus of Samos (341–270 BC). Epicurus' account of physical nature, which largely follows the views of his predecessors Leucippus and Democritus, postulates a universe infinite in extent, without beginning or end, but evolving out of a primordial and immeasurable plurality of uncreated and indivisible particles (*atomoi*). The world was not therefore created by gods or designed by them for some ultimate purpose – the gods themselves are seen as the products of the material universe

The Epicurean hypothesis

---

26. *Dialogues*, ed. Smith, pp. 177–180.
27. *Ibid.*, pp. 177, 179.

and completely indifferent to its functioning – and what changes do occur are the result of the accidental collisions or 'swerves' of these atomic particles.

Epicurus (341–270 BC)

For instance; what if I should revive the old Epicurean hypothesis? This is commonly, and I believe, justly, esteemed the most absurd system, that has yet been proposed; yet, I know not, whether, with a few alterations, it might not be brought to bear a faint appearance of probability. . . . Suppose . . . that matter were thrown into any position, by a blind, unguided force; it is evident that this first position must in all probability be the most confused and most disorderly imaginable, without any resemblance to those works of human contrivance, which, along with a symmetry of parts, discover an adjustment of means to ends and a tendency to self-preservation. . . .

Thus the universe goes on for many ages in a continued succession of chaos and disorder. But is it not possible that it may settle at last, so as not to lose its motion and active force (for that we have supposed inherent in it) yet so as to preserve an uniformity of appearance, amidst the continual motion and fluctuation of its parts? This we find to be the case with the universe at present. Every individual is perpetually changing, and every part of every individual, and yet the whole remains, in appearance, the same. May we not hope for such a position, or rather be assured of it, from the eternal revolutions of unguided matter, and may not this account for all the appearing wisdom and contrivance, which is in the universe? Let us contemplate the subject a little, and we shall find, that this adjustment, attained by matter, of a seeming stability in the forms, with a real and perpetual revolution or motion of parts, affords a plausible, if not a true solution of the difficulty.[28]

Once again the problem presented here is to choose between two rival hypotheses. On the one hand, we have *authentic design* (i.e., the world is the

---

28. *Ibid.*, pp. 182, 184–185.

product of a designer), and on the other, we have *apparent design* (i.e., the world has the appearance of design but is in fact the product of chance). The evidence for each alternative remains the same – the fact of order – but whether this evidence is sufficient to support one hypothesis over the other is hard to see. Certainly we cannot be surprised that, for some people, such degrees of regularity – assuming for the moment that the phenomenon of order *is* a feature of the universe *as a whole* – should provoke feelings of awe and stupefaction and lead them to discount the element of chance in favour of some guiding force. But there are rival hypotheses, Hume contends, about what this guiding force might be: it might be something more akin to an animal instinct or vegetative process, or again some mechanical interaction between particles of matter, or a combination of such forces; but whatever it is, we cannot assume a priori that it is a designing mind because that is precisely what the design argument is seeking to prove. To give an example: If I throw sticks in the air, it is possible that they will fall into a pattern, say, the form of an octagon. Someone who did not see me throw them might conclude that the pattern was deliberate, that I arranged the sticks to produce that effect. But how is that person to know, merely on the evidence before him, that the octagon was the result of a constructing intelligence and not the product of blind chance? Again the fallacy of the 'affirmation of the consequent' applies: there may be a great number of causes (chance being one) which lead to the same effect. Indeed, Hume goes further. We draw analogies from our experiences within our world, and here we find that the creation of intelligent beings follows from some act of animal reproduction and not, so far as we can tell, from the operation of a particular intelligence. To argue by analogy is therefore to draw the more likely conclusion that intelligence is not the originating cause of order and apparent design, and that we should look more to the processes of generation.

According to Hume, then, there appears no good reason to adopt the theistic solution in preference to any other explanation of the causes of order and design. We may initially agree with Cleanthes that the universe, having many properties in common with machines, has the additional property of being designed. But, as we have seen, in several other respects the universe resembles other things that do not possess this property, and this inevitably reduces the likelihood that it actually has it. Certainly it reduces it to the point where the religious preference for a designing intelligence, over against all other causal explanations, is difficult to sustain.

Authentic and apparent design

Of the following which do you consider the most likely causal explanation of the universe?
Explain your answer.

The universe was created by:

a giant insect.   a committee of gods.   the universe itself.

an evil genius.   one God.

EXERCISE 3.6

THE PRINCIPLE OF PROPORTIONALITY

Let us now set aside Hume's criticism of the claim that the cause of the universe is an intelligent being. What of the theistic conclusion that this intelligent being is God? To begin, Hume returns to the inductive principle of proportionality, namely, that *like effects prove like causes*. In the design argument, we remember, this principle allows that the greater the resemblance between the effects – in this case, the universe and human artifacts – the closer the similarity in causes, namely, that both are the product of a designing intelligence. But even if we accept this argument, it still provides insufficient grounds for any additional and religious conclusions about God's nature. Hume's objection, first set out in his *Enquiry*, is simple and effective:

> When we infer any particular cause from an effect, we must proportion the one to the other, and can never be allowed to ascribe to the cause any qualities, but what are exactly sufficient to produce the effect. A body of ten ounces raised in any scale may serve as a proof, that the counter-balancing weight exceeds ten ounces; but can never afford a reason that it exceeds a hundred. . . . The same rule holds, whether the cause assigned be brute unconscious matter, or a rational intelligent being. If the cause be known only by the effect, we never ought to ascribe to it any qualities, beyond what are precisely requisite to produce the effect: Nor can we, by any rules of just reasoning, return back from the cause, and infer other effects from it, beyond those by which it is known to us.[29]

An example will clarify the point Hume is making. If I saw a collection of paintings by Picasso – say, a group associated with his so-called Blue Period of 1901–1904 – I might conclude that the artist was possessed of certain skills and tastes. Here the cause is proportioned to the effect. But what I could not know, merely from the canvasses before me, is that Picasso was also a master of other forms, for example, ceramics, sculpture, *papiers collés*. To credit him with these further skills would be to infer additional qualities from these paintings which, as effects, they are not sufficient to produce. For the design argument this has two important implications. The first is that we cannot apply to God (as the causal agent) any qualities which are not proportionate to his effects – and this may lead to the *exclusion* of certain attributes that the believer wishes to *include*; and the second is, conversely, that what qualities are applicable must be proportionate to those effects – and this may lead to the *inclusion* of certain attributes that the believer wishes to *exclude*. Either way the results are embarrassing.

What, then, is to be *excluded*? The first to go is the claim to *infinity* in any of the attributes of the Deity. From the finite objects we perceive as effects we are asked to infer the existence of an infinite cause; but the most we can legitimately conclude from the cause–effect structure of the design analogy is

29, *Enquiry*, p. 136.

a *finite* cause. Anything else would contravene the principle of proportionality and involve the unjustified and indeed illogical application of empirical concepts beyond the sensible world from which they are drawn and in which they operate. The second attribute to be excluded is that of *perfection*. Again, if the cause be proportionate to the effect, then the fairly obvious and manifold instances of imperfection within the world would lead us more naturally to suppose that their creator is imperfect also, not perfect.[30] And here Hume repeats a by now familiar point. If our universe cannot be compared to any other universe, how do we know that it is perfect and its creator not a bungler?

> But were this world ever so perfect a production, it must still remain uncertain, whether all the excellencies of the work can justly be ascribed to the workman. If we survey a ship, what an exalted idea must we form of the ingenuity of the carpenter, who framed so complicated useful and beautiful a machine? And what surprise must we entertain, when we find him a stupid mechanic, who imitated others, and copied an art, which through a long succession of ages, after multiplied trials, mistakes, corrections, deliberations, and controversies, had been gradually improving? Many worlds might have been botched and bungled, throughout an eternity, ere this system was struck out: Much labour lost: Many fruitless trials made: And a slow, but continued improvement carried on during infinite ages in the art of world-making. In such subjects, who can determine, where the truth; nay, who can conjecture where the probability, lies; amidst a great number of hypotheses, which may be proposed, and a still greater number, which may be imagined?[31]

If the principle of proportionality is to be upheld, therefore, we should by rights have to assert the existence of a finite and imperfect being as God. But other, equally damaging, attributes must be *included* if we are to pursue the design analogy to the end. If the analogy depends on a resemblance between human and natural effects, then it is not merely the effects which must be considered alike but their causes as well. Accordingly, the greater the similarity in effect, the greater the probability that a more *anthropomorphic* or man-like picture of God is the correct one. Hume here considers three alternatives:

Attributes to be included

1. The first possibility is that there is not one God but many. Again, since there are many effects, there might well be many causes. Certainly experience inclines us to the view that the larger the creation, the more people are involved. Why therefore contradict this principle when discussing the creation of a world?

> And what shadow of an argument, continued Philo, can you produce, from your hypothesis, to prove the unity of the Deity? A great number of men join in building a house or ship, in rearing a city, in framing a commonwealth: Why may not several Deities combine in contriving and

---

30. This point introduces Hume's extended discussion of the Problem of Evil in Sections X and XI of the *Dialogues*.
31. *Dialogues*, ed. Smith, p. 167.

framing a world? This is only so much greater similarity to human affairs.[32]

2. The second possibility is that God no longer exists. Just as an architect of a building, being human, may not outlive the building he designed, so the designer (or designers) of the universe may not outlive their creation, even though evidence of his (or their) creativity is still apparent to us:

> But farther, Cleanthes; men are mortal, and renew their species by generation; and this is common to all living creatures. . . . Why must this circumstance, so universal, so essential, be excluded from those numerous and limited Deities?[33]

3. The third possibility is to extend the resemblances between causes to include physical characteristics:

> And why not become a perfect anthropomorphite? Why not assert the Deity or Deities to be corporeal, and to have eyes, a nose, mouth, ears etc. Epicurus maintained, that no man had ever seen reason but in a human figure; therefore the gods must have a human figure. And this argument, which is deservedly so much ridiculed by Cicero, becomes, according to you, solid and philosophical.[34]

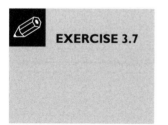

EXERCISE 3.7

Present arguments for and against the possibility that God is . . .

now dead	malevolent
delinquent	one of many gods
incompetent	of human form

This concludes the final phase of Hume's discussion. His contention is that, even if one agrees with the basic premises of the design argument – that there is a resemblance between nature and human artifacts, and that like effects have like causes – one could not thereby attain the sort of knowledge about the nature and existence of God that its proponents desire. Quite the contrary, in fact, since what one comes up with when pursuing the analogy through to its limits is qualities and characteristics totally at variance with those applied to the God of the main Judaeo-Christian tradition. Indeed, the better the analogy, the more one must conclude that the Author of Nature is more like the watchmaker we are familiar with: finite, imperfect, subject to error, and so on. Thus, even if we accept that the universe is caused by some kind of intelligence,

---

this does not of itself discount the possibility that this intelligence is limited, and that universes, like watches, can accordingly be made by fools and bunglers.

DARWIN'S CRITIQUE OF THE DESIGN ARGUMENT

Charles Darwin's criticisms shadow Hume's objections in many respects. While it is difficult to sustain the view that his *Origin of Species* (1859) consciously carries forward the Humean attack – its first edition carries a design argument of its own and in structure, oddly enough, owed much to Paley – we do know from various entries in Darwin's work that at the precise moment when he hit upon his 'theory by which to work' he was reading Hume with care and profit.[35] Nor should we forget that the *Dialogues* contain distinctly evolutionary overtones.[36]

The decisive point of contact between Hume and Darwin lies, as we shall see, in the extent to which Darwin's theory supports Hume's second criticism of the design argument – that dealing with the *diversity of causal explanation*. Here it is worth recalling that, to many religious minds of the nineteenth century, the scandal of Darwinism was not merely to be told that human beings derive from the same stock as animals, but to be informed additionally that the prime mover in the cosmic process was not purpose but chance; in other words, that at least one of Hume's tentative explanations for the *appearance* of design – his so-called Epicurean hypothesis – far from being absurd, in fact had scientific support. How, for example, could one continue to hold to the idea of purposive and intelligent design when, following Darwin's theory of natural selection, it could be shown that living organisms developed as the products not of divine initiative but of a competitive process, a struggle for existence, in which the survival of any particular species depended on the degree to which it could adapt to the particular environment in which it found itself? This conclusion fleshed out Hume's Epicurean hypothesis. It is not *authentic* design that we see in the world around us but *apparent* design, in which chance and adjustment to circumstance determine the order that exists.

So important is Darwin's theory that it may be useful here to give a brief account of its background. In 1831, aged 22, Darwin was offered the post of accompanying naturalist on board HMS *Beagle*, which was to survey the coasts of Patagonia, Tierra del Fuego, Chile and Peru. The voyage lasted five years and was, as Darwin later confessed, the most important event of his life, providing him with a wealth of zoological and botanical specimens. In September 1835

Connection between Darwin and Hume

The voyage of HMS *Beagle*

---

35. See William B. Huntley, 'David Hume and Charles Darwin', *Journal of the History of Ideas*, 33, 1972, pp. 458–470. For two excellent accounts of the development of Darwin's religious beliefs, see John Hedley Brooke, 'The Relations between Darwin's Science and his Religion', in *Darwinism and Divinity*, ed. John Durant, Oxford, Basil Blackwell, 1985, pp. 40–75; and Dov Ospovat, 'God and Natural Selection: The Darwinian Idea of Design', *Journal of the History of Biology*, 13(2), Fall 1980, pp. 169–194.
36. 'Yet may matter be susceptible of many and great revolutions, through the endless periods of eternal duration. The incessant changes, to which every part of it is subject, seem to intimate some such general transformations' (*Dialogues*, ed. Smith, p. 174).

Charles Darwin
(1809–1882)

From a wealthy background, Darwin was educated at Shrewsbury School, and was sent to Edinburgh University to study his father's profession of medicine, which he loathed, and then in 1827 to Cambridge to study divinity, with equal lack of success. Here, however, he met a group of scientists led by the clergyman-botanist John Henslow, who in 1831 recommended Darwin to the Admiralty as the unpaid naturalist on HMS *Beagle*. During his five-year trip Darwin sent back innumerable geologic and biological specimens, which rapidly established his reputation at home. On his return he was promptly elected a Fellow of the Geological Society, and, in 1839, aged 30, a Fellow of the Royal Society. Although Darwin's account of his voyage was published in the same year, in his private notebooks he had already begun work on 'the species problem', two sketches of his evolutionary theory appearing in 1842 and 1844. Although he was always reluctant to publish his thesis in full, the matter was decided for him when, on 18 June 1858, Alfred Wallace, a naturalist working in the Malay Archipelago, sent him a paper largely duplicating Darwin's own conclusions. To avoid embarrassment, a joint paper by Darwin and Wallace was read to the Linnean Society a few days later, on 1 July. *On the Origin of Species by Means of Natural Selection* was published on 24 November 1859 and rapidly sold out, a sixth edition appearing in 1872. Although quickly accepted by most scientists, the theory of natural selection met with fierce opposition from orthodox Christians, the most acrimonious encounter being in Oxford in 1869 between Samuel Wilberforce, the Bishop of Oxford, and T. H. Huxley. Three further books complete Darwin's theory: *The Variation of Animals and Plants under Domestication* (1868), *The Descent of Man* (1871) and *The Expression of the Emotions in Man and Animals* (1872). A semi-invalid for most of his life, Darwin died at Down House on 19 April 1882, and through Parliamentary petition was buried in Westminster Abbey.

HMS *Beagle*

the *Beagle* landed on one of the islands of the Galapagos Archipelago, and it was there that Darwin made a crucial observation. He realized that animals from various islands, which he had previously thought to be of the same species, were in fact of different species – that finches, for example, differed both in structure and behaviour from one island to the next: that some ate insects, others seeds, and that the form of their bills reflected this difference. Two explanations were possible: one explained these differences either on the basis of some independent and immutable creation or on the basis that these species, affected by the different conditions of the different islands, underwent certain transformations. 'It was evident that such facts as these as well as many others could be explained on the supposition that species gradually become modified; and the subject haunted me.'[37]

But what was the mechanism of such modification? Darwin's next step in his search was prompted by two books: Sir Charles Lyell's *Principles of Geology* (1830–1832), the first volume of which Darwin had taken with him on the *Beagle*; and Thomas Malthus' *Essay on Population* (1798), which he read nearly two years after his return. The principal significance of Lyell's work was that it converted Darwin to the theory known as 'uniformitarianism'. This was the view, unfashionable at the time, that the earth had developed over enormous periods of time and as a result of a whole series of disturbances – eruptions, earthquakes, erosion and deposition – which were 'uniform' with what could be observed in our own experience. This thesis contrasted sharply with the more prevalent view – known as 'catastrophism' – which claimed that the earth had changed as a result of violent cataclysms disrupting the regular order of nature, one of these being commemorated in the biblical story of the Flood. Lyell's thesis, which Darwin confirmed for himself when he saw the volcanoes of St Jago and which he developed in his own theory of coral reefs, allowed Darwin later to postulate a more gradual sequence of events in the evolution of the species, and to theorize about what the mechanism of this development might be by analysis of observable phenomena.

Influences on Darwin: Lyell and Malthus

Sir Charles Lyell (1769–1849)

---

37. 'Autobiography' (1903), in *Charles Darwin and T. H. Huxley: Autobiographies*, edited with an Introduction by Gavin de Beer, London, Oxford University Press, 1974, p. 70.

Thomas Malthus (1766–1824)

Equally important was Darwin's reading of the political economist Malthus. In his *Essay on Population* Malthus laid down his famous principle that population increases in a geometrical, and subsistence only in an arithmetical, ratio: i.e., that the universal tendency of all living things to multiply places an intolerable burden upon the resources of the environment, that human beings are no exception to this universal law of nature, and that the result of breaking it is poverty, disease, starvation and war. As an Anglican clergyman, Malthus set his work firmly within the tradition of natural theology – he was, for example, a firm believer in Paley's scheme of design – but the principle he proclaimed, taken completely out of context, nevertheless provided Darwin with the mechanism he sought. For by applying the Malthusian law to plants and animals – neither of which, unlike man, are capable of increasing their resources – he realized that they must die if they multiply beyond the available food supply.

> In October 1838, that is, fifteen months after I had begun my systematic enquiry, I happened to read for amusement 'Malthus on Population', and being well prepared to appreciate the struggle for existence which everywhere goes on from long-continued observation of the habits of animals and plants, it at once struck me that under these circumstances favourable variations would tend to be preserved and unfavourable ones to be destroyed. The result of this would be the formation of new species.[38]

In the notion of a 'struggle for existence' we find Darwin's principal debt to Malthus. For here is the 'theory by which to work', an explanatory, self-regulating and entirely mechanical principle which could explain the evolution of species without recourse to any human or divine intervention. Malthus had drawn his attention to the fact that overproduction and the resulting struggle for life was a universal law; and what Darwin did was to apply this law not merely to human society, which had been Malthus' priority, but to all animal and vegetable kingdoms, thereby concluding that a selection of the fittest individuals or varieties within a species was a necessary result of this competitive struggle. This principle was a notoriously simple one, prompting T. H. Huxley to exclaim 'How extremely stupid not to have thought of it.'[39] Darwin called

38. *The Life and Letters of Charles Darwin*, ed. Francis Darwin, John Murray, 1903, Vol. I, p. 83.
39. *Ibid.*, Vol. II, p. 192..

Malthus requests population information for the United States. In his *Essay on the Principle of Population*, Malthus indicated that 'species may produce large numbers of young, but the species population does not increase accordingly'. Darwin and Wallace credited this very sentence of Malthus for their discovery of the Law of Natural Selection even though each independently discovered that law.

it the principle of 'natural selection', in later editions also adopting the expression popularized by Herbert Spencer: 'the survival of the fittest'.

> If under changing conditions of life organic beings present individual differences in almost every part of their structure, and this cannot be disputed; if there be, owing to their geometrical rate of increase, a severe struggle for life at some age, season, or year, and this certainly cannot be disputed; then, considering the infinite complexity of the relations of all organic beings to each other and to their conditions of life, causing an infinite diversity in structure, constitution, and habits, to be advantageous to them, it would be a most extraordinary fact if no variations had ever occurred useful to each being's own welfare, in the same manner as so many variations have occurred useful to man. But if variations useful to any organic being ever do occur, assuredly individuals thus characterised will have the best chance of being preserved in the struggle for life; and for the strong principle of inheritance, these will tend to produce offspring similarly characterised. This principle of preservation, or the survival of the fittest, I have called Natural Selection.[40]

The principle of natural selection

Having hit upon the idea of natural selection as the mechanism of evolutionary change, Darwin was keen to verify it; and it is interesting to note

40. *The Origin of Species by Means of Natural Selection*, 6th edn, London, John Murray, 1888, pp. 102–103.

that the way in which he did so was initially through a process of inductive-analogical reasoning, prompting further comparisons with Paley.[41] Some time prior to his reading of Malthus, he had been analysing the formation of varieties of plants and animals in *domestic* situations: how, to give some well-known examples, breeders of pigeons, sheep, racehorse or dogs could, by a programme of selective breeding, modify the form and colour of their stock according to their own requirements. The lesson was not lost on Darwin. If the breeder could select, then it was legitimate, by an inductive inference, to suppose that nature could select as well, that nature could operate as if it were the breeder, albeit in a much more various and potent form.

This extrapolation from domestication is quite consciously employed by Darwin, although he speaks rather of 'metaphor' than of 'analogy'. Where the end (*telos*) of domestic selection was an adaptive fitness to man's standard of perfection, so in nature it was an adaptive fitness to the species' own end – namely, survival in the struggle for existence. Thus, to express the analogy or metaphor more pertinently, natural selection could act as an active agent or artificer, determining the innumerable variations in nature through many successive generations, constantly modifying, discarding and improving new species as they arise and rejecting old species in their favour, so that eventually they become extinct.[42]

Here the crucial point to note is the relation between variation and selection. Darwin considered these variations to be extremely slight, not appearing simultaneously but over long intervals of time. What he proposed, however, was that over many generations these differences would become greater, so that organisms possessing *beneficial* modifications would survive – 'beneficial' here being defined by an adaptability to new conditions – while those that did not would be *eliminated*. Thus it is that, by the operation of natural selection, suitably modified forms have a competitive advantage over others, resulting in the production of more offspring and the perpetuation of the type – that is, until such time as further modifications occur and the process begins anew. In itself, then, the natural process by which the *causes* of variation produce the

---

41. The analogy is discussed by Michael Ruse, *Taking Darwin Seriously*, Oxford, Basil Blackwell, 1986, pp. 31–37.

42. More specifically, Darwin proposes five principal causes of variation: (1) *The indirect effect of the Conditions of Life* (i.e., the effect of a changing environment upon the reproductive system); (2) *The direct effect of the Conditions of Life* (i.e., the immediate effect the environment has on the production of variations – e.g., thickness of fur from climate); (3) *Habit, Use, and Disuse*: a unique combination of causes because here the organism is active, not passive, in relation to the environment, bringing about the variation itself – e.g., the habits of plants to flower within a given period changes when they are transported to a different climate; the increase in size of udders habitually milked; the difference in wing-weight between the domestic and wild duck; (4) *Correlation of Growth*: where variations occur in one part of an organism, other parts are modified (e.g., hairless dogs tend to have bad teeth; pigeons with short beaks tend to have small feet); (5) *Compensation or Balancement of Growth*: subsidiary to Correlation, this refers to the withdrawal of nutriment from one part of the organism because of the excessive growth of another part (e.g., cows that give milk cannot be easily fattened). As a supplementary cause of variability Darwin later developed the notion of *sexual selection*, which he developed in his *Descent of Man* (1871). For a detailed discussion of these variations, see Peter J. Vorzimmer, *Charles Darwin: The Years of Controversy*, London, University of London Press, 1972, pp. 71ff.

effects of varieties does very little. It is only when these effects are submitted to the additional natural process of selection that further and substantial change occurs and new species appear.

Before leaving Darwin, it is worth updating his theory in one important respect. Without doubt the greatest weakness in Darwin's presentation was his inability to propose any satisfactory mechanism for the inheritance of favourable traits from one generation to another. If, as we have seen, the adaptation of an organism to its environment proceeds by natural selection, then the question remains: What is it within that organism that natural selection works upon? Or rather: What is the material bond between generations which allows one species to evolve in one direction, and a second in another, while yet coming from the same stock? Darwin admitted that he needed this mechanism of inheritance, but confessed his ignorance: 'The laws governing inheritance are for the most part unknown. No one can say why the same peculiarity in different individuals of the same species, or in different species, is sometimes inherited and sometimes not so.'[43]

Updating Darwin: the discovery of DNA

It is, of course, one of the great achievements of modern biology that this problem has largely been solved. With the discovery of discrete 'primal characters' by the Moravian monk Gregor Mendel (1822–1884), the isolation of deoxyribonucleic acid (DNA) by Oswald Avery in 1944, and the confirmation of its form as a double helix by Watson and Crick in 1953, it is now clear that hereditary information is transmitted from generation to generation in the nucleic acid called DNA, which provides the substance for nearly half of each chromosome. While the molecule of this compound can replicate itself with extraordinary accuracy – a process which accounts for the production of individuals similar to their parents – it does not achieve complete exactitude; and because the chemically coded instructions for development can be misread owing to some alteration in the DNA molecule or in chromosomal structure, a variant form of the DNA will be produced. This explains the structural differences and likenesses between various species. So when we observe the numerous similarities and differences between the gorilla and man – on the one hand, prehensile hands and digits with nails, and, on the other, body size and tooth shape – we are in fact observing the effects of different proteins produced in accordance with the hereditary coding contained in the DNA molecules.

Because of the purely chemical relation between DNA instructions and the evolutionary process, the degree to which natural selection can directly change the codes passed on from parent to parent is limited.[44] This, however, is not a denial of Darwin's doctrine, since selection, we remember, operates on the variations already established (by whatever means), and is therefore still capable of directing genetic variations towards the creation of more fit

---

43. *The Origin of Species by Means of Natural Selection*, p. 10.
44. It is this fact more than any other which disposes of the idea, first proposed by the French naturalist Jean Lamarck (1744–1829), that evolution proceeds through the 'inheritance of acquired characteristics' – a view which Darwin himself partially adopts in the category of 'use and disuse'. But because the transmission of the genetic code is a one-way process, geneticists have discovered no mechanism by which the environment could directly impinge on it.

individuals and populations. A famous example of this can be seen in the effect of measles on the Alaskan Eskimo. The first epidemic, at the beginning of this century, was catastrophic, with 25 per cent of the total population dying; but subsequent epidemics were of decreasing virulence, and today the Eskimos are as resistant to the disease as any other group. Again, the obvious explanation is that the original population, because they had not been previously exposed to the disease, contained few who possessed a mutation capable of resisting it. But as the weaker succumbed in successive epidemics, larger populations came to share the resistant mutation, so that now only a small percentage remains susceptible.[45] Thus Darwin's Malthusian principle remains intact: it is not the single organism or genotype that evolves, but *populations*; and these changes in population result from the greater or lesser rates of reproduction between one gene type and another, and thus from the different rates of survival and elimination.[46]

Darwin acknowledges his debt to 'Malthuses' noble work'. '[When] I began to suspect from geographical distribution, etc., that new species have been forced by descent, I determined to work at domestic production with not one single idea in my head: and no one can know the years of blind labour I had, before I clearly saw that [Natural] Selection was man's chief means . . . When I had got thus far I strongly suspected that this was the key to nature's work, but it was some time before I could conceive how it could be applicable . . . not indeed until I chanced to read Malthuses' noble work.'

45. Witness also the famous case of the Australian rabbit. In order to reduce numbers, a viral disease, myxomatosis, was introduced and between 1950 and 1953 the rabbit population fell by 90 per cent. Thereafter the numbers began to increase again. For while the natural selective forces of the virus had acted to eliminate the more susceptible, the surviving rabbits possessed a mutation which proved resistant. These interbred and thus passed on their mutations to their offspring.
46. For a detailed comparison between evolutionary and genetic theory, see Lawrence S. Dillon, *Evolution: Concepts and Consequences*, St Louis, The C. V. Mosby Company, 1973.

I said earlier that Darwin's critique of the design argument lies in his view that *chance*, rather than purpose, was the prime mover in the cosmic process – thereby giving weight to Hume's original 'Epicurean' hypothesis. However, we need to be cautious here. For where precisely does the element of chance operate? The first thing to say is that, in one important sense, Darwin's theory is not a theory of random occurrences. The principle of natural selection is itself a *causal law*, formulating the primary cause of species development – that an organism survives because of the advantageous properties it possesses – and we may even predict, admittedly in the most rudimentary way and in line with other general laws of nature, that certain general effects will result: namely, that natural selection will never produce a structure inimical to organisms that have those properties; that an organism will never possess a property solely for the good of another; and that selection will always produce adaptation. Indeed, it is fair to say that Darwin maintains that *all* events are caused, including what he terms 'chance variations'. This is no more than an instance of the principle of sufficient reason. While Darwin admits ignorance of the causes governing variation, he does not and cannot admit that variation is uncaused.

The important amendment to make, then, is that for Darwin 'chance' does not mean 'uncaused' or even 'causes unknown' but refers rather to the *unpredictable character of the specific effects*. In this sense we may say that the evolution of life is based on a physical principle – the principle of selection; and that though Darwin considers this the determinative process whenever evolution occurs, it is one which proceeds on an *indeterminate* course, so that particular outcomes cannot be predicted with any degree of accuracy. Thus there is no correlation between the variations that an organism might need for survival and the variations it will receive. This is especially apparent at the microscopic level, where, as we now know in a way that Darwin could not, the chance factor impinges twice. Initially the genetic uniqueness of an individual is due to the *random* reshuffling, reassortment or recombination of the genes originally present in the parents. Thereafter natural selection acts on the heritable variations produced by the resulting mutations. But a new mutation will not increase in frequency and displace the non-mutant gene unless it is favoured by the environment – and here too there is no predicting the conditions that will prevail. So if the idea of an *inconstant* gene is the key to the development of variation, the idea of an *inconstant* environment acting upon that variation is the key to species formation.

What Darwin and his followers exclude in this analysis is not, then, the notion of cause but the notion of purpose or, indeed, any sense of directed creation. This, of course, marks a decisive break with the past and in particular with the view, espoused by both Aquinas and Paley, that it was an implication of an event's being caused that it was intended by some conscious agent – with the corollary that any event which occurs only through the agency of natural necessity is uncaused and accidental. For Darwin, however, selection lacks this orientation towards a controlling intelligence. When, therefore, he proposed that organisms developed not only gradually but through the operation of chance, he demolished the basis of purposive explanation. Whatever the

$\Rightarrow$ laws governing the formation of variation and species may be, they are not *teleological*; and this in turn means that the phenomenon of 'apparent' design in nature is explicable solely in terms of the selective forces of chance. The sting of the theory, as Darwin himself makes clear (**SOURCE 3: PP. 153–156**), lies not so much, then, in the supposition that species develop gradually over long periods of time but in its suggestion that it is mechanical and haphazard factors that govern this development.

> Although I did not think much about the existence of a personal God until a considerably later period of my life, I will here give the vague conclusions to which I have been driven. The old argument from design in nature, as given by Paley, which formerly seemed to me so conclusive, fails, now that the law of natural selection has been discovered. We can no longer argue that, for instance, the beautiful hinge of a bivalve shell must have been made by an intelligent being, like the hinge of a door by man. There seems to be no more design in the variability of organic beings and in the action of natural selection, than in the course which the wind blows.[47]

Darwin supports Hume's critique

Here too the fallacy of the 'affirmation of the consequent' applies. For what Darwin is indicating, on lines that Hume would undoubtedly have approved of, is not only that there *could* be an alternative to the theistic explanation which leads to the same effect – i.e., the adaptation of means to ends – but that there actually *is* one. Hume's own rather fanciful ideas about biological generation and vegetation are accordingly fleshed out by Darwin into a detailed and systematic account of animal and plant development. This, however, is not to exclude the *logical possibility* of God employing evolution as the agent of his creation – after all, Newton had believed that his own law of universal gravitation had been employed by God as his instrument. Thus one could perhaps argue, along with Darwin's friend Asa Gray, that the mechanism of selection is merely the mode of creation, so that each successive variation is 'designed' from the first to be selected. John Dewey dismissed this idea as 'design on the instalment plan',[48] and Darwin himself condemned it as 'mere verbiage'. For quite apart from the fact that there is a profound difference between a God who employs a law of extreme regularity and one whose only law is the law of chance – a God playing dice, to use Einstein's famous phrase – there is also no mention of a guiding intelligence in the formula of universal gravitation, any more than there is in the formula of natural selection.

---

47. 'Autobiography', pp. 52–53.
48. *The Influence of Darwin on Philosophy*, New York, Henry Holt & Co., 1910, p. 12. Dewey's essay was one of the first to show how Darwin's theory upset the traditional idea of final causes. Gray's alternative proposal is found in his *Design Versus Necessity: Discussion between Two Readers of Darwin's Treatise on the Origin of Species, upon its Natural Theology*, 1876, reprinted Cambridge, Mass., Harvard University Press, 1963, pp. 51–71.

No astronomer, in showing how the movements of planets are due to gravity, thinks it necessary to say that the law of gravity was designed, that the planets should pursue the courses which they pursue. I cannot believe that there is a bit more interference by the Creator in the construction of each species than in the course of the planets. It is only owing to Paley and Co., I believe, that this more special interference is thought necessary with living bodies.[49]

For present-day Darwinians, like Richard Dawkins, this, then, is the great achievement of Darwinian biology (SOURCE 4: PP. 156–161). Whereas previously teleologists could not see how undirected natural forces could produce organization, Darwin demonstrated that natural selection, acting on chance variation, could produce just that. This alternative, which Hume could only guess at, seriously impugns the inductive inference that stands at the heart of the design argument. The complexity of the watch requires the mind of the watchmaker; but the still greater complexities of nature do not guarantee any such designing mind but are in fact rather more intelligible, not less, when set within the wheels of chance. Why, then, prefer the theistic solution to a materialist one when nature herself provides innumerable instances of one type of process, but no single instance of the other? Why, then, should Darwin not endow capricious nature with all the attributes of Paley's God? As Dawkins remarks:

⇐

A true watchmaker has foresight: he designs his cogs and springs, and plans their interconnections, with a future purpose in his mind's eye. Natural selection, the blind, unconscious, automatic process which Darwin discovered, and which we now know is the explanation for the existence and apparently purposeful form of all life, has no purpose in mind. It has no mind and no mind's eye. It does not plan for the future. It has no vision, no foresight, no sight at all. If it can be said to play the role of watchmaker in nature, it is the *blind* watchmaker.[50]

In this account of Darwin I have concentrated, naturally enough, on those aspects of his theory which bear directly upon the argument from design. To round off the picture it is worth mentioning that Darwin's religious doubts extended into other areas. Like Hume before him, he doubted the veracity of the biblical texts, he doubted miracles, he doubted the supremacy of one religion over others, and he doubted any religion that could so openly threaten unbelief with punishment. But the doctrine of natural selection impinges directly upon one final area, and here too Darwin's argument mirrors Hume's. Even if we set aside all these arguments against design, what kind of God are

Darwin's supplementary criticisms

---

49. Darwin, letter of 17 June 1860, in *More Letters of Charles Darwin*, ed. F. Darwin and A. C. Seward, London, John Murray, 1903, Vol. 1, p. 154.
50. Richard Dawkins, *The Blind Watchmaker*, London, Penguin Books, 1988, p. 5.

we left with if we strictly adhere to the principle that 'like effects prove like causes'? Hume has already compiled a list of attributes: there may be many gods, there may be no God, there may be anthropomorphic gods, and even these may be adolescent bunglers and fools. To these attributes Darwin now adds the quality of cruelty. In a letter to Asa Gray he writes:

> An innocent and good man stands under a tree and is killed by a flash of lightning. Do you believe (and I really should like to hear) that God *designedly* killed this man? Many and most persons do believe this; I can't and don't. If you believe so, do you believe that when a swallow snaps up a gnat that God designed that that particular swallow should snap up that particular gnat at that particular instant? I believe that the man and the gnat are in the same predicament. If the death of neither man nor gnat are designed, I see no reason to believe that their *first* birth or production should be necessarily designed.[51]

It is worth underscoring Darwin's point. Paley assumed that the watch going wrong would make no difference to its being designed.[52] We might suppose that he had in mind here the inexplicable calamities that occur within the natural world. But it clearly does make a difference to his argument if these calamities are seen to be not merely excessive but *the primary mechanism by which the watch operates*. This is Darwin's point. The mechanism by which species evolve is the process of natural selection, and this process is frequently wasteful and invariably cruel. From this we may suppose that the God implied by evolution, far from being benevolent, is almost totally unconcerned for the welfare of his creatures and almost totally unmoved by the suffering which he has planned for them.

EXERCISE 3.8

Darwin refers to the Ichneumonae as an example of excessive cruelty in nature: a parasitic insect group whose females lay their eggs in or on the larvae or pupae of other insects, often moths and butterflies. These then feed on the fats and body fluids of their hosts, literally eating them alive. Is the existence of the Ichneumonae evidence

for the existence of a benevolent but not omnipotent God?

for the existence of a malevolent but omnipotent God?

for the existence of a God who loves Ichneumonae and hates butterflies?

---

51. *The Life and Letters of Charles Darwin*, Vol. I, p. 315.
52. See above, p. 96.

Conclusion page of *The Origin of Species*, 3rd edn, p.514. 'I have now recapitulated the chief facts and considerations, which have thoroughly convinced me the Species have been modified, during a long course of descent, by the preservation or the natural selection of many successive slight favourable variations. I cannot believe that a false theory would explain, as it seems to me that the theory of natural selection does explain, the several large classes of facts above specified.'

POST-DARWINIAN THEORIES OF DESIGN

If Darwin's theory seriously undermines the design argument, it does not destroy it. This fact was recognized by many of Darwin's contemporaries, who were quick to modify their previous ideas about teleology to accommodate their newly acquired ideas about evolution. For clearly there is a sense in which the theory does not affect the argument. Believers assert that an intelligent being designed and produced the world; and this is not incompatible with the view that *evolution is the process through which God works*. The evidence of design, accordingly, is not impugned by Darwin if evolution can be seen as the manner in which that design was executed.

Evolution as a divine process

Advocates of design also pointed out another feature of evolutionary theory. To admit that natural selection is the process by which species develop is not to accept that this is the way in which the *human species* develops in every particular. Evolution, so they claim, while it may certainly increase man's affinity with the animals, should not at the same time obscure the enormous gap between them. Where, then, does the difference lie? It lies in the fact that *human beings possess characteristics which have no survival benefit*.

One of the first theologians to make this point was the future Archbishop of Canterbury, Frederick Temple (1821–1902), in his Bampton lectures

Frederick Temple (1821–1902)

of 1884. While evolution may lead animals to distinguish between pleasure and pain, between hate and love, even between fear and desire, it cannot instil in them a knowledge of right and wrong. It is therefore man's *moral capacity* – which Temple defines as the primary attribute of his 'spiritual faculty' – which sets him apart. Evolution may thus be able to account for the bodily development of human beings, but it cannot account for their moral development.[53]

While Temple's acceptance of evolution is not representative of the theological opinion of his day – the majority still rejected evolution as 'pure atheism' and still held to a Paleyan notion of design – his views are typical of those who sought an accommodation between natural theology and evolution; and henceforth it becomes almost commonplace for theologians to adopt Temple's form of argument. For example, the Cambridge philosopher F. R. Tennant, in the second volume of his influential *Philosophical Theology* (1930), claims that natural selection cannot account for man's capacity for 'aesthetic awareness'. This, he argues, can only be explained as a function of *revelation*, which in turn suggests the 'invisible and mysterious presence' of God.[54] Somewhat similar arguments are to be found in the work of A. E. Taylor and Peter Bertocci. Taylor argues that human intelligence *transcends* natural selection and cannot therefore be accounted for by it – witness the creative and 'higher' intelligences of Euclid and Newton, human beings who, far from being moulded by their environment, shape and transform it. A more plausible explanation is, therefore, that men and women have been *endowed* with intelligence – that it corresponds to an act of *creation from nothing* – and that this endowment proceeds from an act of divine will.[55] Bertocci, following Tennant, concentrates less on the moral and intellectual life of man and more on his artistic capacities. For him the artist is a man responding to nature, revealing nature to others, making apparent in artistic form a relationship already presupposed between man and his environment. This interconnection between human beings and the natural world is, he claims, inexplicable without postulating a designing intelligence, a Purposer, who has established this interaction and fundamental

---

53. *The Relations between Religion and Science*, London, Macmillan, 1884, p. 186.
54. *Philosophical Theology*, Vol. 2, Cambridge, Cambridge University Press, 1930, p. 93. See also Tennant's article-review, 'The Influence of Darwinism upon Theology', *Quarterly Review*, 211, 1909, pp. 418–440.
55. *Does God Exist?*, London and New York, Macmillan, 1945, p. 66.

harmony.[56] More recently (1996) Keith Ward has argued along similar lines (SOURCE 5: PP. 161–166). For him the Darwinian struggle for survival is only part of the evolutionary story: another is the 'striving to realise values of beauty, understanding and conscious relationship' – values better explained, Ward argues, by the theistic hypothesis than by Darwin's 'gloomy and pessimistic view of nature'.[57]

What are we to make of these arguments? The first thing to note is the move being made by these authors in reclassifying the special effect which requires the special cause. Paley's incredulity at the thought that a purely physical phenomenon (the eye) could have evolved by chance has now been replaced by their incredulity at the suggestion that certain *mental phenomena* (intelligence, moral and aesthetic awareness) could have evolved by natural selection, it being suggested, we remember, that such phenomena have no survival benefit. And we should also remind ourselves that Darwin was quick to see the force of this objection. As he makes clear, any suggestion that the progression from inanimate clay to fully developed male requires a divine intervention – what he calls a 'miraculous addition' – would immediately undermine the evolutionary thesis – the whole point of his thesis being, of course, that natural selection provides a *non-miraculous* account of human development. To suggest, then, that evolution works in one area but not in another is not to modify the theory but, as Darwin saw plainly, to undermine it altogether.

The suggestion, however, that mental activities of this sort cannot originate in purely physical processes is highly questionable, not least because it avoids the whole issue of whether mental phenomena – even if we accept for the moment that they are distinct from physical phenomena – are the results of certain material processes; or, to put the matter more bluntly, whether mental activities are in fact brain-processes and the brain itself is the product of evolutionary change. This was the theory, known as epiphenomenalism, quickly adopted by early evolutionists, most notably by Darwin's famous champion, T. H. Huxley.[58] Part of its attraction for Huxley was the ease with which it could accommodate evolutionism. Darwin's firm conviction was that man was descended from lower animals by gradual transformation, and, beyond this, probably from physical and chemical reactions among inanimate things, which resulted in more intricate forms and eventually in the building-blocks of life itself. From this it is but a short step to conceive of man's mental capacities developing as a by-product (*epiphenomenon*) of these increasing complexities. Man, accordingly, may be unique in his capacity for thought, but this is not to deny his descent from his ape-like progenitors or to preclude the possibility that he evolved from the same basic substances as do rocks, grass, amoebas, and so on. There is nothing outrageous in therefore supposing that, if these other

⇐

Criticisms of post-
Darwinian theories of
design

---

56. *Introduction to the Philosophy of Religion*, Englewood Cliffs, N.J., Prentice-Hall, 1951, pp. 356–357.
57. *God, Chance and Necessity*, Oxford, Oneworld Publications, 1996, pp. 86–88.
58. See *On the Hypothesis that Animals are Automata and its History* (Address, British Association for the Advancement of Science, Belfast, 1874). Reprinted in *Body and Mind*, ed. G. N. A. Vesey, London, George Allen & Unwin, 1964, pp. 134–143.

things are merely material objects without minds, man is either another material object without a mind or, if this seems too far-fetched, an object possessed of a mind which developed solely from these complex material processes.

For our purposes, the merit of this position lies in presenting at least a *plausible* materialist explanation, which early evolutionists like Huxley were quick to spot, of how our so-called higher mental faculties could have developed within the evolutionary process.[59] It is also worth recalling that in 1872 Darwin published his *The Expression of the Emotions in Man and Animals*, and that here he deals with an entire range of emotional conditions shared between man and the lower animals – joy and affection, pain and anger, fear and terror, grief and laughter, love and devotion, attention and curiosity – as well as more complex emotions like hatred, jealousy, sulkiness, disgust, astonishment, admiration and shame. What, then, is so extraordinary in extending this argument still further and projecting a continuity between the development of these emotions and the emergence of a reflective consciousness?

The problem, we have seen, lies with Darwin's mechanism of selection and the suggestion that our human cognitive abilities are superfluous to our survival. But here too there seems to be no difficulty in supposing that our brains have been adapted by natural selection for the purpose of assessing and meeting the dangers that surround us, and that human intelligence is indeed the primary weapon of survival that man possesses, allowing him not only to modify his environment but also to subdue all other species to his will. Granted, this is not selection based on a capacity, say, to do science and higher mathematics; but these capacities could nevertheless have emerged from the demands of survival, provided only that they are correlated with certain simpler skills of reasoning and communication, skills that were originally beneficial to our primitive ancestors.[60]

I have mentioned these theories to challenge the assumption, common among post-evolutionary theories of design, that the existence of such human capacities as goodness and intelligence is sufficient to postulate the existence of a Supreme Mind, which has guided the evolutionary process specifically to develop these qualities. Once again this inference is made on the basis of analogy, admittedly an analogy not as crude as Paley's watch but an analogy nonetheless. The world as a whole is still regarded as an eternal artificial product, as some kind of gigantic mechanism, which has certain characteristics which cannot be explained in terms of evolution but which can be explained in terms of a divine artificer. And again, it is the comparison between competing explanations which leads to this conclusion. But no reformulation of the analogy, it seems to me, can offset the force of Hume's objections at this point or Darwin's update of them.

---

59. For a detailed criticism of epiphenomenalism, see J. B. Pratt, *Matter and Spirit*, New York, Macmillan, 1926, and M. Maher, *Psychology*, London, Longmans, Green, 1940.
60. It is interesting to note that early hominids – such as *Australopithecus*, which first appeared about two million years ago – weighed 27–41 kilograms and had a brain size of a modern ape (350–750 cubic centimeters). By contrast, *Homo sapiens* has a brain capacity of 1,350 cubic centimeters. See also John Hurrell Crook, *The Evolution of Human Consciousness*, Oxford, Clarendon Press, 1980.

To what extent are the following explicable/inexplicable in terms of the Darwinian mechanism of selection?

EXERCISE 3.9

My desire to act morally

My love of music

The genius of Darwin

The plumes of the peacock

THE ANTHROPIC TELEOLOGICAL ARGUMENT

It is at this juncture that advocates of design take a different tack. Evolution may describe the process by which species develop, but it cannot explain why there are species in the first place. How can it be that, at a particular moment in time, so many disparate factors came together to create a world uniquely suited to be the home of living beings? Darwin, in other words, does not present a theory of the *origin* of organisms because he cannot explain the extraordinary series of coincidences that were necessary to produce them. A similar gap in the secular naturalist case is apparent in the arguments of Darwin's apologists, Dawkins providing a case in point. In the passage already quoted,[61] Dawkins slides too easily from the description of how natural selection operates *upon* existence to the assumption that natural selection also provides the explanation *for* that existence. But this is not something that Darwin provides. In Tennant's memorable remark: 'The survival of the fittest presupposes the arrival of the fit, and throws no light thereupon.'[62]

What we have here is a *rejection of the theory of coincidence*: it is absurd to suppose that a structure as complex as the universe could arise from the accumulation of vast numbers of small accidents. It is just as ridiculous to suppose that a dice which consistently throws a six is not loaded: it is logically possible but extremely unlikely. Is it not preferable, then, to suppose that creation itself was 'loaded' by a designing intelligence? During the last decade this argument has become increasingly popular among some scientists and theologians, notable advocates being Roger Penrose (1989), Richard Swinburne (1990), George Ellis (1993) and Hugh Ross (1995). The last-named, a physicist and astronomer, puts the matter thus: the 'fine-tuning' of the universe must originate with a 'personal Entity . . . at least a hundred trillion times more "capable" than are we human beings with all our resources. . . . (This) Entity . . . must be a Personal Being, for only a person can design with anywhere near this degree of precision.'[63]

Coincidence rejected

61. See above. p. 127.
62. *Op. cit.*, p. 85.
63. Ross, *The Creator and the Cosmos: How the Greatest Scientific Discoveries of the Century Reveal God*, Colorado Springs, Navpress, 1995, p. 118. See also Penrose, *The Emperor's New Mind: Concerning Computers, Minds and the Laws of Physics*, Oxford, Oxford University Press, 1989; Swinburne, 'Argument from the Fine-Tuning of the Universe', in John Leslie (ed.), *Physical Cosmology and Philosophy*, New York, Macmillan, 1990, pp. 154–173; and Ellis, *Before the Beginning: Cosmology Explained*, London and New York, Boyars/Bowerdean, 1993.

The anthropic principle

This argument is more generally known as the *anthropic teleological argument* (*anthropos* being the Greek for 'man'). It takes its name from the anthropic principle first suggested by Robert H. Dicke of Princeton University in 1961, whose research dealt with the Hubble constant, which determines the universe's rate of expansion. He concluded that without this constant life could not have arisen. From this was adduced the principle, to give Brandon Carter's well-known formulation, that 'The universe must be such as to admit conscious beings in it at some stage',[64] or, adapting Descartes, 'Cogito ergo mundus talis est' ('I think, therefore the world is as it is'). This is the same as saying that, had the initial conditions of the universe been otherwise (for example, temperature, chemical environment) we human beings (*anthropoi*) would not have existed to observe and reflect upon these conditions.[65] The teleological variant reads as follows. The slightest fluctuation in these conditions would create a universe without intelligent life. So narrow, therefore, is the opportunity for life – so exact do the constants have to be – that it becomes highly improbable that life results from random evolution. A much more probable explanation is that it exists through the activity of a creator.

Certainly the scientific evidence appears impressive. One of the first to adopt this form of argument was the French physiologist Pierre Lecomte du Noüy, who in 1947 calculated that the probability of just one of the basic constituents of life, the protein molecule, appearing by chance was 2.02×10^{-321} or two chances out of a total number of 1 followed by six lines of zeros.[66] More recently (1981) Hoyle and Wickramasinghe calculated that the chance of randomly obtaining all two thousand enzymes in some kind of primaeval soup was one part of $10^{40,000}$, which made the old idea of special creation a far more likely possibility.[67] The theoretical physicist Paul Davies, although agnostic, has drawn attention to other statistical enormities. The steady expansion of the universe requires a perfect balance between gravity and the weak nuclear force. To achieve this, Davies tells us, these two forces have to be tuned to each other with the astonishing accuracy of one part in ten thousand billion billion billion billion.[68] He has added that, had the 'Big Bang' differed in strength by one part in 10^{60}, the universe as we know it would not have existed. This is equivalent to the accuracy a marksman would need to hit a one-inch target at the other end of the universe – twenty billion light years

64. Carter, 'Large Number Coincidences and the Anthropic Principle in Cosmology', *Confrontation of Cosmological Theories with Observational Data*, Dordrecht, Reidel, 1974, pp. 291–298.

65. See J. Barrow and F. Tipler, *The Anthropic Cosmological Principle*, Oxford, Oxford University Press, 1988; Reinhard Breuer, *The Anthropic Principle: Man as the Focal Point of Nature*, Boston, Mass., Birkhäuser, 1991; and William L. Craig, 'The Teleological Argument and the Anthropic Principle', *The Logic of Rational Theism: Exploratory Essays*, Lewiston, Maine, The Edwin Mellen Press, 1990, pp. 127–153.

66. *Human Destiny*, London and New York, Longmans, Green, 1947. Quoted by John Hick, *Arguments for the Existence of God*, London, Macmillan, 1970, pp. 104–111.

67. Sir Fred Hoyle and N. C. Wickramasinghe, *Evolution from Space: A Theory of Cosmic Creationism*, London, Dent, 1981, pp. 96, 130.

68. *The Accidental Universe*, Cambridge, Cambridge University Press, 1982, p. 95.

away.[69] Davies cites one calculation that puts the odds against the observed universe appearing by accident at $10^{10^{30}}$.[70]

I have to say that I regard the anthropic teleological argument as very weak indeed.

1. The argument employs the following logical form: If the existence of A requires the existence of B, and if A exists, then B exists. So much is true. If the existence of Sophie requires the existence of a particular world, and if Sophie exists, then this particular world exists. True again. However, the truism that this world exists does not mean that this is the only form in which this world *could* exist: all it implies is that this is the only world necessary for Sophie's existence; that indeed a different world would have meant no Sophie at all. Now, admittedly Sophie might be awe-struck by the fact that her contingent existence depends on the world being *as it is* and not otherwise; but whether this world is or is not an improbable world is not a matter that she can decide. For this decision requires some antecedent knowledge of other possible worlds that allows her to say that this world is improbable – comparable, that is, to a knowledge of other possible throws of the dice that makes the continual throw of a six a calculable improbability – and this she cannot possess because, to adopt Hume's first criticism of the design argument, no comparison with other worlds is possible, given that this world is unique and all that is. If Sophie cannot therefore say whether this world, in comparison with other worlds, is improbable or not, she cannot go on to say that its existence is best explained by a divine intelligence.

2. Wallace Matson has, I believe, successfully repudiated du Noüy's argument and others of its type. Du Noüy talks of the fantastic improbability of any protein molecule's coming into existence as a result of the chance combination of atoms. But this is not a theory that any Darwinian would advance.

> The chance agglutination of atoms into fully formed men, or protein molecules, would not be evolution but its antithesis. The evolutionary concept is that just as man is the last stage reached to date of an immensely slow and complicated process of successive modifications in less complex creatures, so also the protein molecule itself is the resultant of a very large number of successive stages of synthesis, beginning with quite simple compounds.[71]

In other words, the probability of a protein molecule's existing at all is not the probability (or staggering improbability) that du Noüy calculates but rather 'the product of the probabilities of conditions permitting the steps of the synthesis to be realized in succession'.[72] Frederick Ferré supports Matson here.

Criticisms of the anthropic teleological argument

69. Davies, *God and the New Physics*, London, J. M. Dent, 1983; reprint Harmondsworth, Penguin Books, 1990, p. 179.
70. *Ibid.*
71. *The Existence of God*, Ithaca, N.Y., Cornell University Press, 1965, p. 106.
72. *Ibid.*

What du Noüy and others have omitted is the 'anti-chance factors present in nature itself', namely, the operation of natural laws governing the development of proteins, which therefore makes it unreasonable to infer that the anti-chance factor must be God.

> If I have dropped a rubber ball and know nothing about the properties of rubber, it is quite useless for me to calculate the 'probabilities' of its bouncing. For all I know it might shatter or splatter or run along the floor or do any of an almost infinite number of things when dropped. I drop it; it bounces. How amazing! Out of an almost infinite number of alternatives, this is what it did. And the first time, too, I drop it again; again it bounces. Incredible! Two vastly improbable results from just two 'throws'. I do it ten more times; each time the same result. My conclusion: there must be some 'anti-chance' factor here disturbing the outworkings of pure statistical probability. And of course I am right. The 'anti-chance' factor is the nature of rubber itself! The physical laws that govern it, the chemical bonds between its molecules . . .[73]

The protein molecule and man are, as far as we can tell, unique to this planet. Thus we have no comparable events upon which to compute the probabilities of these entities emerging. What these are may be, and evidently are, sources of wonder; but they are also among the brute facts of our existence – which is not the same as saying that they are so improbable that they cannot be accounted for by some scientific explanation.

3. While the evidence offered by the anthropic teleological argument turns in one direction – the improbability of intelligent life without a creator – the argument is selective in omitting evidence which tends to run in an opposite direction. So even if we allow that it is meaningful to talk of the extreme improbability of certain physical conditions existing for Sophie to exist, we should also take into account those other conditions that Sophie will encounter while she exists – for example, human cruelty and suffering. The first set of evidence may incline us to the view that a creative intelligence exists, but the second set may lead us to the conclusion that, if life does not evolve from a random process, the intelligence that created it is neither benevolent nor worthy of worship.

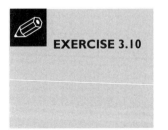

EXERCISE 3.10

The following analogy contains options for and against the anthropic argument. Distinguish between them. Which do you prefer?

You are to be shot by a firing squad of 100 marksmen. The guns are loaded with real bullets, the order to fire is given, the guns go off; but then you realize that you are still alive. Is this because

73. Frederick Ferré, *Basic Modern Philosophy of Religion*, New York, Scribner, 1967, p. 321.

of an amazing coincidence?

of a plan hatched by the marksmen?

the marksmen have been shooting prisoners all week, so were bound to miss sometime?

the marksmen have been shooting prisoners for trillions of years, so were bound to miss sometime?

the marksmen must be blind?

EXERCISE 3.10
continued

SWINBURNE'S DESIGN ARGUMENT

There is one final defence of the design argument which is worth mentioning. This comes from Richard Swinburne in his *The Existence of God* (1979).[74] Like advocates of the anthropic argument, Swinburne takes as his starting-point the wonder that an orderly universe exists.[75]

To marvel at the order of the universe is, according to Swinburne, to wonder at two types of order: (1) what he calls patterns of 'spatial order' (i.e., 'regularities of co-presence', such as a town with all its roads at right angles to each other); and (2) patterns of 'temporal order' (i.e., 'regularities of succession', such as Newton's laws, where objects behave in accordance with certain laws of nature).[76] The kind of argument that Paley presents, and which Hume rejects, is an argument from spatial order, namely, one which concentrates on the remarkable complexity of animals and plants – a complexity which prompts the analogy of a machine-like creation, and thus the inference of a rational machine-maker. But as Swinburne concedes, Darwin has effectively scotched this approach, since natural selection does provide us with an alternative explanation of how such complexity arises.

But what of temporal order? This order – which, to repeat, covers the regularities we find enumerated in the laws of physics, chemistry and biology – is more basic than spatial order, since however we may construe the evolution of the world's complexity, we must still presuppose the operation of these basic and all-pervasive natural laws.

> The orderliness of the universe to which I draw attention here is its conformity to formula, to simple, formulable, scientific laws. The orderliness of the universe in this respect is a very striking fact about it. The universe might so naturally have been chaotic, but it is not – it is very orderly.[77]

Two types of order

---

74. *The Existence of God*, Oxford, Clarendon Press, 1979.
75. Swinburne's argument is extremely complicated, and some readers may care to omit this section. A handy account is given by Stephen T. Davis, *God, Reason and Theistic Proofs*, Edinburgh, Edinburgh University Press, 1997, pp. 116–119.
76. *Ibid.*, p. 133.
77. *Ibid.*, p. 136.

How are we to account for this? Hume's suggestion, we remember, was that the regularity we observe could be no more than a psychological, and quite understandable, disposition on our part to consider nature uniform.[78] But for Swinburne this explanation does not go deep enough. For what strikes our minds as truly extraordinary is not just that there are these natural laws – these regularities of succession – but that things always have and always will conform to them, however various their conditions may be, and however much men may try to interfere with them – for example, that stones will fall tomorrow as they did today and yesterday.

> So the teleological premiss is not just that there has been in nature so far an order which men can recognize and describe; but there has been and will continue to be in nature an order, recognizable and describable by men certainly, but one which exists independently of men. If men are correct in their belief that the order which they see in the world is an order which will hold in the future as in the past, it is clearly not an imposed or invented order. It is there in nature. For man cannot make nature conform subsequently to an order which he has invented. Only if the order is there in nature is nature's future conformity to be expected.[79]

The wonder is, then, that this all-pervasive temporal order exists at all, when there could so easily have been disorder. But how to explain it? Certainly no scientific explanation is sufficient. For while science can explain the 'how?' of order – how phenomena operate according to certain scientific laws – it cannot explain the 'why?' of order: it cannot make clear why there is this relationship between the phenomena and the laws, why objects should have specific and constant characteristics, irrespective of time and space. Here, in other words, scientific explanation comes to an end. But this is not to say that there is no explanation.

> It is strange enough that physical objects should have powers at all – why should they not just be, without being able to make a difference to the world? But that they should all, throughout infinite time and space, have some general powers identical to those of all other objects . . . and yet there be no cause of this at all seems incredible.[80]

Now, if this orderliness were explained by a theory of coincidence, it would leave unexplained not only why one body has a certain power but also why another body has the same power, and why indeed a vast number of different bodies operate in the same way. This, accordingly, is a 'regularity of succession' altogether too striking to occur unexplained, and 'it cries out for an explanation in terms of some single common source with the power to produce it'.[81] By

78. See above, pp. 109–110.
79. *The Existence of God*, p. 137.
80. *Ibid.*, p. 145.
81. *Ibid.*

analogy, we would similarly assume a common mould for coins with an identical pattern or a particular painter for paintings with a common style.

According to Swinburne, then, temporal order is better explained by postulating a common source than it is by any competing theory of coincidence. But why should this common source be God? His answer is (1) that the simplicity of an hypothesis enhances its intrinsic probability; and (2) that theism, being an extremely simple hypothesis, is therefore more probable than any alternative explanation.

Swinburne maintains that theism is an extremely simple hypothesis for three important reasons. First, it postulates a God of a very simple kind, a being whose capacities are as great as they logically can be: he is omnipotent, omniscient, omnipresent (and so non-embodied), eternal, perfectly free and perfectly good. Second, theism reduces all forms of explanation to personal explanation, i.e., ultimately to the actions of God. This second reason enhances the simplicity of theism still further: (1) it means that 'explanation stops at what, intuitively, is the most natural kind of stopping-place for explanation – the choice of an agent';[82] and (2) it implies a significant simplification of our world view. The dichotomy between explanations in terms of science and explanations in terms of an individual's intentions is resolved because scientific explanations are now seen to be expressions of divine choice – in this respect, Newton's laws work because God keeps them in operation. In the last resort, then, explanation is all of one kind. The third and final instance of theism's simplicity lies in its claim that, following on from God's omnipotence and perfect freedom, all things depend on him whereas he depends on nothing. Explanation, in this sense, ends with God.

Theism is therefore an extremely simple hypothesis. But why should this increase its intrinsic probability over theories of coincidence? Swinburne answers:

> the great simplicity of a wide hypothesis outweighs by far its wideness of scope in determining intrinsic probability. Perhaps it seems *a priori* vastly improbable, if one thinks about it, that there should exist anything at all logically contingent. But, given that there does exist something, the simple is more likely to exist than the complex. . . . The intrinsic probability of theism is, relative to other hypotheses about what there is, very high, because of the great simplicity of the hypothesis of theism.[83]

Swinburne's thesis thus turns on the criterion of simplicity. It is far more likely that, in choosing between rival explanations for the existence of anything at all, we shall choose something with the simplicity of God rather than something like the universe, with all its characteristics demanding further explanation: the latter is less likely because it leaves too many crucial questions

Theism: a simple hypothesis

---

82. *Ibid.*, p. 103.
83. *Ibid.*, p. 106.

unanswered. So even if we say that the probability of God creating a universe like this one is not very high, the fact that we have this universe still makes it more probable that it was God who created it. The probability of this world without God is thus lower than the probability of this world with God.

Swinburne's argument has been much criticized and, I think, with good reason.[84] The main difficulties with the theory are as follows:

1. It should first be questioned whether theism is an hypothesis as simple as Swinburne supposes. For while the *definition* of the divine attributes may seem straightforward enough, its implications may be much less so. Let us take just one: omniscience. What is the relation between omniscience and divine providence? Does omniscience impugn the concept of free will? Does omniscience require a knowledge of the evil that is to occur and thus either a malevolent desire that it should occur or an impotent inability to prevent it occurring?

2. For Swinburne theism's explanation of the universe in terms of divine rational agency is an example of its simplicity, since it thereby overcomes the dualism between scientific and personal explanations. But this, it seems to me, leaves far too many questions unanswered. The main problem is not whether Swinburne is correct to reduce all explanations to these two types – a questionable assumption in itself – but whether this dualism is itself legitimate: whether, if regularities of succession can be explained in terms of acts of the will, the opposite cannot also be the case, with mental activity being explicable as regularities of succession, i.e., as some form of brain activity. This materialist alternative, which many modern philosophers espouse and a version of which we have already seen in the theory of epiphenomenalism, would thus reject any claim that the most natural and satisfying 'stopping-place' for explanation is personal explanation. This, of course, is not to say that the materialist alternative is correct; but if it too has a *simplifying* effect by reducing all explanations to mechanistic formulae, it is difficult to see why it cannot be entertained as a rival hypothesis. If the notion of simplicity is central to Swinburne's argument, he has yet to convince us why the simplicity of a thoroughgoing mechanistic explanation has a lower probability than its theistic alternative.

3. This criticism can be maintained from another direction. Swinburne's principle of simplicity may be taken as a variant of William of Ockham's famous razor, namely, that 'Entities are not to be multiplied without necessity' ('entia non sunt multiplicanda praeter necessitatem') – a maxim in logical and scientific analysis which certainly supports the view that, when we are presented with two hypotheses, both of which account for a given fact, the simpler should be preferred. The trouble is that, in Swinburne's case, Ockham's razor is double-edged. While at first it may appear to support personal explanation over any dualistic theory, the 'principle of economy', as it is sometimes called, does not

84. See Gary Doore, 'The Argument from Design: Some Better Reasons for Agreeing with Hume', *Religious Studies*, 16, 1980, pp. 145–161; J. C. A. Gaskin, 'The Design Argument: Hume's Critique of Poor Reason', *Religious Studies*, 12, 1976, pp. 331–345; D. H. Mellor, 'God and Probability', *Religious Studies*, 5, 1969, pp. 223–234; and A. Olding, 'Design – A Further Reply to R. G. Swinburne', *Religious Studies*, 7, 1973, pp. 361–373.

assume that, if the existence of a particular entity makes a particular explanation more 'complete', this is sufficient grounds for believing that that entity exists. Indeed, the more usual interpretation of Ockham's razor is that, in judging between rival hypotheses, the hypothesis to be rejected is the one which introduces an entity, as the basis for its explanation, which is *not* necessary for the explanation of observable phenomena. And this is precisely what, for the materialist, makes his hypothesis more reasonable. Swinburne correctly points out that scientists often consider it reasonable to postulate entities to explain certain effects, so long as these entities provide a simple and coherent explanation for these effects. But this does not meet the objection, earlier made by Hume, that no one has ever 'thought it satisfactory to explain a particular effect by a particular cause which was no more to be accounted for than the effect itself'.[85] It is this which, under the terms of the principle of economy, may be deemed an unnecessary entity – an unnecessary entity here being defined as something totally different from anything in our experience. Indeed, it is worth noting that Ockham's own use of the razor was reserved solely to explain the world and its processes, and that, while always preferring the simplest explanation, he specifically denied that it could be used to make any inferences from experience to what transcends experience, even to the point of determining whether the world was a teleological creation.

4. The issue once again turns on the principle of sufficient reason, which we discussed in the previous chapter.[86] It certainly is true that science, unlike religion, cannot offer a complete explanation of origins; but the trouble here, as we saw before, is that the theistic terminus of explanation (God) eludes further explanation: it may therefore appear to many more satisfying to do without the requirement of absolute comprehensiveness and stay within the realm of the finite. Swinburne rejects this. He argues that Hume's principle of proportionality – 'we never ought to ascribe to it [the cause] any qualities beyond what are precisely requisite to produce the effect' – would spell the end of science, since clearly no new knowledge could thereby be gained. But as J. C. A. Gaskin remarks, this is to miss the point.[87] Hume is not here attacking the *common* situation where it is quite proper, say, to infer inductively from an effect (for example, the building of a house) certain additional attributes to the cause (that whoever built it had two legs), but rather the *special* situation where the cause is known to us *only* through the given effect, and where this effect (the world) is, for all we know, unique. In other words, the strength (or weakness) of an analogical argument, as we saw earlier, is proportionate to the degree and extent of the similarities between the objects concerned. Where, then, the effect is recognized as unique, how can we infer any attributes or qualities to the cause on the basis of an analogical *comparison*, and how then can that cause be subsequently employed as an ultimate *explanation* of that effect? This, indeed, shows that the theistic explanation is *incomplete*. To take an example:

---

85. *Dialogues*, ed. Smith, p. 164.
86. See above, pp. 58–64.
87. *Op. cit.*, p. 335.

the perpetual motion of tiny particles, such as pollen grains, first observed by the Scottish botanist Robert Brown (1773–1858) and known as 'Brownian motion', can be explained by prediction of the existence of even smaller but faster-moving particles. These are molecules which are in random collision with the grains. On Swinburne's theory, however, a more complete analysis would involve some causal property of God acting upon these molecules to determine this collision and produce the resulting incessant jigging motion. The question thereafter remains how God acts in this way, and, in the absence of an answer, the theistic explanation remains incomplete. It is examples like this which prompt Anthony O'Hear to remark:

> one wonders if postulating an independent cause of the universe outside the universe is more or less simple than sticking with the universe alone. Certainly talking of God and the universe gives us a radical dualism of ontological types, where some might find it simpler to settle at this point for things of one type only.[88]

5. Finally there is the question of whether the simplicity of an hypothesis does or does not increase the probability of its being true. Now, there are clearly cases where the principle of simplicity will determine our choices between rival explanations – indeed, this consideration has often played a role in, for example, the discovery of great mathematical theorems; but this is more a question of taste or economy, almost of aesthetics, and not a question of truth. For example, the metrical system is simpler than the system of yards and inches, but there is no difference between them in whether one is true and the other is not. Much the same applies to science.[89] Here the choice between rival hypotheses is not so much dependent on economy, although that may be desired, but more on comparing the explanatory, predictive and corroborative powers of each theory. For example, from our explanation of how water molecules act on freezing (causing expansion) we can safely predict that an unlagged pipe will burst in deep frost, and the confirmation by subsequent events confers a higher probability upon the theory. But it is difficult to see how the additional premiss that 'God has willed that the water molecules should bond in this way' can, in any sense, increase the validity of the original theory. The probability of water expanding in these conditions is increased by the frequency of instances in which this phenomenon is observed; but given that the universe is unique, and given, therefore, that there can be only one instance of it, we cannot increase the probability of the original hypothesis about water being true by introducing the theistic hypothesis about the world (i.e., that it is designed) because no comparison can be made between this world and any other (there being no

88. *Experience, Explanation and Faith*, London, Routledge and Kegan Paul, 1984, p. 114.
89. Cf. R. E. Peierls, *The Laws of Nature*, London, The Scientific Book Guild, 1955, p. 276: 'We may be prejudiced in believing that ultimately the right laws should be simple. We tend to derive an intellectual satisfaction whenever a simple law turns out to fit the facts, though what is simple and what is complicated is, in part, a matter of habits of thought, so that no test of simplicity is absolute.'

other world) and because no confirmation of the probability of this world being designed can be given.[90]

CONCLUSION

Following these criticisms of the various forms taken by the design argument, we must conclude that it fails as an a posteriori proof for the existence of God.

1. Even though it is the case that the universe contains innumerable instances of order, this does not require that the universe be viewed as an artifact, like a watch or a ship or a work of art, i.e., the product of a designing mind. It may be, as Hume suggested, more like a living organism – i.e., a self-originated or self-maintained order such as we find in vegetation and generation – or it may be the result of a chance arrangement, such as Darwin proposes in his theory of natural selection.

2. It is therefore untrue to say that the only cause of order which we know in experience is Intelligence. Why, then, take this cause and apply it to the universe as a whole? For to find intelligence within nature does not guarantee that a Supreme Intelligence created it, any more than it guarantees that Nature created intelligence, although it does require us to place the hypothesis of a Designer alongside the many other possible causes of order, amongst which we must include natural and genetic selection. Thereafter the question is: Which of these possible explanations is to be preferred?

3. In deciding between theistic and non-theistic explanations, we should ask a further question. Even if we admit that the world contains extraordinary phenomena which cannot be explained in terms of the natural order, does this justify the inference that such phenomena are *better* explained by postulating the existence of something *even more extraordinary* as their creator? To this Hume replies that analogical arguments are incapable of leading to the discovery of any new and qualitatively different reality: that is, to a supra-empirical reality utterly distinct from those ordinary empirical experiences from which its existence was first inferred. This is not to say that analogical reasoning cannot lead to the discovery of new information, but rather that the new facts discovered must be of the same general order as those which suggested the hypothesis in the first place. Thus, if we did have the experience of many worlds created by many world-makers, then it would indeed be possible to infer by analogy that this world probably had a maker. But that condition cannot be fulfilled because this world is an object without parallel in our experience. Since, therefore, the whole teleological argument, even in the more recent versions we have considered, implies a divine creator, and since it is admitted even by its modern adherents that there are no empirical analogies for this conception,

---

90. Ockham's razor can be put to another use. It is often held that the idea that many universes exist violates the principle of simplicity (see Ellis, *op. cit.*, p. 97). Max Tegmark has argued that the reverse is the case, and that the idea of a single universe requires more explanation, not less, than the theory of a 'multiverse'. See Tegmark, 'Is "the Theory of Everything" Merely the Ultimate Ensemble Theory?', *Annals of Physics*, 270, 1998, pp. 1–51.

this admission is fatal to the design argument when seeking to convince us that a theistic explanation is preferable to any other. Here the contrast with Darwin's alternative could not be starker. For part of the strength of the evolutionary option lies precisely in the consistency it achieves between effects and causes: both lie within the fold of our experience of the evolutionary process, and neither is explained by the invocation of another realm, which is not directly accessible to us.

?

QUESTIONS

QUESTIONS

1 Give a brief account of the theistic argument that the world is the creation of God.

2 In what respects is the argument from design an argument from analogy?

3 To what extent do you agree with the claim that the uniqueness of the universe undermines the argument from design?

4 Is it fair to say that the argument from design already presupposes what it is seeking to prove?

5 What is the fallacy of 'the affirmation of the consequent'? Is the argument from design guilty of it?

6 What is the principle of proportionality? Is Hume right to employ it as an argument against design?

7 Using the distinction between 'authentic' and 'apparent' design, how far and in what ways does the theory of natural selection develop Hume's argument against design?

8 What difficulties are there in the claim that evolution is the process through which God works?

9 What do you consider to be the strengths and weaknesses of the anthropic teleological argument?

10 Do you think that Swinburne is successful in his defence of the design argument?

SOURCES: THE DESIGN ARGUMENT

I PALEY: THE WATCH AND THE WATCHMAKER[1]

In crossing a heath, suppose I pitched my foot against a *stone*, and were asked how the stone came to be there, I might possibly answer, that, for anything I knew to the contrary, it had lain there forever: nor would it perhaps be very easy to show the absurdity of this answer. But suppose I had found a *watch* upon the ground, and it should be inquired how that watch happened to be in that place: I should hardly think of the answer which I had before given, that, for anything I knew, the watch might have always been there. Yet why should not this answer serve for the watch as well as for the stone? Why is it not admissible in the second case, as in the first? For this reason, and for no other, viz. that, when we come to inspect the watch, we perceive (what we could not discover in the stone) that its several parts are framed and put together for a purpose, e.g., that they are so formed and adjusted as to produce motion, and that motion so regulated as to point out the hour of the day; that if the different parts had been differently shaped from what they are, of a different size from what they are, or placed after any other manner, or in any other order, than that in which they are placed, either no motion at all would have been carried on in the machine, or none which would have answered the use that is now served by it. . . . This mechanism being observed . . . the inference, we think, is inevitable; that the watch must have had a maker; that there must have existed, at sometime, and at some place or other, an artificer or artificers, who formed it for the purpose which we find it actually to answer; who comprehended its construction, and designed its use.

Nor would it, I apprehend, weaken the conclusion, that we had never seen a watch made, that we had never known an artist capable of making one; that we were altogether incapable of executing such a piece of workmanship ourselves, or of understanding in what manner it was performed. . . . Ignorance of this kind exalts our opinion of the artist's skill, if he be unseen and unknown, but raises no doubt in our minds of the existence and agency of such an artist, at some former time, and in some place or other . . .

Neither, secondly, would it invalidate our conclusion, that the watch sometimes went wrong, or that it seldom went exactly right. The purpose of the machinery, the design and the designer, might be evident, and in the case supposed would be evident, in whatever way we accounted for the irregularity of the movement, or whether we could account for it or not. It is not necessary that a machine be perfect, in order to show with what design it was made: still less necessary, where the only question is, whether it were made with any design at all.

Nor, thirdly, would it bring any uncertainty into the argument, if there were a few parts of the watch, concerning which we could not discover, or had not yet discovered, in what manner they conduced to the general effect; . . . if by the loss, or disorder, or decay of the parts in question, the movement of the watch were

---

1. William Paley, *Natural Theology: Evidences of the Existence and Attributes of the Deity*, 9th edn, London, R. Faulder, 1805, pp. 1–8.

found in fact to be stopped, or disturbed, or retarded, no doubt would remain in our minds as to the utility or intention of these parts, although we should be unable to investigate the manner according to which, or the connexion by which, the ultimate effect depended upon their action or assistance; and the more complex is the machine, the more likely is this obscurity to arise . . .

Nor, fourthly, would any man in his sense think the existence of the watch, with its various machinery, accounted for, by being told that it was one out of possible combinations of material forms; that whatever he had found in the place where he found the watch, must have contained some internal configuration or other; and that this configuration might be the structure now exhibited, viz. of the works of a watch, as well as a different structure.

Nor, fifthly, would it yield to his inquiry more satisfaction to be answered, that there existed in things a principle of order, which had disposed the parts of the watch into their present form and situation. He never knew a watch made by the principle of order; nor can he even form to himself an idea of what is meant by a principle of order distinct from the intelligence of the watchmaker.

Sixthly, he would be surprised to hear that the mechanism of the watch was no proof of contrivance, only a motive to induce the mind to think so . . .

Neither, lastly, would our observer be driven out of his conclusion, or from his confidence in its truth, by being told that he knew nothing at all about the matter. He knows enough for his argument. He knows the utility of the end: he knows the subserviency and adaptation of the means to the end. These points being known, his ignorance of other points, affect not the certainty of his reasoning. The consciousness of knowing little need not beget a distrust of that which he does know.

2 HUME: THE DESIGN ARGUMENT[2]

(**Part II**) What I chiefly scruple in this subject, said *Philo*, is not so much that all religious arguments are by *Cleanthes* reduced to experience, as that they appear not to be even the most certain and irrefragable of that inferior kind. That a stone will fall, that fire will burn, that the earth has solidity, we have observed a thousand and a thousand times, and when any new instance of this nature is presented we draw without hesitation the accustomed inference. The exact similarity of the cases gives us a perfect assurance of a similar event, and a stronger evidence is never desired nor sought after. But wherever you depart, in the least, from the similarity of the cases, you diminish proportionally the evidence, and may at last bring it to a very weak *analogy* which is confessedly liable to error and uncertainty. After having experienced the circulation of blood in human creatures, we make no doubt that it takes place in Titius and Maevius: but from its circulation in frogs and fishes, it is only a presumption, though a strong one, from analogy, that it takes place in men and other animals. The analogical reasoning is much weaker when

2. David Hume, *Dialogues Concerning Natural Religion*, edited with an Introduction by Norman Kemp Smith, London, Thomas Nelson, 1935, pp. 144–149, 165–169, 176–177, 182–185.

we infer the circulation of the sap in vegetables from our experience that the blood circulates in animals, and those who hastily followed that imperfect analogy are found, by more accurate experiments, to have been mistaken.

If we see a house, *Cleanthes*, we conclude, with the greatest certainty, that it had an architect or builder, because this is precisely that species of effect which we have experienced to proceed from that species of cause. But surely you will not affirm that the universe bears such a resemblance to a house that we can with the same certainty infer a similar cause, or that the analogy is here entire or perfect. The dissimilitude is so striking that the utmost you can here pretend to is a guess, a conjecture, a presumption concerning a similar cause; and how that pretension will be received in the world I leave you to consider . . . .

Were a man to abstract from every thing which he knows or has seen he would be altogether incapable, merely from his own ideas, to determine what kind of scene the universe must be, or to give the preference to one state or situation or things above another. For as nothing which he clearly conceives could be esteemed impossible or implying a contradiction, every chimera of his fancy would be upon an equal footing; nor could he assign any just reason why he adheres to one idea or system and rejects the others which are equally possible.

Again: after he opens his eyes and contemplates the world as it really is it would be impossible for him, at first, to assign the cause of any one event, much less of the whole of things or of the universe. He might set his fancy a-rambling and she might bring him in an infinite variety of reports and representations. These would all be possible; but being all equally possible, he would never of himself give a satisfactory account for this preferring one of them to the rest.

Now according to this method of reasoning, *Demea*, it follows (and is indeed tacitly allowed by *Cleanthes* himself) that order, arrangement or the adjustment of final causes is not, of itself, any proof of design, but only so far as it has been experienced to proceed from that principle. For aught we can know *a priori*, matter may contain the source or spring of order originally, within itself, as well as mind does; and there is no more difficulty in conceiving that the several elements from an internal unknown cause may fall into the most exquisite arrangement than to conceive that their ideas, in the great, universal mind, from a like internal, unknown cause, fall into that arrangement. The equal possibility of both these suppositions is allowed. By experience we find (according to *Cleanthes*) that there is a difference between them. Throw several pieces of steel together, without shape or form; they will never arrange themselves so as to compose a watch; stone, and mortar, and wood, without an architect, never erect a house. But the ideas in a human mind, we see, by an unknown, inexplicable economy, arrange themselves so as to form the plan of a watch or house. Experience, therefore, proves that there is an original principle of order in mind, not in matter. From similar effects we infer similar causes. The adjustment of means to ends is alike in the universe, as in a machine of human contrivance. The causes, therefore, must be resembling.

I was from the beginning scandalized, I must own, with this resemblance, which is asserted, between the Deity and human creatures and must conceive it to imply such a degradation of the supreme Being as no sound theist could endure. With your assistance, therefore, I shall endeavour to defend what you justly call the adorable mysteriousness of the divine nature, and shall refute this reasoning of *Cleanthes*, provided he allows that I have made a fair representation of it.

When *Cleanthes* has assented, *Philo*, after a short pause, proceeded in the following manner.

That all inferences, *Cleanthes*, concerning fact, are founded on experience and that all experimental reasonings are founded on the supposition that similar causes prove similar effects, and similar effects similar causes, I shall not at present much dispute with you. But observe, I entreat you, with what extreme caution all just reasoners proceed in the transferring of experiments to similar cases. Unless the cases be exactly similar they repose no perfect confidence in applying their past observation to any particular phenomenon. Every alteration of circumstances occasions a doubt concerning the event, and it requires new experiments to prove certainly that the new circumstances are of no moment or importance. A change in bulk, situation, arrangement, age, disposition of the air or surrounding bodies – any of these particulars may be attended with the most unexpected consequences. And unless the objects be quite familiar to us, it is the highest temerity to expect with assurance, after any of these changes, an event similar to that which before fell under our observation. The slow and deliberate steps of philosophers[3] here, if anywhere, are distinguished from the precipitate march of the vulgar, who, hurried by the smallest similitude, are incapable of all discernments or consideration.

But can you think, *Cleanthes*, that your usual phlegm and philosophy have been preserved in so wide a step as you have taken, when you compared to the universe houses, ships, furniture, machines, and from their similarity in some circumstances inferred a similarity in their causes? Thought, design, intelligence, such as we discover in men and other animals, is no more than one of the springs and principles of the universe, as well as heat or cold, attraction or repulsion, and a hundred others which fall under daily observation. It is an active cause by which some particular parts of nature, we find, produce alterations on other parts. But can a conclusion, with any propriety, be transferred from parts to the whole? Does not the great disproportion bar all comparison and inference? From observing the growth of a hair can we learn anything concerning the generation of a man? Would the manner of a leaf's blowing, even though perfectly known, afford us any instruction concerning the vegetation of a tree?

But allowing that we were to take the *operations* of one part of nature upon another for the foundation of our judgment concerning the *origin* of the whole (which can never be admitted) yet why select so minute, so weak, so bounded a principle as the reason and design of animals as found to be upon this planet? What peculiar privilege has this little agitation of the brain which we call thought, that we must thus make it the model of the whole universe? Our partiality in our own favour does indeed present it on all occasions; but sound philosophy ought carefully to guard against so natural an illusion.

So far from admitting, continued *Philo*, that the operations of a part can afford us any just conclusion concerning the origin of the whole, I will not allow any one part to form a rule for another part if the latter be very remote from the former.

---

3. By which Hume means 'scientist' in this context.

Is there any reasonable ground to conclude that the inhabitants of other planets possess thought, intelligence, reason or any thing similar to these faculties in men? When nature has so extremely diversified her manner of operation in this small globe, can we imagine that she incessantly copies herself throughout so immense a universe? And if thought, as we may well suppose, be confined merely to this narrow corner, and has even there so limited a sphere of action, with what propriety can we assign it for the original cause of all things? The narrow views of a peasant who makes his domestic economy the rule for the government of kingdoms is in comparison a pardonable sophism . . .

A very small part of this great system, during a very short time, is very imperfectly discovered to us: and do we thence pronounce decisively concerning the origin of the whole?

Admirable conclusion! Stone, wood, brick, iron, brass have not at this time, in this minute globe of earth, an order or arrangement without human art or contrivance; therefore the universe could not originally attain its order and arrangement without something similar to human art. But is a part of nature a rule for another part very wide of the former? Is it a rule for the whole? Is a very small part a rule for the universe? Is nature in one situation a certain rule for nature in another situation, vastly different from the former? . . .

When two *species* of objects have always been observed to be joined together, I can infer, by custom, the existence of one wherever I *see* the existence of the other: and this I call an argument from experience. But how this argument can have place, where the objects, as in the present case, are single, individual, without parallel, or specific resemblance, may be difficult to explain. And will any man tell me with a serious countenance, that an orderly universe must arise from some thought and art like the human, because we have experience of it? To ascertain this reasoning, it were requisite that we had experience of the origin of worlds; and it is not sufficient surely that we have seen ships and cities arise from human art and contrivance . . . .

(**Part V**) But to show you still more inconveniences, continued *Philo*, in your anthropomorphism, please to take a new survey of your principles. *Like effects prove like causes.* This is the experimental argument; and this you say is the sole theological argument. Now it is certain that the liker the effects are which are seen and the liker the causes which are inferred, the stronger is the argument. Every departure on either side diminishes the probability and renders the experiment less conclusive. You cannot doubt of this principle, neither ought you to reject its principles.

All the new discoveries in astronomy which prove the immense grandeur and magnificence of the works of nature are so many additional arguments for a Deity, according to the true system of theism: but according to your hypothesis of experimental theism they become so many objections, by removing the effect still farther from all resemblance to the effects of human art and contrivance . . . .

Now *Cleanthes*, said *Philo* with an air of alacrity and triumph, mark the consequences. *First*, by this method of reasoning you renounce all claim to infinity in any of the attributes of Deity. For as the cause ought only to be proportioned to the effect, and the effect – so far as it falls under your cognizance – is not infinite:

what pretensions have we, upon your suppositions, to ascribe that attribute to the divine Being? You will still insist that, by removing him so much from all similarity to human creatures, we give into the most arbitrary hypothesis and at the same time weaken all proofs of his existence.

Secondly, you have no reason, on your theory, for ascribing perfection to the Deity, even in his finite capacity, or of supposing him free from every error, mistake or incoherence in his undertakings. There are many inexplicable difficulties in the works of nature which, if we allow a perfect Author to be proved *a priori*, are easily solved, and become only seeming difficulties from the narrow capacity of man, who cannot trace infinite relations. But according to your method of reasoning, these difficulties become all real, and perhaps will be insisted on as new instances of the likeness to human art and contrivance. At least you must acknowledge that it is impossible for us to tell, from our limited views, whether this system contains any great faults or deserves any praise if compared to other possible – or even real – systems. Could a peasant, if the Aeneid were read to him, pronounce that poem to be absolutely faultless, or even assign to it its proper rank among the productions of human wit – he, who had never seen any other production?

But were this world ever so perfect a production, it must still remain uncertain whether all the excellencies of the work can justly be ascribed to the workman. If we survey a ship, what an exalted idea must we form of the ingenuity of the carpenter who framed so complicated, useful and beautiful a machine? And what surprise must we entertain when we find him a stupid mechanic, who imitated others and copied an art which, through a long succession of ages, after multiplied trials, mistakes, corrections, deliberations and controversies, had been gradually improving? Many worlds might have been botched and bungled, throughout an eternity, ere this system was struck out: much labour lost: many fruitless trials made and a slow but continued improvement carried on during infinite ages in the art of world-making. In such subjects, who can determine where the truth – nay, who can determine where the probability – lies, amidst a great number of hypotheses which may be proposed and a still greater number which may be imagined?

And what shadow of an argument, continued *Philo*, can you produce, from your hypothesis, to prove the unity of the Deity? A great number of men join in building a house or ship, in rearing a city, in framing a commonwealth: why may not several Deities combine in contriving and framing a world? This is only so much greater similarity to human affairs. By sharing the work among several, we may so much farther limit the attributes of each and get rid of that extensive power and knowledge which must be supposed in one Deity, and which, according to you, can only serve to weaken the proof of his existence. And if such foolish, such vicious creatures as men can yet often unite in framing and executing one plan, how much more those Deities or Demons, whom we may suppose several degrees more perfect?

To multiply causes without necessity is indeed contrary to true philosophy: but this principle applies not to the present ease. Were one Deity antecedently proved by your theory, who were possessed of every attribute requisite to the production of the universe, it would be needless, I own, though not absurd, to suppose any other Deity existent. But while it is still a question whether all these attributes are united in one subject or dispersed among several independent Beings: by what phenomena in nature can we pretend to decide the controversy? Where we see a body raised in a scale we are sure that there is in the opposite scale, however concealed from sight, some counterpoising weight equal to it; but it is still allowed to doubt whether that weight would be an aggregate of several distinct bodies or one uniformed united mass. And if the weight requisite very much exceeds any thing which we have ever seen conjoined in any single body, the former supposition becomes still more probable and natural. An intelligent Being of such vast power and capacity as is necessary to produce the universe, or, to speak in the language of ancient philosophy, so prodigious an animal, exceeds all analogy and even comprehension.

But farther, *Cleanthes*, men are mortal and renew their species by generation; and this is common to all living creatures. The two great sexes of male and female, says *Milton*, animate the world. Why must this circumstance, so universal, so essential, be excluded from those numerous and limited Deities? Behold then the theogony of ancient times brought back upon us.

And why not become a perfect anthropomorphite? Why not assert the Deity or Deities to be corporeal and to have an eye, a nose, mouth, ears, etc.? *Epicurus* maintained that no man had ever seen reason but in a human figure: therefore the gods must have a human figure. And this argument, which is deservedly so much ridiculed by Cicero, becomes – according to you – solid and philosophical.

In a word, *Cleanthes*, a man who follows your hypothesis is able, perhaps, to assert or conjecture that the universe sometime arose from something like design: but beyond that position he cannot ascertain one single circumstance and is left afterwards to fix every point of this theology by the utmost licence of fancy and hypothesis. The world, for aught he knows, is very faulty and imperfect, compared to a superior standard, and was only the first rude essay of some infant Deity who afterwards abandoned it, ashamed of his lame performance; it is the work only of some dependent, inferior Deity and is the object of derision to his superiors; it is the production of old age and dotage in some superannuated Deity, and ever since his death has run on at adventures, from the first impulse and active force which it received from him – you justly give signs of horror, *Demea*, at these strange suppositions, but these – and a thousand more of the same kind – are *Cleanthes'* suppositions, not mine. From the moment the attributes of the Deity are supposed finite, all these have place. And I cannot for my part think that so wild and unsettled a system of theology is in any respect preferable to none at all . . .

(**Part VII**) But here, continued *Philo*, in examining the ancient system of the soul of the world, there strikes me, all on a sudden, a new idea, which, if just, must go near to subvert all your reasoning, and destroy even your first inferences, on which you repose such confidence. If the universe bears a greater likeness to animal bodies and to vegetables, than to the works of human art, it is more probable that its cause resembles the cause of the former than that of the latter, and its origin ought rather to be ascribed to generation or vegetation than to reason or design. Your conclusion, even according to your own principles, is therefore lame and defective . . .

I affirm, that there are other parts of the universe (besides the machines of human invention) which bear still a greater resemblance to the fabric of the world, and which therefore afford a better conjecture concerning the universal origin of this system. These parts are animals and vegetables. The world plainly resembles more an animal or a vegetable, than it does a watch or a knitting-loom. Its cause, therefore, it is more probable, resembles the cause of the former. The cause of the former is generation or vegetation. The cause, therefore, of the world, we may infer to be some thing similar or analogous to generation or vegetation.

But how is it conceivable, said *Demea*, that the world can arise from any thing similar to vegetation or generation?

Very easily, replied *Philo*. In like manner as a tree sheds its seed into the neighbouring fields, and produces other trees; so the great vegetable, the world, or this planetary system, produces within itself certain seeds, which, being scattered into the surrounding chaos, vegetate into new worlds. A comet, for instance, is the seed of a world; and after it has been fully ripened, by passing from sun to sun, and star to star, it is at last tossed into the unformed elements, which everywhere surround this universe, and immediately sprouts up into a new system . . .

I understand you, says *Demea*: But what wild, arbitrary suppositions are these? What *data* have you for such extraordinary conclusions? And is the slight, imaginary resemblance of the world to a vegetable or an animal sufficient to establish the same inference with regard to both? Objects, which are in general so widely different; ought they to be a standard for each other?

Right, cries *Philo*: This is the topic on which I have all along insisted. I have still asserted, that we have no *data* to establish any system of cosmogony. Our experience, so imperfect in itself, and so limited both in extent and duration, can afford us no probable conjecture concerning the whole of things. But if we must needs fix on some hypothesis; by what rule, pray, ought we to determine our choice? Is there any other rule than the greater similarity of the objects compared? And does not a plant or an animal, which springs from vegetation or generation, bear a stronger resemblance to the world, than does any artificial machine, which arises from reason and design? . . .

(**Part VIII**) . . . Without any great effort of thought, I believe that I could, in an instant, propose other systems of cosmogony, which would have some faint appearance of truth; though it is a thousand, a million to one, if either yours or any one of mine is the true system.

For instance; what if I should revive the old *Epicurean* hypothesis? This is commonly, and I believe, justly, esteemed the most absurd system, that has yet been proposed; yet, I know not, whether, with a few alterations, it might not be brought to bear a faint appearance of probability. Instead of supposing matter infinite, as *Epicurus* did; let us suppose it finite. A finite number of particles is only susceptible of finite transpositions: And it must happen, in an eternal duration, that every possible order or position must be tried an infinite number of times. This world, therefore, with all its events, even the most minute, has before been produced and destroyed, and will again be produced and destroyed, without any bounds and limitations. No one, who has a conception of the powers of infinite, in comparison of finite, will ever scruple this determination . . .

Suppose (for we shall endeavour to vary the expression), that matter were thrown into any position, by a blind, unguided force; it is evident that this first position must in all probability be the most confused and most disorderly imaginable, without any resemblance to those works of human contrivance, which, along with a symmetry of parts, discover an adjustment of means to ends and a tendency to self-preservation. If the actuating force cease after this operation, matter must remain for ever in disorder, and continue an immense chaos, without any proportion or activity. But suppose, that the actuating force, whatever it be, still continues in matter, this first position will immediately give place to a second, which will likewise in all probability be as disorderly as the first, and so on, through many successions of changes and revolutions. No particular order or position ever continues a moment unaltered. The original force, still remaining in activity, gives a perpetual restlessness to matter. Every possible situation is produced, and instantly destroyed. If a glimpse or dawn of order appears for a moment, it is instantly hurried away, and confounded, by that never-ceasing force, which actuates every part of matter.

Thus the universe goes on for many ages in a continued succession of chaos and disorder. But is it not possible that it may settle at last, so as not to lose its motion and active force (for that we have supposed inherent in it), yet so as to preserve an uniformity of appearance, amidst the continual motion and fluctuation of its parts? This we find to be the case with the universe at present. Every individual is perpetually changing, and every part of every individual, and yet the whole remains, in appearance, the same. May we not hope for such a position, or rather be assured of it, from the eternal revolutions, of unguided matter, and may not this account for all the appearing wisdom and contrivance which is in the universe? Let us contemplate the subject a little, and we shall find, that this adjustment, if attained by matter, of a seeming stability in the forms, with a real and perpetual revolution or motion of parts, affords a plausible, if not a true solution of the difficulty.

It is in vain, therefore, to insist upon the uses of the parts in animals and vegetables, and their curious adjustment to each other. I would fain know how an animal could subsist, unless its parts were so adjusted? Do we not find, that it immediately perishes whenever this adjustment ceases, and that its matter corrupting tries some new form? It happens, indeed, that the parts of the world are so well adjusted, that some regular form immediately lays claim to this corrupted matter: And if it were not so, could the world subsist? Must it not dissolve as well as the animal, and pass through new positions and situations; till in a great, but finite succession, it fall at last into the present or some such order?

3 DARWIN: THE EXISTENCE OF A PERSONAL GOD[4]

Although I did not think much about the existence of a personal God until a considerably later period of my life, I will here give the vague conclusions to which

---

4. *Charles Darwin and T. H. Huxley: Autobiographies*, edited with an Introduction by Gavin de Beer, London, Oxford University Press, 1974, pp. 50–54.

1 have been driven. The old argument from design in Nature, as given by Paley, which formerly seemed to me so conclusive, fails, now that the law of natural selection has been discovered. We can no longer argue that, for instance, the beautiful hinge of a bivalve shell must have been made by an intelligent being, like the hinge of a door by man. There seems to be no more design in the variability of organic beings, and in the action of natural selection, than in the course which the wind blows. But I have discussed this subject at the end of my book on the Variation of Domesticated Animals and Plants, and the argument there given has never, as far as I can see, been answered.

But passing over the endless beautiful adaptations which we everywhere meet with, it may be asked how can the generally beneficent arrangement of the world be accounted for? Some writers indeed are so much impressed with the amount of suffering in the world, that they doubt, if we look to all sentient beings, whether there is more of misery or of happiness, – whether the world as a whole is a good or bad one. According to my judgment happiness decidedly prevails, though this would be very difficult to prove. If the truth of this conclusion be granted, it harmonizes well with the effects which we might expect from natural selection. If all the individuals of any species were habitually to suffer to an extreme degree, they would neglect to propagate their kind; but we have no reason to believe that this has ever, or at least often occurred. Some other considerations, moreover, lead to the belief that all sentient beings have been formed so as to enjoy, as a general rule, happiness.

Every one who believes, as I do, that all the corporeal and mental organs (excepting those which are neither advantageous nor disadvantageous to the possessor) of all beings have been developed through natural selection or the survival of the fittest, together with use or habit, will admit that these organs have been formed so that their possessors may compete successfully with other beings, and thus increase in number. Now an animal may be led to pursue that course of action which is most beneficial to the species by suffering, such as pain, hunger, thirst, and fear, – or by pleasure, as in eating and drinking, and in the propagation of the species etc., or by both means combined as in the search for food. But pain or suffering of any kind, if long continued, causes depression and lessens the power of action; yet is well adapted to make a creature guard itself against any great or sudden evil. Pleasurable sensations, on the other hand, may be long continued without any depressing effect; on the contrary, they stimulate the whole system to increased action. Hence it has come to pass that most or all sentient beings have been developed in such a manner, through natural selection, that pleasurable sensations serve as their habitual guides. We see this in the pleasure from exertion, even occasionally from great exertion of the body or mind, – in the pleasure of our daily meals, and especially in the pleasure derived from sociability, and from loving our families. The sum of such pleasures as these, which are habitual or frequently recurrent, give, as I can hardly doubt, to most sentient beings an excess of happiness over misery, although many occasionally suffer much. Such suffering is quite compatible with the belief in Natural Selection, which is not perfect in its action, but tends only to render each species as successful as possible in the battle for life with other species, in wonderfully complex and changing circumstances.

That there is much suffering in the world no one disputes. Some have attempted to explain this with reference to man by imagining that it serves for his moral improvement. But the number of men in the world is as nothing compared with that of all other sentient beings, and they often suffer greatly without any moral improvement. This very old argument from the existence of suffering against the existence of an intelligent first cause seems to me a strong one; whereas, as just remarked, the presence of much suffering agrees well with the view that all organic beings have been developed through variation and natural selection.

At the present day the most usual argument for the existence of an intelligent God is drawn from the deep inward conviction and feelings which are experienced by most persons . . .

Formerly I was led by feelings such as those just referred to (although I do not think that the religious sentiment was ever strongly developed in me), to the firm conviction of the existence of God, and of the immortality of the soul. In my Journal I wrote that whilst standing in the midst of the grandeur of a Brazilian forest, 'it is not possible to give an adequate idea of the higher feelings of wonder, admiration, and devotion, which fill and elevate the mind.' I well remember my conviction that there is more in man than the mere breath of his body. But now the grandest scenes would not cause any such convictions and feelings to rise in my mind. It may be truly said that I am like a man who has become colour-blind, and the universal belief by men of the existence of redness makes my present loss of perception of not the least value as evidence. This argument would be a valid one if all men of all races had the same inward conviction of the existence of one God; but we know that this is very far from being the case. Therefore I cannot see that such inward convictions and feelings are of any weight as evidence of what really exists. The state of mind which grand scenes formerly excited in me, and which was intimately connected with a belief in God, did not essentially differ from that which is often called the sense of sublimity; and however diffcult it may be to explain the genesis of this sense, it can hardly be advanced as an argument for the existence of God, any more than the powerful though vague and similar feelings excited by music.

With respect to immortality, nothing shows me (so clearly) how strong and almost instinctive a belief it is, as the consideration of the view now held by most physicists, namely, that the sun with all the planets will in time grow too cold for life, unless indeed some great body dashes into the sun, and thus gives it fresh life. – Believing as I do that man in the distant future will be a far more perfect creature than he now is, it is an intolerable thought that he and all other sentient beings are doomed to complete annihilation after such long-continued slow progress. To those who fully admit the immortality of the human soul, the destruction of our world will not appear so dreadful.

Another source of conviction in the existence of God, connected with the reason, and not with the feelings, impresses me as having much more weight. This follows from the extreme difficulty or rather impossibility of conceiving this immense and wonderful universe, including man with his capacity of looking far backwards and far into futurity, as the result of blind chance or necessity. When thus reflecting I feel compelled to look to a First Cause having an intelligent mind in some degree analogous to that of man; and I deserve to be called a Theist.

This conclusion was strong in my mind about the time, as far as I can remember, when I wrote the Origin of Species; and it is since that time that it has very gradually, with many fluctuations, become weaker. But then arises the doubt – can the mind of man, which has, as I fully believe, been developed from a mind as low as that possessed by the lowest animals, be trusted when it draws such grand conclusions? May not these be the result of the connection between cause and effect which strikes us as a necessary one, but probably depends merely on inherited experience? Nor must we overlook the probability of the constant inculcation of a belief in God in the minds of children producing so strong and perhaps an inherited effect on their brains, not as yet fully developed, that it would be as difficult for them to throw off their belief in God, as for a monkey to throw off its instinctive fear and hatred of a snake. I cannot pretend to throw the least light on such abstruse problems. The mystery of the beginning of all things is insoluble by us; and I for one must be content to remain an Agnostic.

4 DAWKINS: GOD'S UTILITY FUNCTION[5]

My clerical correspondent of the previous chapter found faith through a wasp. Charles Darwin lost his with the help of another: 'I cannot persuade myself,' Darwin wrote, 'that a beneficent and omnipotent God would have designedly created the Ichneumonidae with the express intention of their feeding within the living bodies of Caterpillars.' Actually Darwin's gradual loss of faith, which he downplayed for fear of upsetting his devout wife Emma, had more complex causes. His reference to the Ichneumonidae was aphoristic. The macabre habits to which he referred are shared by their cousins the digger wasps. . . . A female digger wasp not only lays her egg in a caterpillar (or grasshopper or bee) so that her larva can feed on it but, according to Fabre and others, she carefully guides her sting into each ganglion of the prey's central nervous system, so as to paralyze it *but not kill it*. This way, the meat keeps fresh. It is not known whether the paralysis acts as a general anesthetic, or if it is like curare in just freezing the victim's ability to move. If the latter, the prey might be aware of being eaten alive from inside but unable to move a muscle to do anything about it. This sounds savagely cruel but, as we shall see, nature is not cruel, only pitilessly indifferent. This is one of the hardest lessons for humans to learn. We cannot admit that things might be neither good nor evil, neither cruel nor kind, but simply callous – indifferent to all suffering, lacking all purpose.

We humans have purpose on the brain. We find it hard to look at anything without wondering what it is 'for', what the motive for it is, or the purpose behind it. When the obsession with purpose becomes pathological it is called paranoia – reading malevolent purpose into what is actually random bad luck. But this is just an exaggerated form of a nearly universal delusion. Show us almost any object or process, and it is hard for us to resist the 'Why' question – the 'What is it for?' question.

---

5. Richard Dawkins, *River Out of Eden: A Darwinian View of Life*, London, Weidenfeld & Nicolson, 1995, pp. 95–98, 102–106, 120–122, 131–133.

The desire to see purpose everywhere is a natural one in an animal that lives surrounded by machines, works of art, tools and other designed artifacts; an animal, moreover, whose waking thoughts are dominated by its own personal goals. A car, a tin opener, a screw-driver and a pitchfork all legitimately warrant the 'What is it for?' question. Our pagan forebears would have asked the same question about thunder, eclipses, rocks, and streams. Today we pride ourselves on having shaken off such primitive animism. If a rock in a stream happens to serve as a convenient stepping-stone, we regard its usefulness as an accidental bonus, not a true purpose. But the old temptation comes back with a vengeance when tragedy strikes – indeed, the very word 'strikes' is an animistic echo: 'Why, oh why, did the cancer/earthquake/hurricane have to strike *my* child?' And the same temptation is often positively relished when the topic is the origin of all things or the fundamental laws of physics, culminating in the vacuous existential question 'Why is there something rather than nothing?'

I have lost count of the number of times a member of the audience has stood up after a public lecture I have given and said something like the following: 'You scientists are very good at answering "How" questions. But you must admit you're powerless when it comes to "Why" questions.' Prince Philip, Duke of Edinburgh, made this very point when he was in an audience at Windsor addressed by my colleague Dr Peter Atkins. Behind the question there is always an unspoken but never justified implication that since science is unable to answer "Why" questions, there must be some other discipline that is qualified to answer them. This implication is, of course, quite illogical.

I'm afraid that Dr Atkins gave the Royal Why fairly short shrift. The mere fact that it is possible to frame a question does not make it legitimate or sensible to do so. There are many things about which you can ask, "What is its temperature?" or 'What color is it?" but you may not ask the temperature question or the color question of, say, jealousy or prayer. Similarly, you are right to ask the "Why" question of a bicycle's mudguards or the Kariba Dam, but at the very least you have no right to assume that the "Why" question deserves an answer when posed about a boulder, a misfortune, Mt Everest or the universe. Questions can be simply inappropriate, however heartfelt their framing.

Somewhere between windscreen wipers and tin openers on the one hand and rocks and the universe on the other lie living creatures. Living bodies and their organs are objects that, unlike rocks, seem to have purpose written all over them. Notoriously, of course, the apparent purposefulness of living bodies has dominated the classic Argument from Design, invoked by theologians from Aquinas to William Paley to modern "scientific" creationists.

The true process that has endowed wings and eyes, beaks, nesting instincts and everything else about life with the strong illusion of purposeful design is now well understood. It is Darwinian natural selection. Our understanding of this has come astonishingly recently, in the last century and a half. Before Darwin, even educated people who had abandoned "Why" questions for rocks, streams and eclipses still implicitly accepted the legitimacy of the "Why" question where living creatures were concerned. Now only the scientifically illiterate do. But "only" conceals the unpalatable truth that we are still talking about an absolute majority.

Actually, Darwinians do frame a kind of "Why" question about living things, but they do so in a special, metaphorical sense. Why do birds sing, and what are wings for? Such questions would be accepted as a shorthand by modern Darwinians and would be given sensible answers in terms of the natural selection of bird ancestors. The illusion of purpose is so powerful that biologists themselves use the assumption of good design as a working tool. . . .

I now want to introduce two technical terms, "reverse engineering" and "utility function." In this section, I am influenced by Daniel Dennett's superb book *Darwin's Dangerous Idea*. Reverse engineering is a technique of reasoning that works like this. You are an engineer, confronted with an artifact you have found and don't understand. You make the working assumption that it was designed for some purpose. You dissect and analyze the object with a view to working out what problem it would be good at solving: "If I had wanted to make a machine to do so-and-so, would I have made it like this? Or is the object better explained as a machine designed to do such-and-such?"

The slide rule, talisman until recently of the honorable profession of engineer, is in the electronic age as obsolete as any Bronze Age relic. An archaeologist of the future, finding a slide rule and wondering about it, might note that it is handy for drawing straight lines or for buttering bread. But to assume that either of these was its original purpose violates the economy assumption. A mere straight-edge or butter knife would not have needed a sliding member in the middle of the rule. Moreover, if you examine the spacing of the graticules you find precise logarithmic scales, too meticulously disposed to be accidental. It would dawn on the archaeologist that, in an age before electronic calculators, this pattern would constitute an ingenious trick for rapid multiplication and division. The mystery of the slide rule would be solved by reverse engineering, employing the assumption of intelligent and economical design.

"Utility function" is a technical term not of engineers but of economists. It means "that which is maximized." Economic planners and social engineers are rather like architects and real engineers in that they strive to maximize something. Utilitarians strive to maximize "the greatest happiness for the greatest number" (a phrase that sounds more intelligent than it is, by the way). Under this umbrella, the utilitarian may give long-term stability more or less priority at the expense of short-term happiness, and utilitarians differ over whether they measure "happiness" by monetary wealth, job satisfaction, cultural fulfillment or personal relationships. Others avowedly maximize their own happiness at the expense of the common welfare, and they may dignify their egoism by a philosophy that states that general happiness will be maximized if one takes care of oneself. By watching the behavior of individuals throughout their lives, you should be able to reverse-engineer their utility functions. If you reverse-engineer the behavior of a country's government, you may conclude that what is being maximized is employment and universal welfare. For another country, the utility function may turn out to be the continued power of the president, or the wealth of a particular ruling family, the size of the sultan's harem, the stability of the Middle East or maintaining the price of oil. The point is that more than one utility function can be imagined. It isn't always obvious what individuals, or firms, or governments are striving to maximize. But it is probably safe to assume that they are maximizing something. This is because *Homo sapiens* is a deeply purpose-ridden species. The principle holds good even if the utility function turns out to be a weighted sum or some other complicated function of many inputs.

Let us return to living bodies and try to extract their utility function. There could be many but, revealingly, it will eventually turn out that they all reduce to one. A good way to dramatize our task is to imagine that living creatures were made by a Divine Engineer and try to work out, by reverse engineering, what the Engineer was trying to maximize: What was God's Utility Function?

Cheetahs give every indication of being superbly designed for something, and it should be easy enough to reverse-engineer them and work out their utility function. They appear to be well designed to kill antelopes. The teeth, claws, eyes, nose, leg muscles, backbone and brain of a cheetah are all precisely what we should expect if God's purpose in designing cheetahs was to maximize deaths among antelopes. Conversely, if we reverse-engineer an antelope we find equally impressive evidence of design for precisely the opposite end: the survival of antelopes and starvation among cheetahs. It is as though cheetahs had been designed by one deity and antelopes by a rival deity. Alternatively, if there is only one Creator who made the tiger and the lamb, the cheetah and the gazelle, what is He playing at? Is He a sadist who enjoys spectator blood sports? Is He trying to avoid overpopulation in the mammals of Africa? Is He maneuvering to maximize David Attenborough's television ratings? These are all intelligible utility functions that might have turned out to be true. In fact, of course, they are all completely wrong. We now understand the single Utility Function of life in great detail, and it is nothing like any of those.

. . . The true utility function of life, that which is being maximized in the natural world, is DNA survival. But DNA is not floating free; it is locked up in living bodies and it has to make the most of the levers of power at its disposal. DNA sequences that find themselves in cheetah bodies maximize their survival by causing those bodies to kill gazelles. Sequences that find themselves in gazelle bodies maximize their survival by promoting opposite ends. But it is DNA survival that is being maxiized in both cases . . . .

Peacocks are burdened with finery so heavy and cumbersome that it would gravely hamper their efforts to do useful work, even if they felt inclined to do useful work – which, on the whole, they don't. Male songbirds use dangerous amounts of time and energy singing. This certainly imperils them, not only because it attracts predators but because it drains energy and uses time that could be spent replenishing that energy. A student of wren biology claimed that one of his wild males sang itself literally to death. Any utility function that had the long-term welfare of the species at heart, even the long-term survival of this particular individual male, would cut down on the amount of singing, the amount of displaying, the amount of fighting among males. Yet, because what is really being maximized is DNA survival, nothing can stop the spread of DNA that has no beneficial effect other than making males beautiful to females. Beauty is not an absolute virtue in itself. But inevitably, if some genes do confer on males whatever qualities the females of the species happen to find desirable, those genes, willy-nilly, will survive.

Why are forest trees so tall? Simply to overtop rival trees. A "sensible" utility function would see to it that they were all short. They would get exactly the same amount of sunlight, with far less expenditure on thick trunks and massive supporting buttresses. But if they were all short, natural selection couldn't help favoring a variant individual that grew a little taller. The ante having been upped, others would have to follow suit. Nothing can stop the whole game escalating until all trees are ludicrously and wastefully tall. It is ludicrous and wasteful only from the point of view of a rational economic planner thinking in terms of maximizing efficiency. But it all makes sense once you understand the true utility function – genes are maximizing their own survival. Homely analogies abound. At a cocktail party, you shout yourself hoarse. The reason is that everybody else is shouting at top volume. If only the guests could come to an agreement to whisper, they'd hear one another exactly as well with less voice strain and less expenditure of energy. But agreements like that don't work unless they are policed. Somebody always spoils it by selfishly talking a bit louder, and, one by one, everybody has to follow suit. A stable equilibrium is reached only when everybody is shouting as loudly as physically possible, and this is much louder than required from a "rational" point of view. Time and again, cooperative restraint is thwarted by its own internal instability. God's Utility Function seldom turns out to be the greatest good for the greatest number. God's Utility Function betrays its origins in an un-coordinated scramble for selfish gain.

Humans have a rather endearing tendency to assume that welfare means group welfare, that "good" means the good of society, the future well-being of the species or even of the ecosystem. God's Utility Function, as derived from a contemplation of the nuts and bolts of natural selection, turns out to be sadly at odds with such utopian visions. To be sure, there are occasions when genes may maximize their selfish welfare at their level, by programming unselfish cooperation, or even self-sacrifice, by the organism at its level. But group welfare is always a fortuitous consequence, not a primary drive. This is the meaning of "the selfish gene."

. . . To return to this chapter's pessimistic beginning, when the utility function – that which is being maximized – is DNA survival, this is not a recipe for happiness. So long as DNA is passed on, it does not matter who or what gets hurt in the process. It is better for the genes of Darwin's ichneumon wasp that the caterpillar should be alive, and therefore fresh, when it is eaten, no matter what the cost in suffering. Genes don't care about suffering, because they don't care about anything.

If Nature were kind, she would at least make the minor concession of anesthetizing caterpillars before they are eaten alive from within. But Nature is neither kind nor unkind. She is neither against suffering nor for it. Nature is not interested one way or the other in suffering, unless it affects the survival of DNA. It is easy to imagine a gene that, say, tranquilizes gazelles when they are about to suffer a killing bite. Would such a gene be favored by natural selection? Not unless the act of tranquilizing a gazelle improved that gene's chances of being propagated into future generations. It is hard to see why this should be so, and we may therefore guess that gazelles suffer horrible pain and fear when they are pursued to the death – as most of them eventually are. The total amount of suffering per year in the natural world is beyond all decent contemplation. During the minute it takes me to compose this sentence, thousands of animals are being eaten alive; others are running for their lives, whimpering with fear; others are being slowly devoured from within by rasping parasites; thousands of all kinds are dying of starvation, thirst, and disease. It must be so. If there is ever a time of plenty, this very fact will automatically lead to an increase in population until the natural state of starvation and misery is restored.

Theologians worry away at the "problem of evil" and a related "problem of suffering." On the day I originally wrote this paragraph, the British newspapers all carried a terrible story about a bus full of children from a Roman Catholic school that crashed for no obvious reason, with wholesale loss of life. Not for the first time, clerics were in paroxysms over the theological question that a writer on a London newspapers (The *Sunday Telegraph*) framed this way: "How can you believe in a loving, all-powerful God who allows such a tragedy?" The article went on to quote one priest's reply: "The simple answer is that we do not know why there should be a God who lets these awful things happen. But the horror of the crash, to a Christian, confirms the fact that we live in a world of real values: positive and negative. If the universe was just electrons, there would be no problem of evil or suffering."

On the contrary, if the universe were just electrons and selfish genes, meaningless tragedies like the crashing of this bus are exactly what we should expect, along with equally meaningless good fortune. Such a universe would be neither evil nor good in intention. It would manifest no intentions of any kind. In a universe of blind physical forces and genetic replication, some people are going to get hurt, other people are going to get lucky, and you won't find any rhyme or reason in it, nor any justice. The universe we observe has precisely the properties we should expect if there is, at bottom, no design, no purpose, no evil and no good, nothing but blind, pitiless indifference. As that unhappy poet A. E. Housman put it:

For Nature, heartless, witless Nature
Will neither know nor care.

DNA neither knows nor cares. DNA just is. And we dance to its music.

5 WARD: DARWIN'S GLOOMY VIEW[6]

. . . Another important feature of his [Darwin's] theory is its reliance on a particular set of metaphors for understanding the natural world. These are metaphors of battle, struggle and the survival of the fittest. Is it really an objective, dispassionate and non-evaluative view of nature which sees it as a constant battlefield of competing powers, each ruthlessly seeking survival at any cost to others, 'red in tooth and claw'?

One cannot deny that there is much suffering in nature, that whole species become extinct, that death is the universal fate of organic beings and that all animal life-forms have to destroy other organic forms in order to survive. But does it

---

6. Keith Ward, *God, Chance and Necessity*, Oxford, Oneworld Publications, 1996, pp. 86–95.

follow from this that it is appropriate to see life on earth as a 'war of nature', where the strong survive and the weak die? Such a way of seeing the world is in stark contrast to a theistic vision of the world, for which the earth belongs to God, while humans are to hold it in trust, and for which the righteous are to inherit the earth.

It is also in strong contrast with views that see nature as a much more holistic, integrated web of interactions. Darwin himself is not wholly blind to such aspects of the natural world. 'How infinitely complex and close-fitting are the mutual relations of all organic beings,' he writes.[7] At this point, he seems to glimpse a very different vision of nature as a web of relationships, adapted beautifully to one another, in a developing and ever more complex harmony. Moreover, he occasionally seems to see this process as destined to continue in ways that increase beauty, harmony and complexity without limit: 'I can see no limit to the amount of change, to the beauty and infinite complexity of the coadaptations between all organic beings.'[8]

The metaphor of a war of nature here gives way to a different metaphor; that of a developing emergent whole, with increasingly complex and beautiful co-adaptedness among organic life-forms, and which pictures nature as expressing a continuous growth in harmonious complexity. Instead of selfish genes, ruthlessly competing, Darwin sees a finely balanced interplay of forms within an emergent totality, generating new states of organisation and beauty. This change of metaphor reflects a change that has also taken place in physics, from the atomism of Newton to the interconnected fields of energy that characterise relativity theory. In biology, the model of isolated units in competition has for some time now been opposed by a model of a unified web of interrelated and intricately balanced forces.[9]

On the newer, more holistic, picture, suffering and death are inevitable parts of a development that involves improvement through conflict and generation of the new. But suffering and death are not the predominating features of nature. They are rather necessary consequences or conditions of a process of emergent harmonisation which inevitably discards the old as it moves on to the new.

Competition and struggle exist, as parts of the mechanism by which organic life evolves to new and superior forms. But co-operation and self-sacrifice also exist, even at quite basic levels of conscious animal life. It is not just a blind will to power that drives evolution forward. It is also a striving to realise values of beauty, understanding and conscious relationship. This becomes quite overt at the level of *Homo sapiens*, but it is also plausible to see it as underlying the whole evolutionary process from the start. For it is, after all, that process which has produced *Homo sapiens*. The theist does not have to introduce any mysterious 'vital force' into the process, or any supposition that simple organisms are somehow trying to achieve higher goals by some semi-conscious effort. The theistic

7. *Origin of Species*, p. 130.
8. *Ibid.*, p. 153.
9. A more holistic and positive picture of the biosphere is given by James Lovelock's Gaia hypothesis, outlined in *A New Look at Life on Earth*, Oxford, Oxford University Press, 1979.

hypothesis is that there is a cosmic intelligence, God, which intends the evolutionary process to produce such values, and causes it to do so.

The goal of the process is a fully conscious goal, formulated in the mind of God. What God wills, and consequently what the process will eventually produce, is not the triumph of the strong, but the triumph of virtue, of beneficence, compassion and love. The ultimate evolutionary victory, on the theistic hypothesis, does not go to the most ruthless exterminators and most fecund replicators. It will go to beings who learn to co-operate in creating and contemplating values of many different sorts, to care for their environment and shape it to greater perfection. It will go to creatures who can found cultures in which scientific understanding, artistic achievement, and religious celebration of being can flourish.

Evolution and the Fall

From a theistic point of view, the natural world that Darwin sees is a corruption of what the world is meant to be. It is not true that the will to power alone characterises the animal world. Rather, there is a quite extraordinary development of organised bodies and nervous systems which allow brains to form, which carry the first stirrings of conscious life. The natural world is a world of great beauty, and it proves to be conducive to the emergence of forms of consciousness that can react to and appreciate that beauty, which can rejoice in life, in its times of struggle as well as in its times of peaceful relaxation.

When one comes to the complex personal consciousness of humans, the picture is changed by the emergence of moral responsibility, of the possibility of self-centred action and of a willed self-alienation from the harmonious web of emergent organic relationships. The will to power, to dominate and use nature for selfish ends, only really comes to exist with the first human lives. When it comes to exist, it corrupts the natural course of things, as the human will to power corrodes and undermines the rhythms of the natural order. Far from denying that such a corruption exists, it is an essential part of the theistic vision that human life is estranged from its creator and is trapped in the bondage of self-will. But theists see this as a responsible choice that the first humans made, when they came to be able to make such a choice.

This entails a modification of early religious pictures of life on earth, in the biblical traditions, as having been created without suffering and death, which only came into the world after the selfish disobedience of Adam. Certainly we now know that suffering and death existed among animals long before the appearance of the first human beings. Bacteria and carnivores existed before *Home sapiens* came into existence. Thus we must understand the death that the first conscious sin brought, not as a physical end of life, but as a spiritual death, a separation from God, the only true source of life. Sin, it seems clear, makes suffering, for all creatures encountered by humans as well as for humans themselves, much worse than it might otherwise have been. It creates a fear of death, now seen not as a natural process but as a possibly final separation from God.

The will to power and self is not, for the theist, the normal condition of all organic life, as Darwin's talk of a 'battle of nature' suggests. It is precisely a perversion of the natural tendency towards the realisation of value, a willed and conscious turning aside from one's natural, proper, destiny. The emergent web of nature is torn by human beings, as they turn aside from their divinely willed vocation towards lives of selfish desire. It is because humans are trapped in an alienated consciousness that they tend to project their own fears and passions onto the natural order itself, and see it as a blind struggle of selfish entities. They begin to see the basic carriers of heredity, the genes, as themselves 'selfish', the mutations that carry forward the emergent process as 'mistakes in copying', and striving for new forms of life as 'struggles for survival'. These metaphors are all projections of a wholly negative and reductionist view of human existence onto the natural order. The theist thinks instead of genes as organic parts of the building up of complex carriers for consciousness, of mutations as vehicles of emergence, and of the striving for life as a striving for the realisation of new values. This is a much more positive view, and of course it derives directly from the hypothesis of God, as one who gives a positive goal and value to the natural order.

If one looks at the natural world, and asks which hypothesis seems more adequate to the facts, it seems to me that the 'emergent web' hypothesis is the more adequate of the two. The 'selfish gene' theory . . . has great difficulty in accounting for the genesis of culture, of scientific understanding and the powerful sense of moral obligation. It has to see these things as by-products of a struggle for dominance on the planet, and thus as without intrinsic value. It is extraordinary that they have come to exist at all, and no very convincing reasons have been given for their survival value. Moral obligations, in particular, often restrain conduct which would effectively exterminate one's competitors in the evolutionary battle, and scientists often show a biologically inexplicable preference for truth over expediency. The effect of the selfish gene theory is to undermine truth and moral obligations altogether, by claiming them to be only survival mechanisms, now perhaps counter-productive.

The 'emergent web' theory, on the other hand, gives truth and beauty a primary place in its account of the nature of things, and has no problem in accounting for the genesis of societies of rational moral agents, responding to moral and scientific imperatives in responsible freedom. It can also account for the 'struggle and death' aspects of evolution, as necessary conditions for the gradual emergence of ever more complex forms of sentient life. And it can account for the 'will to power' aspect of life on earth, as one that is introduced to the planet by the acts of responsible human agents who have chosen the path of egoistic desire rather than of dispassionate care. It gives a better account of all the relevant facts, and is thus the preferable hypothesis.

EVOLUTION AND PURPOSE

However, as with all such rather metaphor-based visions of nature, which one seems more appealing will largely depend on one's own personal reactions to existence and its value. The theistic hypothesis leads us to expect that this would be so, since a rejection of God will cause one to evaluate and react to existence in a much more negative and pessimistic way. Since people will probably continue to accept or reject

God on very personal grounds, this means that there are likely to remain disputes in this area, based on deep personal evaluations rather than on strictly evidential considerations. If one asks whether the strong will inherit the earth, an answer will depend as much on one's own hopes and commitments as on an allegedly dispassionate survey of the evidence. For a theistic view, the 'strong' – those who depend solely on violence and oppression – will in the long run destroy themselves. The 'weak' – those who are prepared to give their lives in the cause of love – will in the long run be supported by the divine intention for the flourishing of goodness. The theist hopes for the fulfilment of the natural order that humans can bring about through a conscious relationship of knowledge and love with the creator. It is the righteous who will inherit the earth becaues they are taken up into the current of divine concern for the fulfilment of all things which is cosmically irresistible.

I suggest that Darwin's theory of natural selection is partly motivated by a gloomy and pessimistic view of nature as a battleground of irreconcilably hostile forces. Malthus' gloomy picture of human life seems to many contemporary commentators much too atomistic and adversarial. Darwin's gloomy picture of life on earth shares a similar worldview of adversarial atomism. The *laissez-faire* capitalist ethic of ruthlessly competing individuals lies just under the surface, determining Darwin's choice of metaphors and images. Those who find Lovelock's Gaia hypothesis more apt will see all planetary life interlinked in a web of mutually supporting relationships. This may help one to see the beauty and wisdom of the natural world in a much more positive light.

Connected with his gloomy assessment of life is Darwin's increasing inability to find any sign of purpose in the evolutionary process. In my view, this is largely due to the fact that he saw purpose very much in terms of particular design. Any sign of randomness or malfunction in nature would then count against the existence of a benevolent designer. The thought that millions of species have become extinct can lead to an impression of waste and destructiveness in evolution which looks inconsistent with good design.

The best way to deal with this difficulty is to discard all naive ideas of God as a parent who would like to eliminate all waste and randomness if he could. Such ideas can stand in the way of seeing the true purposiveness of the evolutionary process. One must look at the evolutionary process in terms of the underlying physical laws that drive it. These laws, far from being wasteful and random, are supremely elegant and efficient. It may seem that the element of randomness in genetic change is not very efficient. But the apparently random element is in fact the best way of achieving a goal-directed outcome, while leaving the process itself non-deterministic. Thus, a space is left for the free actions of intelligent beings, which will later be so important to the development of the cosmos. The apparently wasteful extermination of individuals and species is, in fact, the best way of achieving a gradual improvement of organic life-forms, while not permitting autocratic 'interferences' which miraculously effect improvements from outside the system. Moreover, it seems virtually undeniable that the process brings into existence states of very great value (like the appreciation of beauty, moral action and rational understanding), which could not otherwise exist in the same way. Thus the process is purposive, in the important sense that it is an elegant and efficient law-like system for realising states of great value.

I have suggested that natural selection alone does not provide a very good explanation of this fact. It makes the whole process highly improbable, is unable to predict what is likely to happen, and gives no reason for expecting any trend towards complexity and consciousness. By far the best hypothesis is that there is a cosmic mind of immense wisdom, creating a system which will shape itself to realise states of value. In that case, the existence of mind will not be an accidental by-product of a blind conflict of hostile atoms. It will be the fundamental reality that underlies the whole cosmic process. The intended goal of the process will be to produce minds, capable of creating and appreciating values. Natural selection is undoubtedly an important part of evolution. But to say that it wholly explains evolution is something that Darwin himself did not believe, and it is to fail to see the purposes and values that evolution alone is capable of realising.

KEY TEXTS

Barrow, J. (with F. Tipler). *The Anthropic Cosmological Principle*, Oxford, Oxford University Press, 1988.

Darwin, Charles. 'Autobiography' (1903), in *Charles Darwin and T. H. Huxley: Autobiographies*, edited with an Introduction by Gavin de Beer, London, Oxford University Press, 1974.

Dawkins, Richard. *The Blind Watchmaker*, London, Penguin Books, 1988.

Hume, David. *Dialogues Concerning Natural Religion* (1779), edited with an Introduction by Norman Kemp Smith, 2nd edn, London and Edinburgh, Thomas Nelson & Sons, 1947.

—— *Enquiry Concerning Human Understanding*, ed. L. A. Selby-Bigge, 3rd edn revised by P. H. Nidditch, Oxford, Clarendon Press, 1975.

Matson, Wallace. *The Existence of God*, Ithaca, N.Y., Cornell University Press, 1965.

Swinburne, Richard. *The Existence of God*, Oxford, Oxford University Press, 1979.

BIBLIOGRAPHY

Barrow, J. and F. Tipler. *The Anthropic Cosmological Principle*, Oxford, Oxford University Press, 1988.

Bertocci, Peter. *Introduction to the Philosophy of Religion*, Englewood Cliffs, N.J., Prentice-Hall, 1951.

Breuer, Reinhard. *The Anthropic Principle: Man as the Focal Point of Nature*, Boston, Birkhäuser, 1991.

Brewster, D. *Memoirs of the Life, Writings, and Discoveries of Sir Isaac Newton*, Edinburgh, T. Constable, 1850.

Brooke, John Hedley. 'The Relations between Darwin's Science and his Religion', in *Darwinism and Divinity*, ed. John Durant, Oxford, Basil Blackwell, 1985, pp. 40–75.

Carter, Brandon. 'Large Number Coincidences and the Anthropic Principle in Cosmology', *Confrontation of Cosmological Theories with Observational Data*, Dordrecht, Reidel, 1974, pp. 291–298.

Clark, Robert. *The Universe – Plan or Accident?* Philadelphia, Muhlenburg Press, 1961.

Craig, William L. 'Barrow and Tipler on the Anthropic Principle vs. Divine Design', *British Journal for the Philosophy of Science*, 39, 1988, pp. 389–395.

—— 'The Teleological Argument and the Anthropic Principle', *The Logic of Rational Theism: Exploratory Essays*, Lewiston, Maine, The Edwin Mellen Press, 1990, pp. 127–153.

Crook, John Hurrell. *The Evolution of Human Consciousness*, Oxford, Clarendon Press, 1980.

Darwin, Charles. 'Autobiography' (1903), in *Charles Darwin and T. H. Huxley: Autobiographies*, edited with an Introduction by Gavin de Beer, London, Oxford University Press, 1974.

—— *The Life and Letters of Charles Darwin*, ed. Francis Darwin, John Murray, 1903.

—— *More Letters of Charles Darwin*, ed. F. Darwin and A. C. Seward, 2 vols, London, John Murray, 1903.

—— *The Origin of Species by Means of Natural Selection*, London, John Murray, 1859.

Davies, Brian. *An Introduction to the Philosophy of Religion*, Oxford, Oxford University Press, 1982.

Davies, Paul. *The Accidental Universe*, Cambridge, Cambridge University Press, 1982.

—— *God and the New Physics*, London, J. M. Dent, 1983.

Davis, Stephen T. *God, Reason and Theistic Proofs*, Edinburgh, Edinburgh University Press, 1997.

Dawkins, Richard. *The Blind Watchmaker*, London, Penguin Books, 1988.

—— *River Out of Eden: A Darwinian View of Life*, London, Weidenfeld & Nicolson, 1995.

Dewey, John. *The Influence of Darwin on Philosophy*, New York, Henry Holt & Co., 1910.

Dillon, Lawrence S. *Evolution: Concepts and Consequences*, St Louis, The C. V. Mosby Company, 1973.

Doore, Gary. 'The Argument from Design: Some Better Reasons for Agreeing with Hume', *Religious Studies*, 16, 1980, pp. 145–161.

Du Noüy, Pierre Lecomte. *Human Destiny*, London and New York, Longmans, Green, 1947.

Ellis, George. *Before the Beginning: Cosmology Explained*, London and New York, Boyars/Bowerdean, 1993.

Evans, Stephen. *Philosophy of Religion*, Leicester, Inter-Varsity Press, 1982.

Ferré, Frederick. *Basic Modern Philosophy of Religion*, New York, Scribner, 1967.

Flew, Antony. *David Hume: Philosopher of Moral Science*, Oxford, Basil Blackwell, 1986.

—— *God and Philosophy*, London, Hutchinson, 1966.

—— *Hume's Philosophy of Belief*, London, Routledge & Kegan Paul, 1961.

—— 'Hume's Philosophy of Religion', in *Philosophers Ancient and Modern*, ed. Godfrey Vesey, Cambridge, Cambridge University Press, 1986.

Gaskin, J. C. A. 'The Design Argument: Hume's Critique of Poor Reason', *Religious Studies*, 12, 1976, pp. 331–345.

Gray, Asa. *Design Versus Necessity: Discussion between Two Readers of Darwin's Treatise on the Origin of Species, upon its Natural Theology* (1876), reprinted Cambridge, Mass., Harvard University Press, 1963, pp. 51–71.

Himmelfarb, G. *Darwin and the Darwinian Revolution*, London, Chatto & Windus, 1959.

Hoyle, Fred and N. C. Wickramasinghe. *Evolution from Space: A Theory of Cosmic Creationism*, London, Dent, 1981.

Hume, David. *Dialogues Concerning Natural Religion* (1779), edited with an Introduction by Norman Kemp Smith, 2nd edn, London and Edinburgh, Thomas Nelson & Sons, 1947.

—— *Enquiry Concerning Human Understanding*, ed. L. A. Selby-Bigge, 3rd edn revised by P. H. Nidditch, Oxford, Clarendon Press, 1975.

—— *A Treatise of Human Nature*, ed. L. A. Selby-Bigge, London, Oxford University Press, 1896.

Huntley, William B. 'David Hume and Charles Darwin', *Journal of the History of Ideas*, 33, 1972, pp. 458–470.

Huxley, T. H. *On the Hypothesis that Animals are Automata and its History*, Address, British Association for the Advancement of Science, Belfast, 1874. Reprinted in *Body and Mind*, ed. G. N. A. Vesey, London, George Allen & Unwin, 1964.

McPherson, Thomas. *Philosophy and Religious Belief*, London, Hutchinson University Library, 1974.

Maher, M. *Psychology*, London, Longmans, Green, 1940.

Mandelbaum, M. 'Darwin's Religious Views', *Journal of the History of Ideas*, 19, 1958, pp. 363–378.

Matson, Wallace. *The Existence of God*, Ithaca, N.Y., Cornell University Press, 1965.

Mellor, D. H. *The Argument from Design*, London, Macmillan, 1972.

—— 'God and Probability', *Religious Studies*, 5, 1969, pp. 223–234.

Moore, J. R. 'Creation and the Problem of Charles Darwin', *British Journal of the History of Science*, 14, 1981, pp. 189–200.

O'Hear, Anthony. *Beyond Evolution*, Oxford, Clarendon Press, 1998.

—— *Experience, Explanation and Faith*, London, Routledge & Kegan Paul, 1984.

Olding, A. 'Design – A Further Reply to R. G. Swinburne', *Religious Studies*, 7, 1973, pp. 361–373.

Ospovat, Dov. 'God and Natural Selection: The Darwinian Idea of Design', *Journal of the History of Biology*, 13(2), Fall 1980, pp. 169–194.

Paley, William. *Natural Theology* (1802), abridged and edited by Frederick Ferré, Indianapolis, Bobbs-Merrill, 1963.

Peierls, R. E. *The Laws of Nature*, London, The Scientific Book Guild, 1955.

Penelhum, Terence. *Hume*, London, Macmillan, 1975.

Penrose, Roger. *The Emperor's New Mind: Concerning Computers, Minds and the Laws of Physics*, Oxford, Oxford University Press, 1989.

Plantinga, Alvin. *God and Other Minds*, Ithaca, N.Y., Cornell University Press, 1967.

Pratt, J. B. *Matter and Spirit*, New York, Macmillan, 1926.

Ross, Hugh. *The Creator and the Cosmos: How the Greatest Scientific Discoveries of the Century Reveal God*, Colorado Springs, Navpress, 1995.

Ruse, Michael. *The Darwinian Paradigm: Essays on its History, Philosophy and Religious Implications*, London, Routledge, 1989.

—— *Taking Darwin Seriously*, Oxford, Basil Blackwell, 1986.

Smith, Quentin. 'Atheism, Theism and Big Bang Cosmology', *Australasian Journal of Philosophy*, 69, 1991, pp. 48–66.

Stenger, Victor. *Not by Design: The Origin of the Universe*, Amherst, N.Y., Prometheus Books, 1988.

—— *The Unconscious Quantum: Metaphysics in Modern Physics and Cosmology*, Amherst, N.Y., Prometheus Books, 1995.

Stephen, Leslie. *English Thought in the Eighteenth Century*, 3rd edn, London, Murray, 1902.

Swinburne, Richard. 'The Argument from Design', *Philosophy*, 43, 1968, pp. 199–212.

—— 'Argument from the Fine-Tuning of the Universe', in John Leslie (ed.), *Physical Cosmology and Philosophy*, New York, Macmillan, 1990, pp. 154–173.

—— *The Existence of God*, Oxford, Clarendon Press, 1979.

Taylor, A. E. *Does God Exist?* New York, Macmillan, 1945.

Taylor, Richard. *Metaphysics*, Englewood Cliffs, N. J., Prentice-Hall, 1963.

Tegmark, Max. 'Is "the Theory of Everything" Merely the Ultimate Ensemble Theory?', *Annals of Physics*, 270, 1998, pp. 1–51.

Temple, Frederick. *The Relations between Religion and Science*, London, Macmillan, 1884.

Tennant, F. R. 'The Influence of Darwinism upon Theology', *Quarterly Review*, 211, 1909, pp. 418–440.

—— *Philosophical Theology*, 2 vols, Cambridge, Cambridge University Press, 1928–1930.

Tipler, Frank. *The Physics of Immortality: Modern Cosmology, God and the Resurrection of the Dead*, New York, Doubleday, 1994.

Vorzimmer, Peter J. *Charles Darwin: The Years of Controversy*, London, University of London Press, 1972.

Ward, Keith. *God, Chance and Necessity*, Oxford, Oneworld Publications, 1996.

chapter 4 THE ARGUMENT FROM MIRACLES

COMMENTARY

INTRODUCTION

All the major theistic religions testify to a belief in miracles (Latin, *miraculum*, from *mirari*, 'to wonder'); and many of their principal personalities (for example, Moses, Muhammad, Buddha) have their status confirmed by their ability to perform miracles. This is particularly true of Christianity, where it has become usual to consider Jesus' miracles as evidences of his divine nature, with one Christian miracle (the resurrection) being regarded by St Paul as so essential that the religion becomes impossible without it.[1] Apart from the New Testament, Christianity also includes, to name but a few, miracles associated with the bones of martyrs and the relics of saints, miracles of bodily preservation, miracles of stigmatization and miracles following the apparition of the Virgin Mary, the last of these establishing Lourdes as probably the greatest shrine of miraculous healing in the world. Even today the performance of at least two miracles, before or after death, is required for papal canonization.

    The extraordinary nature of miraculous events largely explains the peculiar nature of the argument which employs them as evidences for the existence of God. By drawing on certain features of experience, albeit very unusual experience, the argument is evidently a posteriori in form; but the experience being cited is manifestly so uncommon that it clearly cannot be counted among those more familiar experiences – for example, the experience of movement, causality or contingency – which have hitherto been employed within the cosmological argument. In other words, we are considering an argument which does not stake its case upon such rational inferences as could be drawn from normal experience but upon the occurrence of events so abnormal that they are construed as revelations of supernatural power, as divinely given signs attesting to the creator's intervention within his own creation.

Distinctive form of the argument

In what senses is the word 'miracle' being used in the following sentences? What do you consider an appropriate 'religious' definition of the term?

The discovery of penicillin was a miracle of medical science.

It was a miracle that I won the lottery.

He's a miracle of a footballer.

She's a miracle for her age: she still runs ten miles a day.

EXERCISE 4.1

---

1. So St Paul in I Corinthians 15.14–15: 'If Christ has not been raised, then our preaching is in vain and your faith is in vain. We are even found to be misrepresenting God, because we testified of God that he raised Christ, whom he did not raise if it is true the dead are not raised.'

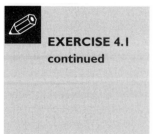

EXERCISE 4.1
continued

She's a miracle for her age: she'll live for ever.

He prayed for a miracle and it happened: his daughter was cured.

It was a miracle that I met you when I did.

It was a miracle that the Virgin Mary appeared to me.

The faith-healer told me that I would walk and I did: it was a miracle.

It was a miracle that Lazarus rose from the dead.

The extraordinary character of miraculous occurrences not only sets the argument from miracles apart from other cosmological arguments, but also indicates the particular direction that criticism of it takes. When we were looking at Aquinas' arguments, for example, the issue to be decided was whether the evidence adduced by him was sufficient to support his conclusions; whether, say, the existence of contingent things did require the existence of a necessary being. What was not questioned was the main premiss, that things are contingent. But in the argument from miracles, it is precisely the main premiss – that miracles can and do occur – that is disputed. There are two main reasons for this. It is alleged (a) that these events, being so extraordinary, could not have happened as they are reported to have happened; and (b) that the evidence to support the occurrence of miracles is simply insufficient. The first criticism is *philosophical* in form: no matter how strong the evidence may appear to be, there never can be good evidence of a miracle because of the nature of the event itself. The second criticism concerns itself mainly with *practical* issues and casts doubt upon the veracity of witnesses and the accuracy of texts.

DAVID HUME: 'OF MIRACLES'

The classic presentation of these two arguments is given by David Hume in his essay 'Of Miracles' (SOURCE 1: PP. 204–211). This essay, which in his own lifetime was the most famous and controversial of all his works, constitutes Section 10 of Hume's *Enquiry Concerning Human Understanding* (1748).[2] Hume rated his argument very highly, claiming from the outset that he had here discovered an argument 'which, if just, will, with the wise and

2. *Enquiries Concerning Human Understanding and Concerning the Principles of Morals*, ed. L. A. Selby-Bigge; 3rd edn with text revised and notes by P. H. Nidditch, Oxford, Clarendon Press, 1975, pp. 109–131. For an historical background to the essay, see Norman Kemp Smith in his edition of the *Dialogues*, 2nd edn, Edinburgh, Thomas Nelson & Sons, 1947, pp. 45–50. At the beginning of his essay Hume tells us that his argument is indebted to one earlier deployed against the doctrine of transubstantiation by Archbishop John Tillotson (1630–1694). For more on this connection, see Dennis M. Ahern, 'Hume on the Evidential Impossibility of Miracles', in *Studies in Epistemology*, ed. Nicholas Rescher, Oxford, Basil Blackwell, 1975, pp. 1–32.

learned, be an everlasting check to all kinds of superstitious delusion, and consequently, will be useful as long as the world endures'.[3]

HUME'S PHILOSOPHICAL ARGUMENT: MIRACLES AND INDUCTIVE PROBABILITY

Hume's philosophical argument is intended to demonstrate that evidence for miracles is intrinsically improbable. Hume begins by referring back to his earlier theory of causation, which we have already discussed.[4] It is, we recall, a fundamental principle of inductive reasoning that the more I see A followed by B, the greater is my expectation that A will be followed by B in the future. That I expect a rubber ball to bounce is dependent on my having seen a rubber ball bounce not once but many times. To put this another way, our belief that the ball will bounce will *increase* and *decrease* proportionately to the amount of evidence for it. For example, if in 99 cases out of 100 the ball bounces (i.e., in one case the ball did not bounce), we expect the ball to bounce in the next case. If, however, this had not happened in, say, 50 per cent of the cases, we should be less inclined to believe that the ball would bounce in the next instance.

Now, the same inductive principle, argues Hume, applies when we evaluate the testimony of others. Here, too, the 'wise man . . . proportions his belief to the evidence'.[5] If, for example,

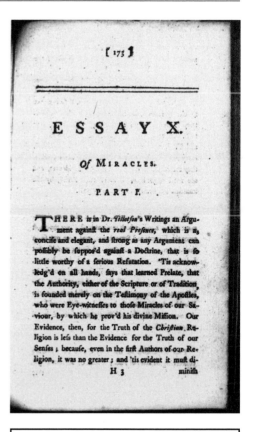

Hume's 'Of Miracles', first edition

one person says that X has occurred and another says that it hasn't, we cannot decide on the matter because we have as much reason to believe that it happened as that it did not. But what if all the witnesses agree that X occurred? In that case our belief in them will depend on two factors: (a) it will be reinforced or weakened by our knowledge of their characters, whether they are generally honest and trustworthy, whether they have a vested interest in saying what they do, whether they hesitate in saying it, and so on; (b) it will be reinforced or weakened by our consideration of the *intrinsic probability or improbability of X occurring*. If X is a type of event that has often happened, I should be inclined to believe the witnesses. But what if, while still believing the witnesses to be trustworthy, I regard X as a type of event that has not often happened or indeed is highly unlikely to happen? Then, says Hume, a struggle takes place between two competing, but equally justifiable, positions, and one

Induction and the
assessment of testimony

3. *Enquiries*, p. 110. J. C. A. Gaskin makes out a strong case for saying that Hume was here replying to Bishop Thomas Sherlock's *The Tryal of the Witnesses of the Resurrection* (1729) and his claim that the evidence of the apostles was sufficient to establish the miracle of Jesus' resurrection. See Gaskin, 'David Hume and the Eighteenth Century Interest in Miracles', *Hermathena*, 99, 1964, pp. 80–92; and his *Hume's Philosophy of Religion*, London, Macmillan, 1968, Ch.7.
4. See above, pp. 65–68.
5. *Enquiries*, p. 110.

would have to decide whether the possibility of the witnesses misleading you or indeed being misled themselves is greater or less than the possibility of the event itself occurring. Nor does the fact that one can make a wrong decision invalidate the correctness of the procedure.

> The Indian prince, who refused to believe the first relations concerning the effects of frost, reasoned justly; and it naturally required very strong testimony to engage his assent to facts, that arose from a state of nature, with which he was unacquainted, and which bore so little analogy to those events, of which he had had constant and uniform experience. Though they were not contrary to his experience, they were not conformable to it.[6]

Let us now suppose, Hume continues, that the event we are examining is not just extraordinary but *miraculous*. How, then, are we to assess the trustworthiness of those who testify to its occurrence? To do this we must first determine what a miracle is. Hume defines a miracle as *a transgression of a law of nature by a particular volition of the Deity, or by the interposition of some invisible agent.*[7] If, for example, a healthy man dies suddenly, we should not regard this as miraculous because this sort of thing, although unusual, has been observed to happen before. If, on the other hand, a dead man came back to life, we would properly regard this as miraculous because it would contravene the known laws of nature.

Hume's definition of a miracle

Hume's argument turns, then, on his view that a miracle is a *violation of a law of nature*. A law of nature is a statement of an invariance or 'uniform experience' that has so far been observed to be the case. The law, to put the matter another way, is the summary of an *induction*.[8] If countless A's have been observed to be B's, and indeed no A's have ever been observed that are not B's, then we may correctly and inductively infer that all A's are B's – certainly to the point where we may exclude the likelihood that some A's are not B's, there being no empirical evidence for this at all. Here, then, the empirical invariance of A's being B's has been elevated to the natural law that 'All A's are B's'. This law, we should note, is not arrived at *deductively*. The universal proposition that 'All A's are B's' cannot claim to be analytically true – i.e., that it is a necessary implication of A's that they are B's – but only synthetically true, that is, a matter of contingent fact. The inductive conclusion that 'All A's are B's' does not therefore exclude the possibility of this statement's being false – if it did, we would have to reclassify it as a necessary truth – but it may properly exclude the probability that it is. The story of the saint who, following his beheading, walked a few hundred yards to a cathedral with his head under his arm and there sang a Te Deum is therefore dismissed not because it is a priori impossible but because it is a posteriori improbable: it runs counter to our common and invariable experience of the world.

---

6. *Ibid.*, pp. 113–114.
7. *Ibid.*, p. 115.
8. For induction and deduction, see above, pp. 97–98.

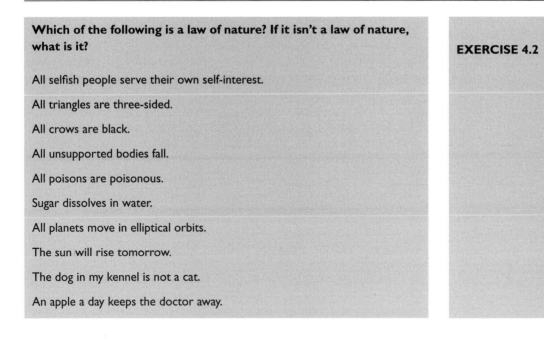

Which of the following is a law of nature? If it isn't a law of nature, what is it?

EXERCISE 4.2

All selfish people serve their own self-interest.

All triangles are three-sided.

All crows are black.

All unsupported bodies fall.

All poisons are poisonous.

Sugar dissolves in water.

All planets move in elliptical orbits.

The sun will rise tomorrow.

The dog in my kennel is not a cat.

An apple a day keeps the doctor away.

To resume: Hume is concerned with the balance of probabilities, with whether it is more or less likely that a particular event happened – in this case, an event which violates a law which has been inductively confirmed to hold without exception. Again, the 'wise man' must make his judgment on the basis of the evidence before him. Let us suppose that a number of trustworthy people maintain that they saw a miracle, that they saw Lazarus rising from the dead. Is it more probable that these witnesses are deceived about what they claim to have seen, or more probable that a human being, once dead, is now alive? Now, if it is a miracle it will be incompatible with the natural law, which designates an absolutely uniform experience, i.e., the experience of those innumerable instances in which human beings have not been brought back to life. Thus the weight of evidence always lies with those who deny the miracle. Denying that Lazarus rose from the dead is, therefore, always the reasonable thing to do, no matter how trustworthy the witnesses.

> There must, therefore, be a uniform experience against every miraculous event, otherwise the event would not merit that appellation. And as a uniform experience amounts to a proof, there is here a direct and full *proof*, from the nature of the fact, against the existence of any miracle; nor can such a proof be destroyed, or the miracle rendered credible, but by an opposite proof, which is superior.[9]

A reasonable person cannot, therefore, be expected to affirm both (1) that a miracle has occurred (that Lazarus rose from the dead); and (2) that there is

---

9. *Enquiries.*

a law of nature which it violates (that no human being can rise from the dead). For if an event is to be counted a miracle, it must violate the uniform experience that makes up the law; and since all the empirical evidence relevant to the law has confirmed it as having no exceptions, the evidence supporting the event being a violation must be discounted in favour of the evidence which says that no such violations occur. Thus to call anything a 'miracle' is *to admit to a proportionate lack of evidence.* This conclusion allows Hume to provide a useful rule of thumb for assessing miracles. As a general rule, no testimony is sufficient to establish a miracle unless its falsehood would be more miraculous than the event it is reporting. Thus testimony will establish that Lazarus rose from the dead only if it would be more a violation of natural law for the witnesses to have lied or been deceived than for that event to have occurred.

Evidence always weighted against miracles

> When anyone tells me, that he saw a dead man restored to life, I immediately consider with myself, whether it be more probable, that this person should either deceive or be deceived, or that the fact, which he relates, should really have happened. I weigh the one miracle against the other; and according to the superiority, which I discover, I pronounce my decision, and always reject the greater miracle. If the falsehood of his testimony would be more miraculous, than the event which he relates; then, and not till then, can he pretend to command my belief or opinion.[10]

Two test-cases

Towards the end of his essay, Hume returns to his philosophical argument and provides some test-cases, which are worth mentioning here. Two of these are of particular interest, the first historical, the second fictional. In the first Hume cites the famous case of the miracles alleged to have taken place at the tomb of the famous Jansenist Abbé Paris. What was remarkable about this case was not just the quantity and quality of supporting evidence but the fact that the Jesuits, opponents of the Jansenists, were never able successfully to refute it. 'Where shall we find', Hume asks, 'such a number of circumstances, agreeing to the corroboration of one fact?' But this does not mean that these miracles occurred. 'And what have we to oppose to such a cloud of witnesses, but *the absolute impossibility or miraculous nature of the events, which they relate?* And this surely, in the eyes of all reasonable people, will alone be regarded as a sufficient refutation.'[11]

In his second example, Hume imagines the resurrection of Queen Elizabeth I. What if 'after having been interred a month, she again appeared, resumed the throne, and governed England for three years'? What if this extraordinary event were a publicly attested fact, witnessed by her physicians and the whole court? Again, Hume is adamant that this simply could not be the case, and that an altogether more plausible explanation would be that these witnesses had been deceived in some way, or that some hoax had been practised upon them, or indeed that Elizabeth had not died in the first place.

---

10. *Ibid.*, p. 116.
11. *Ibid.*, p. 125 (my italics).

I should not have doubted of her pretended death, and of those other public circumstances that followed it: I should only assert it to have been pretended, and that it neither was, nor possibly could be real. You would vain object to me the difficulty, and almost impossibility of deceiving the world in an affair of such consequence; the wisdom and solid judgement of that renowned queen; with the little or no advantage which she could reap from so poor an artifice: All this might astonish me; but I would still reply, that the knavery and folly of men are such common phenomena, that I should rather believe the most extraordinary events to arise from their concurrence, *than admit of so signal a violation of the laws of nature.*[12]

These cases indicate how the intrinsic improbability of the alleged miracle allows Hume to discard any amount of evidence, no matter how reliable that evidence may appear to be. Admittedly, he is here dealing with the reports of miracles, with the evaluation of testimony, and not with our own eye-witnessing of them. What, then, one wonders, would Hume have said if he had himself seen a miracle? It is not difficult, I think, to imagine his reply. The general rule – the greater the miracle, the less likely its occurrence – holds true even in cases of direct eye-witness. For even here, when faced with one's own immediate experience, one has to ask whether it is more likely that what one has seen is the result of natural causes or not, and so whether one has been deceived into believing it a violation of uniform experience or not. Again the more reasonable conclusion is that one has somehow been deceived – that things were not as they appeared to be – because the weight of evidence, the innumerable instances when such a thing did not occur, remains against one. Thus believing in miracles is never a reasonable thing to do, however reliable the witnesses may appear to be, and even when that witness is oneself.

Before we leave Hume's philosophical objections, there is one early reply to them that I should like to mention now, if only because it draws specific attention to the nature of Hume's argument at this point. This was given by Joseph Butler (1692–1752), whom Hume had used as a model for his 'Cleanthes' in the *Dialogues Concerning Natural Religion*. In his *The Analogy of Religion* (1736), Butler argues that the intrinsic improbability of a miracle should have no bearing on the credibility of reports about it. He writes:

Butler's reply to Hume

Bishop Joseph Butler (1692–1752)

---

12. *Ibid.*, p. 128 (my italics).

There is a very strong presumption against common speculative truths, and against the most ordinary facts before the proof of them, which yet is overcome by almost any proof. There is a presumption of millions to one against the story of Caesar, or of any other man. For suppose a number of common facts so and so circumstanced, of which one had no kind of proof, should happen to come into one's thoughts, every one would, without any possible doubt, conclude them to be false. And the like may be said of a single common fact; and from hence it appears, that the question of importance . . . is concerning the degree of the peculiar presumption supposed against miracles; not whether there be any peculiar presumption at all against them. For, if there be the presumption of millions to one against the most common facts, what can a small presumption additional to this amount to, though it be peculiar? It cannot be estimated and it is as nothing.[13]

What Butler is saying here is that miracles are no more improbable than any other events: that indeed the occurrence of ordinary events is also unpredictable, and that we do not, on that account, say that reports about them should be dismissed as unreliable. Just as the low predictability of there being a Julius Caesar does not therefore impugn the credibility of stories about him, so the low predicatability of miracles should not invalidate reports about them.

Reply to Butler

This objection is, I believe, misplaced, and this is so because the 'additional presupposition' against a miraculous fact is not, as many critics of Butler have since noted, as slight as he supposes. J. S. Mill complained, for instance, that Butler had here confused the question of probability before the report of an event with the probability after it: in the case of a reported miracle, the probability against it *remains* enormous even after its reported occurrence.[14] In other words, we are here dealing with events of two qualitatively different types: (1) with events that fall within the normal scope of empirical experience, and which therefore determine the kind of events that are said to be probable or improbable; and (2) with events that are unique and unparalleled within experience, in which the 'additional presupposition' is that they are of a different kind, i.e., that they contravene the known laws of nature. So even if we could calculate, for purposes of argument, that the appearance of a Caesar is 'many millions to one against', his appearance would not be considered extraordinary in the first sense because it does not violate our understanding of human beings and what they are capable of – indeed, as Butler says, in this respect Caesar's appearance is no different from the appearance of any other persons: it is a 'single *common* fact'; but his appearance would be extraordinary in the second sense if we were additionally asked to believe that he was born of a virgin or that, instead of crossing the Rubicon, he walked or flew across it – these would be single *uncommon* facts that the 'wise man' could justifiably discount because they remain outside the whole range of his experience, because there is no

13. *The Analogy of Religion*, London, 1736; New York, Ungar, 1961, pp. 142–143.
14. *System of Logic*, Vol. II, London, Longmans, Green, Reader & Dyer, 1843, p. 173.

known regularity in nature with which to compare them. This explains why, when the wise man evaluates testimony, he is entitled to discard some stories and not others. He will not say, if he is wise, that all miracle-stories should be admitted because the probability of a miracle occurring is not significantly greater than the probability of any other event occuring; he will rather exclude these stories because there are no known analogies to them in his experience: the events they report violate the relevant and known causal laws. It is one thing therefore to assess the chances of a Caesar appearing within the rules or laws governing events of that type, but it is quite another to assess his chances of adopting a particular mode of transport for which there is no known equivalence.

Butler's criticism of Hume has been revived in recent times by Robert Hambourger (**SOURCE 2: PP. 212–213**). Hambourger argues that Hume's argument depends on the 'principle of relative likelihood', a principle which, through examples drawn from lotteries, can be shown to be fallacious as applied to miracles. For just as we would not question the veracity of *The Times* reporting that Smith had won the lottery – not even when the odds against his doing so may be many millions to one – so we should not question the veracity of reports of a miracle simply on the basis that miracles are statistical improbabilities. Whether or not we accept such reports depends more properly on whether we view *The Times* as a reliable newspaper. Hambourger's argument, however, has been criticized, most notably by Dorothy Coleman (**SOURCE 3: PP. 213–216**), on the Humean grounds that a miracle violates the known laws of nature, whereas winning the lottery does not violate the known laws of lotteries: indeed, that someone should win is an expected and regular feature of these events and so reports of this occurring remain unexceptional. As my earlier remarks will have already indicated, I believe that this is a valid reply and that accordingly Hume's point still stands: that there is a correlation between one's scepticism about a report of an event, no matter how unimpeachable the source, and the intrinsic improbability of the event being reported, that is, when that event conforms to no known pattern of experience.[15]

⇐

A modern debate: the principle of relative likelihood

⇐

Provide a 'Humean' evaluation of the following claims:

I am Moses and I saw the Red Sea part.

According to scripture, Christ rose from the dead.

EXERCISE 4.3

---

15. See Robert Hambourger, 'Belief in Miracles and Hume's Essay', *Noûs*, 14, 1980, pp. 587–604; and Dorothy Coleman, 'Hume, Miracles and Lotteries', *Hume Studies*, 14, 1988, pp. 328–345. For further criticisms of Hambourger, see Keith Chrzan, 'Vindicating the "Principle of Relative Likelihood"', *International Journal for Philosophy of Religion*, 16, 1984, pp. 13–18; and for a defence, see Bruce Langtry, 'Miracles and Principles of Relative Likelihood', *International Journal for Philosophy of Religion*, 18, 1985, pp. 123–131. An argument rather similar to Hambourger's is also presented by Roy A. Sorensen, 'Hume's Skepticism Concerning Reports of Miracles', *Analysis*, 43, 1983, p. 60.

**EXERCISE 4.3
continued**

I read today in the newspaper a report of my own death.

I must be dead: I cast no shadow.

Fifty thousand people can't be wrong: we saw the Martians land.

Fifty thousand people can't be wrong: we saw the battleship levitate.

I am in London and I spoke to George in New York.

She's 98: she can't live much longer.

When you have exhausted the possible, try the impossible (Sherlock Holmes).

HUME'S PRACTICAL ARGUMENT: THE INSUFFICIENCY OF EVIDENCE

In Part I of his essay 'Of Miracles' Hume has argued that, however good the testimony for miracles may appear to be, we should reject it on the grounds of the intrinsic improbability of such a violation of natural law occurring. We should reject it not because such an event is theoretically impossible but because of its intrinsic improbability when compared with those other innumerable and uniform events upon which the law, as an empirical generalization, depends. In Part II of his essay Hume now shows that, from a practical point of view, the corroborative testimony for miracles is never very good anyway, 'that there never was a miraculous event established on so full an evidence'.[16] He produces four arguments:

Four arguments against testimonial evidence for miracles

(a) There never has been a sufficient number of witnesses of 'such un-questioned good-sense, education, and learning' to ensure that they are not deluding themselves, or of such unimpeachable honesty that they are not deluding others. Nor has a miracle been performed so publicly as to discount any chance of fraud.

(b) Human beings are naturally attracted to anything out of the ordinary or surprising and love to gossip about such things. This is particularly true of religious people, who will often accept the story of a miracle on the basis of evidence they would have dismissed outright in any other context; nor indeed are they averse to telling lies to promote something they believe to be basically true.

> With what greediness are the miraculous accounts of travellers received, their descriptions of sea and land monsters, their relations of wonderful adventures, strange men, and uncouth manners? But if the spirit of religion join itself to the love of wonder, there is an end of common sense; and human testimony, in these circumstances, loses all pretensions to

---

16. *Enquiries*, p. 116.

authority. A religionist may be an enthusiast, and imagine he sees what has no reality: he may know his narrative to be false, and yet persevere in it, with the best intentions in the world, for the sake of promoting so holy a cause.[17]

(c) It is unfortunate for miracles that 'they are observed chiefly to abound among ignorant and barbarous nations';[18] and that the more educated people become, the less miracles are said to occur. This strongly suggests that the belief in miracles is due to the fact that the uneducated can be easily deceived and that, being ignorant, they are unaware of the natural laws that would otherwise explain the miracle.

(d) Religious systems are incompatible: it is impossible, for example, to say that both Christianity and Islam are true. This means that evidence for an Islamic miracle will support Islam, and so discredit Christianity and its evidence for miracles; and evidence for a Christian miracle will support Christianity, and so discredit the Islamic evidence for miracles, and so on.

> Every miracle, therefore, pretended to have been wrought in any of these religions (and all of them abound in miracles), as its direct scope is to establish the particular system to which it is attributed; so has it the same force, though more indirectly, to overthrow every other system. In destroying a rival system, it likewise destroys the credit of those miracles, on which that system was established; so that all the prodigies of different religions are to be regarded as contrary facts, and the evidences of these prodigies, whether weak or strong, as opposite to each other.[19]

This argument is different from the preceding three: the unreliability of the evidence for miracles derives not only from the unreliability of the witnesses, which has already been established, but also and more particularly from the fact that their evidence is further contradicted by other witnesses telling a different story. Every set of witnesses states that its miracles have occurred (i.e., that its own religion is true), and this implies that the miracles of any other set have not occurred (i.e., that its religion is false). Thus evidence for one is evidence against the other, and vice versa. This conflict, however, irretrievably undermines the evidence of any set of witnesses – any statement that a miracle has occurred implies its contradiction – and so tends to increase the probability that miracles have never happened.

---

17. *Ibid.*, p. 117.
18. *Ibid.*, p. 119.
19. *Ibid.*, pp. 121–122.

EXERCISE 4.4

Present a 'Humean' evaluation of the following claims:

The President is a Christian Democrat, and, as a Christian Democrat, I proclaim his innocence.

Miracles do not occur in Manhattan.

The peasants saw the Virgin Mary and she spoke to them.

I shouted 'Alleluia', and was cured.

My illness is God's punishment for my past sins.

Jesus could do no miracles there because of their unbelief.

I do not doubt what I saw, only that you will believe me.

The miracle converted me.

We can't all be wrong: we saw the paralysed child walk.

Review of Hume's argument

Let us now place the philosophical and practical sections of Hume's argument together. Hume, as we have seen many times, is not concerned with whether any miracles have happened or do happen but with an evaluation of the evidence for them, with how we can *come to know* that they have happened or do happen. And his answer is that no such knowledge is forthcoming, and for two reasons: (1) The event reported is intrinsically improbable; (2) The witnesses to this event are utterly unreliable. Hume's own conclusion is worth quoting in full:

> Upon the whole, then, it appears, that no testimony for any kind of miracle has ever amounted to a probability, much less to a proof; and that, even supposing it amounted to a proof, it would be opposed by another proof; derived from the very nature of the fact, which it would endeavour to establish. It is experience only, which gives authority to human testimony; and it is the same experience, which assures us of the laws of nature. When, therefore, these two kinds of experience are contrary, we have nothing to do but substract the one from the other, and embrace an opinion, either on one side or the other, with that assurance which arises from the remainder. But according to the principle here explained, this substraction, with regard to all popular religions, amounts to an entire annihilation; and therefore we may establish it as a maxim, that no human testimony can have such force as to prove a miracle, and make it a just foundation for any such system of religion.[20]

So forthright is Hume in attacking the probability of miracles that it is not difficult to see why some commentators have taken his argument as an attack

---

20. *Ibid.*, p. 127.

upon the *possibility* of miracles. Certainly Hume's language creates that impression, particularly when, to quote a passage already cited, he characterizes his argument as 'entire as any argument from experience can possibly be imagined', and as a 'full *proof*, from the nature of the fact, against the existence of any miracle'.[21] But we have to be careful here. The 'proof' being spoken of is not a priori but a posteriori, not deductive but inductive – indeed, the kind of proof, as Hume was fond of saying, that a judge encounters in a courtroom when weighing up the evidence. Thus it would be quite proper for Hume to say: 'I must allow for the theoretical possibility that X occurred; but I do not and cannot believe that it actually did occur or that evidence will ever be forthcoming to demonstrate that it did'. As Gaskin has remarked, here the 'effective *practical* difference between "never reasonable to believe" and "impossible" becomes negligible'.[22]

For Hume, then, and contrary to some interpretations, the possibility of miracles, however remote, remains. This is so because, to put the matter more specifically, it is a characteristic of a law of nature that what it expresses is not logically true but an empirical generalization; that the law which says that A causes B is not stating a necessary connection between them but the well-established invariability of their relation. If, then, we reject the *possibility* of an exception to the law of nature – that there can be no miracle, given this uniform experience – we are construing the law as an analytic truth which it would be self-contradictory to deny, and this Hume does not do. Nor would Hume concede that allowing this exception weakens his argument: it rather clarifies the direction of its thrust. The wise man is here proportioning his belief to the *evidence*; and on those grounds he is right to conclude that the case against miracles has been proven beyond rational doubt.

EXTENDING HUME'S ARGUMENT: MCKINNON AND FLEW

Before leaving Hume's argument, it is worth considering two elaborations of his position provided by Alastair McKinnon and Antony Flew.

McKinnon's argument is the more extreme of the two. He claims that it is, after all, correct to say that a miracle is *impossible* because 'the idea of a suspension of natural law is self-contradictory'.[23] Natural laws, McKinnon contends, are 'simply highly generalized shorthand descriptions of how things

---

21. *Ibid.*, pp. 114–115.

22. 'Hume on Religion', in *The Cambridge Companion to Hume*, ed. David Fate Norton, Cambridge, Cambridge University Press, 1993, p. 332. Part of the difficulty here lies in Hume's use of the word 'proof'. In the *Enquiry* (p. 56) he distinguishes proof from *demonstrations* and *probabilities*, the former providing knowledge a priori (e.g., mathematics). A proof, however, is an 'argument from experience', one which, although carrying great conviction, is yet corrigible – hence the case of the Indian prince already cited.

23. '"Miracle" and "Paradox"', *American Philosophical Quarterly*, 4, 1967. Reprinted in *Miracles*, ed. Richard Swinburne, London, Collier Macmillan, 1989, p. 49.

do in fact happen'; they describe, in other words, the 'actual course of events'.[24] To say, therefore, that a miracle violates the natural law is to claim that this real and historical event involves the 'suspension of the actual course of events', and this is clearly impossible: one cannot say that this event both is and is not an event. Thus one either has to affirm that the event is an event but not miraculous or a miracle but not an event. McKinnon does not claim, however, that we are never confronted with events that do appear, initially at least, as violations of the natural law; but in these cases, he says, the proper thing to do is not to say that a miracle has occurred, that a real violation has taken place, but that our original conception of the law was *inadequate*. So if Lazarus did indeed rise from the dead, this is not a miracle but evidence that our original notions about bodily decomposition will have to be reassessed. The natural laws state what happens and thus can be constantly adjusted to account for everything that occurs, even alleged violations.

McKinnon: the impossibility of miracles

Asserting that miracles are *impossible* makes McKinnon's position much more vulnerable than Hume's. For Hume, to repeat, miracles could happen, although the evidence suggests that they never have happened. McKinnon, by contrast, rules out the possibility of miracles by definition: given that it is an a priori truth that laws of nature state what happens, anything that happens must conform to those laws. Thus anything that may at first appear a violation *must in principle always be something else*, that is, an instance of an amended law. Thus there can be no violations of the laws and so no miracles. But this argument, I believe, is hard to sustain. If it is *not* contradictory to say that what happened in all our yesterdays might not happen today – that counter-instances of an empirical regularity are possible (e.g., lead floats) – then it is difficult to see why it *is* contradictory to say that an event has occurred that violates natural law (e.g., Jesus walked on water). McKinnon's reasoning is that, while extraordinary events may occur, their *causes*, even if unknown, must themselves be natural. But again there is no *logical* reason why this should be the case, and why therefore such events could not be brought about by a cause that is supranatural, i.e., by a god. Unless therefore it can be shown that the existence of God is impossible, it is conceptually legitimate to conceive of the laws of nature being violated by divine intervention – in other words, *if* there is a God, miracles could occur. Of course, the fact that in the past natural explanations of extraordinary events have been found may well lead us to suppose, with Hume, that miracles also fall into this category; but this does not mean that (by definition) there never can be cases in which we prefer the theistic explanation. To return to Lazarus: if Lazarus' resurrection is a violation of 'the actual course of events', then this may be a sufficient reason for saying that such a thing never happened; but the alternative cannot be excluded a priori: that Lazarus' resurrection, being a violation, cannot be explained by natural laws and may therefore be better explained as a miracle.[25]

---

24. *Ibid.*, p. 50.
25. F. R. Tennant reaches the same conclusion, claiming that, since laws do not precede facts, no facts can be ruled out as impossible. 'Facts do not presuppose laws, but laws facts. Or, more correctly, there is no presupposing either way, but cosupposing. As Boutroux happily expresses it,

A more successful amendment to Hume's argument comes from Antony Flew (SOURCE 4: PP. 216–219). Flew was one of the first to see that Hume's argument allows for the logical possibility of miracles: not regarding laws of nature as analytic truths, Hume cannot establish that miracles cannot occur. But then this was not Hume's primary concern anyway. The weight of Hume's argument falls rather against the testimonial evidence for such occurrences, namely, that the historical evidence in their favour will forever remain inadequate. Accordingly, whether or not miracles occur is something which, on testimonial grounds, can never be decided.[26] It is at this point that Flew strengthens Hume's argument. We discard miracles not only for these evidential reasons but also because the *historical method* by which we assess *any* evidence from the past militates against such things happening.

Flew: the historian's rejection of miracles

Antony Flew

> The heart of the matter is that the criteria by which we must assess historical testimony, and the general presumptions which alone make it possible for us to construe the detritus of the past as historical evidence, must inevitably rule out any possibility of establishing, upon purely historical grounds, that some genuinely miraculous event has indeed occurred.[27]

Flew's thesis is that the historian has only one direct way of assessing whether something happened in the past, and that is to be present when the event occurred. Given that this is generally impossible, the only other way is indirect:

if laws are the channels along which the stream of fact rushes, the channels have themselves been hollowed by the facts. We assert, then, that the possibility of miracle as an exception to law is not precluded *a priori*.' *Miracles and its Philosophical Presuppositions*, Cambridge, Cambridge University Press, 1925, p. 13.

26. So Flew: 'What he [Hume] was trying to establish was: not that miracles do not occur, although he does make it very plain that this was his own view as well as that of all other men of sense; but that, whether or not they did or had, this is not something we can any of us ever be in a position positively to know. This is why the label "Hume's Check" fits, whereas "Hume's Checkmate" would not.' *David Hume: Philosopher of Moral Science*, Oxford, Basil Blackwell, 1986, p. 80. However, for an alternative interpretation, see Robert J. Fogelin, 'What Hume Actually said about Miracles', *Hume Studies*, 16(1), 1990, pp. 81–86. Cf. R. M. Burns, *The Great Debate on Miracles: From Glanville to David Hume*, Lewisburg, Bucknell University Press, 1981.

27. *God and Philosophy*, London, Hutchinson, 1966, p. 145. Flew's argument was first presented in his *Hume's Philosophy of Belief*, London, Routledge & Kegan Paul, 1961, pp. 186–187. Other statements of it are to be found in Flew's article on 'Miracles' in *The Encyclopedia of Philosophy*, New York, Macmillan, 1967, Vol. V, p. 350; in 'Parapsychology Revisited: Laws, Miracles, and Repeatability', *The Humanist*, 36, May–June, 1976, pp. 28–30; and in 'Hume's Check', the *Philosophical Quarterly*, 9(34), 1959, pp. 1–18.

to reconstruct the past on the basis of the evidence still available to us. In evaluating this evidence the historian appeals to what he now knows about how the world operates, to what he now considers to be probable or improbable, possible or impossible. What he now knows is, for example, that there are certain universal natural laws upon which he relies, and that these laws can be, and often are, subject to repeated verification. So the reason for saying that a dead person cannot come back to life is that it conforms to a well-known law which has been, and continues to be, tested and confirmed.

For these reasons, Flew contends, there never can be genuine historical evidence to support a belief in miracles. For the historical method by which we seek to discover whether a miracle did actually occur requires that the evidence be assessed on the basis of evidence *still available to us*, and this present evidence, rather than confirming that a violation did take place, confirms the opposite: a miracle being precisely that which, in the light of present knowledge, is thought to be physically impossible. Thus the historian, in weighing up the pros and cons of the evidence, can never have better reasons for saying that a miracle has occurred than that it has not. It is not just that his first-hand knowledge of the laws of nature, of those regularities in the world *directly verifiable*, outweighs the testimonial evidence that in the past things were different and that violations *not directly verifiable* did take place; it is more exactly that a miracle is something that the historian, applying the rules of historical judgment, *cannot know*. For in assessing the evidence for any past event, let alone miracles, he must appeal to criteria that accept the body of scientific knowledge as given. In this way the reason for calling an event miraculous becomes at the same time a sufficient reason for the historian calling it physically impossible.

Flew's argument is an important strengthening of Hume's case, and one of which, I feel sure, Hume would have approved. Flew, like Hume, does not deny the logical possibility of miracles. It may be, then, that violations of natural law have actually happened; but if they have, then the evidence must be other than historical and appeal must be made to some non-natural criteria, such as a divine revelation from God – a point to which we shall return. For Hume and Flew, however, this type of appeal suggests in turn that miracles do not provide any substantial and independent evidence 'so as to be the foundation of a system of religion', unless it be first accepted that God exists – an argument, in other words, that will carry little weight with those who either do not hold such a belief or who are seeking independent evidence to establish whether God exists or not.

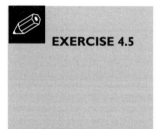

EXERCISE 4.5

Read the New Testament account of Jesus walking on the water (Matthew 14: 22–33). Assess the following possible explanations for this event. Which, if any, do you consider the most likely? If none are likely, must we accept that the event was a miracle?

Jesus was walking on floating timber.

The boat was in fact closer to the shore and so Jesus was walking on rocks.

The whole story is a fiction told by the disciples to boost Jesus' prestige.

The disciples were deluded or drunk.

If Jesus walked on water then the laws of hydrostatics will have to be rewritten.

People don't walk on water *now*: so I have no reason to suppose that Jesus walked on water *then*.

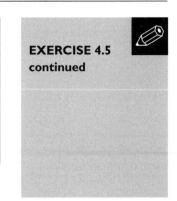

EXERCISE 4.5
continued

CRITICISM OF HUME (1): LAWS OF NATURE

As might be expected, criticisms of Hume have been many and various. The first and perhaps most obvious criticism focuses upon Hume's understanding of a *law of nature*: that a law is based on an inductive inference made on past experiences. It was this, we recall, that allows the 'wise man' to discount the miracle-event as at all likely: since a miracle is by definition a violation of a natural law, there will always be by definition a greater weight of evidence against a miracle than for it. Critics, however, have been quick to point out that this argument depends on assumptions that Hume has already rejected elsewhere in his philosophy. We should here recall Hume's attack upon the causal argument: that this argument depends on the principle that *nature is uniform*, and that this principle cannot be established. Thus the repetition of instances, which certainly leads us to suppose that A causes B, is no guarantee that this is indeed the case, even to the point where we must allow that B may have no cause at all.[28] It is difficult, however, to see how these two arguments can be held together: how, having established the principle that there can be no natural impossibilities because nature is *not* necessarily uniform, Hume can proceed to his 'proof' that miracles as alleged natural impossibilities must be excluded because nature *is* uniform, 'firm and unalterable'. I am not the first critic to indicate this inconsistency between Hume's essay 'Of Miracles' and his earlier work, the most prominent being C. S. Lewis.[29]

Inconsistency of Hume's argument

Setting aside this fairly obvious confusion on Hume's part, it has further been suggested that his argument, by being directed against anything which contradicts experience, makes it hard to determine when a revision of a known law of nature is in fact legitimate. Hume allows that such revisions will take place; but if it is the exception that prompts the revision, why should we not, even here, apply Hume's argument and discount the exception in favour of the known law based on past experience? So C. D. Broad writes:

---

28. See above, pp. 64–68.
29. *Miracles*, London, Collins, 1947; edition used, London, Collins, Fount Paperbacks, 1990, pp. 106–111. See also *Hume's Dialogues Concerning Natural Religion*, edited with an Introduction by Norman Kemp Smith, London and Edinburgh, Thomas Nelson, 1935, p. 47. Even Flew, a dedicated Humean, in his edition of Hume's essay, does not seek to excuse his hero for the confusion. See *Of Miracles*, La Salle, Ill., Open Court, 1985, p. 11.

Clearly many propositions have been accounted laws of nature because of an invariable experience in their favour, then exceptions have been observed, and finally these propositions have ceased to be regarded as laws of nature. But the first reported exception was, to anyone who had not himself observed it, in precisely the same position as a story of a miracle, if Hume be right.[30]

When are exceptions to natural laws acceptable?

In other words, Hume, in advancing his case against miracles, has so weighted the evidence against exceptions to the laws of nature that it militates against the acceptance of any new scientific information. Admittedly this was not his intention, and he makes clear that scientific discovery does indeed proceed on the basis of investigating such exceptions. But if this is so, then the admission that exceptions to the natural law occur is not unreasonable, and Hume's rejection of miracle because it is such an exception also becomes unreasonable. In this sense, the scientist has placed himself in exactly the same position as the believer: he is rejecting the evidence of invariable experience in favour of a violation. How, then, can Hume lay down the principle that no amount of evidence is sufficient to establish a miracle?

CRITICISM OF HUME (2): HISTORICAL EVIDENCE FOR MIRACLES: FLEW AND SWINBURNE

But is it true that the scientist and believer are in the same position? Here it is worth returning to Flew's important amendment: there is a difference between them, and the difference is that the scientist, unlike the believer, can immediately *verify* that a violation has occurred; that against the *indirect* and testimonial evidence for a miracle we can set the *direct* and experimental evidence which can be tested and revised at any time and by any person. Thus it is only these *repeated* and verifiable exceptions that can falsify natural laws; and as long as exceptions of this type are not forthcoming, we must stand by the known empirical regularities of nature and so discount any event, or report of an event, which does not conform to them.

This is a strong argument. The question remains, however, whether Flew is right to say that the historian, in assessing whether a miracle has occurred, would apply criteria that are scientific: i.e., whether in this case an historical judgment must follow the pattern established by science, and that, accordingly, the historian should always reject testimonial evidence in favour of what is, after all, immediately verifiable.

Direct and indirect evidence

One way of assessing Flew's argument is to pursue the distinction between the *direct* and *indirect* evidence for miracles. Let us turn first to direct evidence, by which I mean 'eye-witness' evidence. I have already suggested one way in which Hume could dismiss even this evidence: the more intrinsically improbable the event, the more likely it is that things are not as they appear

30. 'Hume's Theory of the Credibility of Miracles', *Proceedings of the Aristotelian Society*, 17, 1916–1917, p. 87.

and that the witness has somehow been deceived.[31] But if this be a legitimate Humean reply, it does not necessarily cover the case at hand. For although the witness may agree that the event he sees is improbable – given that he accepts that it does run counter to invariable experience – the fact that he has seen it may lead him to suppose that the improbable has indeed occurred. This can be put another way. By saying that an event is 'improbable' the witness is not admitting to the probability that any claims that he makes that he saw it must be mistaken. What he is admitting to is that what he saw was something he did not expect to see, that it was contrary to the normal course of events and so is to be distinguished from all other events within his experience – that this, indeed, was why he *described* the event as 'miraculous' in the first place. Nor is it fanciful to suppose that, knowing this, our witness would be particularly scrupulous in his observations: that he would check to see whether others had experienced the same event, perhaps take photographs, take advice from experts, etc., etc. After all these checks had been completed, it would, I think, be unreasonable to maintain that the evidence remained unreliable and that, accordingly, the witness could not have seen what he said he saw.

What does the following dialogue tell you about what is necessary for an event to be a miracle? Do you agree with the sceptic's conclusion?

EXERCISE 4.6

Believer: It is preposterous to deny the possibility of a miracle like Jesus' resurrection. Resurrections are quite commonplace here: they've happened in Maine, in Florida, in Georgia, in New York, and in many other places besides.

Sceptic: That's incredible! Well, if what you say is true, I'll have to change my mind about Jesus' resurrection. So it probably did happen after all! But so what?

Believer: So what? Is that all you've got to say? How can you be so indifferent to the most significant event in history?

Sceptic: But the resurrection can't be that if the same kind of event has happened elsewhere. So take your pick: either that event was a miracle because naturally impossible or it was not a miracle because naturally possible. You really can't have it both ways.

Thus we may conclude that, on the basis of direct evidence, an eye-witness would be justified in saying (1) that a miracle is a violation of a law of nature (or counter-instance of an empirical invariable); and (2) that he had seen such a violation – i.e., that in this particular case the evidence of his own senses had outweighed the evidence of uniform experience.[32] We must be clear, however,

31. See above, p. 177.
32. On this point, see Keith Ward, 'Miracles and Testimony', *Religious Studies*, 21, 1985, p. 133.

that this admission does not undermine the epistemological status of natural law. This is because what would count as a genuine counter-instance of a natural law is not the *singular* exception, such as a miracle, but, to quote Ninian Smart, a *repeatable* 'small-scale law'. Miracles, as he makes clear,

> are not experimental, repeatable. They are particular, peculiar events occurring in idiosyncratic human situations. They are not small-scale laws. Consequently they do not destroy large-scale laws. Formally they may seem to destroy the 'always' statements of the scientific laws; but they have not the genuine deadly power of the negative instance.[33]

It may be argued, however, and with some justification, that the argument here being defended is not one that either Hume or Flew attacks: that, having allowed for the logical possibility of a miracle occurring, they would concede not only that it could be seen to occur but also that the witness could satisfy himself that it had occurred on the lines I have just indicated. But this is not where the Humean attack lies. We should rather ask: What happens when the eye-witness tells somebody else about what he has seen, when we move from direct to *indirect evidence*? Here, surely, their criticism stands: that, *not being an eye-witness*, the 'wise man' can only proceed on the basis of what is directly accessible to him – the immediately verifiable conclusions of science – and so he must be led to dismiss out of hand any claims to the contrary as unthinkable, no matter how reliable the witnesses. The admission, in other words, that, logically, there could be a miraculous event does not offset the legitimate demand from those *who did not see it* for a proportionately greater amount of evidence, a strong 'opposite proof', to use Hume's words, to outweigh what science now says could not happen.

Swinburne's argument

This argument has been disputed, most notably by Richard Swinburne.[34] Swinburne first considers the four claims advanced by Hume in his practical argument to undermine the veracity of miracle-testimony, namely, that it proceeds generally from those who are uneducated, credulous, mendacious, and so on.[35] Swinburne is willing to concede that Hume's argument incorporates many of the criteria employed for assessing evidence: for example, that we are extremely cautious about the testimony of those 'with axes to grind' or whose upbringing 'conditions them to expect unusual events'.[36] The trouble with Hume's argument is, however, that it is altogether too imprecise. We do not know, for example, what would count as a 'sufficient number of men' – how small or large should the sample be? – nor does the fact that people are often swayed by their 'love of the marvellous' necessarily mean that they have

---

33. *Philosophers and Religious Truth*, London, SCM Press, 1964, p. 41.
34. In his *The Concept of Miracle*, London, Macmillan, 1970, pp. 33–51. A shortened version is found in *Miracles*, ed. Swinburne, London, Collier Macmillan, 1989, pp. 133–151. For other criticisms of Flew, see Dennis Ahern, 'Miracles and Physical Impossibility', *Canadian Journal of Philosophy*, 7(1), 1977, pp. 71–79; and R. C. Wallace, 'Hume, Flew, and the Miraculous', *Philosophical Quarterly*, July 1970, pp. 230–243.
35. See above, pp. 180–181.
36. *The Concept of Miracle*, p. 46.

been so swayed when they report a miracle. Similarly, we do not know what is required of a nation to be 'ignorant and barbarous'. If we mean by this 'not scientific', then we should have to say that this still applies to many nations today; if we mean by this that a nation is generally uncultured, lacking a literature or any sort of science, then Hume's claim is historically dubious: many nations in the Middle Ages had a considerable literature and a solid scientific knowledge, neither of which prevented them from believing in miracles. Hume's fourth point – that miracles

Richard Swinburne

cancel themselves out by being credited in different religions – is admittedly more substantial. But again, as Swinburne makes clear, it is difficult to imagine two cases where the conflict is sufficiently precise to constitute a contradiction. One such would be a Roman Catholic miracle specifically required to demonstrate the doctrine of transubstantiation (the tabernacle levitates), and a Protestant miracle demonstrating that the doctrine is idolatrous (the tabernacle is struck by lightning).

> But it is enough to give this example to see that most alleged miracles do not give rise to conflicts of this kind. Most alleged miracles, if they occurred as reported, would show at most the power of a god or gods and their concern for the needs of men, and little more specific in the way of doctrine. A miracle wrought in the context of the Hindu religion and one wrought in the context of the Christian religion will not in general tend to show that specific details of their systems are true, but, at most, that there is a god concerned with the needs of those who worship, which is a proposition accepted in both systems.[37]

With Hume's argument behind him, Swinburne now seeks to show that there could be good indirect evidence to believe that a law of nature had been violated, or, as he puts it, that 'a non-repeatable counter-instance to a law of

---

37. *Ibid.*, p. 61. We might add, as an additional point, that it is possible to construe the diversity of religions as so many different experiences of the same, but immensely complex, divine reality. The idea has been explored in particular by John Hick in *God and the Universe of Faiths*, London, Macmillan, 1973, and in *An Interpretation of Religion*, London, Macmillan, 1989. A useful collection of critical responses to Hick's thesis is to be found in *Problems in the Philosophy of Religion*, ed. Harold Hewitt, London, Macmillan, 1991.

$\Rightarrow$ nature'[38] had occurred (SOURCE 5: PP. 219–221). He distinguishes between four types of evidence: our own apparent memories, the testimony of others, physical traces (for example, footprints, fingerprints), and finally 'our contemporary understanding of what things are physically impossible or improbable'.[39] As Swinburne correctly remarks, Hume says a great deal about the second and fourth kinds of evidence (testimony and probability) but nothing at all about the first and third kinds (memories and physical traces). Since I have already discussed eye-witness evidence, we need not linger over Swinburne's account of memory, except to say that his qualification of it as 'apparent' allows him to count it as direct evidence that would still in all probability outweigh the evidence of other witnesses, while yet itself retaining the possibility of error. More important is his treatment of physical traces, which may be employed to confirm that certain past events, although extraordinary, probably happened.

Four types of evidence

> Thus we might have evidence of footprints in soft mud that Jones was on one side of a broad river one minute ago, and evidence of Jones on the other side now not in the least wet, with not the slightest indication of water having touched his body or clothes (viz. no traces of his having swum across the river), and no bridge, boats, aeroplanes or rope by which he could have crossed. Hence the evidence indicates that he must have walked or flown across. Traces alone, unsupported by testimony, could thus provide evidence that such an event occurred.[40]

The trouble here, as Swinburne points out, is that physical traces are more useful in the analysis of alleged miracles of the recent past than of long ago: it is, after all, a truism of the detective's trade that traces of this kind are all too rapidly obliterated. But this is not true of all traces – one thinks, for instance, of carbon dating – and science is continually discovering other methods for assessing evidence of past events.

Swinburne's reply to Flew

Swinburne's reply to Flew now follows. Flew's case rests on the principle that scientific propositions, unlike statements about the past, can be repeatedly verified. This presumption, however, is mistaken because 'in the historical as in the scientific case, there is no limit to the testing which we can do'.[41] For in seeking to establish whether a past event has occurred – even an event that would constitute a violation of a natural law – we bring to bear evidence that can accumulate (for example, actual physical traces, apparent memories and testimony) and that can be constantly updated and tested. It is quite possible, therefore, that this indirect evidence for a miraculous event could 'mount up in just the same way in which the evidence of the physical impossibility of an event could mount up'.[42] Flew's principle is therefore 'an unreasonable principle

38. *The Concept of Miracle*, p. 26.
39. *Ibid.*, p. 34.
40. *Ibid.*, p. 36.
41. *Ibid.*, p. 42.
42. *Ibid.*, p. 43.

since claims that some formula L is a law of nature, and claims that apparent memory, testimony or traces of certain types are to be relied on are claims established ultimately in a similar kind of way . . . and will be strong or weak for the same reasons, and so neither ought to take automatic preference over the other. To make the supposition that they are to be treated differently is to introduce a complicating *ad hoc* procedure for assessing evidence.'[43]

Set up a test-case of an alleged miracle, using Swinburne's criteria of

apparent memory

the testimony of others

physical traces

our contemporary understanding of what is physically impossible or improbable.

Do you think these criteria would be sufficient to establish that a miracle had occurred? If not, why not?

EXERCISE 4.7

Swinburne's criticism is, then, that Flew's principle is positivistic – that it makes historical study dependent on science – whereas in fact the criteria employed by these two disciplines are essentially the same. Accordingly Flew cannot employ the verifiability of scientific claims as part of his case against any alleged violations of a natural law because the evidence for these alleged violations could be investigated by an historian in an appropriately scientific manner.[44]

I think that Swinburne has made a convincing case. There could be good indirect evidence sufficient to justify belief that a 'counter-instance' to a law of nature has occurred, and so sufficient to outweigh any more general doubts we may have about the reliability of people who believe in miracles. Indeed, to return to an earlier point, the fact that such events are possible – conceded by Hume and Flew – requires that there might be evidence sufficient to show that what is possible has, after all, happened. The only thing, therefore, that we could not say is that there could be no such evidence a priori. So I agree with Swinburne that there could be occasions in which the investigator, having examined an event very thoroughly, and by using the four kinds of evidence Swinburne mentions, could conclude, on good historical grounds, that it is a violation of the currently known laws of nature. Nor does this conclusion mean that we have to abandon science altogether, as Malcolm Diamond and others

43. *Ibid.*
44. Other arguments very similar to Swinburne's have been presented by Margaret Boden, 'Miracles and Scientific Explanation', *Ratio*, 11, 1969, pp. 137–141; and by Grace Jantzen, 'Hume on Miracles, History, and Politics', *Christian Scholars' Review*, 8, 1979, pp. 318–325.

⇒   have suggested (**SOURCE 6: PP. 221–223**).[45] This is because, as Swinburne makes clear, the conclusion itself is corrigible and as such constantly subject to the strains of empirical research. To say, then, that an event is miraculous is to offer an explanation on the best available evidence: it does not veto other possible explanations on the grounds that this event *must* be miraculous, and so does not discount the possibility that, after all, what was once thought to be miraculous may yet fall within the compass of a natural law.

The importance of Swinburne's argument is that, Flew notwithstanding, we must now agree that evidence for a non-repeatable counter-instance of a natural law is legitimate historical evidence, and must accordingly view it as an admissible candidate for historical evaluation. This allows us to dismiss the claim that any so-called 'proof' of a law of nature *must always* be stronger than any so-called 'proof' to the contrary: having admitted that certain evidence is a genuine candidate, we cannot thereafter dismiss it a priori. What Swinburne has done, in fact, is to reformulate the nature of the decision Hume requires of us, namely, that it is a decision between two contrasted but comparable sets of evidence. These we may now restate as: (1) evidence that is past, testable and unrepeatable, and (2) evidence that is present, testable and repeatable. The question yet remains, however, which of the two is to be preferred. At what point, we may ask, is it *reasonable to conclude* that evidence of the first set has sufficiently 'mounted up' to override evidence of the second set?

In one sense, of course, this question cannot be decided here: everything, after all, will depend on the case at hand. All that one can fairly indicate, at this juncture, is where in all probability *the burden of proof* lies when one is comparing the two sets of evidence just noted. Suppose that indirect evidence for a past and unrepeatable event E is forthcoming, and that E involves, for example, the instantaneous transmutation of base metal into gold or the audible prayers of a saint recently beheaded. What can be said in its favour? It might be replied that, no matter how extraordinary E is, it fulfils all the criteria stipulated by Swinburne (physical traces, apparent memory, testimony) and that, on these grounds, it is historically legitimate to conclude that the event did happen as it is reported to have happened.

But although historically legitimate, this conclusion does not, I believe, take sufficient account (following Hume) of the *intrinsic implausibility of the E-event*. Now, given the truism that the investigator cannot tackle this matter directly – in the sense of his not being an eye-witness – he must tackle it indirectly; and here not only can he apply Swinburne's criteria but also – and crucially – he can set up conditions in which the intrinsic plausibility or implausibility of other E-type events can be immediately and repeatedly verified. I said earlier that *direct* evidence that a miracle (E) has occurred – that I saw it occur – could legitimately outweigh any *indirect* evidence that no such event (of the E-type) could occur.[46] But this argument works both ways. For, by the same token, *direct* evidence that no E-type event has occurred – that I have never seen it

Where lies the burden of proof?

---

45. See also Guy Robinson, 'Miracles', *Ratio*, 9, 1967, pp. 155–166.
46. See above, p. 193.

occur – would legitimately cast considerable doubt upon the *indirect* evidence that it had: the direct evidence here being the repeated and verifiable conclusions of empirical testing (for example, I have beheaded many saints and none has subsequently spoken). If, in other words, the comparison with other ordinary events indicates why an E-event is extra-ordinary, this comparison may also be utilized to indicate why this particular event is also implausible: in both it is the contrast with current experience that is decisive.

It is this implausibility which indicates, in my view, where the burden of proof lies: it lies with those who continue to insist that a miraculous E-event occurred. Certainly such an event is practically possible, and testable evidence may be gathered for it: it stands therefore as a genuine historical option among other options, as an event that cannot be ruled out as unhistorical merely because of its extraordinary nature. But that this is an option, and that there is indirect evidence for it, does not increase its likelihood: that, indeed, can only be established when we set it against other options. When we realize, however, that these other options are consistent with what we already know to be the case – when we see that at least part of their evidence is present and repeatable and not past and unrepeatable – then the burden of proof falls on those who continue to insist that accounts of an E-event occurring are true, that this indirect evidence is correctly reporting something which is inconsistent with our present knowledge of how the world proceeds

That the burden of proof has fallen where it has does, I believe, constitute a *prima facie* case for doubting these reports. We are in a position not dissimilar from that of a jury-member hearing a case of theft. The innocence of the accused is unlikely to be established by the plea that the wine found in his possession was not, after all, the wine stolen but water miraculously transformed into the finest claret. Of course, it may be argued in mitigation that this places undue weight upon the invariability of natural law – that the change from water into wine could have happened and that therefore the innocence of the accused cannot be logically excluded. This is true. It is, however, an alternative difficult to reconcile with what we already know about water and wine, and, given that, the accused is under an obligation to provide pertinent and *additional* evidence to show that, in his particular and unique case, the scientific evidence marshalled against him does not apply. Again, the burden of proof lies with him. Thereafter it is for the jury to decide whether guilt or innocence has been established beyond all reasonable doubt. Here, as Hume would have it, wise men can do no more than proportion their belief to the evidence.

CRITICISM OF HUME (3): EVIDENCE OF GOD'S ACTIVITY

Additional evidence to support miracles

A number of philosophers have suggested, however, that additional evidence could be provided in the case just cited, and that this evidence could be sufficient to establish not just that an extraordinary event had occurred but that this event was *caused by God*. Swinburne suggests that the following would count as appropriate evidence: (1) the violation occurs in answer to a request (a prayer); (2) the request was specifically addressed to a named individual ('O Apollo', 'O Allah'); (3) the request is often followed by a voice, not that of an embodied agent, giving reasons for granting or refusing the request (for example, allowing for the relief of suffering but not for the punishment of enemies); and (4) the voice praises some requests and rebukes petitioners for others.[47] Kellenberger further suggests that even without a disembodied voice or request, the innate benevolence of an event – say, the instantaneous curing of paralysis – could be counted as evidence that its cause is a benevolent God.[48] A more specific example has been given by Tan Tei Wei to support this line of argument. He asks us to suppose not only that Lazarus did rise from the dead after Jesus' direct appeal to God but that such feats were not uncommon after calls from Jesus for divine intervention; we may further suppose that such events have continued to occur after calls for divine intervention from other religious people. Under these circumstances, says Tan, it would be unreasonable to remain sceptical and seek for 'an ordinary natural regularity, that relates such exceptional events with the intentions and commands of this sort of religious personage'. At some point, therefore, abandoning scepticism becomes the reasonable thing to do 'because here some of our ordinary criteria . . . governing the rational acceptability of purported coincidences as merely ordinary ones, would not be met'.[49]

Whether or not such additional evidence would be sufficient to convince rational individuals that a miraculous event had occurred is again hard to say, and can only be determined on a case-by-case basis. The question remains, however, whether the introduction of such evidence would significantly shift the burden of proof towards those who were not themselves petitioners for or recipients of divine intervention; or whether, to put the matter otherwise, ascribing to God an event that is already deemed implausible – that without God no E-event could occur – will make it *more* plausible, to the extent that continued scepticism about, say, the transformation of water into wine becomes unreasonable. I do not think that it does, and for two reasons:

Two criticisms of additional evidence

1. We should first recall Hume's caution about explaining one extraordinary event by another. Since I have already mentioned this in some detail in the preceding chapter,[50] I shall not labour this point here, except to say that the plausibility of one divine intervention is hardly advanced by the introduction of another intervention as its authentication: all it does is push the question of plausibility further back. For if it is said that a 'divine voice' provides some kind of extra warrant for the connection between an extraordinary event and divine causation, what we then require is some additional warrant to establish the authenticity of this 'divine voice' as itself a revelation of divine activity and not, as some might suppose, a symptom of psychological disturbance.

2. The argument suggests that it would be unreasonable for us to deny that a leper had been divinely healed if we had already established that his recovery

---

47. *The Concept of Miracle*, pp. 58–59.
48. J. Kellenberger, 'Miracles', *International Journal for Philosophy of Religion*, 10, 1979, p. 154.
49. Tan Tei Wei, 'Recent Discussions on Miracles', *Sophia*, 11, 1972, p. 24.
50. See above, p. 143.

followed from a direct and public petition to God to perform this precise miracle. This, so it is said, is *prima facie* evidence of divine causation that we cannot ignore. Nor should we. But then neither should we ignore other evidence that may be properly advanced at this point. This evidence, however, deals not so much with the case at hand, with whether this particular individual's request was answered in this particular and dramatic way, but with the more general question of whether the notion of divine causation, which has been introduced here, is or is not compatible with the more common experiences that all of us share: with, for instance, the experience of human suffering, of the wicked prospering, and so on. While one set of evidence may therefore support the claim that God has been revealed in a particular event, another set may support the claim that there is no God to be revealed. In what ever way we resolve this issue, all we can say at this point is that it is clearly not 'unreasonable' or a matter of intellectual dishonesty to reject one set of evidence in favour of another; and that however strong the corroborative evidence for God's activity is in one area, it may be insufficient to outweigh the evidence for his apparent lack of activity in others. Thus scepticism about miracles remains a rational and responsible alternative, no matter how many voices may be heard or prayers answered.[51]

It is an implication of the preceding remarks that the introduction of this kind of supplementary evidence will not advance the case for miracles for those already disposed towards atheism or agnosticism: having no good reason to believe that God exists, they will not be inclined to think that these additional evidences support belief in violations of natural law due to his activity. By the same token, of course, for those who do have good reasons for believing that God exists, these additions may well be regarded as highly significant: if the world is God's creation, it becomes much more likely that he would wish to intervene and indeed respond to requests to do so. In other words, relative to our belief in the invariability of natural law, miracles (and their additional warrants) are highly improbable, and relative to our belief in God, highly probable. What this serves to demonstrate, however, is the more general truth that miracles are 'theory-laden', and that whether one believes in them or not does not derive solely from the assessment of testimonial evidence – whether, given the data, one will be more or less inclined to believe what has been reported. For, as we have just noted, neither belief nor denial can be isolated from other attitudes and perspectives, and each presupposes and expresses fundamental assumptions about the nature of reality: about whether, for example, a theistic explanation is or is not a more plausible explanation than any other. To this extent, then, the debate about miracles is also a debate between competing interpretive standpoints, between distinctive world views, about whether or not the only forces in the universe are natural forces, forces which empirical science alone can measure and evaluate.

---

51. For further discussion of Tan's argument, see David and Randall Basinger, *Philosophy and Miracle*, Lewiston, The Edwin Mellen Press, 1986, pp. 82–93.

CRITICISM OF HUME (4): THE CONTINGENCY DEFINITION OF MIRACLES: HOLLAND AND TILLICH

Coincidences as divine acts

Thus far in this discussion I have concentrated on the Humean definition of miracle as a 'violation' of natural law, as an event therefore contrary to inductive probability. It is, however, a further criticism of Hume that this is not the only definition that can be offered, and that indeed this next definition obviates many of the difficulties mentioned by him. This is sometimes known as the *contingency definition of the miraculous*. Contingency miracles we may describe as extremely rare coincidences, which, when set within a religious framework, have religious significance. As coincidences these events are entirely natural events and so are capable of natural explanation. To put this another way, a direct act of God may be wholly explicable in natural terms and yet be deemed miraculous. Consider, for example, the following well-known story told by R. F. Holland, which I quote in full:

Holland's example

> A child riding his toy motor car strays on to an unguarded railway crossing near his house and a wheel of his car gets stuck down the side of one of the rails. An express train is due to pass with the signals in its favor and a curve in the track makes it impossible for the driver to stop his train in time to avoid any obstruction he might encounter on the crossing. The mother coming out of the house to look for her child sees him on the crossing and hears the train approaching. She runs forward shouting and waving. The little boy remains seated in his car looking downward, engrossed in the task of pedaling it free. The brakes of the train are applied and it comes to rest a few feet from the child. The mother thanks God for the miracle; which she never ceases to think of as such although, as she in due course learns, there was nothing supernatural about the manner in which the brakes of the train came to be applied. The driver had fainted, for a reason that had nothing to do with the presence of the child on the line, and the brakes were applied automatically as his hand ceased to exert pressure on the control lever. He fainted on this particular afternoon because his blood pressure had risen after an exceptionally heavy lunch during which he had quarreled with a colleague, and the change in blood pressure caused a clot of blood to be dislodged and circulate. He fainted at the time when he did on the afternoon in question because this was the time at which the coagulation in his bloodstream reached the brain.[52]

It is a crucial feature of Holland's example that the mother continues to thank God for what has happened *after* discovering the natural explanation for why the train stopped. Her calling it a miracle does not, therefore, require her to say that a violation of the natural order has occurred, as Hume might suppose, only that she has witnessed something for which God must be thanked. What makes this a miracle for the mother is that she attributes a

---

52. 'The Miraculous', *American Philosophical Quarterly*, 2, 1965, pp. 43–44. Reprinted in *Miracles*, ed. Richard Swinburne, London, Collier Macmillan, 1989, pp. 53–69.

particular meaning to this event: unlike a non-believer witnessing the same event, she does not see it merely as a coincidence but as an act of divine agency, for which giving thanks is the appropriate response. Here, then, the concept of miracle is placed squarely within the religious tradition: it is itself a religious concept, utilized only by those disposed to see the hand of God at work in the world and to thank him for it. To designate an event as a miracle is therefore to view it as a *religiously significant occurrence*, as an event whose truth or falsehood cannot be settled solely by an analysis of the available evidence, because indeed what will count as evidence cannot be isolated from the perspective of the believer.

Many theologians have adopted a very similar position to Holland's; and they do this not because, as Flew seems to think, they are 'simply changing the subject' in order to avoid Hume's criticisms but because of a variety of other reasons.[53] Some, for example, reject the violation concept as incoherent; some believe that the biblical accounts of miracles should not be taken literally but symbolically; and still others argue that miracles cannot be substantiated scientifically but only from within the context of belief. One distinguished theologian who adopts all three positions is Paul Tillich.

A leading twentieth-century theologian, often contrasted with Karl Barth, Tillich served as an army chaplain during the First World War, a traumatic experience which led to a deep pessimism about the future of European civilization. His practical response was to become a founder-member of Religious Socialism, as a result of which he became profoundly interested in Marxist philosophy. Many teaching posts in leading universities followed (1919–1933), but, as an early critic of Hitler, he was barred from academic life and fled to the United States, teaching at the Union Theological Seminary in New York and at Harvard and Chicago Universities. Although often daunting in style, Tillich's work is marked by a passionate conviction to relate the everyday questions of human existence to the answers given in Christian revelation. This so-called 'method of correlation' often led him to employ concepts drawn from a remarkable intellectual and cultural range: from expressionist art, from psychoanalysis, and from the existentialist ideas of his philosophical heroes, Kierkegaard and Heidegger. His many books brought him world-wide fame, particularly *The Courage To Be* (1952) and *The Dynamics of Faith* (1957). Just before his death, he completed his *Systematic Theology*, begun in 1925, a monumental work now generally regarded as one of the great theological works of our time.

Paul Tillich (1886–1965)

Tillich's theology is notoriously complex, and accordingly what follows can be only a brief summary of his argument.[54] He begins by rejecting out of hand

---

53. See Flew's article 'Miracles' in *The Encyclopedia of Philosophy*, Vol. V, p. 353.
54. See particularly his *Systematic Theology*, Vol. I, London, James Nisbet, 1953, pp. 128–131. I have here relied heavily on my own *Paul Tillich's Philosophy of Art*, Berlin and New York, Walter de Gruyter, 1984.

the 'ordinary definition' of a miracle as a 'happening that contradicts the laws of nature'. This definition is responsible for the development of what Tillich calls 'irrationalist rationalism', in which 'the degree of absurdity in a miracle story becomes the measure of its religious value. The more impossible, the more revelatory!'[55] Accordingly Tillich prefers the New Testament *sêmeion*, meaning 'sign'. As a sign-event a miracle manifests what he calls the 'mystery of being', which is the revelation of the power or 'ground of being', which is God as 'being-itself'. This revelation has further distinguishing features: it possesses a 'shaking and transforming power' and is received in a state of 'ecstasy'. There are therefore no such things as public and 'objective' miracles: miracles are given only to those for whom they are sign-events, to those who receive them ecstatically.

Tillich: miracles as 'signs'

> A genuine miracle is first of all an event which is astonishing, unusual, shaking, without contradicting the rational structure of reality. In the second place, it is an event which points to the mystery of being, expressing its relation to us in a definite way. In the third place, it is an occurrence which is received as a sign-event in an ecstatic experience.[56]

Behind Tillich's rather tortuous terminology lies a fairly straightforward argument. Miracles are essentially expressions of a two-fold revelation, the one side negative, the other positive. The negative side is expressed by our own finitude or, as Tillich has it, by the possibility of non-being that is a constituent feature or ontological fact of the whole of reality. The positive side is expressed in the awareness of that which overcomes the threat of non-being by its own infinite and inexhaustible power to be. This is the revelation of God as the creative ground of all that is, without which nothing could exist. If we translate this in terms of Holland's earlier example, we may say that the mother, by witnessing her son's danger and escape, simultaneously experienced the shock of non-being and the power of being overcoming it. This is why she gave thanks to God. What occurred had become the means by which God was revealed to her as being-itself, or, what amounts to the same thing, as the infinite ground or power of being in everything, resisting and conquering non-being. And it is important to note that this revelation was not brought about by any disruption of natural law but by an event explicable in rational terms. That there are structures of reality that endure amidst change – i.e., laws of nature – is a further revelation of God's *sustaining* creativity, and any violation of them would be, as it were, an act of God against himself. 'If such an interpretation were true, the manifestation of the ground of being would destroy the structure of being; God would be split within himself.'[57] In this sense, then, the fact that things exist bears witness to the participation of everything in God, and to that

The revelation of God as the ground of being

---

55. *Op. cit.*, p. 128.
56. *Ibid.*, p. 130.
57. *Ibid.*, p. 129.

extent anything – a tree, a painting, a person, anything at all – can, by virtue of the fact that it cannot exist without God's existence, be the means of disclosing God's infinite power to be. It need be hardly said that we are now as far from Hume as it is possible to be. The revelation of God occurs through the ordinary and familiar objects of experience – they do not, in other words, have to be 'extraordinary' to accomplish this – and any definition of miracle which departs from this view, such as the violation concept, only serves to make the concept of God incoherent.

Tillich, however, has to resolve another difficulty. If a miraculous event is, in the terms described above, an ordinary event – i.e., one that takes place within the structure of being without in any sense disrupting it – why is it that the believer yet feels compelled to call it a 'miracle', that is, a revelation of God? If no public and objective verification of its being a miracle is or can be forthcoming, how can Tillich avoid the conclusion that miracles are simply relative to the psychological disposition of the believer, and that, for all we know, nothing was revealed at all? How, in other words, can the mother justifiably claim that her son's narrow escape was not a mere coincidence but that here *God* directly intervened to save him?

Tillich insists, we remember, that revelations are not products of the imagination but specific occurrences of a particular type: that they involve the 'ecstatic' response to something that is *given* as a sign-event of 'shaking and astonishing' power. He further insists, however, that faith can, of itself, guarantee that this is the case. How so? Because 'revelation', as we have noted, refers neither to ecstasy nor miracle alone, but to those occurrences in which the two are held 'in strict interdependence' and 'cannot be separated';[58] because, in other words, it is the a priori of ecstasy that it be correlated with the miracle that occasioned it and to which it responds. Such, then, is the constitution of revelatory events that the *fact of faith* in relation to an event constitutes the immediate evidence for the actual manifestation of revelation through the medium of that event. *Faith therefore can certify by its own existence in relation to an event that this event reveals the mystery of being, namely, God as being-itself.*

Faith itself can guarantee miraculous events

The key to this slightly puzzling argument lies in the qualities that a genuine miracle is said to possess. To repeat: it is a characteristic of a revelatory event that it produces a particular kind of *effect*, namely, that it is accompanied by astonishing, unusual, and shaking power. If therefore it is the case that this power can only be actualized by the revelation of the mystery of being – God as being-itself – then it is true to say that the experience of it in relation to a particular event confirms and guarantees that God was revealed there. If something *is* a genuine miracle, it *will* mediate to us the transforming power of the mystery it is expressing. An event is thus deemed miraculous by *what it does*: nothing can be received as a miracle that does not involve the transformation of the existence of the receiver; and an event that does not shake one by its

---

58. *Ibid.*, pp. 123–124.

transforming power is not a miracle. Accordingly the mother, seeing her son narrowly escape death on the railway track, can immediately and unequivocally know that she has witnessed a miracle; and this she knows because of the ecstatic and transforming experience it has produced in her. Because this experience can only be correlated with the revelation of God – because only this revelation can be the cause of this transforming effect – she is therefore right to assert that a revelation has taken place and for which God may be thanked.

Criticisms of Tillich

The most frequent criticism levelled against Tillich at this point is the charge of 'subjectivism': that despite his attempt to produce a notion of miracle that safeguards its status as a real and not imagined revelation, it is the believer's experience of transformation that remains paramount, his subjective conviction that something has happened being the only evidence provided. But this appeal to experience, while it may direct attention to some human psychological state induced by an event, remains totally unsatisfactory as an argument for establishing this event as a revelation, as something that has been *given* and not just received. For it clearly is not the case that a statement is true simply because someone is convinced that it is, however beneficial or transforming that conviction may be. A proposition like 'The mother is certain that B is a miracle' may be true in so far as it tells us something of the psychological state of the mother in relation to B; but the truth of the assertion that the mother was certain in this respect does not entail that she was correct in her judgment about B, that it was in fact a revelation of God as being-itself. Subjective certainty, in other words, is not the measure of historical truth. That I may experience a particular sensation through the medium of an event does not of itself justify the conclusion that there exists something distinct from that sensation as its cause, and which I may thus discount as a fiction.

This does not, of course, exclude the possibility that what the mother saw was an actual revelation, and that this revelation did indeed transform her. What we lack, however, and what Tillich never gives us, is some criterion by which to distinguish this experience from any other. If we are told that there is something absolutely distinctive about a miracle, but that what that is cannot be empirically established, we must suppose that there is therefore something distinctive in the experience that accrues from it – something such that we can say, by inspection of our own transformation, that one event does indeed reveal the mystery of being and another does not. But no such distinction is made by Tillich. No justification is here given for the juxtaposition of a particular experience with the particular reality that is said to cause it. All that Tillich does is to identify the experience as the reception of something that *must be given*. This, however, is to do no more than secure the distinctiveness of the experience by means of a *definition*: it is the a priori of faith that its reception of transforming power be correlated with a revelation. In other words, from the definition that faith is the subjective state of one to whom the transforming power of the mystery of being has been mediated through a miracle, Tillich has here deduced that, say, the mother's affirmation of faith – giving thanks to God – in relation to a particular event *implies* that her son's survival was a miracle. What he fails to see is that this is a tautology – a deduction of a conclusion already implicit within a previous definition – and so quite empty. Thus X is Y because by X we mean Y.[59]

CONCLUSION

In this chapter we have considered two definitions of miracle, which we may for convenience categorize as 'strong' and 'weak'. In the strong definition a miracle is taken to be an event disruptive of the normal course of events and so incapable of explanation within the terms of natural law. In the weak definition, by contrast, a miracle is an event within the natural order but perceived by faith to be of religious significance. For Hume, as we have seen, the strong definition renders the occurrence of such an event, on evidential grounds, extremely improbable, if not impossible. The weak definition, on the other hand, although admittedly avoiding Hume's criticisms, does so by jettisoning the notion of inexplicability in favour of faith's response: a shift in emphasis that makes it objectionable on other grounds, not least because it is now difficult to determine when faith's response to a given event is or is not appropriate.

The strong and the weak views do, however, share the conviction that, whether contravening laws of nature or not, miracles are by definition revelatory events – events through which God manifests himself – and to that extent both operate within the framework of religious conviction. Belief in miracles is not therefore, as Tillich correctly saw, a matter of assessing 'objective' evidence because, in this instance, what one accepts as evidence is in part controlled by one's prior disposition to believe or not. For the believer miracles are religiously significant because they provide an important corroboration of the claim that God does reveal himself within his own creation; but for the non-believer there is no God to be revealed and so miracles are without any religious significance whatsoever, except perhaps in the more restricted sense of providing evidence of psychological aberration. Accordingly miracles cannot be considered *in vacuo*, as evidences sufficient in themselves to establish the truth of God's existence. On this point at least Hume is unassailable: it is not so much that there are no miracles as that 'a miracle can never be proved, so as to be the foundation of a system of religion'.[60]

> **Strong and weak definitions of 'miracle'**

1 Assess Hume's argument that miracles are intrinsically improbable events.

2 Why does Hume regard miracles as improbable but not impossible events?

QUESTIONS ?

---

59. In many respects Tillich's argument, by its emphasis on the subjective disposition of the believer, is strikingly similar to the psychological account of belief given by Carl Gustav Jung. Jung's arguments, however, are open to many of the same objections. See my *Freud and Jung on Religion*, London and New York, Routledge, 1998.
60. *Op. cit.*, p. 127.

QUESTIONS

continued

3 'Since there can be no violations of the laws of nature, the definition of a miracle as a violation is nonsensical.' Evaluate this claim.

4 'The fact that I have been transformed by a miracle is sufficient for me to claim that a miracle has occurred.' Discuss.

5 Can an event be a miracle if it can be naturally explained?

6 Assess Hume's practical argument against miracles. Construct a case which you think avoids his criticisms.

7 Provide a natural explanation of a famous Old or New Testament miracle.

8 Why does Flew believe that there can never be genuine historical evidence for miracles? Do you agree with him?

9 Evaluate Swinburne's argument that legitimate historical evidence can be gathered for a non-repeatable counter-instance of a natural law.

10 After reading this chapter, what is your conclusion about miracles? Do they occur or not?

SOURCES: ARGUMENT FROM MIRACLES

1 HUME: 'OF MIRACLES'[1]

PART ONE

A wise man . . . proportions his belief to the evidence. In such conclusions as are founded on an infallible experience, he expects the event with the last degree of assurance, and regards his past experience as a full *proof* of the future existence of that event. In other words, he proceeds with more caution: He weighs the opposite experiments: He considers which side is supported by the greater number of experiments: to that side he inclines, with doubt and hesitation; and when at last he fixed his judgement, the evidence exceeds not what we properly call *probability*. All probability, then, supposes an opposition of experiments and observations, where the one side is found to overbalance the other, and to produce a degree of evidence, proportioned to the superiority. A hundred instances or experiments on one side, and fifty on another, afford a doubtful expectation of any event; though a hundred uniform experiments, with only one that is contradictory, reasonably begets a pretty strong degree of assurance. In all cases, we must balance the opposite experiments, where they are opposite, and deduct

1. David Hume, *Enquiries Concerning Human Understanding and Concerning the Principles of Morals* (1777), ed. L. A. Selby-Bigge; 3rd edn with text revised and notes by P.H. Nidditch, Oxford, Clarendon Press, 1975, pp. 110–122, 124–125, 126–129, 130–131.

the smaller number from the greater, in order to know the exact force of the superior evidence.

To apply these principles to a particular instance; we may observe, that there is no species of reasoning more common, more useful, and even necessary to human life, than that which is derived from the testimony of men, and the reports of eye-witnesses and spectators. This species of reasoning, perhaps, one may deny to be founded on the relation of cause and effect. I shall not dispute about a word. It will be sufficient to observe that our assurance in any argument of this kind is derived from no other principle than our observation of the veracity of human testimony, and of the usual conformity of facts to the reports of witnesses. It being a general maxim, that no objects have any discoverable connexion together, and that all the inferences, which we can draw from one to another, are founded merely on our experience of their constant and regular conjunction; it is evident, that we ought not to make an exception to this maxim in favour of human testimony, whose connexion with any event seems, in itself, as little necessary as any other. Were not the memory tenacious to a certain degree; had not men commonly an inclination to truth and a principle of probity; were they not sensible to shame, when detected in a falsehood: Were not these, I say, discovered by *experience* to be qualities, inherent in human nature, we should never repose the least confidence in human testimony. A man delirious, or noted for falsehood and villany, has no manner of authority with us.

And as the evidence, derived from witnesses and human testimony, is founded on past experience, so it varies with the experience, and is regarded either as *proof* or a *probability*, according as the conjunction between any particular kind of report and any kind of object has been found to be constant and variable. There are a number of circumstances to be taken into consideration in all judgements of this kind; and the ultimate standard, by which we determine all disputes, that may arise concerning them, is always derived from experience and observation. Where this experience is not entirely uniform on any side, it is attended with an unavoidable contrariety in our judgements, and with the same opposition and mutual destruction of argument as in every other kind of evidence. We frequently hesitate concerning the reports of others. We balance the opposite circumstances, which cause any doubt or uncertainty; and when we discover a superiority on one side, we incline to it; but still with a diminution of assurance, in proportion to the force of its antagonist.

This contrariety of evidence, in the present case, may be derived from several different causes; from the opposition of contrary testimony; from the character or number of the witnesses; from the manner of their delivering their testimony; or from the union of all these circumstances. We entertain a suspicion concerning any matter of fact, when the witnesses contradict each other; when they are but few, or of a doubtful character; when they have an interest in what they affirm; when they deliver their testimony with hesitation, or, on the contrary, with too violent asseverations. There are many other particulars of the same kind, which may diminish or destroy the force of any argument, derived from human testimony.

Suppose, for instance, that the fact, which the testimony endeavours to establish, partakes of the extraordinary and the marvellous; in that case, the evidence, resulting from the testimony, admits of a diminution, greater or less, in proportion as the fact is more or less unusual. The reason why we place any credit in witnesses and historians is not derived from any *connexion*, which we perceive *a priori*, between testimony and reality, but because we are accustomed to find a conformity between them. But when the fact attested is such a one as has seldom fallen under our observation, here is a contest of two opposite experiences; of which the one destroys the other, as far as its force goes, and the superior can only operate on the mind by the force which remains. The very same principle of experience, which gives us a certain degree of assurance in the testimony of witnesses, gives us also, in this case, another degree of assurance against the fact, which they endeavour to establish; from which contradiction there necessarily arises a counterpoize, and mutual destruction of belief and authority.

I should not believe such a story were it told me by Cato, was a proverbial saying in Rome, even during the lifetime of that philosophical patriot. The incredibility of a fact, it was allowed, might invalidate so great an authority.

The Indian prince, who refused to believe the first relations concerning the effects of frost, reasoned justly; and it naturally required very strong testimony to engage his assent to facts, that arose from a state of nature, with which he was unacquainted, and which bore so little analogy to those events, of which he had had constant and uniform experience. Though they were not contrary to his experience, they were not conformable to it.

But in order to encrease the probability against the testimony of witnesses, let us suppose, that the fact, which they affirm, instead of being only marvellous, is really miraculous; and suppose also, that the testimony considered apart and in itself, amounts to an entire proof; in that case, there is proof against proof, of which the strongest must prevail, but still with a diminution of its force, in proportion to that of its antagonist.

A miracle is a violation of the laws of nature; and as a firm and unalterable experience has established these laws, the proof against a miracle, from the very nature of the fact, is as entire as any argument from experience can possibly be imagined. Why is it more than probable, that all men must die; that lead cannot, of itself, remain suspended in the air; that fire consumes wood, and is extinguished by water; unless it be, that these events are found agreeable to the laws of nature, and there is required a violation of these laws, or in other words, a miracle to prevent them? Nothing is esteemed a miracle, if it ever happen in the common course of nature. It is no miracle that a man, seemingly in good health, should die of a sudden: because such a kind of death, though more unusual than any other, has yet been frequently observed to happen. But it is a miracle, that a dead man should come to life; because that has never been observed in any age or country. There must, therefore, be a uniform experience against every miraculous event, otherwise the event would not merit that appellation. And as a uniform experience amounts to a proof, there is here a direct and full *proof*, from the nature of the fact, against the existence of any miracle; nor can such a proof be destroyed, or the miracle rendered credible, but by an opposite proof, which is superior.

[Sometimes an event may not, *in itself*, *seem* to be contrary to the laws of nature, and yet, if it were real, it might, by reason of some circumstances, be denominated a miracle; because, in *fact*, it is contrary to these laws. Thus if a person, claiming a divine authority, should command a sick person to be well, a healthful man to fall down dead, the clouds to pour rain, the winds to blow, in short, should order many natural events, which immediately follow upon his command; these might justly be esteemed miracles, because they are really, in this case, contrary to the laws of nature. For if any suspicion remain, that the event and command concurred by accident, there is no miracle and no transgression of the laws of nature. If this suspicion be removed, there is evidently a miracle, and a transgression of these laws; because nothing can be more contrary to nature than that the voice or command of a man should have such an influence. A miracle may be accurately defined, *a transgression of a law of nature by a particular volition of the Deity, or by the interposition of some invisible agent*. A miracle may either be discoverable by men or not. This alters not its nature and essence. The raising of a house or ship into the air is a visible miracle. The raising of a feather, when the wind wants ever so little of a force requisite for that purpose, is as real a miracle, though not so sensible with regard to us.][2]

The plain consequence is (and it is a general maxim worthy of our attention), 'That no testimony is sufficient to establish a miracle, unless the testimony be of such a kind, that its falsehood would be more miraculous, than the fact, which it endeavours to establish; and even in that case there is a mutual destruction of arguments, and the superior only gives us an assurance suitable to that degree of force, which remains, after deducting the inferior.' When anyone tells me, that he saw a dead man restored to life, I immediately consider with myself, whether it be more probable, that this person should either deceive or be deceived, or that the fact, which he relates, should really have happened. I weigh the one miracle against the other; and according to the superiority, which I discover, I pronounce my decision, and always reject the greater miracle. If the falsehood of his testimony would be more miraculous, than the event which he relates; then, and not till then, can he pretend to command my belief or opinion.

PART II

In the foregoing reasoning we have supposed, that the testimony, upon which a miracle is founded, may possibly amount to an entire proof, and that the falsehood of that testimony would be a real prodigy: But it is easy to show, that we have been a great deal too liberal in our concession, and that there never was a miraculous event established on so full an evidence.

For *first*, there is not to be found, in all history, any miracle attested by a sufficient number of men, of such unquestioned good sense, education, and learning, as to secure us against all delusion in themselves; of such undoubted integrity, as to place them beyond all suspicion of any design to deceive others; of such credit and reputation in the eyes of mankind, as to have a great deal to lose in case of their being detected in any falsehood; and at the same time, attesting facts performed in such a public manner and in so celebrated a part of the world, as to render the detection unavoidable: All which circumstances are requisite to give us a full assurance in the testimony of men.

---

2. In the original text, this paragraph appears as a footnote.

Secondly. We may observe in human nature a principle which, if strictly examined, will be found to diminish extremely the assurance, which we might, from human testimony, have, in any kind of prodigy. The maxim, by which we commonly conduct ourselves in our reasonings, is, that the objects, of which we have no experiences, resemble those, of which we have; that what we have found to be most usual is always most probable; and that where there is an opposition of arguments, we ought to give the preference to such as are founded on the greatest number of past observations. But though, in proceeding by this rule, we readily reject any fact which is unusual and incredible in an ordinary degree; yet in advancing farther, the mind observes not always the same rule; but when anything is affirmed utterly absurd and miraculous, it rather the more readily admits of such a fact, upon account of that very circumstance, which ought to destroy all its authority. The passion of *surprise* and *wonder*, arising from miracles, being an agreeable emotion, gives a sensible tendency towards the belief of those events, from which it is derived. And this goes so far, that even those who cannot enjoy this pleasure immediately, nor can believe those miraculous events, of which they are informed, yet love to partake of the satisfaction at second-hand or by rebound, and place a pride and delight in exciting the admiration of others.

With what greediness are the miraculous accounts of travellers received, their descriptions of sea and land monsters, their relations of wonderful adventures, strange men, and uncouth manners? But if the spirit of religion join itself to the love of wonder, there is an end of common sense: and human testimony, in these circumstances, loses all pretensions to authority. A religionist may be an enthusiast, and imagine he sees what has no reality: he may know his narrative to be false, and yet persevere in it, with the best intentions in the world, for the sake of promoting so holy a cause: or even where this delusion has no place, vanity, excited by so strong a temptation, operates on him more powerfully than on the rest of mankind in any other circumstances; and self-interest with equal force. His auditors may not have, and commonly have not, sufficient judgement to canvass his evidence: what judgement they have, they renounce by principle, in these sublime and mysterious subjects: or if they were ever so willing to employ it, passion and a heated imagination disturb the regularity of its operations. Their credulity increases his impudence: and his impudence overpowers their credulity.

Thirdly. It forms a strong presumption against all supernatural and miraculous relations, that they are observed chiefly to abound among ignorant and barbarous nations; or if a civilized people has ever given admission to any of them, that people will be found to have received them from ignorant and barbarous ancestors, who transmitted them with that inviolable sanction and authority, which always attend received opinions. When we peruse the first histories of all nations, we are apt to imagine ourselves transported into some new world; where the whole frame of nature is disjointed, and every element performs its operations in a different manner, from what it does at present. Battles, revolutions, pestilence, famine and death, are never the effect of those natural causes, which we experience. Prodigies, omens, oracles, judgements, quite obscure the few natural events, that are intermingled with them. But as the former grow thinner every page, in proportion as we advance nearer the enlightened ages, we soon learn, that there is nothing mysterious or supernatural in the case, but that all proceeds from the usual propensity of mankind towards the marvellous, and that, though this inclination may at intervals receive a check from sense and learning, it can never be thoroughly extirpated from human nature.

It is strange, a judicious reader is apt to say, upon the perusal of these wonderful historians, *that such prodigious events never happen in our days*. But it is nothing strange, I hope, that men should lie in all ages. You must surely have seen instances enough of that frailty. You have yourself heard many such marvellous relations started, which, being treated with scorn by all the wise and judicious, have at last been abandoned even by the vulgar. Be assured, that those renowned lies, which have spread and flourished to such a monstrous height, arose from like beginnings; but being sown in a more proper soil, shot up at last into prodigies almost equal to those which they relate . . .

I may add as a *fourth* reason, which diminishes the authority of prodigies, that there is no testimony for any, even those which have not been expressly detected, that is not opposed by an infinite number of witnesses; so that not only the miracle destroys the credit of testimony, but the testimony destroys itself. To make this the better understood, let us consider, that, in matters of religion, whatever is different is contrary; and that it is impossible the religions of ancient Rome, of Turkey, of Siam, and of China should, all of them, be established on any solid foundation. Every miracle, therefore, pretended to have been wrought in any of these religions (and all of them abound in miracles), as its direct scope is to establish the particular system to which it is attributed; so has it the same force, though more indirectly, to overthrow every other system. In destroying a rival system, it likewise destroys the credit of those miracles, on which that system was established; so that all the prodigies of different religions are to be regarded as contrary facts; and the evidences of these prodigies, whether weak or strong. as opposite to each other. According to this method of reasoning, when we believe any miracle of Mahomet or his successors, we have for our warrant the testimony of a few barbarous Arabians: And on the other hand, we are to regard the authority of Titus Livius, Plutarch, Tacitus, and, in short, of all the authors and witnesses, Grecian, Chinese, and Roman Catholic, who have related any miracle in their particular religion; I say, we are to regard their testimony in the same light as if they had mentioned that Mahometan miracle, and had in express terms contradicted it, with the same certainty as they have for the miracle they relate. This argument may appear over subtle and refined; but is not in reality different from the reasoning of a judge, who supposes, that the credit of two witnesses, maintaining a crime against any one, is destroyed by the testimony of two others, who affirm him to have been two hundred leagues distant, at the same instant when the crime is said to have been committed . . .

There surely never was a greater number of miracles ascribed to one person, than those, which were lately said to have been wrought in France upon the tomb of Abbé Paris, the famous Jansenist, with whose sanctity the people were so long deluded. The curing of the sick, giving hearing to the deaf, and sight to the blind, were every where talked of as the usual effects of that holy sepulchre. But what is more extraordinary; many of the miracles were immediately proved upon the spot, before judges of unquestioned integrity, attested by witnesses of credit and distinction, in a learned age, and on the most eminent theatre that is now in the world. Nor is this all: a relation of them was published and dispersed every where; nor were the *Jesuits*, though a learned body, supported by the civil magistrate, and determined enemies to those opinions, in whose favour the miracles were said to have been wrought, ever able distinctly to refute or detect them. Where shall we find such a number of circumstances, agreeing to the corroboration of one fact? And what have we to oppose to such a cloud of witnesses, but the absolute impossibility or miraculous nature of the events, which they relate? And this surely, in the eyes of all reasonable people, will alone be regarded as a sufficient refutation . . .

How many stories of this nature have, in all ages, been detected and exploded in their infancy? How many more have been celebrated for a time, and have afterwards sunk into neglect and oblivion? Where such reports, therefore, fly about, the solution of the phenomenon is obvious; and we judge in conformity to regular experience and observation, when we account for it by the known and natural principles of credulity and delusion. And shall we, rather than have a recourse to so natural a solution, allow of a miraculous violation of the most established laws of nature? . . .

Upon the whole, then, it appears, that no testimony for any kind of miracle has ever amounted to a probability, much less to a proof; and that, even supposing it amounted to a proof it would be opposed by another proof; derived from the very nature of the fact, which it would endeavour to establish. It is experience only, which gives authority to human testimony; and it is the same experience, which assures us of the laws of nature. When, therefore, these two kinds of experience are contrary, we have nothing to do but substract the one from the other, and embrace an opinion, either on one side or the other, with that assurance which arises from the remainder. But according to the principle here explained, this substraction, with regard to all popular religions, amounts to an entire annihilation; and therefore we may establish it as a maxim, that no human testimony can have such force as to prove a miracle, and make it a just foundation for any such system of religion.

I beg the limitations here made may be remarked, when I say, that a miracle can never be proved, so as to be the foundation of a system of religion. For I own, that otherwise, there may possibly be miracles, or violations of the usual course of nature, of such a kind as to admit of proof from human testimony; though, perhaps, it will be impossible to find any such in all the records of history. Thus, suppose, all authors, in all languages, agree, that, from the first of January 1600, there was a total darkness over the whole earth for eight days: suppose that the tradition of this extraordinary event is still strong and lively among the people: that all travellers, who return from foreign countries, bring us accounts of the same tradition, without the least variation or contradiction: it is evident, that our present philosophers, instead of doubting the fact, ought to receive it as certain, and ought to search for the causes whence it may be derived. The decay, corruption, and dissolution of nature, is an event rendered probable by so many analogies, that any phenomenon, which seems to have a tendency towards that catastrophe, comes within the reach of human testimony, if that testimony be very extensive and uniform.

But suppose, that all the historians who treat of England, should agree, that, on the first of January 1600, Queen Elizabeth died; that both before and after her death she was seen by her physicians and the whole court, as is usual with persons of her rank; that her successor was acknowledged and proclaimed by the parliament; and that, after being interred a month, she again appeared, resumed the throne, and governed England for three years: I must confess that I should be surprised at the concurrence of so many odd circumstances, but should not have the least inclination to believe so miraculous an event. I should not doubt of her pretended death, and of those other public circumstances that followed it: I should only assert it to have been pretended, and that it neither was, nor possibly could be real. You would in vain object to me the difficulty, and almost impossibility of deceiving the world in an affair of such consequence; the wisdom and solid judgement of that renowned queen; with the little or no advantage which she could reap from so poor an artifice: All this might astonish me; but I would still reply, that the knavery and folly of men are such common phenomena, that I should rather believe the most extraordinary events to arise from their concurrence, than admit of so signal a violation of the laws of nature.

But should this miracle be ascribed to any new system of religion; men, in all ages, have been so much imposed on by ridiculous stories of that kind, that this very circumstance would be a full proof of a cheat, and sufficient, with all men of sense, not only to make them reject the fact, but even reject it without farther examination. Though the Being to whom the miracle is ascribed, be, in this case, Almighty, it does not, upon that account, become a whit more probable; since it is impossible for us to know the attributes or actions of such a Being, otherwise than from the experience which we have of his productions, in the usual course of nature. This still reduces us to past observation, and obliges us to compare the instances of the violation of truth in the testimony of men, with those of the violation of the laws of nature by miracles, in order to judge which of them is most likely and probable. As the violations of truth are more common in the testimony concerning religious miracles, than in that concerning any other matter of fact; this must diminish very much the authority of the former testimony, and make us form a general resolution, never to lead any attention to it, with whatever specious pretence it may be covered . . .

What we have said of miracles may be applied, without any variation, to prophecies; and indeed, all prophecies are real miracles, and as such only, can be admitted as proofs of any revelation. If it did not exceed the capacity of human nature to foretell future events, it would be absurd to employ any prophecy as an argument for a divine mission or authority from heaven. So that, upon the whole, we may conclude, that the *Christian Religion* not only was at first attended with miracles, but even at this day cannot be believed by any reasonable person without one. Mere reason is insufficient to convince us of its veracity: And whoever is moved by *Faith* to assent to it, is conscious of a continued miracle in his own person, which subverts all the principles of his understanding, and gives him a determination to believe what is most contrary to custom and experience.

2 HAMBOURGER: THE PRINCIPLE OF RELATIVE LIKELIHOOD[3]

. . . The heart of Hume's essay is an argument, given in Part I of the essay, to show that, in principle, it can never be reasonable to believe in a miracle on the basis of the testimony of others. It is this argument that I believe to be fallacious. . . . It rests on the *principle of relative likelihood*.

Suppose that someone or, perhaps, a group of people testify to the truth of a proposition *P* that, considered by itself, is improbable. Then to evaluate the testimony, one must weight the probability that *P* is true against the probability that the informants are lying or mistaken. If it is more likely that *P* is true than that the informants are lying or mistaken, then, on balance, the testimony renders *P* more likely than not, and it may be reasonable for one to believe that *P*. However, if it as likely, or even more likely, that the informants are lying or mistaken than that it is that *P* is true, then, on balance, the testimony does not render *P* more likely true than false, and it would not be reasonable for one to believe that *P*.

Hume's principle of relative likelihood seems quite plausible on its face. Further, the principle seems to capture reasoning that might actually be used to reject an otherwise believable account of a miraculous occurrence. Suppose that I told you that last night I walked across a friend's swimming pool. Then no matter how high a regard you had for my probity, and no matter how plausibly I presented my story, I trust that you would have little doubt that the story was false. And what would your reason be, except that, implausible as it might be that I should be so badly deluded or so brilliantly playing an elaborate charade, it would be still more improbable that I actually walked across a friend's pool?

Nonetheless, I believe the principle of relative likelihood is open to counter-examples and, indeed, that counter-examples to it are very common. Let me present two such examples here.

First, suppose that a lottery is held in which there are one million entrants each with one chance in a million of winning, and suppose that a reliable newspaper, say the *New York Times*, reports that a given entrant, Smith, is the winner. Then the probability that what the *Times* reports is true, that is, the probability that Smith is the winner, considered on our evidence apart from the *Times*' testimony, is one in one million, while the probability that the *Times* should misreport the winner is certainly greater than one in one million. Say, to give them the benefit of the doubt, that it is one in ten thousand. Nevertheless, it clearly would be reasonable in this case to believe that Smith is the winner. One would not respond, 'Look, I grant that it is very unlikely that the *Times* should misreport the winner of a lottery. However, to evaluate the *Times*' testimony we must weight the probability that they misreported the winner against the probability that Smith really was the winner. As it happens, it is even more unlikely that Smith should win than that the *Times* should make a mistake, and, therefore, on balance, it is more probable that Smith lost the lottery, and the *Times* misreported the winner, than that Smith won the lottery.'

3. Robert Hambourger, 'Belief in Miracles and Hume's Essay,' *Noûs*, 14, 1980, pp. 590–592, 599.

Indeed, in this case the improbability of the occurrence the *Times* reports will play no role whatever in our evaluation of its testimony. If we believe that the *Times* misreports a simple piece of information of this sort about one time in ten thousand, then, unless we have special reason to believe they are either more or less likely to make a mistake in reporting this story than in reporting others of the same sort, we will come to hold that the probability that Smith is the winner is about all but one in ten thousand. We will not weigh this probability against any other and then choose that which is greater . . .

What is important in the lottery case is this. We do not evaluate the *Times*' testimony that Smith is the winner by first considering how likely the *Times* is to be right when reporting similar stories and then weighing that fact against another. Once we know how likely the *Times* is to be correct in a given sort of case, then unless we have reason to believe they are more likely to err in this particular case than in others of the sort, we are done. If the *Times* is right all but one time out of ten thousand, then, unless we have reason to think this story is different, once they say Smith is the winner, we should conclude that the probability that he is is all but one ten thousand.

If we apply these considerations, now, to the case of testimony in favor of a miracle, then we can conclude that what we want to know to evaluate such a piece of testimony is the likelihood that a piece of testimony of just that sort is true; that is, roughly, what we want to ask is, how frequently are reports of similar miracles, given in similar situations, true? The answer to this question, however, unfortunately, is not something that can be easily discovered. One who is confident that there are no miracles can be expected to hold that miracle reports of any kind are always false. One who believes in miracles, on the other hand, might well believe that, though miracle reports frequently are the result of delusion or dishonesty, under certain circumstances some are true. Whichever view is correct, though, I doubt that one can hope to evaluate the extent to which a miracle report supports the hypothesis that a miracle has occurred independently of considerations concerning the plausibility that there are miracles of the sort reported. Hume, then, I think, is certainly correct in believing that the plausibility of what someone reports is one of the important considerations affecting whether it is reasonable to believe his report, but I doubt that we can hope, as it were, to factor out the plausibility of what one reports, consider the remaining factors without it, and then, by weighing the two together, arrive at the probability that a report is true. And, thus, I think that Hume's principle of relative likelihood . . . can be of no help to us in evaluating testimony for miracles.

3 COLEMAN: MIRACLES AND LOTTERIES[4]

. . . Hambourger's lottery example does not prove to be the counterexample to Hume's principle of relative likelihood he believed it to be. The principle is to be invoked only when evaluating reports of events that do not conform to

---

4. Dorothy Coleman, 'Hume, Miracles and Lotteries,' *Hume Studies*, 14, 1988, pp. 334–340.

general rules or laws pertaining to events of its type. But Smith's winning the lottery is not an exception to rules governing lotteries: although Smith's chances of winning are only one in a million, the 'laws of lottery' make it certain that some individual will win the lottery and that Smith has a chance equal to any other lottery ticket-holder of winning. Thus, in evaluating the *Times*' report that Smith is a winner, one would not invoke the principle of relative likelihood but would instead, as Hambourger himself points out, ascertain the reliability of the *Times* in making such reports or seek further evidence that would corroborate the *Times*' report.

However, it is possible to construct an example involving lotteries that would require an application of Hume's principle of relative likelihood. We would want this example to be analogous to the problem of evaluating the credibility of a report of an improbable event, improbable not in the sense that the statistical odds are against it, but in the sense that the event reported does not conform to causal regularities pertaining to its type. Moreover, this example should be analogous to our situation with respect to having knowledge of the laws of nature. The secret springs and principles of nature, Hume often wrote, are unknown to us. The farthest we can go towards knowing these secret springs and principles is to form generalizations based on observed uniformities in nature. To set up an analogous situation involving a lottery, we must suppose a type of lottery for which the precise rules of the lottery are unknown to its players. Knowledge of the rules of the lottery would be derived from generalizing from observed uniformities in the way the lottery is conducted. Therefore, we would want there to be several examples of the lottery on which to base these generalizations. In order to meet these conditions, let us suppose there exists a small country, call it Lottovania, that has sponsored a lottery every month for the past hundred years. It is known that the governors of Lottovania print up an indefinitely large number of tickets each month, but distribute only some of them. Each month a winning ticket is announced, but as it happens, in all the one hundred years of the Lottovania lottery, there has never been a citizen with a winning ticket. That is, while there has always been a winning ticket, the winning ticket has always been selected from one of the undistributed tickets. Based on the observation that in every known drawing the winning ticket has been selected from among the undistributed tickets, one would reasonably infer that one of the 'rules of lottery' is that all winning tickets are undistributed tickets.

Now suppose that a newspaper, the *Lottovania Times*, reports that Smith of Lottovania won this month's lottery. Suppose that the *Lottovania Times* has a good track record of accurate reporting, say, erring only once in every 10,000 reports. In reporting that there is a winner of the Lottovania lottery the *Lottovania Times* would be reporting an event which is not consistent or conformable with past experience, and hence, an improbable event (the fact that it is Smith or anybody else is not relevant to its improbability). How do we determine whether the *Lottovania Times*' report should be believed? In this case, the probability that the report is correct or in error is not to be determined by its track record alone, although it may be a relevant factor. We should also want to know if the event it reports is an instance of a regular pattern or type known to occur. While it may be possible that either the governors of Lottovania changed the rules or the rules were not what they were thought to be, the fact that the event the *Times* reports does not conform to past experience provides grounds for adopting a cautious skepticism regarding the report. To determine the credibility of the report, we would want to know if there is additional confirming evidence that the report is true . . . .

Now let us consider how the principle of relative likelihood can be applied to the evaluation of reports of miracles. Hambourger maintains that it may be reasonable to infer a miracle actually has occurred provided an event is (1) sufficiently well testified to warrant the belief that the event has occurred, (2) without any plausible natural explanation and (3) the type of event which would be appropriate for God to cause. While not advancing an argument supporting the adequacy of these conditions, he provides hypothetical examples that he believes intuitively establish this case, one of which is the following:

> If all the records and accounts from the beginning of the last century agreed that on January 1, 1800, in all parts of the earth, the clouds of each region began to spell out the Old Testament with perfect precision and in the language of the region, and that they continued to do so for several weeks until the New Testament was completed, then I think it would be hard to escape the conclusion that a miracle had occurred. Thus I believe that, at least in principle, testimony could give one adequate reason to believe in a miracle.[5]

To simplify matters, let us grant straight off that the event Hambourger describes could have occurred and that the amount of testimony said to be available would provide sufficient grounds for believing the event did occur. Doing so would be consistent with Hume's own views. . . . The question remains whether it would be reasonable to believe that the event, admittedly anomalous, is a miracle. This is a question about the nature or cause of the event rather than about the occurrence of the event. We are asking whether it is more reasonable to believe that such an event has a supernatural, as opposed to natural cause. Criteria (1) and (3) together are not sufficient justification for believing an event is miraculous because even the most ordinary natural events can meet these conditions. The two criteria thus do not by themselves provide a means for rationally discriminating between the natural and the miraculous. This leaves criterion (2) for identifying events as miraculous. But an event that has no ready natural explanation is not necessarily an event that has no natural cause. To be a miracle an event must be inexplicable not in terms of what *appears* to us to be laws of nature but in terms of what laws of nature actually are. On what grounds would it be reasonable to infer that this condition is met in Hambourger's hypothetical example?

Other hypotheses would be possible. The event could be evidence that the laws of nature are not what we thought them to be. Perhaps someone or some group of people, not God, without anyone else's knowledge, could have learned the true causes of cloud formation and used this knowledge to produce some amazing

---

5. *Op. cit.*, p. 603.

effect, like spelling out the Old and New Testaments. Or the event could be of a different nature than it is thought to be. Perhaps the clouds were not really clouds but laser images produced by creatures from outer-space. Perhaps these space-creatures were carrying out a religious mission, or perhaps they were simply toying with the gullibility of a less intellectually advanced species. Applying Hume's principle of relative likelihood, one must ask if it is always more likely, i.e., conformable to experience, that those claiming the event to be a miracle are mistaken rather than that the event is a genuine violation of a law of nature. Counter-instances of what are taken to be natural laws are not by themselves evidence establishing that no natural law could possibly explain them: at most they provide grounds for revising our formulations of natural laws or seeking an improved understanding of the nature of the phenomena in question. At the very least they provide grounds for suspending judgments about the nature of their cause until more evidence is available. On the other hand, past experience shows that what are at one time considered violations of natural laws are frequently found at some later time not to be so. Proportioning belief to evidence, therefore, it is more reasonable to believe that the claim that an event is a miracle is mistaken than it is that the event is a violation of natural law.

It might be objected that insisting that the weight of evidence will *always* be against inferring that laws have been violated through divine agency is merely a dogmatic rejection of supernatural causation: if one assumes that God exists, that it is consistent with divine nature to intervene with nature, and that a certain event, having no ready natural explanation, is the type of event that is appropriate for God to cause, then it would be reasonable to hypothesize a divine origin for the event. The difficulty with this argument is that it justifies too much. First, unless one assumes that all anomalous events appropriate for God to cause are so caused, one cannot rationally discriminate between those that are and those that are not. Second, one can no more reasonably assume that an anomalous event is caused by God given a set of assumptions about the existence and nature of God any more than one can say the event is caused by unknown alien life-forms, gremlins, demons, fairies or any other fanciful creature given a similar set of assumptions about their existence and imagined pattern of behavior. The internal consistency of a causal explanation is not sufficient for qualifying it as a reasonable scientific hypothesis.

4 FLEW: MIRACLES AND REPEATABILITY[6]

. . . In the *History* of Herodotus, we read that some Phoenician sailors at the time of Pharaoh Necho II (about 600 B.C.) claimed to have circumnavigated the continent of Africa. They sailed south from the Red Sea and arrived at the Mediterranean coast of Egypt nearly three years later. The interesting thing for us is their report that during the voyage the position of the sun shifted from the south to the north. Herodotus, recording that they said this, states that he himself does

6. Antony Flew, 'Parapsychology Revisted: Laws, Miracles, and Repeatability', *The Humanist*, 36, May–June, 1976, pp. 28–30.

not believe what they said. He had two good reasons for disbelief: first, he knew that Phoenician, and not only Phoenician, sailors are apt to tell tall stories; and second, he believed that he knew that what the sailors reported was impossible. Herodotus therefore had good reason to dismiss this story, and did in fact, dismiss it.

But for us, of course, what was for Herodotus an excellent reason for incredulity is the decisive ground for believing that the Phoenicians did in fact circumnavigate Africa at this time. They could not have reported the changing relative position of the sun correctly unless they had actually made the voyage that they said they had made.

We can learn from all this something about historical method. What a historian tries to do is to reconstruct what actually happened in the past by interpreting the present detritus of the past as historical evidence. He interprets this detritus – documents, ruins, and so on – as historical evidence only and precisely by appealing to what he knows or thinks he knows about how things in fact happen in the world, what is in fact possible or impossible. Thus, Herodotus, in trying to interpret the evidence of the Phoenicians, rightly appealed to what he knew, or rather to what he thought he knew, about astronomy and geography. We, following exactly the same fundamental principles of historical reconstruction, but having the advantage over him of knowing more about astronomy and geography, reach different conclusions by fundamentally the same methods.

Now it seems to me, as it seemed to Hume two centuries ago, that there is one very important general consequence to be drawn from this understanding of the nature of historical inquiry. It is that, whether or not anything did in fact happen in the past inconsistent with what we at present believe to be a law of nature, one cannot possibly know on historical evidence that it did so happen. The reason is simply that, if something miraculous is to have occurred, the miracle is precisely something that in the light of present knowledge is thought to be impossible; it is precisely an event overriding, or an account inconsistent with, what we presently believe to be a law of nature. To the extent that we have good reasons for thinking that there are laws of nature, that there are nomological regularities or necessities in the world that rule out such-and-such ongoings, as historians we have to say that one thing we cannot know on historical grounds is that a miracle occurred. After all, what we are doing as historians is applying all we know, or think we know, to the interpretation of the evidence. Suddenly to say that in the past things were different and that miracles occurred is to abandon quite arbitrarily fundamental principles of historical inquiry. On what principles, then, could we say when a miracle had occurred and when not?

Of course, it may well happen that through some independent advances in the natural sciences our successors as historians may have to take another look at the historical evidence and conclude that what their predecessors refused to believe, because on the evidence available to them it would have had to be rated as miraculous, was entirely possible in the light of what they will then know. This is still not discovering that a genuine miracle did occur, or probably did occur. Their reason for saying that it may in fact have occurred is that they will then know, or think they know, that had it occurred it would not in fact have been miraculous.

Consider there the instructive case of the miracles alleged to have been performed by the Roman emperor Vespasian. Eighteenth-century skeptics – including Hume, the greatest of them – maintained that these stories were altogether incredible, notwithstanding that the evidence for their truth was far and away better than the evidence for any of the miracles of the New Testament. Suppose that we actually look up the accounts in Suetonius and Tacitus – something that almost no one seems ever to have done in this connection. According to Suetonius, when the Emperor was in Egypt 'two labourers, one blind and the other lame, approached him, begging to be healed; apparently the god Serapis had promised them in a dream that if Vespasian would consent to spit in the blind man's eye and touch the lame man's leg with his heel, both would be cured.' According to the longer account in Tacitus (in which the lame man had a withered hand), Vespasian 'asked the doctors for an opinion whether blindness and atrophy of this sort were curable by human means. The doctors were eloquent about the various possibilities: the blind man's vision was not completely destroyed, and if certain impediments were removed his sight would return; the other man's limb had been dislocated, but could be put right by correct treatment . . . . Anyway, if a cure were effected, the credit would go to the ruler; if it failed, the poor wretches would have to bear the ridicule.'

Vespasian, who was a shrewd old soldier, did what was asked. The men were cured. In the light of what we now know, or think we know, about psychosomatic possibilities, we have to say, not that two genuine miracles occurred and that we now know this on historical grounds, but that what Hume had dismissed in the *Inquiry Concerning Human Understanding* as something that would have been miraculous and therefore did not occur in fact did occur but was not miraculous . . .

What, we now ask, justifies us in asserting logically contingent nomological universal propositions, and what justifies us in ruling out in our historical work evidence for what would have been miraculous if it were to have occurred? It is, surely, only the fact that those universal propositions upon which we thus rely have been and still can be tested, given certain conditions, anywhere and at any time, or else that they are logical consequences of others of which this can be said. The reason for saying that such and such a thing is in fact impossible is that either we or other people have tested the nomological proposition that rules out this occurrence as being impossible; that we can too; and that its truth guarantees that certain things will necessarily and repeatably happen, given the appropriate and stated preconditions.

Compare the nomological universal proposition in this respect with the singular past-tense proposition, saying that such and such a thing did happen in the past. The only possibility of directly testing the truth of the latter was at the time that it occurred. For us, the only way of discovering whether what is said to have occurred did in fact occur is to reconstruct somehow the story, inferring what actually happened on the basis of what evidence is still available today. The proposition on the basis of which we rule out the ostensible miracle is one on which we have far better reason for relying than we can possibly have for relying on the singular past-tense proposition that affirms that something occurred that would have been miraculous if it did occur.

Someone may well maintain that the so-called miracle genuinely was an overriding of what elsewhere is a natural necessity, that the miracle did in fact actually happen. To this, we must reply that maybe it did happen. But what we have to insist is that we certainly cannot now know, on historical evidence, that it did in fact happen.

5 SWINBURNE: EVIDENCE OF MIRACLES[7]

I need to spell out what I understand by a miracle and what would be evidence that an event was a miracle in my sense . . . I understand by a miracle a violation of the laws of nature, that is, a non-repeatable exception to the operation of these laws, brought about by God. Laws of nature have the form of universal statements 'all *A*s are *B*', and state how bodies behave of physical necessity. Thus Kepler's three laws of planetary motion state how the planets move. The first law states that all planets move in ellipses with the sun at one focus. If this purported law is to be a law of nature, planets must in general move as it states. What however is to be said about an isolated exception to a purported law of nature? Suppose that one day Mars moves out of its elliptical path for a brief period and then returns to the path. There are two possibilities. This wandering of Mars may occur because of some current condition of the Universe (e.g. the proximity of Jupiter drawing Mars out of its elliptical path), such that if that condition were to be repeated the event would happen again. In this case the phenomenon is an entirely regular phenomenon. The trouble is that what might have appeared originally to be a basic law of nature proves now not to be one. It proves to be a consequence of a more fundamental law that the original purported law normally holds, but that under circumstances describable in general terms (e.g. 'when planets are close to each other') there are exceptions to it. Such repeatable exceptions to purported laws merely show that the purported laws are not basic laws of nature. The other possibility is that the exception to the law was not caused by some current condition, in such a way that if the condition were to recur the event would happen again. In this case we have a non-repeatable exception to a law of nature. But how are we to describe this event further? There are two possible moves. We may say that if there occurs an exception to a purported law of nature, the purported law can be no law. If the purported law says 'all *A*s are *B*' and there is an *A* which is not *B*, then 'all *A*s are *B*' is no law. The trouble with saying that is that the purported law may be a very good device for giving accurate predictions in our field of study; it may be by far the best general formula for describing what happens in the field which there is. (I understand by a general formula a formula which describes what happens in all circumstances of a certain kind, but does not mention by name particular individuals, times, or places.) To deny that the purported law is a law, when there is no more accurate general formula, just because there is an isolated exception to its operation, is to ignore its enormous ability to predict what happens in the field.

---

7. Richard Swinburne, *Faith and Reason*, Oxford, Clarendon Press, 1981, pp. 185–189.

For this reason it seems not unnatural to say that the purported law is no less a law for there being a non-repeatable exception to it; and then to describe the exception as a 'violation' of the law. At any rate this is a coherent way of talking, and I think that it is what those who use such expressions as 'violation' of a law of nature are getting at. In this case we must amend our understanding of what is a law of nature. To say that a generalization 'all *As* are *B*' is a universal law of nature is to say that being *A* physically necessitates being *B*, and so that any *A* will be *B* – apart from violations.

But how do we know that some event such as the wandering of Mars from its elliptical path is a non-repeatable rather than a repeatable exception to a purported law of nature? We have grounds for believing that the exception is non-repeatable in so far as any attempt to amend the purported law of nature so that it predicted the wandering of Mars as well as all the other observed positions of Mars, would make it so complicated and *ad hoc* that we would have no grounds for trusting its future predictions. It is no good for example amending the law so that it reads: 'all planets move in ellipses with the Sun at one focus, except in years when there is a competition for the World Chess Championship between two players both of whose surnames begin with *K*.' Why not? Because this proposed law mentions properties which have no other place in physics (no other physical law invokes this sort of property) and it mentions them in an *ad hoc* way (that is, the proposed new law has the form 'so-and-so holds except under such-and-such circumstances', when the only reason for adding the exceptive clause is that otherwise the law would be incompatible with observations; the clause does not follow naturally from the theory). What we need if we are to have a more adequate law is a general formula, of which it is an entirely natural consequence that the exception to the original law occurs when it does.

In these ways we could have grounds for believing that an exception to a purported law was non-repeatable and so a violation of a natural law. Claims of this sort are of course corrigible – we could be wrong; what seemed inexplicable by natural causes might be explicable after all. But then we could be wrong about most things, including claims of the opposite kind. When I drop a piece of chalk and it falls to the ground, every one supposes that here is an event perfectly explicable by natural laws. But we could be wrong. Maybe the laws of nature are much more complicated than we suppose, and Newton's and Einstein's laws are mere approximations to the true laws of mechanics. Maybe the true laws of mechanics predict that almost always when released from the hand, chalk will fall to the ground, but not today because of a slightly abnormal distribution of distant galaxies. However although the true laws of nature predict that the chalk will rise, in fact it falls. Here is a stark violation of natural laws, but one which no one detects because of their ignorance of natural laws. 'You could be wrong' is a knife which cuts both ways. What seem to be perfectly explicable events might prove, when we come to know the laws of nature much better, to be violations. But of course this is not very likely. The reasonable man goes by the available evidence here, and also in the converse case. He supposes that what is, on all the evidence, a violation of natural laws really is one. There is good reason to suppose that events such as the following if they occurred would be violations of laws of nature: levitation, that is, a man rising in the air against gravity without the operation of magnetism or any other known physical force; resurrection from the dead of a man whose heart has not been beating for twenty-four hours and who counts as dead by other currently used criteria; water turning into wine without the assistance of chemical apparatus or catalysts; a man growing a new arm from the stump of an old one.

Since the occurrence of a violation of natural laws cannot be explained in the normal way, either it has no explanation or it is to be explained in a different way. The obvious explanation exists if there is a God who is responsible for the whole order of nature, including its conformity to natural laws, and who therefore can on occasion suspend the normal operation of natural laws and bring about or allow some one else to bring about events, not via this normal route. We should suppose that events have explanations if suggested explanations are at all plausible. If there is quite a bit of evidence that there is a God responsible for the natural order, then any violations are plausibly attributed to his agency and so plausibly recognized as miracles – at least so long as those violations are not ruled out by such evidence as we may have from other sources about God's character.[8] God's permitting a law of nature to be violated is clearly necessary for this to occur if he is the author of Nature; and in the absence of evidence that any other agent had a hand in the miracle, it ought to be attributed to God's sole agency. But if there is evidence, say, that it happens after a command (as opposed to a request to God) for it to happen issued by another agent, then the miracle is to be attributed to a joint agency.

I have not considered here the kind of historical evidence needed to prove the occurrence of an event which if it occurred would be a violation, but clearly it will be of the same kind as the evidence for any other historical event. There is the evidence of one's own senses, the testimony of others (oral and written) and the evidence of traces (effects left by events, such as footprints, fingerprints, cigarette ash, etc.). I see no reason in principle why there should not be evidence of this kind to show the occurrence of a levitation or a resurrection from the dead.

6 DIAMOND: MIRACLES AND SCIENTIFIC AUTONOMY[9]

I claim that accepting the possibility of a class of supernatural exceptions to scientific laws would involve the sacrifice of scientific autonomy. I shall deploy this argument by sketching a farfetched scenario.

Imagine that the government of the United States has scheduled thermonuclear tests on an island in the Pacific. A well-known pacifist, who is a priest, determines to stop it. He fails to influence the government's policy and the tests proceed. He then prays in the hope that he can at least keep the explosions from polluting the atmosphere.

---

8. I argue in *The Coherence of Theism* that necessarily an omnipotent, omniscient and perfectly free God must be perfectly good.
9. Malcolm Diamond, *Contemporary Philosophy and Religious Thought*, New York and London, McGraw-Hill, 1974, pp. 64–67.

The military leaders give the signal to fire a bomb. The exploding mechanisms are properly triggered, but there is no gigantic mushroom cloud. They rush to check the machinery. To their astonishment they find that all the pointer readings and other available data indicate that the 1,000-megaton bomb being tested had actually exploded. It seemed to have gone off, in the sense of energy exchanges, yet there had been no visible signs of an explosion, nor had any damage been done to the island. They try to fire the bomb again, but it is futile. It is dead, and the money invested in it has gone down the drain. Baffled, the military leaders order another 1,000-megaton bomb to be exploded. It is with the same astonishing result.

At this point, the military leaders are dissatisfied with the scientists on hand who cannot handle these amazing occurrences. They call for a full-scale investigation. One of the leading physicists in the country undertakes the job of research and assembles a crack team.

Let's assume that these scientists are prepared to allow for the possibility of supernatural exceptions to the scientific status quo. They investigate the possibility that the extraordinary patterns displayed by the thermonuclear weapons are attributable to the prayers of the priest. We are now in a position to see why, allowing for the possibility of supernatural explanations, naturally observable occurrences are something that would, in effect, drive working scientists to opt right out of the scientific enterprise. In a situation of this kind, these scientists would not be able to investigate the effectiveness of the priest's prayers because, as scientists, they would not be able to determine whether the exception was supernatural. Therefore, the head of the investigating team would have to phone the Pope to ask him to send one of *his* investigating teams (the Vatican has trained personnel to investigate claims of the miraculous) to the area. The conversation might run something like this:

> *Scientist*: Your Holiness, this is Professor Grendl, and I have a problem. Thermonuclear tests are taking place in the South Pacific under the auspices of my government, and all sorts of incredible things are happening. Gigantic discharges of energy are taking place with no observable effects on the environment. My government has called me in to investigate it.
> *The Pope*: Fine, from what I hear you're just the man to do it. Go ahead!
> *Scientist*: Well, Your Holiness, it isn't that simple. These investigations cost a fortune, and our present administration is economy-minded. So we don't want to spend all that money investigating these extraordinary occurrences unless we're sure that these exceptions are ours. I mean unless we're sure that they're *natural* exceptions. Now, you must have heard about the priest who is conducting a prayer vigil in this area. Some people say that his prayers are being answered miraculously and that's why the bombs are discharging without damaging anything and without polluting the atmosphere. Could you send one of your best teams out here to check this out?

By this time, the point should be clear. Scientists cannot function as scientists if they have to appeal to leading figures in some other enterprise to tell them what to do. Scientists, as scientists, must operate with autonomy, that is, they must set their own rules and referee their own games. Even though no logical prohibition prevents scientists from accepting the supernatural interpretation of an extraordinary occurrence, on the functional level, it involves a sellout of science.

The discussion of autonomy has helped to determine the price of accepting the class of supernaturally caused exceptions to supernatural laws, but it does not settle the question of whether the price is worth paying. Supernaturalists argue that in undercutting the work of scientists we interfere with a merely human enterprise, whereas the naturalistic interpretation cuts us off from the possibility of responding to the grace of God.

The answer that I offer on behalf of the naturalistic interpretation is practical. It recommends reliance on scientific explanations without pretending to be a conclusive refutation of supernaturalism.

In discussing the interpretation of miraculous occurrences, we are dealing with naturally observable events like the sudden healing of a totally withered leg. We are not dealing with such elusive phenomena as intelligence and freedom. Any educated person knows that the record of scientists in handling observable occurrences is vastly superior to that of magicians, shamans, witch doctors, faith healers, and other types who have claimed to both understand and control nature. It is, therefore, unreasonable to propose a policy, like the sacrifice of autonomy, which would interfere with the work of scientists at the operative level.

To summarize: It is reasonable to reject the supernatural interpretations of 'miraculous' occurrences because (1) the record shows that, in the long run, scientists come up with explanations of events that seem – even for long periods of time – to defy natural explanation, (2) to accept supernatural interpretations of events that can be naturally observed would impede the work of scientists at the operative level by forcing them to sacrifice their autonomy, and (3) by contrast, naturalistic interpretations of naturally observable events do not require a sacrifice of any concepts that are important and integral to religion.

The natural/supernatural contrast should not be equated with a contrast between science and religion. Leading religious thinkers of the past two centuries have fought the tendency to identify Christian faith with supernaturalist views that claim that the activity of God must be invoked to explain extraordinary observable occurrences. They have insisted that we can understand God's relation to men on the model of freedom. I do not wish to explore the complexities of philosophical discussions of freedom and determinism. For my purposes I need only note that no philosopher who defends the notion of freedom would claim that a free decision could enable a human being to jump out of a twelfth-story window and to fly up instead of falling down. So too, religious thinkers who reject the traditional view of miracles insist that God's relation to mankind must be understood within the fabric of scientific understanding. This position does not force religion to demand a sacrifice of the scientists' autonomy or of any other significant operative principles of science.

KEY TEXTS

Basinger, David and Randall. *Philosophy and Miracle*, Lewiston, The Edwin Mellen Press, 1986.

Broad, C. D. 'Hume's Theory of the Credibility of Miracles', *Proceedings of the Aristotelian Society*, 17, 1916–1917, pp. 77–94.

Brown, Colin. *Miracles and the Critical Mind*, Grand Rapids, Mich., Eerdmans, 1983.

Hume, David. *Enquiries Concerning Human Understanding and Concerning the Principles of Morals*, ed. L. A. Selby-Bigge; 3rd edn with text revised and notes by P. H. Nidditch, Oxford, Clarendon Press, 1975.

Lewis, C. S. *Miracles*, London, Collins, 1947; edition 1960.

Swinburne, Richard (ed.). *The Concept of Miracle*, London, Macmillan, 1970.

—— *Miracles*, London, Collier Macmillan, 1989.

BIBLIOGRAPHY

Ahern, Dennis M. 'Hume on the Evidential Impossibility of Miracles', in *Studies in Epistemology*, ed. Nicholas Rescher, Oxford, Basil Blackwell, 1975, pp. 1–32.

—— 'Miracles and Physical Impossibility', *Canadian Journal of Philosophy*, 7(1), 1977, pp. 71–79.

Basinger, David and Randall. *Philosophy and Miracle*, Lewiston, The Edwin Mellen Press, 1986.

Boden, Margaret. 'Miracles and Scientific Explanation', *Ratio*, 11, 1969, pp. 137–141.

Broad, C. D. 'Hume's Theory of the Credibility of Miracles', *Proceedings of the Aristotelian Society*, 17, 1916–1917, pp. 77–94.

Brown, Colin. *Miracles and the Critical Mind*, Grand Rapids, Mich., Eerdmans, 1983.

Burns, R. M. *The Great Debate on Miracles: From Granville to David Hume*, Lewisburg, Bucknell University Press, 1981.

Butler, Joseph. *The Analogy of Religion*, London, 1736; New York, Frederick Ungar, 1961.

Coleman, Dorothy. 'Hume, Miracles and Lotteries', *Hume Studies*, 14, 1988, pp. 328–346.

Colwell, Gary. 'On Defining Away Miracles', *Philosophy*, 57, 1982, pp. 327–336.

Diamond, Malcolm. *Contemporary Philosophy and Religious Thought*, New York and London, McGraw-Hill, 1974, pp. 57–71.

Flew, Antony. *David Hume: Philosopher of Moral Science*, Oxford, Basil Blackwell, 1986.

—— *God and Philosophy*, London, Hutchinson, 1966.

—— 'Hume's Check', *Philosophical Quarterly*, 9(34), 1959, pp. 1–18.

—— *Hume's Philosophy of Belief*, London, Routledge & Kegan Paul, 1961.

—— 'Miracles', *The Encyclopedia of Philosophy*, New York, Macmillan, 1967, Vol. V, pp. 346–353.

—— 'Parapsychology Revisited: Laws, Miracles, and Repeatability', *The Humanist*, 36, May–June, 1976, pp. 28–30.

Fogelin, Robert J. 'What Hume Actually said about Miracles', *Hume Studies*, 16(1), 1990, pp. 81–86.

Gaskin, J. C. A. 'David Hume and the Eighteenth Century Interest in Miracles', *Hermathena*, 99, 1964, pp. 80–92.

—— 'Hume on Religion', in *The Cambridge Companion to Hume*, ed. David Fate Norton, Cambridge, Cambridge University Press, 1993, pp. 313–344.

—— *Hume's Philosophy of Religion*, London, Macmillan, 1968.

Hambourger, Robert. 'Belief in Miracles and Hume's Essay', *Noûs*, 14, 1980, pp. 587–604.

Hewitt, Harold (ed.). *Problems in the Philosophy of Religion*, London, Macmillan, 1991.

Hick, John. *God and the Universe of Faiths*, London, Macmillan, 1973.

—— *An Interpretation of Religion*, London, Macmillan, 1989.

Holland, R. F. 'The Miraculous', *American Philosophical Quarterly*, 2, 1965, pp. 43–51. Reprinted in *Miracles*, ed. Richard Swinburne, London, Collier Macmillan, 1989, pp. 53–69.

Hume, David. *Dialogues Concerning Natural Religion*, edited with an Introduction by Norman Kemp Smith, 2nd edn, London and Edinburgh, Thomas Nelson & Sons, 1947.

—— *Enquiries Concerning Human Understanding and Concerning the Principles of Morals*, ed. L. A. Selby-Bigge; 3rd edn with text revised and notes by P. H. Nidditch, Oxford, Clarendon Press, 1975.

—— *Of Miracles*, edited, with an Introduction, by Antony Flew, La Salle, Ill., Open Court, 1985.

Jantzen, Grace. 'Hume on Miracles, History, and Politics', *Christian Scholars' Review*, 8, 1979, pp. 318–325.

Kellenberger, J. 'Miracles', *International Journal for Philosophy of Religion*, 10, 1979, pp. 145–162.

Keller, Ernst and Marie-Louise. *Miracles in Dispute*, London, SCM Press, 1969.

Langtry, Bruce. 'Hume on Miracles and Contrary Religion', *Sophia*, 22, 1983, pp. 3–14.

—— 'Miracles and Rival Systems of Religion', *Sophia*, 24, 1985, pp. 21–31.

Lewis, C. S. *Miracles*, London, Collins, 1947; London, Collins, Fount Paperbacks, 1990.

McKinnon, Alastair. '"Miracle" and "Paradox"', *American Philosophical Quarterly*, 4, 1967, pp. 308–314. Reprinted in *Miracles*, ed. Richard Swinburne, London, Collier Macmillan, 1989, pp. 53–69.

Mill, J. S. *System of Logic*, 2 vols, London, Longmans, Green, Reader & Dyer, 1843.

Palmer, Michael. *Freud and Jung on Religion*, London and New York, Routledge, 1998.

—— *Paul Tillich's Philosophy of Art*, Berlin and New York, Walter de Gruyter, 1984.

Robinson, Guy. 'Miracles', *Ratio*, 9, 1967, pp. 155–166.

Smart, Ninian. *Philosophers and Religious Truth*, London, SCM Press, 1964.

Swinburne, Richard (ed.). *The Concept of Miracle*, London, Macmillan, 1970.

—— *Miracles*, London, Collier Macmillan, 1989.

Tan Tei Wei. 'Recent Discussions on Miracles', *Sophia*, 11, 1972, pp. 21–28.

Tennant, F. R. *Miracles and its Philosophical Presuppositions*, Cambridge, Cambridge University Press, 1925.

Tillich, Paul. *Systematic Theology*, Vol. 1, London, James Nisbet, 1953.
Wallace, R. C. 'Hume, Flew, and the Miraculous', *Philosophical Quarterly*, July 1970, pp. 230–243.
Ward, Keith. 'Miracles and Testimony', *Religious Studies*, 21, 1985, pp. 131–145.
Williams, T. C. *The Idea of the Miraculous*, London, Macmillan, 1990.

INTRODUCTION: OBJECTIVE AND RELATIVE MORAL VALUES

The moral argument takes its place among the a posteriori arguments for God's existence and to that extent is based on a universally acknowledged experience. This is the experience of *human moral activity*: that men and women are frequently required to make moral decisions, and that these decisions, so it is alleged, could not justifiably be made without the presupposition of divine reality, that in some sense God is the source of moral obligation. We have met this argument briefly before. Both Frederick Temple and A. E. Taylor claimed that Darwin's theory of natural selection could not account for man's moral capacity – it having no survival benefit – and that our recognition that there is an *objective moral law* of universal validity – that everyone admits, say, that 'Murder is wrong' – carries with it the implication, to use Taylor's words, of an 'intelligence which recognizes and upholds it'.[1]

The Karamazov defence

    This argument often appears in tandem with another, rather different in type. This is the view, admittedly not common among philosophers but a favourite among popular apologists for religion, which holds that any divorce between moral values and theism will lead to a kind of moral degeneration; that religion, in other words, functions as a necessary check upon the undesirable impulses that human beings often succumb to, and that without it civilized behaviour would be impossible. This line of argument is sometimes called the 'Karamazov defence', taking its cue from Dostoevsky's figure of Ivan Karamazov, who remarked that 'if there is no God, then everything is permitted'. Interestingly enough, an almost identical claim is made by Friedrich Nietzsche, admittedly for very different reasons, in his *On the Genealogy of Morals* (1887).[2] Although he vehemently attacks religion for being motivatated by the expedient fear of divine wrath and for requiring of its adherents a slave-like readiness to obey without thinking, Nietzsche concedes that its 'God hypothesis' provides the most powerful antidote to what he himself was seeking to establish – i.e., moral nihilism, that there are no moral values.

    The moral argument for God proceeds, then, on the initial presupposition that there is an *objective* moral law – i.e., that our moral obligation to do what we ought to do is not based on our individual and *subjective* estimate of what is right but on the fact that there exists, somehow independently of us, absolute moral rules which it is our duty to obey, whether we like it or not. Advocates of the argument willingly concede that this is an assumption on their part, and so one which must first be defended if their argument is to get under way. Not least it must be defended against the popular alternative, philosophically known

1. *Does God Exist?*, New York, Macmillan, 1945, p. 106.
2. *Basic Writings of Nietzsche*, translated and edited, with commentaries, by Walter Kaufmann, New York, Random House, The Modern Library, 1968, p. 586.

as *ethical relativism.*

Ethical relativism comes in various guises. To name a few: there is *cultural* relativism, which states that the ethical standards adopted will vary according to the culture or society of the individual concerned; *class* relativism, with its roots in Marxist theory, which maintains that moral obligations are relative to an individual's economic class; and *historical* relativism, which makes moral criteria relative to the particular historical period of the person concerned. All these forms of ethical relativism coordinate in the view that, given the undisputed fact that people clearly do adopt divergent ethical standards, the claim that there are objective moral rules, binding on individuals *irrespective* of their culture, class or historical time, must be incorrect. If ethical relativism is true, then it would appear that the moral argument is based on an initial assumption which is demonstrably false.

Forms of ethical relativism

Defenders of the moral argument, it has to be said, rarely lose sleep over this alternative, however initially attractive, and that for three main reasons:

1. The first is that very often what appears as a difference in ethical standards is not so in fact but a difference in how the *same* standard is applied in the context of other *beliefs*. So the principle 'Honour thy father and mother' may be the adopted standard of two societies but yet produce very different results: in Japan, a respect bordering on worship, and in Eskimo culture, the practice of parental euthanasia – the latter alternative following from the belief that parents should enter the after-life in as healthy a state as possible. These, then, are societal differences masking common principles. And these principles, as some anthropologists have indicated, may be widely adhered to: group loyalty, courage and care for the young being generally praised, and deceit, ingratitude and theft being invariably condemned.

2. Even if there are genuinely divergent moral beliefs, this does not imply that there are no objective ethical standards. The fact that what X thinks is right is not what Y thinks is right does not mean that nothing is right, any more than does the suggestion that because, once upon a time, people believed the world to be flat, whereas we now believe it to be round, it therefore has no shape at all. All that can be inferred is that, if one person believes in one ultimate standard, and another believes in another standard, one (or both) of these individuals is mistaken, not that there is no true criterion of morality. The possibility of these differences is not therefore incompatible with moral absolutism. For it still remains an invalid inference to suppose that, because what people *hold* to be morally true differs relatively to societies, moral truth itself is relative and there is no ultimate standard of moral action.

Three criticisms of ethical relativism

3. More serious still, in the absence of any absolute moral law, no individual or society, however abhorrent, could be judged immoral: intersocietal moral conflicts become impossible and demands for social reform untenable. For if there are divergent moral principles, and if these principles are justified by no more than the fact that they are believed to be true, it will be impossible to condemn them on the grounds that, say, infanticide, racism or genocide, although believed, are just plain wrong because it is the fact that they *are* believed that makes them right. But again, multiplicity of beliefs does not prove that any is right: it only demonstrates that each believes itself to be right. If

relativists should argue, in reply, that they at least allow for a more tolerant attitude towards the diverse customs of different cultures, then they are in grave danger of asserting that one value – the need to be tolerant – has objective worth and so of contradicting their original position.

By and large, these objections to relativism have led proponents of the moral argument to reaffirm their belief that there are objective moral values.[3] Relativism is not just philosophically unsound, for the reasons just given, but contrary to our basic moral intuitions that certain moral values, irrespective of time or place, are intrinsically important and must be upheld. This, then, guarantees the first stage of the moral argument. It remains to be seen, however, whether the second stage can be so easily upheld: that without God's existence there would be no objective moral values.

EXERCISE 5.1

Would you approve of the following practices if they were commonplace in your own society? Upon what grounds would you disapprove of them? Do your conclusions lead you to suppose that there are absolute moral rules or not?

Hunting foxes for sport

Having more than one wife at a time

Compulsorily sterilizing the mentally retarded

Refusing a blood transfusion to a dying child

Killing Jews because they are racially inferior

Killing rats for medical experiments

THE MORAL ARGUMENT OUTLINED

In its simplest form, then, the moral argument runs as follows:

SUMMARY: THE MORAL ARGUMENT

1 If absolute moral laws exist, then God exists.
2 Absolute moral laws exist.
3 Therefore God exists.

Brief history of the argument

This argument falls within a tradition of long standing. In Christian thinking it dates back to the late medieval writings of Duns Scotus (c. 1266–1308) and William Ockham (?–1347), achieving prominence in the Reformation

---

3. For further discussions on ethical relativism, see John Ladd (ed.), *Ethical Relativism*, Belmont, Calif., Wadsworth, 1973.

theology of Martin Luther (1483– 1546) and John Calvin (1509–1564).[4]
Other important exponents are René Descartes (1596–1650), John Locke
(1632–1704), George Berkeley (1685–1753) and, perhaps surprisingly,
given his criticisms of the theistic proofs, Immanuel Kant, whom I shall
turn to in a moment. In our own time, the argument appears in the work
of many distinguished twentieth-century theologians – Karl Barth, Emil
Brunner, Reinhold Niebuhr and
Rudolf Bultmann all subscribe –
while undoubtedly its most popular
advocate was C. S. Lewis (1898–
1963), who in 1952 gave a classic
account of it in his widely read
book *Mere Christianity* (**SOURCE 2:
PP. 264–267**).[5] Still fresher versions
have come to be known as 'divine
command theories', which, as their
name suggests, concentrate on God's
role as authoritative legislator of the
moral law, and these I shall discuss
later on in this chapter. It is fair to say,
however, that there are far more critics
than advocates, and that these are
not necessarily agnostics and atheists.
The Thomistic philosophical tradition
stands largely opposed to an ethics of
divine commands, Aquinas himself
teaching that there is an unchangeable

C. S. Lewis (1898–1963)

and universal moral law, not unlike the laws of logic and mathematics, which
makes it possible for individuals to act morally irrespective of whether there is
a God or not. Much later, Gottfried Wilhelm Leibniz (1646–1716), even
though one of the most committed theists, rejected the argument on the
grounds that it destroyed any notion of God's love, and in our own day Richard
Swinburne is equally dismissive.[6] For the most part, however, critics of the

---

4. William of Ockham is usually cited as the most extreme exponent of the argument, being
renowned for his claim that acts of theft, adultery and 'hating God' could be performed
meritoriously if proceeding from a divine command. The most extended defence of the theory
among known medieval sources is by the French Franciscan Andrew of Neufchateau. See his
Questions on an Ethics of Divine Commands, edited, translated and with an Introduction by Janine
Marie Idziak, Notre Dame, Ind., University of Notre Dame Press, 1997.
5. London, Collins, 1952.
6. See Leibniz, *Discourse on Metaphysics* (1686), edited and translated with an Introduction, notes
and glossary by R. N. D. Martin and Stuart Brown, Manchester and New York, Manchester
University Press, 1988. Leibniz' remarks are worth quoting: 'Also, if we say that things are good
by no rule of goodness beyond the will of God alone, we thoughtlessly destroy, I feel, all the love
and glory of God. For why praise Him for what He had done if He would be equally praiseworthy
for doing the opposite? Where will His justice and His wisdom be, if all that remains of Him is
some kind of despotic power, if His will takes the place of reason, and if, by the very definition
of tyranny, what pleases the Almighty is *ipso facto* just?' (p. 40). Cf. Swinburne, *The Existence of*

argument have tended to follow the example of philosophers like Thomas Hobbes (1588–1679) and David Hume, both of whom advanced entirely *secular* theories of morality: the former claiming that moral standards are necessary human conventions to secure the safety of the individual in society, the latter that such standards help to control our selfish instincts. Today perhaps the most outspoken critic is the Canadian philosopher Kai Nielsen.[7]

De A. Theuet, Liure II.   59
PLATON PHILOSOPHE GREC.
Chap. 29.

Plato (*c.* 427–347 BC)

Plato was born in Athens, of wealthy and aristocratic parents. As a youth he had political ambitions but became quickly disillusioned with the excesses of political life. This was in part due to his association with Socrates, and was confirmed by Socrates' execution by rabid conservative groups. Socrates' defence, imprisonment and death are magnificently described by Plato in three dialogues: *Apology, Crito* and *Phaedo.* Thereafter Plato travelled widely in Egypt, Sicily and Italy. On his return to Athens Plato founded, in about 387 BC and near the grove of the hero Academus, his 'Academy' – often acknowledged as the first university – a school of learning devoted to philosophy and the sciences, and over which he presided until his death. All Plato's writings have come down to us, and are generally recognized as the most influential works in all philosophy. They are for the most part in dialogue form – 26 in all – with Socrates as the protagonist.

THE EUTHYPHRO DILEMMA

It is customary to formulate the issue at hand – whether moral rules are or are not dependent on God's existence – in terms of a question posed by Socrates in Plato's dialogue *Euthyphro* (SOURCE 1: PP. 261–264). Socrates had recently been charged by the Athenians with impiety (worshipping false gods) and of corrupting the young. At the entrance to the law courts, he meets Euthyphro, a young theologian, who he discovers has also been charged with impiety because he is bringing a case against his father – his father, he alleges, has murdered a labourer on Euthyphro's estate at Naxos. Given the similarity of their cases, it is natural for Socrates and Euthyphro to consider the nature of piety and impiety, and an important philosophical discussion ensues about what is, in this instance, the good or 'holy' thing to do.

Socrates and Euthyphro

Euthyphro is a conceited young man, and his first definition of piety is unsurprising: it is to follow his example and prosecute anyone who is guilty of murder, sacrilege or any other such crime. Socrates is quick to point out that this is not a definition of the 'holy' but a list of examples: it still does not provide us with a standard by which to judge whether these actions are holy or not.

God, Oxford, Clarendon Press, 1979, pp. 175–179; and 'Duty and the Will of God', in *Divine Commands and Morality*, ed. Paul Helm, Oxford, Oxford University Press, 1981, pp. 120–134.
7. See his *Ethics Without God*, Buffalo, N.Y., Prometheus Books, 1973; revised edn, 1990.

Euthyphro accordingly suggests a second definition: 'what is pleasing to the gods is holy, and what is not pleasing to them is unholy.'[8] But this definition still does not satisfy Socrates. The gods, after all, might differ about what they consider right and wrong, so that what will be pleasing to Zeus might be hateful to Cronus and Uranus, and so on. Euthyphro, exasperated, offers a third definition: 'that holiness is what the gods all love, and its opposite is what the gods all hate, unholiness.' It is at this point that Socrates asks the all-important question: '*Is what is holy holy because the gods approve it, or do they approve it because it is holy?*'[9]

I do not propose at this point to go into the precise meanings of the Socratic vocabulary or indeed into how the objection can be variously deployed.[10] All that we need to see for the present is the nature of the dilemma that Euthyphro was incapable of resolving. The usual formulation of this is:

The Euthyphro dilemma

Either:

a right action is right because God approves (or commands) it;

Or:

God approves (or commands) a right action because it is right.

The alternatives presented here are clearly intended to be exhaustive, the first proposition asserting the dependence of A (moral action) on B (God), the second its independence. In the former case, 'X is good' is equivalent to 'God wills X', so that in this case the moral agent, faced with a moral perplexity, knows that he ought to do X because he has made the logically prior judgment that there is a God, that this God is good, and that accordingly what this God commands, wills or ordains (X) will be good. In the latter case, however, no such assumption is made. This is not because the existence of God is *denied* but because it is argued that no moral agent would describe any action (X) as a 'divine command' unless he *first* thought that he ought to obey it; that, in other words, he ascribes to God a command that he considers worthy of God because it has been independently validated as good. It is not so much, then, that nothing is morally wrong unless God has forbidden it, but rather that God would not forbid anything that was not morally wrong – i.e., that what he forbids depends upon some *prior standard of goodness*.

It does not take much to see that this second option is highly damaging for any argument that proceeds from objective moral values to the existence

8. *Plato: The Collected Dialogues*, ed. Edith Hamilton and Huntingdon Cairns, trans. Lane Cooper, Bollingen Series 71, New York, Pantheon Books, 1966, p. 174.
9. *Ibid.*, p. 178.
10. But see Paul Faber, 'The *Euthyphro* Objection to Divine Normative Theories: A Response', *Religious Studies*, 21, 1985, pp. 559–572; Peter Geach, 'Plato's Euthyphro – An Analysis and Commentary', *Monist*, 50, 1966, pp. 369–382; John C. Hall, 'Plato: Euthyphro 10a1–11a10', *Philosophical Quarterly*, 18, 1968, pp. 1–11; Mark McPherran, 'Socratic Piety in the "Euthyphro"', *Journal of the History of Philosophy*, 23, 1985, pp. 283–310; and Richard Sharvy, 'Euthyphro 9b–11b: Analysis and Definition in Plato and Others', *Noûs*, 6, 1972, pp. 119–137.

of God. For the ability to invoke a prior and independent standard of goodness means that whether an action is right or wrong may be decided by reference to that standard alone and requires no appeal to theistic premisses. Thus even if God does exist, his existence makes no difference to the moral situation. It is not then from the moral situation that his existence may be adduced.

There is, however, one argument which rejects this conclusion, and it comes from Immanuel Kant. The peculiarity and strength of his argument consist in the fact that he rejects the implication of the preceding paragraph, namely, that the existence of universal and independent moral obligations makes God irrelevant to exercise of them. Indeed, as he will seek to show, the *practical exercise* of such obligations requires God's existence as a precondition, since without God moral action would become virtually meaningless, little better than an exercise in futility. We must now examine this hypothesis in some detail.

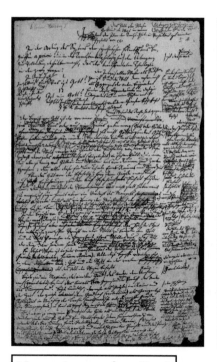

Manuscript page from Kant's *Opus Postumum*

Kant's moral case for God is without question the most important and influential in the history of the argument, to the point indeed that it is sometimes said, admittedly erroneously, that the moral argument effectively begins with Kant. It appears in various places within his philosophy but primarily in his *Critique of Practical Reason* (1786) and additionally in his *Critique of Judgment* (1790) and *Religion within the Limits of Reason Alone* (1792). For Kant's anti-religious contemporaries his return to a theistic defence was deeply disappointing, sufficiently so for some of them to suggest ulterior motives. One well-known story at the time, put about by the poet Heinrich Heine, was that Kant had only introduced religion into his system to placate the feelings of his devout servant, Lampe, or that Kant, as Heine more scurrilously suggested, was simply afraid of what the police might do if God did not put in a brief appearance.[11] Others, on reading the *Opus Postumum*, a fragmentary work discovered after Kant's death in 1804, have since claimed that Kant in old age had abandoned his moral argument altogether.[12]

11. *Religion and Philosophy in Germany*, trans. J. Snodgrass, Boston, Mass., Beacon Press, 1959, pp. 119, 276–277.
12. A view discussed in detail and rejected by G. A. Schrader, 'Kant's Presumed Repudiation of the "Moral Argument" in the Opus Postumum', *Philosophy*, 26, 1951, pp. 228–241.

KANT'S MORAL ARGUMENT (1): AUTONOMY AND CATEGORICAL DUTY

We should first begin where we left off: with Kant's concluding remarks following his demolition of the traditional proofs for God. In the *Critique of Pure Reason* (1781) we read:

> Now I maintain that all attempts to employ reason in theology in any merely speculative manner are altogether fruitless and by their very nature null and void, and that the principles of its employment in the study of nature do not lead to any theology whatsoever. Consequently, the only theology of reason which is possible is that which is based upon *moral laws or seeks guidance from them*.[13]

Contrary to appearances, then, Kant's moral argument for God is not bought at the expense of any last-minute repudiation of the epistemological position taken in the *Critique of Pure Reason*. Quite the reverse, in fact. Kant's rejection of the cosmological and design arguments still stands, and with it the following general principle: that no argument from experience can prove (or disprove) the existence of anything that lies beyond the boundaries of human experience, and so it cannot establish the reality of any transcendent and super-sensible entity, such as God. This does not imply, however, that God does not exist, nor does it expose the futility of religious belief – indeed, as Kant makes clear in his Preface to the second edition of the *Critique*, these limitations on human knowledge are defined precisely in order to 'make room for faith'.[14] In other words, religious conviction is independent of any theoretical attempts to demonstrate God's existence, and resides elsewhere. It resides, so Kant will argue, in the human capacity for moral thought, this capacity requiring the existence of something outside the individual which impels him to think and act in a moral way, and that this something is God. Thus, although the purely rational proofs of God are rejected, the immediate and undeniable experience of moral obligation makes it necessary nevertheless for us to *postulate* God's existence. In this way, God ceases to be an object of knowledge and becomes a moral certainty, an inner conviction born of individual moral experience.

> No one, indeed, will be able to boast that he *knows* that there is a God, and a future life. . . . No, my conviction is not *logical*, but *moral* certainty; and since it rests on subjective grounds (of the moral sentiment), I must not even say, '*It is* morally certain that there is a God, etc.', but '*I am* morally certain, etc.' In other words, belief in a God and in another world is so interwoven with my moral sentiment that as there is little danger of

Kant: 'making room for faith'

God as the postulate of moral obligation

---

13. *Critique of Pure Reason*, trans. Norman Kemp Smith, London, Macmillan, 1929, p. 528 (my italics).
14. *Ibid.*, p. 29.

my losing the latter, there is equally little cause for fear that the former can ever be taken from me.[15]

I should like to begin by taking note of two features of Kant's 'moral belief' (*moralischer Glaube,* to use his term) which make it abundantly clear where he stands on the Euthyphro question. There can be no theological system of morality because (1) such a system would destroy the *autonomy* of morals; and because (2) moral laws are independent of any lawgiver (divine or otherwise) and proceed solely from the *imperative of duty.*

THE AUTONOMY OF MORAL ACTION

The autonomy of moral action

In Kantian ethics an autonomous act is a free and self-legislative act of the will, implicit within any moral act: it is not so much that any free act will be necessarily a moral act but that any moral act must be free and autonomous, that is, one undertaken without interference or constraint and for which one is therefore individually responsible. The usual philosophical way of expressing Kant's point here is to say that 'Ought implies can'. If we say that somebody *ought* to perform a certain action, we are implying that this person could do it if he wished: it is an action *possible* for him; he has a choice, to do it or not. But if this person simply cannot perform this action, no matter how hard he may try, then there is clearly no sense in our still saying that he ought to do it. If Smith cannot swim, he cannot save the drowning child; and if someone should complain that Smith ought to have saved the infant, Smith can reasonably reply that this accusation is absurd: he cannot be blamed for what he cannot do but only for not doing what he could do. For Kant, then, the degree of moral responsibility depends on the degree of freedom exercised.

> Man *himself* must make or have made himself into whatever, in a moral sense, whether good or evil, he is or is to become. Either condition must be an effect of his free choice; for otherwise he could not be held responsible for it and could therefore be morally neither good nor evil.[16]

The incompatibility of autonomy and divine command

This fundamental principle of Kantian ethics – that moral action is autonomous action and so independent of any constraining influences – allows Kant to assert that the individual is never obligated to do that which he is commanded to do, not even when that command comes from God, and so to reject the first of the Euthyphro alternatives: that what is right is determined by what God conceives right to be. For this definition requires our deference to rules imposed by an external authority and so undermines the moral validity

---

15. *Ibid.,* p. 650.
16. *Religion within the Limits of Reason Alone,* trans. T. M. Greene and H. Hudson, Chicago, 1934, p. 40.

of our actions. We come to think of God as the rewarding and avenging power behind the moral law, turning our obedience into a prudential act, motivated more by the hope of reward and the fear of punishment than by any recognition of the intrinsic value of the action being commended. *Thus fidelity to God's will, if imposed on free men as a duty, is immoral.*

THE IMPERATIVE OF DUTY

In the second and much more elaborate strand of his argument Kant demonstrates why the second of the Euthyphro alternatives is the correct one: that the determination of what is right is not logically dependent on the existence of God, and that accordingly it is not only believers who are good, still less that theological assertions must be presupposed as the necessary basis for the generation of moral assertions. This is so because there exists a formal principle of moral duty enabling us to distinguish between those actions which we ought and ought not to do, irrespective of our religious commitments. This principle takes the form of duties derived from the *categorical imperative* and which we autonomously impose on ourselves, recognizing that we ought to obey them for their own sake *because this is the rational thing to do.*

> The categorical imperative

Kant's clearest explanation of his argument at this point is found in his remarkable little book *Groundwork of the Metaphysic of Morals* (1783).[17] He begins by saying that the 'sole aim of the present Groundwork is to seek out and establish *the supreme principle of morality*',[18] a principle which, if it is to be universally binding upon us, must contain that which is good in itself and the highest good (*summum bonum*). After reviewing various candidates for the highest good or 'good without qualification' Kant presents his own proposal: that it is 'impossible to conceive of anything at all in the world, or even out of it, which can be taken as good without qualification, except a *good will*'.[19] This we may interpret as meaning that the goodness of an action depends not on its results but on the *motive* for the action. This follows from the fact that, if the moral value of the good will were dependent on its effects, it could no longer be considered as of unconditional value: in that case it would be merely a means to an end (i.e., an instrumental good) and not the good without qualification (i.e., an intrinsic good). One condition that is instrumental rather than intrinsic is *happiness* – I mention it here because it plays a decisive role later on in Kant's argument. For if our duty were done because of the happiness it brought, the possibility would remain that our duty would be secondary to this effect, and that we would do what we ought to do only so long as we enjoyed doing it.

> The *summum bonum*

---

17. Translated, with analysis and notes, by H. J. Paton in *The Moral Law*, London, Hutchinson & Co., 1972. The following analysis of Kant's argument relies heavily on an earlier account in my *Moral Problems*, Cambridge, Lutterworth Press, 1991, pp. 97–102.
18. *Groundwork*, p. 57.
19. *Ibid.*, p. 60.

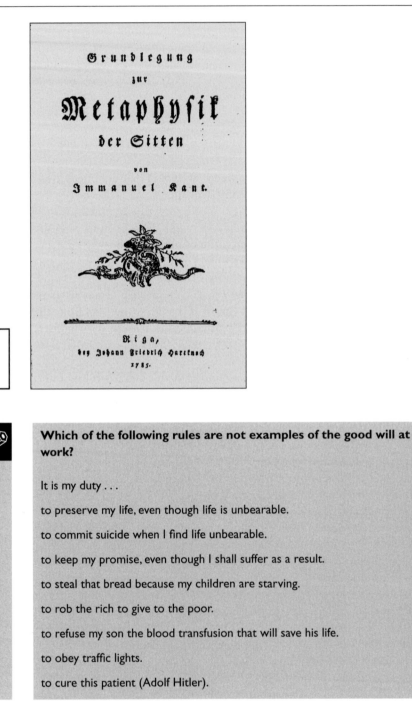

Grundlegung

zur

Metaphysik

der Sitten

von

Immanuel Kant.

Riga,
bey Johann Friedrich Hartknoch
1785.

Groundwork of the Metaphysic of Morals, title page, first edition

EXERCISE 5.2

Which of the following rules are not examples of the good will at work?

It is my duty . . .

to preserve my life, even though life is unbearable.

to commit suicide when I find life unbearable.

to keep my promise, even though I shall suffer as a result.

to steal that bread because my children are starving.

to rob the rich to give to the poor.

to refuse my son the blood transfusion that will save his life.

to obey traffic lights.

to cure this patient (Adolf Hitler).

Duty and the categorical imperative

For Kant, therefore, it is not the consequences of an act that make that act moral but the motive behind the act: it is having the right intention that makes the good will good. But what kind of intention? Kant's famous reply is that a good will's only motive is *to act for the sake of duty*; and that our duty, so conceived, lies in obeying those rules generated by the categorical imperative. This imperative, as its name implies, thus distinguishes moral action in the form of a *command*, expressed by 'I ought'. Kant presents three versions of the categorical imperative, the first of which is: *I ought never to act except in such a way that I can also will that my maxim become a universal law.*[20]

The most important feature of the categorical imperative, as just stated, is its emphasis on *universalizability*, that the will, as Kant puts it in his third formulation, can make 'universal law through its maxim'.[21] In other words, the method by which we can determine which rules have universal moral worth is that of asking whether the rule in question can be universally applied. Here, remember, it is the consistency of the rule that is decisive: any rule that, when universalized, becomes contradictory must be rejected. Kant gives two methods for distinguishing such contradictions. The first he calls *contradictions in the law of nature* (i.e., rules that cannot be universalized because they are straightforwardly self-contradictory – for example, 'Do this but don't'). The second he calls *contradictions in the will* (i.e., rules that can be universalized but which would produce situations unacceptable to any rational agent). The imperative 'Always accept help and never give it' is of this type. For while it may be possible for me to obey it, it would be impossible for everybody to obey it because, if everybody refused to help, there would be no help to receive – and it is irrational for an individual to propose a rule that may be later used against him. In both cases, then, the inability to universalize a command entails that it is no part of our moral duty to obey it.[22]

Contradictions in the law of nature and contradictions in the will

EXERCISE 5.3

Which of the following imperatives are not universalizable because of contradictions in the law of nature or in the will?

Come first in examinations.

Never speak until you are spoken to.

Jump the queue.

Give no money to the poor.

Lie when it is convenient to do so.

Shoot first and argue later.

Defend yourself but never start the fight.

Take what you want.

---

20. *Ibid.*, p. 67.
21. *Ibid.*, p. 96.
22. *Ibid.*, pp. 85–86.

Kant and the Euthyphro dilemma

Kant's conclusions require him to opt decisively for the second of the two Euthyphro alternatives: that religious belief is not a prerequisite for the exercise of moral judgment. Moral duty, as Kant has made clear, lies in obedience to a principle of universal application, applicable to everyone irrespective of their situation, and so regardless of personal self-interest, individual belief or particular consequences. This duty is autonomously and rationally undertaken, since it is an essential component of the categorical imperative that it should appeal to that aspect of human nature which already binds man to man, namely, his *reason*. Since reason, Kant argues, is an innate intellectual power existing more or less equally in all men, it enables the individual to resolve his problems in a way more or less acceptable to everyone. So if person A, reasoning logically, concludes that a particular argument is self-contradictory, then person B, going through the same argument and also reasoning logically, will arrive at the same conclusion. Here, in other words, reason dictates that their answers will be the same. Kant holds that this is equally true when we apply our reason to moral problems. If, for instance, I conclude, using my reason, that a particular action is right, then this, says Kant, is the conclusion that would be reached by anyone in my position. What is right for me, using my reason, is right for everyone, using their reason. This is so because, to repeat, if reason is universal, the moral commands generated by reason will be universal and so applicable to all moral situations.

The supreme principle of morality is thus a construct of reason, not imposed on an individual from without but proceeding from his own nature *as* a rational agent, allowing him autonomously to assess moral rules according to their self-consistency and universality, signalling thereby the independence of his good will from God's will. To this extent, the source of morality is the agent's own autonomy, rationally deployed, by means of which he can determine where his moral duty lies; and any attempt to subvert the self-sufficiency of this procedure, not least by invoking divine authority as the source of moral obligation, undermines the inherent value of human beings as rational beings. Every man, that is, has an inalienable right to be treated as an autonomous being, rightfully insisting on yielding only to rational argument.[23] Thus to speak at all of the morality of obeying God's will requires the equation of God's will with the

Kant: a contemporary silhouette

23. A view implicit within Kant's second formulation of the categorical imperative, and itself one of the great humanistic doctrines of the Enlightenment: 'Act in such a way that you always treat humanity, whether in your own person or in the person of any other, never simply as a means, but always at the same time as an end' (*ibid.*, p. 91).

rational principle of the categorical imperative. For it is not a divine command which makes a duty moral but *rather the universalizability of the duty which makes it divine.* As Kant remarks, 'we shall not look upon actions as obligatory because they are commands of God, but shall regard them as divine commands because we have an inward obligation to obey them'.[24] Indeed, for Kant the very notion of God's will is opaque and 'we have no conception of such a will, except as formed in accordance with these [moral] laws'.[25] Accordingly, we shall

> believe ourselves to be acting in conformity with the divine will in so far only as we hold sacred the moral law which reason teaches us from the nature of the actions themselves; and we shall believe that we can serve that will only by furthering what is best in the world, alike in ourselves and in others.[26]

KANT'S MORAL ARGUMENT (2): GOD AS THE POSTULATE OF MORAL ACTION

In his *Groundwork* Kant has shown that men and women are rational agents who perceive that they are under moral obligation, and who know where their moral duty lies: that it lies in their autonomous submission to the rules that they themselves generate through the application of the categorical imperative. For this reason any attempt to make their good will subservient to God's will as 'the basis for a moral system' would be 'in direct opposition to morality'.[27] Following this uncompromising conclusion, Kant is now faced with the difficult task of showing that, although this may be true from a *theoretical* viewpoint, it is not true from a *practical* viewpoint, and that human beings, in their everyday and immediate experience of moral activity, are driven to *postulate* (if not demonstrate) that God is the moral governor of the world; that the moral person is, in the very act of being moral, committing himself to a belief in God. The *Groundwork* contains no indication of how this uneasy transition from the independent laws of morality to divine sovereignty is to be be secured. Kant provided it three years later, in 1788, with the publication of his *Critique of Practical Reason* (SOURCE 3: PP. 268–272), the purpose of which was to extend its author's philosophical enquiry to include the whole range of individual moral experience.

The picture that Kant has so far presented of the moral man – as someone who neither needs nor seeks further explanation of his duty, or indeed motive for it, other than his obedience to the moral law – is not exhaustive. For while this description is, as far as it goes, correct, the moral man also wants to know whether doing his duty will indeed bring about the desired result: whether it will or will not achieve the 'highest good' (*summum bonum*). This is by no

---

24. *Critique of Pure Reason*, p. 644.
25. *Ibid.*
26. *Ibid.*
27. *Groundwork*, p. 104.

The *bonum consummatum*

Critique of Practical Reason, title page, first edition

means guaranteed. It is true that we do our duty by obeying the moral law; but other contingent factors may intrude, outside our control, which prevent the realization of the highest good: natural events may conspire against us, we may ourselves misread the situation we are in, others may wish to obstruct us. We are thus faced with the daunting possibility that the *summum bonum*, which the moral law commands us to promote, is in fact unrealizable, a practical impossibility.

To clarify his argument at this point, Kant introduces an important distinction within his definition of the *summum bonum*. It may mean either the *supremum bonum* (the supreme good) or the *bonum consummatum* (the completed good). The *supremum bonum* characterizes moral goodness, the goodness that Kant has thus far described as good in itself, dependent on nothing other than itself. Yet this good is evidently not the entire good – i.e., the best possible state of goodness – because, as we have just seen, other factors may intrude to prevent its realization. This contrasts, therefore, with the *bonum consummatum*, which is the realized good, and which must consist therefore in something additional to moral goodness. And what makes the latter form of goodness the perfect and most complete good is the *happiness of the moral agent*. For, in this context, the happiness of the moral person, acting in accordance with his duty, presupposes that he will not be made *unhappy* by the likely non-attainment (for whatever reason) of the highest good. More exactly, then, where happiness and duty combine in the pursuit of the highest good, we must presume the possibility of the highest good being obtained, for clearly no man could be happy if convinced of the inevitable failure of his whole moral enterprise. So, while virtue (conceived as 'worthiness to be happy') without actual happiness is still morally admirable, and while happiness without virtue is morally deplorable, the union of the two, virtue and happiness, is still a greater good, the realization of the *bonum consummatum*.

The union of virtue and happiness

Now, inasmuch as virtue and happiness together constitute possession of the highest good in a person, and happiness distributed in exact proportion to morality (as the worth of a person and his worthiness to be happy) constitutes the *highest good* of a possible world, the latter means the whole, the complete good, in which, however, virtue as the condition is always the supreme good, since it has no further condition above it, whereas happiness is something that, although always pleasant to the possessor of it, is not of itself absolutely and in all respects good but always presupposes morally lawful conduct as its condition.[28]

There is nothing, then, in doing our duty (i.e., acting morally in obedience to the moral law) that guarantees our eventual happiness, and there is nothing in being happy that guarantees that our duty is being or will be done. So while an autonomous individual, doing his duty, may achieve virtue for himself, he cannot thereby ensure, simply by acting in this way, that the greatest good – the *summum bonum* conceived as the *bonum consummatum*, which is the union of happinees and virtue – will be realized. This leaves Kant with a perplexity. The man of good will has been enjoined to seek the highest good as a moral and practical necessity, to seek, in other words, the union of that which is demanded by morality but which human beings cannot of their own volition achieve. This being the case, *some other agency* must be postulated capable of bringing about the union of virtue and happiness, and which constitutes the essence of the *bonum consummatum*. This is God. God, in other terms, makes moral action rational by making the goal of morality attainable; or rather, the moral injunction to do one's duty, although itself still categorically authoritative, is now given still extra force within the personal moral dimension through the realization of its divine completion, this perception driving the moral individual forward towards a religious commitment. What was first seen as a theoretical and universal moral obligation is now transformed into a practical and universal moral need:

> the postulate of the possibility of the *highest derived good* (the best world) is likewise the postulate of the reality of a *highest original good*, namely of the existence of God. Now, it was a duty for us to promote the highest good; hence there is in us not merely the warrant but also the necessity, as a need connected with duty, to presuppose the possibility of this highest good, which, since it is possible only under the condition of the existence of God, connects the presupposition of the existence of God inseparably with duty; that is, it is morally necessary to assume the existence of God.[29]

The guiding premiss of this argument is, once again, that 'ought implies can', that it is meaningless to say that someone ought to do X unless he can do X. So, if we ought to promote the *summum bonum*, this highest good must be possible, and so realizable; and if this highest good is not, as we have seen, realizable solely through human agency, it is necessary to postulate God's existence as the only means by which the required union of virtue and happiness can be achieved. Without, then, the existence of God man would have to

'Ought' implies 'can'

---

28. *Critique of Practical Reason*, translated and edited by Mary Gregor, with an Introduction by Andrews Reath, Cambridge, Cambridge University Press, 1997, p. 93.
29. *Ibid.*, p. 105.

The *absurdum practicum*

abandon his pursuit of the moral law as impossible. By 'impossible' Kant does not mean that without God the moral law itself becomes invalid because *logically self-contradictory* – its inherent validity as a law determined by the categorical imperative remains – but rather that without God what I know to be valid (the moral law) places me under no obligation to uphold it, since that is *practically impossible*. What results, in other words, is what Kant calls elsewhere an *absurdum practicum*. This is not an inconsistency in the moral law as such but in the behaviour and attitude of the moral man who seeks to uphold the law. If the goal of morality is practically impossible, he need not be committed to what his duty requires, need expect no happiness from doing his duty, and is thus more likely to give way to his vices and become a 'knave'.[30]

Unpacking this argument we can see that it depends on three fundamental premises. These are:

SUMMARY: KANT'S MORAL ARGUMENT

1 That moral individuals are obligated to seek the highest good (i.e., the fusion of happiness and duty).
2 That that which moral individuals are obligated to seek (the highest good) must be possible to attain.
3 That it is impossible for moral individuals to attain the highest good.

Now, as Kant points out, these three propositions cannot be held simultaneously. For if (1) and (2) are true, then (3) is false; and if (2) and (3) are true, then (1) is false; and if (1) and (3) are true, then (2) is false. All these contradictions are resolved, however, with the postulation of God's existence, i.e., with the assumption that, through God's agency, the attainment of the highest good is practically possible. It is, therefore, a practical requirement of being moral that God's existence be presumed.

The case of Spinoza

Does this mean that there can be no moral atheists? In his *Critique of Judgment* Kant provides an illuminating answer to this question. He imagines 'the case of a righteous man, such, say, as Spinoza, who considers himself firmly persuaded that there is no God'.[31] Here we have someone who has rejected the old speculative arguments for God's existence but who yet 'reveres' the moral law in practice: he agrees that he must disinterestedly direct all his energies to

---

30. Kant, *Lectures on Metaphysics*, Cambridge, Cambridge University Press, 1997, p. 133. God's existence, I should add, is not the only practical postulate demanded by morality. There are two others: freedom and immortality. The first, as we have seen already, follows from the fact that the moral law commands us to act autonomously. The second arises from the fact that achieving the highest good is not a factual possibility within the lifetime of men but nevertheless a practical necessity if moral action is to be rational. Immortality should therefore be postulated, thereby providing human beings with an 'endless progress' towards the complete fulfilment of the moral law. Like God's existence, then, life after death is not a matter of theoretical knowledge but is nevertheless a profoundly reasonable belief, inseparably connected as it is with our experience of moral obligation. *Ibid.*, pp. 102–103.
31. Translated with Analytical Indexes by James Creed Meredith, Oxford, Clarendon Press, 1928; reprint 1986, p. 120.

establish the *summum bonum*. But such a man, Kant continues, is all too aware of the gulf separating the ideal world, in which people do what they ought, from the actual world, in which people do what they like. In reality, then, a Spinoza finds a world in which the virtuous are invariably surrounded by 'deceit, violence, and envy', where they are seldom rewarded for their efforts, and where indeed the wicked, more often than not, prosper. The result is that the virtuous man, while certainly deserving of happiness, cannot achieve it, and is thus severely 'circumscribed in his endeavour'. He still strives to do his duty; but he is at the same time forced to conclude that his moral goal is unattainable.

> But perhaps he resolves to remain faithful to the call of his inner moral vocation and would fain not let the respect with which he is immediately inspired to obedience by the moral law be weakened owing to the nullity of the one ideal final end that answers to its high demand – which could not happen without doing injury to moral sentiment. If so he must assume the existence of a *moral* author of the world, that is, of a God.[32]

For Kant, then, the combination of prolonged moral effort and genuine atheism is impossible, for the former requires 'the one ideal final end' that the latter rejects. From this it follows that where we do find a sustained attempt to do one's duty, even in an unbeliever like Spinoza, we find nevertheless a *practical* belief in God. So once again, however dismissive a moral individual may be of the *theoretical* demonstrations of God's existence, his actions are in themselves sufficient witness to an implicit and unmistakable religious commitment.

This argument, we should stress again and as Kant makes clear in an important footnote, is not intended 'to supply an *objectively* valid proof of the existence of God',[33] but rather to show that the failure of such proofs, which he himself had done so much to expose, does not mean that God cannot be vindicated as the legitimate focus of belief. There is, as he says, 'still enough left to satisfy us', namely, a practical proof dependent on the immediate and indubitable experience of having moral obligations, an argument which accordingly satisfies the moral side of our nature.

> Since, therefore, the moral precept is at the same time my maxim (reason prescribing that it should be so), I inevitably believe in the existence of God and in a future life, and I am certain that nothing can shake this belief, since my moral principles would thereby be themselves overthrown, and I cannot disclaim them without becoming abhorrent in my own eyes.[34]

---

32. *Ibid.*, p. 121.
33. *Ibid.*, p. 119.
34. *Critique of Pure Reason*, p. 650.

CRITICISMS OF KANT'S MORAL ARGUMENT

When Kant famously denies knowledge 'in order to make room for faith', he is expressing his conviction that the impossibility of achieving a theoretical proof that God exists is no justification for *acting* as though God does not exist. This conviction is central to Kant's moral argument. The hypothesis of God's existence is established as the only principle which makes conducting a moral life a meaningful activity. For without it the gap between what is and what ought to be would be recognized as unbridgeable and the moral life deemed ultimately futile. The philosophical *tour de force* of Kant's case lies in how he resolves this *absurdum practicum*. He takes the 'ought' of the categorical imperative – the duty imposed upon us by the moral law – as the one element within our immediate experience that can guarantee the reality of a being alone capable of realizing the demands of this duty, that is, of so ordering the natural world that a union of happiness and virtue can be realized. All moral action, we might say, has an irreducible *teleological* aspect – i.e., to attain the highest good – which, since we cannot attain it by our own effort, is only rendered rational (and so intelligible) by the postulation of its eventual divine fulfilment. This does not mean that it is God who makes the moral law good – that has been independently and autonomously established; but it does mean that it is by God that the moral law is converted into an appropriable rule of life, something by which human beings can in fact live. Thus our immediate and tangible sense of being under an obligation that is neither false nor fantastic becomes our immediate and tangible evidence of being under God, evidence that is not denied by any Spinoza-like ignorance of it.

Even on its first appearance Kant's argument was subjected to fierce and prolonged criticism. The main objection was that, on two counts at least, it was inconsistent with his own previously held philosophical position.

1. If the existence of God is postulated as necessary for the *telos* of morality to be achieved, then it would seem that God is being introduced as the only *causal* explanation of how this occurs. The question is whether this solution in the *Critique of Practical Reason*, if it be a form of teleological argument, is

---

Is Kant's argument a
teleological argument?

Kant's house in
Königsberg

vulnerable to the criticisms of any speculative cosmological proof in the *Critique of Pure Reason*. Kant, to be fair to him, does not think that it is. He claims that the denial of any knowledge of God through 'theoretical reason' does not prohibit its attainment through 'practical reason': we can affirm or postulate *that* God exists, even while admitting that we can know nothing of *how* he exists, and that this is sufficient for religious belief. This, however, looks suspiciously like trying to keep your cake and eat it. For it is difficult to see how the requirement of *some* knowledge, albeit practically grounded, can be intelligibly advanced without incorporating some residual knowledge on the speculative level – i.e., that God's existence, at the very least, must incorporate a quite specific *causal* activity in which he achieves the ultimate end of morality by uniting virtue and happiness. Despite Kant's earlier strictures about all metaphysical approaches to God, it would appear, then, that he is nevertheless required to make some speculative assessment of a transcendental reality; and that he is, in short, trying to do what he has already forbidden.

2. The second criticism focuses on Kant's account of 'happiness' and an apparent contradiction between that given in the moral argument of the second *Critique* and in the earlier *Groundwork*. In the latter, happiness is deliberately discarded as having any place in the determination of the *summum bonum*, not merely because what is counted as happiness differs from person to person but because it presupposes that one would not do one's duty if it made one unhappy – a state of affairs that makes the impulse of moral action dependent on individual self-interest and so not categorical, i.e., not applicable to everyone, equally and alike. This, it has to be said, sits uneasily with Kant's treatment of happiness in the *Critique of Practical Reason*. Here happiness, in combination with virtue, constitutes the *bonum consummatum*, the completed and most perfect good. What human beings thus fail to achieve in the sensible world – where being happy is not necessarily productive of virtue, and where being virtuous is not necessarily productive of happiness – is thus postulated as being what human beings nevertheless seek to achieve when doing their moral duty. Happiness thus becomes an essential component of the highest good, which is the *telos* of all moral volition.

Now, even if we concede that it may be true that *in general* we like to think that our moral efforts will produce some satisfaction, Kant has not shown why this ambition should be considered a moral *necessity*, or even why a rational will should not be satisfied, as the *Groundwork* previously stipulated, by acting solely in accordance with its categorical duty – that is, in a disinterested way – and not with an eye to whether such obedience will be rewarded with happiness. Indeed, it is not difficult to think of situations in which a virtuous act requires the deliberate renunciation of happiness – Peter Byrne, in his forceful criticism of Kant at this point, gives the example of a self-sacrificing carer looking after an elderly relative[35] – or of those cases, almost too numerous to mention, in which, having achieved an ambition, we find that it does not bring the expected satisfaction but indeed the reverse. In these examples, then,

> Is happiness necessary to virtue?

---

35. *The Moral Interpretation of Religion*, Edinburgh, Edinburgh University Press, 1998, p. 73.

we might be more inclined to say that our moral development is better served by a more sceptical expectation of a possible mis-match between having a goal and achieving happiness.

Now, if this be the case, then the connection between happiness and virtue is certainly not *analytic*. Kant has not even shown that it is *synthetic*, namely, that some kind of practical and empirical invariance exists between the two, such as would override the examples just given. All he has shown (assuming, for the moment, that he has shown this) is that it is not irrational for the moral man to pursue their union as a moral goal because certain extra-sensible factors have made its realization possible. But the fact that God can achieve the highest good does not demonstrate that a moral individual can do so or that he or she ought to do so. Indeed, there is a case for saying that, by knowing that this happy state will be achieved, not through our will but through the agency of God's omnipotence, we shall be less inclined to do what we ought to do because, in the final reckoning, what we ought to do will be done.

Despite recent attempts to iron out some of Kant's difficulties at this point,[36] these two criticisms do, I believe, cast serious doubt on the first of Kant's three fundamental premisses – 'that moral individuals are obligated to seek the highest good' (i.e., the fusion of happiness and duty).[37] But still more telling objections can be levelled against the second of his premisses, namely, 'that that which moral individuals are obligated to seek (the highest good) must be possible to attain'. The question is: Is it the case that the exercise of moral duty requires that the *summum bonum* be realizable? For if it is not, then no *absurdum practicum* occurs – moral obligation is no longer demanding the impossible – and we need not postulate God's existence as necessary to resolve this absurdity.

The backbone of Kant's argument is, as we have seen, that 'ought implies can', i.e., that if someone is obligated to do something, it must be possible for them to do it, and conversely, that no one is obligated to do that which is impossible. But the principle that *moral obligation implies possibility* is by no means as straightforward as it appears. We should first understand what Kant does not mean: he does not mean that our moral duty requires that the highest good be simply *logically possible*, since by that he would be saying no more than that the *summum bonum* is a coherent concept, not self-contradictory (i.e., in the sense that I could not strive to become a married bachelor). Kant would be the first to point out that one is never entitled to deduce from a concept that anything exists as an instance of it. And the same applies here. The fact that the *summum bonum* is a coherent concept does not of itself indicate that there is a *summum bonum* to be realized and thus that there must be something existing sufficient to bring it about.

What Kant clearly does mean is that the *summum bonum* should be *practically possible*, and that the *ought* of moral duty requires that the object of

Does moral obligation imply possibility?

---

36. Most notably by Allen W. Wood, *Kant's Moral Religion*, Ithaca and London, Cornell University Press, 1970, pp. 10–37.
37. See above, p. 248.

that duty can be in fact realized. But this is plainly false. For a moral obligation can still be exercised if the good will – following Kant's own reading of it in the *Groundwork* – fulfils a right *intention*: i.e., if it *seeks* to attain (not actually attains) the highest good. In this way, our knowing that the *summum bonum* is not humanly possible does not mean that we cannot act morally *as if* it were possible; that we cannot, in other words, derive moral value from our *pursuit* of what we know to be impossible, and cannot by our example encourage in others a similar determination to pursue this moral ideal. After all, the political desire to achieve full employment may result in a decrease in the numbers unemployed; and this decrease, and the effort it took to secure it, we may regard as morally laudable; but they are no less laudable because falling short of what is recognized to be an unattainable perfection. Indeed, pursuing this example, I cannot see why full employment is not a social possibility. In that case, the *summum bonum* would in this instance be a realizable goal, brought about solely through the human ambition to achieve it.

No *absurdum practicum* in moral conduct therefore results if my duty consists in promoting the highest good as far as my abilities and situation permit. An *absurdum practicum* would, however, result if my duty to act in this way required the denial of that through which my duty was exercised, namely, my autonomy. But this is not implied in Kant's moral argument, but rather safeguarded. Thus the only possibility which is a requisite of the *ought* of moral action is whether or not I *can* autonomously subject my good will to its categorical duties, and not whether, by so doing, it is or is not possible to attain what the good will projects as its ultimate goal (the *summum bonum*).

If no *absurdum practicum* results, then the third premiss – 'that it is impossible for moral individuals to attain the highest good' – becomes little more than a (debatable) Kantian truism without the slightest relevance to whether or not God exists. But even if we were to admit, for the purposes of argument, that the pursuit of an impossibility would be *psychologically* difficult to sustain – that a Spinoza would remain uneasy about dedicating his life to an unrealizable ideal – it remains hard to see how the extra demands of religion would in practice alleviate his situation. For the person faced with the decision whether to do X or Y, God's existence provides no extra warrant, additional to the categorical imperative, for identifying where his or her duty lies; nor does it provide any present help in deciding which option has the greater likelihood of bringing the individual the happiness that is the reward of virtuous action, or indeed whether such action will contribute to the greater collective happiness of mankind. It may be true, of course, that the believer, by accepting that there is a moral governor of the universe, will feel greater confidence than the unbeliever that these goals will be achieved, and that affairs will be so ordered that success is assured; but this is a psychological condition of its own in which such confidence may well be misplaced, given that Kant never specifies how God will actually overcome the human and natural obstacles that are said to thwart the union of happiness and virtue. It remains unclear, then, how belief in a union with an unrealizable present but inevitable future can contribute in any way to the resolution of moral problems here and now. If we believe that mathematics is worth doing because God is a mathematician, no doubt the desire to 'think God's thoughts' can provide an important educational incentive; but nonetheless, little of educational value is achieved by telling a child that mathematics is not a difficult subject because God can do the sums.

The failure of Kant's argument

For these various reasons, Kant's moral argument, although undoubtedly the most important in the argument's history, must be considered a failure. Either human beings are capable of independent moral action or they are not. If they are, then it is unnecessary to postulate a transcendent causal agent to explain how this is possible: the only thing that is necessary is our apprehension of our categorical duty. But if they are not, then it is difficult to see how Kant can square this conclusion with his demand that our duty be autonomously undertaken or how he can avoid breaking his own embargo on theoretical speculation into the nature of God's existence as a causal agent: of how, for example, God actually achieves the union between two otherwise unconnected states (virtue and happiness), and of how this accomplishment actually impinges upon the moment of moral decision.

POST-KANTIAN MORAL ARGUMENTS: DIVINE COMMAND THEORY

Kant's moral case for God, albeit unsuccessful, remains unsurpassed in the history of the moral argument and it set the agenda for the majority of subsequent attempts to succeed where he had failed, his general scepticism about all metaphysical speculation driving his successors to re-explore the moral dimension of human experience as an alternative source of theistic evidence. Some of these I must mention briefly.

Hastings Rashdall (1907) proposed, for example, that the relation between God's existence and the existence of absolute moral laws was a *logical* one. We believe, he says, in an absolute and real standard of right and wrong, but we do not believe that such a standard exists in nature or in the mind of this or that individual. Thus the belief in God is 'the logical presupposition' of an objective morality. 'Our moral ideal can only claim objective validity in so far as it can rationally be regarded as the revelation of a moral ideal eternally existing in the mind of God.'[38] Another version, suggested by W. R. Sorley (1919), sees the relation as a *causal* one, thereby converting the argument into a type of cosmological argument. While it is illegitimate (following Kant and Hume) to infer from the laws of nature that there is a divine cause, the same does not apply to ethical values: while we accept their absolute validity, we also accept that their truth cannot be established by observation of the course of nature. How then does moral truth arise? 'The question is answered', Sorley contends, 'if we regard the moral order as the order of a Supreme Mind and the ideal of goodness as belonging to this Mind.'[39]

---

38. *The Theory of Good and Evil*, 2 vols, Oxford, 1907, Vol. II, p. 212.
39. Sorley, *Moral Values and the Idea of God*, Cambridge, Cambridge University Press, 1919, p. 352.

Among more recent versions of the moral arguments, it is the so-called 'divine command theory' that has attracted most attention. This, too, begins from a Kantian starting-point, namely, the categorical form in which morality commonly expresses itself, i.e., as laws and commands. So H. P. Owen (1965) has suggested that God is the 'legislator' of morality, creating the moral law by legislative act and thus functioning in much the same way as human lawgivers.[40] Another alternative, proposed by Robert Adams (1979) and Robert Burch (1980), is that God acts as a 'commander': that it is by divine command that 'X is good' becomes the exclusive criterion of moral action, thereby requiring unconditional obedience.[41]

Divine command theory has attracted many criticisms, of which the following are perhaps the most important.

1. The first is the most obvious: How are the commands of God communicated to men and women? It is sometimes claimed by believers that knowledge of what God commands is acquired through some form of scriptural revelation (for example, the Bible or Koran). Now, quite apart from the fact that opinions differ as to how much textually God is directly responsible for – everything, including the punctuation, or merely the basic ethical concepts? – this argument runs into a well-known difficulty. This is that, even if we were to accept that God's commands can on occasion be quite specific as to *what* he requires, this does not explain why there is such diversity amongst believers as to *how* such instructions should be practically applied. Thus, while the general prohibition against taking a life accounts for the extreme pacifism of the Quakers, it has not prevented other Christian groups from arguing that killing is justified in time of war or in the defence of the innocent. This ethical diversity within the same religious tradition certainly weakens the view that this tradition has access to an authoritative and divinely revealed moral truth.

One of the more venerable ways of resolving this problem has been to suggest that it is our *conscience* that allows us to distinguish between what is right and wrong, and that the voice of conscience is the voice of God. The most influential advocate of this view is Cardinal John Henry Newman in his *The Grammar of Assent* (1870). Going against the dictates of conscience, says Newman, makes a person 'ashamed and frightened'; and since these emotions have no visible and empirical source, 'the Object to which his perception is directed must be Supernatural and Divine; and thus the phenomena of Conscience, as a dictate, avail to impress the imagination with the picture of

God as legislator and commander

Conscience as the voice of God

40. Owen, *The Moral Argument for Christian Theism*, London, George Allen & Unwin, 1965; Philip Quinn, *Divine Commands and Moral Requirements*, Oxford, Clarendon Press, 1978.
41. Adams, 'Moral Arguments for Theistic Belief' (1979), in Adams, *The Virtue of Faith*, New York, Oxford University Press, 1981, pp. 144–163; Burch, 'Objective Values and the Divine Command Theory of Morality', *New Scholasticism*, 54, 1980, pp. 279–304. Other arguments worth mentioning are those of Stephen Clark, 'God, Good, and Evil', *Proceedings of the Aristotelian Society*, 77, 1977, pp. 247–264; Edward Wierenga, 'A Defensible Divine Command Theory', *Noûs*, 17, 1983, pp. 387–407; Philip Devine, *Relativism, Nihilism and God*, Notre Dame, Ind., University of Notre Dame Press, 1989; and Franklin Gamwell, *The Divine Good: Modern Moral Theory and the Necessity of God*, San Francisco, Harper, 1990.

**John Henry Newman
(1801–1890)**

a Supreme Governor'.[42] This argument is, however, liable to one fatal criticism. Setting aside the immediate objections that this argument would do as well for polytheism as for theism, and that it provides no criteria for distinguishing a divine voice from a demonic one, it is not at all difficult to think of non-theistic naturalistic explanations for the emotions felt when doing something we ought not to do, the most obvious being that these occur when we contravene the social values of our upbringing. Freud, for example, calls conscience the 'super-ego', which he describes as an internalized, cultural means of controlling our aggressive and asocial instincts. So the guilt we experience when acting against the norms of society 'expresses itself as a need for punishment'.[43]

EXERCISE 5.4

What problems arise from the following?

I do good when I do whatever . . .

| my church commands. |
my master commands.	my instinct commands.
my society commands.	my conscience commands.
scripture commands.	God commands.

2. A second objection, brought to the fore by the philosopher A. C. Ewing, is that divine command theory makes the claim 'What God commands is good' trivial and so irrelevant to the individual deciding what he or she ought to do. For if we have determined that 'X is good' because 'God commanded X', then it is not a question of God commanding X *because* it is good – because in some way God perceives X to be good and then commands us to do it – but because whatever God will command *must* be good, the good being defined by his command. This reduces 'God commands what is good' to 'God commands what God commands' or 'God does what is good' to 'God does what he wills', that is, to the level of a tautology, giving the individual therefore no occasion to ask the moral question: Ought I to do what God commands? This question

---

42. Edited with a Preface and Introduction by Charles Frederick Harrold, New York and London, Longmans, Green & Co., 1870, p. 83.
43. Freud, *Civilization and its Discontents* (1930), in *The Penguin Freud Library*, London, Penguin Books, 1985, Vol. 12, pp. 315–316.

becomes, as it were, morally redundant. For I cannot ask whether I ought to obey God when what God orders is by definition good; when indeed the maxim of my actions has become the rather convoluted 'I must always do what God wills because what God wills is willed by God.'

This criticism can be better seen if we here employ G. E. Moore's 'open question' technique, a method he devised for testing whether proposed definitions of moral terms were correct or not.[44] Take the word 'brother'. This has the definition 'being male and being a sibling'. This definition makes the question 'I know Jim is a brother, but is he male and a sibling?' pointless because the first part of the sentence has already supplied the answer to the question. It is what Moore calls a 'closed question': the properties denoted by the words 'male' and 'sibling' represent a necessary condition for anyone to be a brother. But if I then ask the question 'I know Jim is a brother, but is he a teacher at Lancing College?', this is not a senseless question since the definition of Jim as a brother says nothing about whether he is at Lancing and teaching there. This is what Moore calls an 'open question': the properties denoted by the words 'teacher at Lancing College' do not represent a necessary condition for anyone being a brother. Moore concludes that a definition is correct when the question asked is closed and incorrect when the question is open. Asking an open question, in other words, means that the two expressions being used do not mean the same thing. This open question technique can be directly applied to divine command theory and its definition that 'What is good is what God commands.' For since it is not senseless to ask 'God commands X, but is it good?', this question is an open question, revealing thereby that 'God commands X' is not equivalent to 'X is good'.

Moore: the open question technique

3. The third objection to divine command theory is that, if the rightness of an action did depend on God's will or command, morality would be entirely arbitrary, depending on divine whim. So if God ordered us to slaughter a hostile tribe, with thirty thousand virgins as our reward (as he does in the Old Testament book of Numbers, Chapter 31), we are morally obliged to obey him because it is our duty to do what is right, and what is right is defined by what God orders. But if, on the other hand, we view this order as, to say the least, ethically suspect – if we reply that such arbitrary cruelty is unworthy of a God who is good, and that this command could not therefore have come from him – we are in effect abandoning the divine command theory because we have now judged this action morally reprehensible according to our own rational criteria about what is morally right or not and so have discarded the proposition that it must be right because God commanded it. Since, then, as Michael Martin has persuasively argued (SOURCE 5: PP. 275–278), doing what is right in this instance runs counter to our basic moral intuitions – that such wholesale

Can God command morally repugnant acts?

⇐

---

44. *Principia Ethica*, Cambridge, Cambridge University Press, 1903, pp. 5–11. This method was devised by Moore to expose what he called the 'naturalistic fallacy', that is, the impossibility of equating goodness with any natural property, such as pleasure. Whether or not this means that goodness is a quality without definition, as Moore contends, is arguable; but his method does expose the difficulties of *defining* moral properties, particularly when the definition is not in terms of natural properties at all but in terms of a super-natural being such as God.

slaughter and rape should never become a moral duty – disobeying God cannot be wrong, and so here *not* doing what God orders is right. Thus the dependence of morality on God's will must be rejected.

EXERCISE 5.5

What criticism of the moral argument is implied in the following story?

Moses (coming down from Mt Sinai): Well, lads, I've spoken to God, and there's good news and bad news.
Israelites: Let's have the good news first.
Moses: The good news is that there are only ten commandments.
Israelites: Great! Now what's the bad news?
Moses: The bad news is that he's kept in the rule about adultery.

Divine command theory is to be rejected, then, on the grounds that we cannot obey a divine command which is contrary to our basic moral intuitions. But there is a way round this difficulty. That is to interpret divine command theory so that it precludes the possibility of God ordering morally repugnant acts. This suggestion has been developed by the ethicist Robert Adams. Adams agrees that the believer would be right not to do evil even though God commanded it; but this is because, Adams contends, divine commands can be considered worthy of obedience 'only if certain conditions are assumed – namely, only if it is assumed that God has the character which I believe Him to have, of *loving His human creatures*'.[45] When I say, then, that 'What God commands is morally right' I am presuming – as the believer has the right to presume – that these commands are given by a *loving God* and that accordingly I would be justified in disobeying any instruction to act in an *unloving manner*. While, therefore, it may be logically possible that God could command cruelty for its own sake, it is 'unthinkable that God should do so. To have *faith* in God is not just to believe that He exists, but also to trust in His love for mankind.'[46]

This modification of divine command theory has problems of its own. The first and most obvious is that it works only by crediting God with what our own moral sensibilities take to be an excellence of character – a loving nature. But this, frankly, gets us nowhere. For if love is a moral excellence, then it is so either (1) because God wills or commands loving – in which case we cannot so blithely discount hating as a moral quality if God commanded hating, thus making the incident of Numbers 31 not just a logical possibility but a practical possibility; or (2) because we *independently* apprehend loving as a moral quality, one which God must possess as a necessary quality if God is God – in which case it is a quality independent of his will and one which we think should be ascribed to him. And to this objection we should add another. If the reason that God commands X and not Y is that X is an act of love and Y is not, then

45. 'A Modified Divine Command Theory of Ethical Wrongness', in *Divine Commands and Morality*, ed. Paul Helm, Oxford, Oxford University Press, 1981, p. 86 (my italics).
46. *Ibid.*, p. 88.

why may we not adopt the maxim 'A moral act is an act of love' as alone sufficient for us in the determination of our moral obligations? If the determination of a good act is, even for God, that it be an act of love, we do not need God's commands to justify what has already justified his commands as good. Like Socrates, we are thus driven to recognize that the gods command virtue because it is good (i.e., loving, following this version of the theory) and not that virtue is good because the gods command it.

Evaluate the following as a disproof of the existence of God:

EXERCISE 5.6

1   If God exists, then he is a being who is omnipotent and all-good.

2   If he is omnipotent and all-good, he can ensure that the good be done through obedience to his commands.

3   His good commands are not obeyed and people act morally and immorally.

4   Therefore God does not exist.

4. The fourth and final objection to divine command theory is invariably cited as the most powerful of all. We recall that, according to the first part of the Euthyphro dilemma, moral duty is defined as being in accordance with God's will, that where God commands we must obey. But, as we have just seen, the fact that 'God commands me to do X' does not mean that 'I ought to do X'. There is thus no necessary connection between my moral obligation to do X and God willing that X be done because, after all, there may be moral reasons for not doing what God wants me to do (i.e., killing infants). If it is argued in response that this unqualified subservience to God nevertheless remains – that it is precisely this submission to God's will that constitutes, like it or not, part of the believer's unconditional moral obligation to a divine sovereign of unlimited authority – then the next objection follows: that this may certainly be an obligation of belief but it is not, for all that, a moral obligation. For a moral obligation, as Kant stipulated, proceeds from a free and *autonomous* decision on the part of the human agent – that a moral decision is one freely undertaken in a situation of choice – and that accordingly any act motivated by obedience (or fear of divine retribution) is morally worthless. Indeed, one philosopher, James Rachels, has gone so far as to construct a formal *disproof* of God's existence on this basis (**SOURCE 4: PP. 272–275**). Paralleling Findlay's earlier reworking of the ontological argument,[47] Rachels argues that only a being with an 'unqualified claim on our obedience' is worthy of worship. Since, however, such obedience requires the abdication of our autonomy, no being who is worthy of worship can make this demand. Thus there is no God whom a moral agent can worship.

47. See above, pp. 19–20.

SUMMARY: RACHELS' DISPROOF OF GOD

1 If any being is God, he must be a fitting object of worship.

2 No being could possibly be a fitting object of worship, since worship requires the abandonment of one's role as an autonomous moral agent.

3 Therefore, there cannot be any being who is God.[48]

The key element in Rachels' argument is the view that the unconditional obedience required of the worshipper runs counter to the necessary exercise of the worshipper's autonomy in a moral decision. So being a moral agent means that one cannot be a worshipper (i.e., subservient to God's commands), and, conversely, being a worshipper means that one cannot be a moral agent. For these reasons God is unworthy to be worshipped, a conclusion that contradicts the requirement that God is to be worshipped. Hence there is no God.

EXERCISE 5.7

Whose side do you take in the following judgement-day dialogue?

God: You must be feeling foolish! What have you to say for yourself before I punish you with everlasting torments?

Atheist: Well, sir, I was obviously wrong; but I won't apologize. In fact, I'm furious. Why should I be blamed? If you'd made the evidence for your existence a little more obvious, I'd have been happy to believe in you. So it's your fault!

God: My fault? How dare you! Others have believed on the same evidence.

Atheist: So good for them! But you gave me the ability to make a free decision, and I made that decision. But what did you expect? That I'd always get it right? You gave me the freedom to choose, and so you are now punishing me for doing what you wanted me to do.

God: That I gave you the freedom to choose does not make me responsible for the decisions you make. And being responsible for them means accepting the blame and the punishment.

Atheist: So I am to suffer infinite pain for a genuine mistake? In that case, sir, you're not nice. So why expect me to worship somebody so unpleasant?

Quinn's reply to Rachels

Philip Quinn has, however, suggested one way in which this apparent contradiction can be resolved. It is quite possible that God can require that autonomy be exercised in moral situations, and thus remain worthy of worship, because it is not contrary to his nature to allow individuals to *deny* that the commands they have received *are* genuine divine commands.

---

48. 'God and Human Attitudes', *Religious Studies*, 17, 1971, pp. 325–337. Reprinted in *Divine Commands and Morality*, ed. Paul Helm, Oxford, Oxford University Press, 1981, pp. 34–48.

In other words, an autonomous moral agent can admit the existence of God if he is prepared to deny that any putative divine command which is inconsistent with his hard-core reflective moral judgements really is a divine command. He can resolve the supposed role-conflict by allowing that genuine divine commands ought to be obeyed unconditionally but also maintaining that no directive which he does not accept on moral grounds is a genuine divine command.[49]

What Quinn is saying here is that obedience to God's commands does not negate autonomous moral judgment because it is only through its exercise that a believer can give good moral reasons why he ought to do what God is commanding him to do. Rachels, in other words, has failed to distinguish between (a) unqualified *obedience* to a divine command and (b) unqualified *acceptance of the claim* that a command is of divine origin. In the latter case, the believer may rightly apply 'particularly stringent epistemic conditions' before accepting whether certain commands are genuinely God's – such as whether the command is demonic or divine, whether it coheres with scripture and dogma, and so on. This is not a case of the believer 'sitting in judgement' on divine commands and so qualifying his obedience; but rather of him laudably 'qualifying his assent to claims of moral authority made on religious grounds. This he must do somehow if he is not to become a fanatic or the victim of charismatic religious charlatans.'[50]

By way of example Quinn cites the well-known story of Abraham and Isaac. Abraham may have good reasons for saying that God's command to kill Isaac ought to be obeyed – after all, obeying God's commands has in the past brought him rich rewards, not least having a son when he was 100 years old. On the other hand, Abraham may have equally good reasons for disobeying God's command – he is a proto-Kantian, who believes that the killing of the innocent is morally inexcusable. Here, then, there is a conflict of duties which Abraham must resolve, and resolve in the only way he can, by the exercise of his autonomous reason.

Quinn's criticism of Rachels' argument is justified. For it is clearly not contradictory for the believer to say that the being he worships requires that he act autonomously, if, like Abraham, he must decide *before* being obedient to a command whether it is or is not worthy of the God he worships. To this extent Quinn is not presenting a simple definitional version of divine command theory – which, as we have seen, is vulnerable to the objection that, if God commands what is by definition right, killing the innocent would be right if he commanded it – but rather a modification in which the believer may offer good reasons for disputing that a reported command of God *is* of divine origin. This modification would thus allow him to reject, through the exercise of his autonomy, a command like 'Kill Isaac' if killing him was held to be contrary to his 'hard-core reflective moral judgements'.

---

49. Quinn, *Divine Commands and Moral Requirements*, Oxford, Clarendon Press, 1978, pp. 6–7.

50. *Ibid.*, p. 10.

But Quinn's success against Rachels is bought at a high price, since his reply now requires us to jettison divine command theory altogether, even in its modified form. As the Abraham case makes clear, the autonomous decision to obey God is *preceded* by the autonomous evaluation of what things are goods and evils: what we autonomously assess as being good is subsequently applied to God as being worthy of him (he would command it), whereas what is autonomously assessed as evil is not so applied (he would forbid it). Here, then, and contrary to divine command theory, the ultimate criterion of moral action is not that right actions are right *only because* God commands them but because our autonomous reason has previously decided that they possess the property of being right, which explains why we subsequently describe them as acts that God would command. If this be the case, we may apply to Quinn the criticism already made of Adams. Whatever moral values we may autonomously decide to attribute to God (whether these would require killing Isaac or not), *the act of attribution means that the divine command theory has been relinquished*, and that whatever reason we had for saying that a certain moral act *is* worthy of God may be held as the same reason why we *ought* to perform it. The fact, of course, that 'God commands X' may certainly provide an additional reason for the believer to do X; but a sufficient reason already exists for his doing it, and that independent of God's will.[51]

EXERCISE 5.8

God has ordered you (Abraham) to sacrifice Isaac. But how do you determine that the command comes from God? Which of the following options would help you decide?

I'll obey because I recognize his voice.

I'll obey because obeying God brings rich rewards.

I'll obey because killing Isaac will show God that I love him the most.

I'll obey because I expect a miracle afterwards: he'll bring him back to life.

I'll disobey because God would never command me to kill a child.

I'll disobey because hearing voices is a sure sign of psychological disorder.

CONCLUSION: ABSOLUTE MORAL LAWS WITHOUT GOD

Of all the arguments for God's existence reviewed in this book, the moral argument is the weakest. It seldom stands alone and acts more as a supplement to other arguments, appealing by and large to those who already have grounds

---

51. For further criticisms, see John Chandler, 'Is the Divine Command Theory Defensible?', *Religious Studies*, 20, 1984, pp. 443–452; and 'Divine Command Theories and the Appeal to Love', *American Philosophical Quarterly*, 22, 1985, pp. 231–239; also T. A. Roberts, 'Morality and Divine Commands', *Proceedings of the Aristotelian Society*, 68, 1968, pp. 49–62.

for their religious belief. That God is the source of all moral obligation – that in some sense he 'created' the moral law in much the same way that he created the universe (as Descartes believed)[52] – is true if it is true that no other cosmological explanation of the origin of things (including moral phenomena) is possible. But other competing cosmological explanations are possible and these alternatives have first to be evaluated before we can proceed to the moral argument.

But even if we set these alternatives aside, and state that we have arrived, by whatever route, at a belief in God's existence, it is difficult to see what additional warrants the moral argument could of itself provide for us. The claim that 'There is a God and what is good is created by him: thus I do good when I obey him' is a perfectly sound *description* of what a believer *affirms* to be true; but as a form of *proof* it remains either cosmological in form – requiring first and foremost a demonstration of the truth of its first premiss – or a particularly instructive example of the fallacy known as *petitio principii* – i.e., the fallacy of begging the question – by presupposing its first premiss and so depending upon the very point at issue, namely, that there is a God who is the source of all moral truth. Either, then, the moral argument, as a species of cosmological proof, is open to all the objections of an earlier chapter; or its reasoning is circular and thus fallacious: the existence of an objective moral law being first used to establish the argument's first premiss – that there is a God – and this first premiss being then employed to establish its conclusion, that without God's existence no objective moral law would exist. This conclusion, we should add, is perhaps the greatest source of embarrassment for even the doughtiest believer, the argument's *reductio ad absurdum* being that atheists and agnostics (for example, Lucretius, Spinoza, Mill, Hume, George Eliot, Darwin, Einstein and Russell) must evidently have a hard time of it trying to be moral – this list of names, it is hoped, being sufficient to demonstrate that moral degeneracy is not a necessary consequence of indifference or denial.[53] Indeed, as Kai Nielsen has argued, the desire to live in obedience to a command may be construed as an infantile abdication of moral responsibility, carrying with it therefore less chance of attaining moral maturity (SOURCE 6: PP. 279–281).

As Swinburne aptly remarks, 'man's moral knowledge does not wear its source on its face'.[54] Indeed, the history of philosophy is sufficiently full of alternative theories of morality to make it unlikely that the moral argument is the only, or even the most convincing, candidate; and whatever initial success the moral argument may have had against the claims of ethical relativism – that there are no absolute moral laws and that therefore morality is subjective and so culturally and personally diverse – this success is quickly dissipated before a

The failure of the moral argument

⇐

---

52. So: 'You asked me by what kind of causality God established the eternal truths. I reply: By the same kind of causality as He created all things, that is to say, as their efficient and total cause.' *Philosophical Letters*, trans. and ed. by Antony Kenny, Minneapolis, University of Minnesota Press, 1981, p. 11.

53. A more specific example: a study by Samuel and Pearl Oliner revealed that, of those who helped Jews escape the Holocaust, many were non-religious, their actions defining them as moral persons. *The Altruistic Personality: Rescuers of the Jews*, New York, Free Press, 1988, pp. 174–175.

54. *The Existence of God*, p. 179.

much more powerful set of opponents, which claims that absolute moral laws may be generated without the presumption of a deity. 'That there is a God' is certainly one explanation of why there are shared moral values – like 'Murder is wrong' – but it competes with many others, less metaphysically ambitious. We may say, just to mention some, that this is an absolute moral rule because, to adopt a Kantian view, it is categorically applicable to everyone and safeguards the rights of every autonomous individual; or because, to follow Hobbes, it reflects a fundamental human need, shared by different societies, to protect citizens; or because, viewed from an evolutionary perspective, it fosters a more secure and stable environment, makes the rearing of vigorous individuals more likely, and so increases the chances of species survival.

These, then, are just a few of the many attempts to show that morality can have an objective basis without religion, and a much more extensive catalogue, although beyond the scope of this book, could be introduced here.[55] The important point to note, however, is that it is precisely these systems of ethics, formulated without reference to God, which advocates of the moral argument must show to be unsuccessful if their argument is to be successful. But as yet no comprehensive critique of these alternatives has been forthcoming, understandably perhaps, and for two good reasons. First, it is difficult to see how the theistic alternative is to be preferred when it first requires as its warrant the assumption of a divine existence far more extraordinary than anything it may be said to explain; and second, in calling this existence 'good', and thus the origin of goodness, it is hard to see how it can escape the following dilemma: If goodness is a defining attribute of God, the theory is circular and so uninformative; but if it is not a defining attribute, the theory is false, since we now have no guarantee that what God commands is good. In neither case, then, does the argument provide a tenable theory of morality.

To return to the Euthyphro dilemma: it is unreasonable to believe that an action is right because God commands it to be done. One may, on the other hand, more reasonably believe that God commands an action to be done because it is right; but believing this is to hold that an action is right, irrespective of whether there is a God or not. In the final analysis, then, the view that the moral law requires a divine lawgiver cannot be sustained because in the moment we credit goodness *to* God we undermine any argument that goodness comes *from* God alone.

---

55. See also Roderick Firth, 'Ethical Absolutism and the Ideal Observer', in *Readings in Ethical Theory*, ed. Wilfrid Sellars and John Hospers, 2nd edn, Englewood Cliffs, N.J., Prentice-Hall, 1970, pp. 200–221; Richard Boyd, 'How to be a Moral Realist', and Peter Railton, 'Moral Realism', in *Moral Discourse and Practice*, ed. S. Darwell, A. Gibbard and P. Railton, Oxford, Oxford University Press, 1997, pp. 105–135, pp. 137–163; and David Brink, *Moral Realism and the Foundations of Ethics*, Cambridge, Cambridge University Press, 1989; Bernard Gert, *Morality: A New Justification of the Moral Rules*, New York, Oxford University Press, 1988. See also the collection *Prospects for a Common Morality*, ed. Gene Outka and John P. Reeder Jr, Princeton, N.J., Princeton University Press, 1993.

1 What evidence is there to support the view that there are universal moral values? How would you reply to the criticisms of ethical relativism?

2 Analyse Plato's discussion of morality in the dialogue *Euthyphro*. What is his conclusion and what is its relevance for the moral argument?

3 What is the *absurdum practicum* and how does Kant resolve it? Does he resolve it successfully?

4. What does the expression 'Ought implies can' signify for moral action? What role does it play in Kant's argument?

5 What do you consider the principal weaknesses of Kant's moral argument?

6 Analyse and discuss Rachels' disproof of the existence of God.

7 'What God commands must be good.' What problems follow from this assertion?

8 Examine the view that, in claiming that God is good, the believer is presupposing an independent standard of goodness.

9 'No autonomous individual can act morally in obeying a divine command.' Discuss.

10 Is it the case that, if there is no God, everything is permitted?

SOURCES: THE MORAL ARGUMENT

1 PLATO: THE EUTHYPHRO DILEMMA[2]

Socrates: Then come, dear Euthyphro, teach me as well, and let me grow wise. What proof have you that all the gods think that your servant died unjustly, your hireling, who, when he had killed a man, was shackled by the master of the victim, and perished, dying because of his shackles before the man who shackled him could learn from the seers what ought to be done with him? What proof have you that for a man like him it is right for a son to prosecute his father, and indict him on a charge of murder? Come on. Try to make it clear to me beyond all doubt that under these conditions the gods must all consider this action to be right. If you can adequately prove it to me, I will never cease from praising you for your wisdom.

Euthyphro: But, Socrates, that, very likely, would be no small task, although I could indeed make it very clear to you.

Socrates: I understand. You think that I am duller than the judges; obviously you will demonstrate to them that what your father did was wrong, and that the gods all hate such deeds.

---

1. *Plato: The Collected Dialogues*, ed. by Edith Hamilton and Huntington Cairns, Bollingen Series 51, New York, Pantheon Books, 1966, pp. 172–185.

Euthyphro: I shall prove it absolutely, Socrates, if they will listen to me.

Socrates: They are sure to listen if they think that you speak well. But while you were talking, a notion came into my head, and I asked myself, Suppose that Euthyphro proved to me quite clearly that all the gods consider such a death unjust; would I have come one whit the nearer for him to knowing what the holy is, and what is the unholy? The act in question, seemingly, might be displeasing to the gods, but then we have just seen that you cannot define the holy and unholy in that way, for we have seen that a given thing may be displeasing, and also pleasing to gods. So on this point, Euthyphro, I will let you off; if you like, the gods shall all consider the act unjust, and they all shall hate it. But suppose that we now correct our definition, and say what the gods all hate is unholy, and what they love is holy, whereas what some of them love, and others hate, is either both or neither. Are you willing that we now define the holy and unholy in this way?

Euthyphro: What is there to prevent us, Socrates?

Socrates: Nothing to prevent me, Euthyphro. As for you, see whether when you take this definition you can quite readily instruct me, as you promised.

Euthyphro: Yes, I would indeed affirm that holiness is what the gods all love, and its opposite is what the gods all hate, unholiness.

Socrates: Are we to examine this position also, Euthyphro, to see if it is sound? Or shall we let it through, and thus accept our own and others' statement, and agree to an assertion simply when somebody says that a thing is so? Must we not look into what the speaker says?

Euthyphro: We must. And yet, for my part, I regard the present statement as correct.

Socrates: We shall soon know better about that, my friend. Now think of this. Is what is holy holy because the gods approve it, or do they approve it because it is holy?

Euthyphro: I do not get your meaning.

Socrates: Well, I will try to make it clearer. We speak of what is carried and the carrier, do we not, of led and leader, of the seen and that which sees? And you understand that in all such cases the things are different, and how they differ?

Euthyphro: Yes, I think I understand.

Socrates: In the same way what is one thing, and what loves is another?

Euthyphro: Of course.

Socrates: Tell me now, is what is carried 'carried' because something carries it, or is it for some other reason?

Euthyphro: No, but for that reason.

Socrates: And what is led, because something leads it? And what is seen, because something sees it?

Euthyphro: Yes, certainly.

Socrates: Then it is not because a thing is seen that something sees it, but just the opposite – because something sees it, therefore it is seen. Nor because it is led, that something leads it, but because something leads it, therefore it is led. Nor because it is carried, that something carries it, but because something carries it, therefore it is carried. Do you see what I wish to say, Euthyphro? It is this.

Whenever an effect occurs, or something is effected, it is not the thing effected that gives rise to the effect; no, there is a cause, and then comes this effect. Nor is it because a thing is acted on that there is this effect; no, there is a cause for what it undergoes, and then comes this effect. Don't you agree?

Euthyphro: I do.

Socrates: Well then, when a thing is loved, is it not in process of becoming something, or of undergoing something, by some other thing?

Euthyphro: Yes, certainly.

Socrates: Then the same is true here as in the previous cases. It is not because a thing is loved that they who love it love it, but it is loved because they love it.

Euthyphro: Necessarily.

Socrates: Then what are we to say about the holy, Euthyphro? According to your argument, is it not loved by all the gods?

Euthyphro: Yes.

Socrates: Because it is holy, or for some other reason?

Euthyphro: No, it is for that reason.

Socrates: And so it is because it is holy that it is loved; it is not holy because it is loved.

Euthyphro: So it seems.

Socrates: On the other hand, it is beloved and pleasing to the gods just because they love it?

Euthyphro: No doubt of that.

Socrates: So what is pleasing to the gods is not the same as what is holy, Euthyphro, nor, according to your statement, is the holy the same as what is pleasing to the gods. They are two different things.

Euthyphro: How may that be, Socrates?

Socrates: Because we agree that the holy is loved because it is holy, and is not holy because it is loved. Isn't it so?

Euthyphro: Yes.

Socrates: Whereas what is pleasing to the gods is pleasing to them just because they love it, such being its nature and its cause. Its being loved of the gods is not the reason of its being loved.

Euthyphro: You are right.

Socrates: But suppose, dear Euthyphro, that what is pleasing to the gods and what is holy were not two separate things. In that case if holiness were loved because it was holy, then also what was pleasing to the gods would be loved because it pleased them. And, on the other hand, if what was pleasing to them pleased because they loved it, then also the holy would be holy because they loved it. But now you see that it is just the opposite, because the two are absolutely different from each other, for the one [what is pleasing to the gods] is of a sort to be loved because it is loved, whereas the other [what is holy] is loved because it is of a sort to be loved. Consequently, Euthyphro, it looks as if you had not given me my answer – as if when you were asked to tell the nature of the holy, you did not wish to explain the essence of it. You merely tell an attribute of it, namely, that it appertains to holiness to be loved by all the gods. What it is, as yet you have not said. So, if you please, do not conceal this from me. No begin again. Say what the holy is, and never mind if gods do love it, nor if it has some

other attribute; on that we shall not split. Come, speak out. Explain the nature
of the holy and unholy.

Euthyphro: Now, Socrates, I simply don't know how to tell you what I think.
Somehow everything that we put forward keeps moving about us in a circle,
and nothing will stay where we put it.

2 C. S. LEWIS: THE LAW OF NATURE[1]

Each man is at every moment subjected to several different sets of law but there
is only one of these which he is free to disobey. As a body, he is subjected to
gravitation and cannot disobey it; if you leave him unsupported in mid-air, he has
no more choice about falling than a stone has. As an organism, he is subjected to
various biological laws which he cannot disobey any more than an animal can.
That is, he cannot disobey those laws which he shares with other things; but the
law he does not share with animals or vegetables or inorganic things, is the one
he can disobey if he chooses.

The law was called the Law of Nature because people thought that every one
knew it by nature and did not need to be taught it. They did not mean, of course,
that you might not find an odd individual here and there who did not know it,
just as you find a few people who are colour-blind or have no ear for a tune. But
taking the race as a whole, they thought that the human idea of decent behaviour
was obvious to every one. And I believe they were right. If they were not, then all
the things we said about the war were nonsense. What was the sense in saying the
enemy were in the wrong unless Right is a real thing which the Nazis at bottom
knew as well as we did and ought to have practised? If they had had no notion of
what we mean by right, then, though we might still have had to fight them, we
could no more have blamed them for that than for the colour of their hair.

I know that some people say the idea of a Law of Nature or decent behaviour
known to all men is unsound, because different civilisations and different ages
have had quite different moralities.

But this is not true. There have been differences between their moralities, but
these have never amounted to anything like a total difference. If anyone will take
the trouble to compare the moral teaching of, say, the ancient Egyptians,
Babylonians, Hindus, Chinese, Greeks and Romans, what will really strike him
will be how very like they are to each other and to our own. . . . Men have differed
as regards what people you ought to be unselfish to – whether it was only your
own family, or your fellow countrymen, or every one. But they have always agreed
that you ought not to put yourself first. Selfishness has never been admired. Men
have differed as to whether you should have one wife or four. But they have always
agreed that you must not simply have any woman you liked . . .

It seems, then, we are forced to believe in a real Right and Wrong. People may
be sometimes mistaken about them, just as people sometimes get their sums wrong;
but they are not a matter of mere taste and opinion any more than the

---

2. *Mere Christianity*, London, Fontana Books, 1964, pp. 16–19, 29–33.

multiplication table. Now if we are agreed about this, I go on to my next point, which is this. None of us are really keeping the Law of Nature. If there are any exceptions among you, I apologise to them. They had much better read some other book, for nothing I am going to say concerns them. And now, turning to the ordinary human beings who are left . . .

I do not succeed in keeping the Law of Nature very well, and the moment anyone tells me I am not keeping it, there starts up in my mind a string of excuses as long as your arm. The question at the moment is not whether they are good excuses. The point is that they are one more proof of how deeply, whether we like it or not, we believe in the Law of Nature. If we do not believe in decent behaviour, why should we be so anxious to make excuses for not having behaved decently? The truth is, we believe in decency so much – we feel the Rule or Law pressing on us so – that we cannot bear to face the fact that we are breaking it, and consequently we try to shift the responsibility. For you notice that it is only for our bad behaviour that we find all these explanations. It is only our bad temper that we put down to being tired or worried or hungry; we put our good temper down to ourselves.

These, then, are the two points I wanted to make. First, that human beings, all over the earth, have this curious idea that they ought to behave in a certain way, and cannot really get rid of it. Secondly, that they do not in fact behave in that way. They know the Law of Nature; they break it. These two facts are the foundation of all clear thinking about ourselves and the universe we live in . . .

Let us sum up what we have reached so far. In the case of stones and trees and things of that sort, what we call the Laws of Nature may not be anything except a way of speaking. When you say that nature is governed by certain laws, this may mean that nature does, in fact, behave in a certain way. The so-called laws may not be anything real – anything above and beyond the actual facts which we observe. But in the case of Man, we saw that this will not do. The Law of Human Nature, or of Right and Wrong, must be something above and beyond the actual facts of human behaviour. In this case, besides the actual facts, you have something else – a real law which we did not invent and which we know we ought to obey.

I now want to consider what this tells us about the universe we live in. Ever since men were able to think, they have been wondering what this universe really is and how it came to be there. And, very roughly, two views have been held. First, there is what is called the materialist view. People who take that view think that matter and space just happen to exist, and always have existed, nobody knows why; and that the matter, behaving in certain fixed ways, has just happened, by a sort of fluke, to produce creatures like ourselves who are able to think. By one chance in a thousand something hit our sun and made it produce the planets; and by another thousandth chance the chemicals necessary for life, and the right temperature, occurred on one of these planets, and so some of the matter on this earth came alive; and then, by a very long series of chances, the living creatures developed into things like us. The other view is the religious view. According to it, what is behind the universe is more like a mind than it is like anything else we know. That is to say, it is conscious, and has purposes, and prefers one thing to another. And on this view it made the universe, partly for purposes we do not know, but partly, at any rate, in order to produce creatures like itself – I mean, like itself to the extent of having minds. Please do not think that one of these views was held a long time ago and that the other has gradually taken its place. Wherever there have been thinking men both views turn up. And note this too. You cannot find out which view is the right one by science in the ordinary sense. Science works by experiments. It watches how things behave. Every scientific statement in the long run, however complicated it looks, really means something like, 'I pointed the telescope to such and such a part of the sky at 2.20 a.m. on January 15th and saw so-and-so,' or 'I put some of this stuff in a pot and heated it to such-and-such a temperature and it did so-and-so.' Do not think I am saying anything against science: I am only saying what its job is. And the more scientific a man is, the more (I believe) he would agree with me that this is the job of science – and a very useful and necessary job it is too. But why anything comes to be there at all, and whether there is anything behind the things science observes – something of a different kind – this is not a scientific question. If there is 'Something Behind,' then either it will have to remain altogether unknown to men or else make itself known in some different way. The statement that there is any such thing, and the statement that there is no such thing, are neither of them statements that science can make. And real scientists do not usually make them. It is usually the journalists and popular novelists who have picked up a few odds and ends of half-baked science from textbooks who go in for them. After all, it is really a matter of common sense. Supposing science ever became complete so that it knew every single thing in the whole universe. Is it not plain that the questions, 'Why is there a universe?' 'Why does it go on as it does?' 'Has it any meaning?' would remain just as they were.

Now the position would be quite hopeless but for this. There is one thing, and only one, in the whole universe which we know more about than we could learn from external observation. That one thing is Man. We do not merely observe men, we *are* men. In this case we have, so to speak, inside information; we are in the know. And because of that, we know that men find themselves under a moral law, which they did not make, and cannot quite forget even when they try, and which they know they ought to obey. Notice the following point. Anyone studying Man from the outside as we study electricity or cabbages, not knowing our language and consequently not able to get any inside knowledge from us, but merely observing what we did, would never get the slightest evidence that we had this moral law. How could he? for his observations would only show what we did, and the moral law is about what we ought to do. In the same way, if there were anything above or behind the observed facts in the case of stones or the weather, we, by studying them from outside, could never hope to discover it.

The position of the question, then, is like this. We want to know whether the universe simply happens to be what it is for no reason or whether there is a power behind it that makes it what it is. Since that power, if it exists, would be not one of the observed facts but a reality which makes them, no mere observation of the facts can find it. There is only one case in which we can know whether there is anything more, namely our own case. And in that one case we find there is. Or put it the other way round. If there was a controlling power outside the universe, it could not show itself to us as one of the facts inside the universe – no more than the architect of a house could actually be a wall or staircase or fireplace in that house. The only way in which we could expect it to show itself would be inside ourselves as an influence or a command trying to get us to behave in a certain way. And that is just what we do find inside ourselves. Surely this ought to arouse our suspicions? In the only case where you can expect to get an answer, the answer turns out to be Yes; and in the other cases, where you do not get an answer, you see why you do not. Suppose someone asked me, when I see a man in a blue uniform going down the street leaving little paper packets at each house, why I suppose that they contain letters? I should reply, 'Because whenever he leaves a similar little packet for me I find it does contain a letter.' And if he then objected – 'But you've never seen all these letters which you think the other people are getting,' I should say, 'Of course not, and I shouldn't expect to, because they're not addressed to me. I'm explaining the packets I'm not allowed to open by the ones I am allowed to open.' It is the same about this question. The only packet I am allowed to open is Man. When I do, especially when I open that particular man called Myself, I find that I do not exist on my own, that I am under a law; that somebody or something wants me to behave in a certain way. I do not, of course, think that if I could get inside a stone or a tree I should find exactly the same thing, just as I do not think all the other people in the street get the same letters as I do. I should expect, for instance, to find that the stone had to obey the law of gravity – that whereas the sender of the letters merely tells me to obey the law of my human nature, He compels the stone to obey the laws of its stony nature. But I should expect to find that there was, so to speak, a sender of letters in both cases, a Power behind the facts, a Director, a Guide . . .

All I have got to is a Something which is directing the universe, and which appears in me as a law urging me to do right and making me feel responsible and uncomfortable when I do wrong. I think we have to assume it is more like a mind than it is like anything else we know – because after all the only other thing we know is matter and you can hardly imagine a bit of matter giving instructions . . .

3 IMMANUEL KANT: THE EXISTENCE OF GOD AS A POSTULATE OF PURE PRACTICAL REASON[3]

In the preceding analysis the moral law led to a practical task that is set by pure reason alone and without the aid of any sensible incentives, namely that of the necessary completeness of the first and principal part of the highest good, **morality**; and, since this can be fully accomplished only in an eternity, it led to the postulate of *immortality*. The same law must also lead to the possibility of the second element of the highest good, namely **happiness** proportioned to that morality, and must do so as disinterestedly as before, solely from impartial reason; in other words, it must lead to the supposition of the existence of a cause adequate to this effect, that is, it must postulate the *existence of God* as belonging necessarily to

---

3. *Critique of Practical Reason*, translated and edited by Mary Gregor, with an Introduction by Andrews Reath, Cambridge, Cambridge University Press, 1997, pp. 103–110.

the possibility of the highest good (which object of our will is necessarily connected with the moral lawgiving of pure reason). We shall present this connection in a convincing manner.

Happiness is the state of a rational being in the world in the whole of whose existence *everything goes according to his wish and will*, and rests, therefore, on the harmony of nature with his whole end as well as with the essential determining ground of his will. Now, the moral law as a law of freedom commands through determining grounds that are to be quite independent of nature and of its harmony with our faculty of desire (as incentives); the acting rational being in the world is, however, not also the cause of the world and of nature itself. Consequently, there is not the least ground in the moral law for a necessary connection between the morality and the proportionate happiness of a being belonging to the world as part of it and hence dependent upon it, who for that reason cannot by his will be a cause of this nature and, as far as his happiness is concerned, cannot by his own powers make it harmonize thoroughly with his practical principles. Nevertheless, in the practical task of pure reason, that is, in the necessary pursuit of the highest good, such a connection is postulated as necessary: we *ought* to strive to promote the highest good (which must therefore be possible). Accordingly, the existence of a cause of all nature, distinct from nature, which contains the ground of this connection, namely of the exact correspondence of happiness with morality, is also *postulated*. However, this supreme cause is to contain the ground of the correspondence of nature not merely with a law of the will of rational beings but with the representation of this *law*, so far as they make it the *supreme determining ground of the will*, and consequently not merely with morals in their form but also with their morality as their determining ground, that is, with their moral disposition. Therefore, the highest good in the world is possible only insofar as a supreme cause of nature having a causality in keeping with the moral disposition is assumed. Now, a being capable of actions in accordance with the representation of laws is *an intelligence* (a rational being), and the causality of such a being in accordance with this representation of laws is his *will*. Therefore the supreme cause of nature, insofar as it must be presupposed for the highest good, is a being that is the cause of nature by *understanding* and *will* (hence its author), that is, **God**. Consequently, the postulate of the possibility of the *highest derived good* (the best world) is likewise the postulate of the reality of a *highest original good*, namely of the existence of God. Now, it was a duty for us to promote the highest good; hence there is in us not merely the warrant but also the necessity, as a need connected with duty, to presuppose the possibility of this highest good, which, since it is possible only under the condition of the existence of God, connects the presupposition of the existence of God inseparably with duty; that is, it is morally necessary to assume the existence of God.

It is well to note here that this moral necessity *is subjective*, that is, a need, and not *objective*, that is, itself a duty; for, there can be no duty to assume the existence of anything (since this concerns only the theoretical use of reason). Moreover, it is not to be understood by this that it is necessary to assume the existence of God *as a ground of all obligation in general* (for this rests, as has been sufficiently shown, solely on the autonomy of reason itself). What belongs to duty here is only the striving to produce and promote the highest good in the world, the possibility of which can therefore be postulated, while our reason finds this thinkable only on the presupposition of a supreme intelligence; to assume the existence of this supreme intelligence is thus connected with the consciousness of our duty, although this assumption itself belongs to theoretical reason; with respect to theoretical reason alone, as a ground of explanation, it can be called a *hypothesis*; but in relation to the intelligibility of an object given us by the moral law (the highest good), and consequently of a need for practical purposes, it can be called *belief* and, indeed, a pure *rational belief* since pure reason alone (in its theoretical as well as in its practical use) is the source from which it springs.

From this *deduction* it now becomes comprehensible why the *Greek* schools could never solve their problem of the practical possibility of the highest good: it was because they made the rule of the use which the human will makes of its freedom the sole and sufficient ground of this possibility, without, as it seemed to them, needing the existence of God for it. They were indeed correct in establishing the principle of morals by itself, independently of this postulate and solely from the relation of reason to the will, so that they made it the *supreme* practical condition of the highest good; but this principle was not on this account the *whole* condition of its possibility. The Epicureans had indeed assumed an altogether false principle of morals as supreme, namely that of happiness, and had substituted for a law a maxim of each choosing as he pleased according to his inclination; they proceeded, however, *consistently* enough in this by demeaning their highest good in the same way, namely in proportion to the meanness of their principle, and expecting no greater happiness than can be acquired by human prudence (including temperance and moderation of the inclinations), which, as we know, has to be paltry enough and turn out very differently according to circumstances, not to mention the exceptions which their maxims had to constantly admit and which made them unfit for laws. The Stoics, on the contrary, had chosen their supreme practical principle quite correctly, namely virtue, as the condition of the highest good; but inasmuch as they represented the degree of virtue required by its pure law as fully attainable in this life, they not only strained the moral capacity of the *human being*, under the name of a *sage*, far beyond all the limits of his nature and assumed something that contradicts all cognition of the human being, but also and above all they would not let the second *component* of the highest good, namely happiness, hold as a special object of the human faculty of desire but made their *sage*, like a divinity in his consciousness of the excellence of his person, quite independent of nature (with respect to his own contentment), exposing him indeed to the ills of life but not subjecting him to them (at the same time representing him as also free from evil); and thus they really left out the second element of the highest good, namely one's own happiness, placing it solely in acting and in contentment with one's personal worth and so including it in consciousness of one's moral cast of mind – though in this they could have been sufficiently refuted by the voice of their own nature.

The doctrine of Christianity, even if it is not regarded as a religious doctrine, gives on this point a concept of the highest good (of the kingdom of God) which alone satisfies the strictest demand of practical reason. The moral law is holy (inflexible) and demands holiness of morals, although all the moral perfection that a human being can attain is still only virtue, that is, a disposition confirmed with law *from respect* for law, and thus consciousness of a continuing propensity to transgression or at least impurity, that is, an admixture of many spurious (not moral) motives to observe the law, hence a self-esteem combined with humility; and so, with respect to the holiness that the Christian law demands, nothing remains for a creature but endless progress, though for that reason he is justified in hoping for his endless duration. The *worth* of a disposition *completely* conformed with the moral law is infinite, since all possible happiness in the judgment of a wise and all-powerful distributor of it has no restriction other than rational beings' lack of conformity with their duty. But the moral law of itself still does not *promise* any happiness, since this is not necessarily connected with observance of the law according to our concepts of a natural order as such. The Christian doctrine of morals now supplements this lack (of the second indispensable component of the highest good) by representing the world in which rational beings devote themselves with their whole soul to the moral law as a *kingdom of God*, in which nature and morals come into a harmony, foreign to each of them of itself, through a holy author who makes the derived highest good possible. *Holiness* of morals is prescribed to them as a rule even in this life, while the well-being proportioned to it, namely *beatitude*, is represented as attainable only in an eternity; for, the *former* must always be the archetype of their conduct in every state, and progress toward it already possible and necessary in this life, whereas the *latter*, under the name of happiness, cannot be attained at all in this world (so far as our own capacity is concerned) and is therefore made solely an object of hope. Nevertheless, the Christian principle of *morals* itself is not theological (and so heteronomy); it is instead autonomy of pure practical reason by itself, since it does not make cognition of God and his will the basis of these laws but only of the attainment of the highest good subject to the condition of observing these laws, and since it places even the proper *incentive* to observing them not in the results wished for but in the representation of duty alone, faithful observance of which alone constitutes worthiness to acquire the latter.

In this way the moral law leads through the concept of the highest good, as the object and final end of pure practical reason, *to religion, that is, to the recognition of all duties as divine commands, not as sanctions – that is, chosen and in themselves contingent ordinances of another's will –* but as essential *laws* of every free will in itself, which must nevertheless be regarded as commands of the supreme being because only from a will that is morally perfect (holy and beneficent) and at the same time all-powerful, and so through harmony with this will, can we hope to attain the highest good, which the moral law makes it our duty to take as the object of our endeavors. Here again, then, everything remains disinterested and grounded only on duty, and there is no need to base it on incentives of fear and hope, which if they became principles would destroy the whole moral worth of actions. The moral law commands me to make the highest possible good in a world the final object of my conduct. But I cannot hope to produce this except by the harmony of my will with that of a holy and beneficent author of the world; and although in the concept of the highest good, as that of a whole in which the greatest happiness is represented as connected in the most exact proportion with the greatest degree of moral perfection (possible in creatures), *my own happiness* is included, this is nevertheless not the determining ground of the will that is directed to promote the highest good; it is instead the moral law (which, on the contrary, limits by strict conditions my unbounded craving for happiness).

For this reason, again, morals is not properly the doctrine of how we are to *make* ourselves happy but of how we are to become *worthy* of happiness. Only if religion is added to it does there also enter the hope of some day participating in happiness to the degree that we have been intent upon not being unworthy of it.

Someone is *worthy* of possessing a thing or state when it harmonizes with the highest good that he is in possession of it. It can now be readily seen that all worthiness depends upon moral conduct, since in the concept of the highest good this constitutes the condition of the rest (which belongs to one's state), namely, of one's share of happiness. Now, from this it follows that *morals* in itself must never be treated as a *doctrine of happiness*, that is, as instruction in how to become happy; for morals has to do solely with the rational condition (*conditio sine qua non*) of happiness and not with the means of acquiring it. But when morals (which merely imposes duties and does not provide rules for selfish wishes) has been set forth completely, then – after the moral wish, based on a law, to promote the highest good (to bring the kingdom of God to us) has been awakened, which could not previously have arisen in any selfish soul, and for the sake of this wish the step to religion has been taken – then for the first time can this ethical doctrine also be called a doctrine of happiness, because it is only with religion that the *hope* of happiness first arises.

From this it can also be seen that if one asks about *God's final end* in creating the world, one must not name the *happiness* of the rational beings in it but *the highest good*, which adds a condition to that wish of such beings, namely the condition of being worthy of happiness, that is, the *morality* of these same rational beings, which condition alone contains the standard in accordance with which they can hope to participate in the former at the hands of a *wise* author. For, since *wisdom* considered theoretically signifies *cognition of the highest good*, and practically *the fitness of the will for the highest good*, one cannot attribute to a highest independent wisdom an end that would be based merely on beneficence. For one cannot conceive the effect of this beneficence (with respect to the happiness of rational beings) as befitting the highest original good except under the limiting conditions of harmony with the *holiness* of his will. Hence those who put the end of creation in the glory of God (provided this is not thought anthropomorphically, as inclination to be praised) perhaps hit upon the best expression. For, nothing glorifies God more than what is most estimable in the world, respect for his command, observance of the holy duty that his law lays upon us, when there is added to this his magnificent plan of crowning such a beautiful order with corresponding happiness. If the latter (to speak humanly) makes him worthy of love, by the former he is an object of worship (adoration). Human beings themselves can acquire love by beneficence, but by it alone they can never acquire respect, so that the greatest beneficence procures them honor only when it is exercised in accordance with worthiness.

It now follows of itself that in the order of ends the human being (and with him every rational being) is an *end in itself*, that is, can never be used merely as a means by anyone (not even by God) without being at the same time himself an end, and that humanity in our person must, accordingly, be *holy* to ourselves: for he is the *subject of the moral law* and so of that which is holy in itself, on account of which and in agreement with which alone can anything be called holy. For, this moral law is based on the autonomy of his will, as a free will which, in accordance with its universal laws, must necessarily be able at the same time *to agree* to that to which it is to *subject* itself.

4 JAMES RACHELS: GOD AND AUTONOMY[4]

(The) idea that any being could be *worthy* of worship is much more problematical than we might have at first imagined. For in admitting that a being is worthy of worship we would be recognising him as having an unqualified claim on our obedience. The question, then, is whether there could be such an unqualified claim. It should be noted that the description of a being as all-powerful, all-wise, etc., would not automatically settle the issue; for even while admitting the existence of such an awesome being we might still question whether we should recognise him as having an unlimited claim on our obedience.

In fact, there is a long tradition in moral philosophy, from Plato to Kant, according to which such a recognition could never be made by a moral agent. According to this tradition, to be a moral agent is to be an autonomous and self-directed agent; unlike the precepts of law or social custom, moral precepts are imposed by the agent upon himself, and the penalty for their violation is, in Kant's words, 'self-contempt and inner abhorrence.' The virtuous man is therefore identified with the man of integrity, i.e., the man who acts according to precepts which he can, on reflection, conscientiously approve in his own heart. Although this is a highly individualistic approach to morals, it is not thought to invite anarchy because men are regarded as more or less reasonable and as desiring what we would normally think of as a decent life lived in the company of other men.

On this view, to deliver oneself over to a moral authority for directions about what to do is simply incompatible with being a moral agent. To say 'I will follow so-and-so's directions no matter what they are and no matter what my own conscience would otherwise direct me to do' is to opt out of moral thinking altogether; it is to abandon one's role as a moral agent. And it does not matter whether 'so-and-so' is the law, the custom of one's society, or God. This does not, of course, preclude one from seeking advice on moral matters, and even on occasion following that advice blindly, trusting in the good judgment of the adviser. But this is to be justified by details of the particular case, e.g. that you cannot in that case form any reasonable judgment of your own due to ignorance or inexperience in dealing with the types of matters involved. What *is* precluded is that a man should, while in possession of his wits, adopt this style of decision-making (or perhaps we should say this style of *abdicating* decision-making) as a general strategy of living, or abandon his own best judgment in any case where he can form a judgment of which he is reasonably confident.

---

4. Extracted from 'God and Human Attitudes', *Religious Studies*, 7, 1971, pp. 325–337. Reprinted in *Divine Commands and Morality*, ed. Paul Helm, Oxford, Oxford University Press, 1981, pp. 34–48.

What we have, then, is a conflict between the role of worshipper, which by its very nature commits one to total subservience to God, and the role of moral agent, which necessarily involves autonomous decision-making. The point is that the role of worshipper takes precedence over every other role which the worshipper has – when there is any conflict, the worshipper's commitment to God has priority over any other commitments which he might have. But the first commitment of a moral agent is to do what in his own heart he thinks is right. Thus the following argument might be constructed:

(a) If any being is God, he must be a fitting object of worship.
(b) No being could possibly be a fitting object of worship, since worship requires the abandonment of one's role as an autonomous moral agent.
(c) Therefore, there cannot be any being who is God.

The concept of moral agency underlying this argument is complex and controversial; and, although I think it is sound, I cannot give it the detailed treatment here that it requires. Instead, I will conclude by answering some of the most obvious objections to the argument.

(1) What if God lets us go our own way, and issues no commands other than that we should live according to our own consciences? In that case there would be no incompatibility between our commitment to God and our commitments as moral agents, since God would leave us free to direct our own lives. The fact that this supposition is contrary to major religious traditions (such as the Christian tradition) doesn't matter, since these traditions could be mistaken. The answer here is that this is a mere contingency, and that even if God did not require obedience to detailed commands, the worshipper would still be committed to the abandonment of his role as a moral agent, *if* God required it.

(2) It has been admitted as a necessary truth that God is perfectly good; it follows as a corollary that He would never require us to do anything except what is right. Therefore in obeying God we would only be doing what we should be doing in any case. So there is no incompatibility between obeying him and carrying out our moral commitments. Our primary commitment as moral agents is to do right, and God's commands *are* right, so that's that.

This objection rests on a misunderstanding of the assertion that (necessarily) God is perfectly good. This can be intelligibly asserted only because of the principle that *No being who is not perfectly good may bear the title 'God'*. We cannot determine whether some being is God without first checking on whether he is perfectly good; and we cannot decide whether he is perfectly good without knowing (among other things) whether his commands to us are right. Thus our own judgment that some actions are right, and others wrong, is logically prior to our recognition of any being as God. The upshot of this is that we cannot justify the suspension of our own judgment on the grounds that we are deferring to God's command (which, as a matter of logic, *must* be right); for if, by our own best judgment, the command is wrong, this gives us good reason to withhold the title 'God' from the commander.

(3) The following expresses a view which has always had its advocates among theologians: 'Men are sinful; their very consciences are corrupt and unreliable

guides. What is taken for conscientiousness among men is nothing more than self-aggrandisement and arrogance. Therefore, we cannot trust our own judgment; we must trust God and do what he wills. Only then can we be assured of doing right.'

This view suffers from a fundamental inconsistency. It is said that we cannot know for ourselves what is right and what is wrong; and this is because our judgment is corrupt. But how do we know that our judgment is corrupt? Presumably, in order to know that, we would have to know (a) that some actions are morally required of us, and (b) that our own judgment does not reveal that these actions are required. However, (a) is just the sort of thing that we can*not* know, according to this view. Now it may be suggested that while we cannot know (a) by our own judgment, we can know it as a result of God's revelation. But even setting aside the practical difficulties of distinguishing genuine from bogus revelation (a generous concession), there is still this problem: if we learn that God (i.e. some being that we take to be God) requires us to do a certain action, and we conclude on this account that the action is morally right, then we have *still* made at least one moral judgment of our own, namely that whatever this being requires is morally right. Therefore, it is impossible to maintain the view that we do have some moral knowledge, and that *all* of it comes from God's revelation.

Many philosophers, including St Thomas, have held that the voice of individual conscience is the voice of God speaking to the individual, whether he is a believer or not. This would resolve the alleged conflict because in following one's conscience one would at the same time be discharging his obligation as a worshipper to obey God. However, this manoeuvre is unsatisfying, since if taken seriously it would lead to the conclusion that, in speaking to us through our 'consciences', God is merely tricking us: for he is giving us the illusion of self-governance while all the time he is manipulating our thoughts from without. Moreover, in acting from conscience we are acting under the view that our actions are right and not merely that they are decreed by a higher power. Plato's argument in the *Euthyphro* can be adapted to this point: If, in speaking to us through the voice of conscience, God is informing us of what is right, then there is no reason to think that we could not discover this for ourselves – the notion of 'God informing us' is eliminable. On the other hand, if God is only giving us arbitrary commands, which cannot be thought of as 'right' independently of his promulgating them, then the whole idea of 'conscience', as it is normally understood, is a sham.

(5) Finally, someone might object that the question of whether any being is *worthy* of worship is different from the question of whether we *should* worship him. In general, that X is worthy of our doing Y with respect to X does not entail that we should do Y with respect to X. For example, Mrs Brown, being a fine woman, may be worthy of a marriage proposal, but we ought not to propose to her since she is already married. Or, Seaman Jones may be worthy of a medal for heroism but perhaps there are reasons why we should not award it. Similarly, it may be that there is a being who is worthy of worship and yet we should not worship him since it would interfere with our lives as moral agents. Thus God, who is worthy of worship, may exist; and we should love, respect, and honour him, but not worship him in the full sense of the word. If this is correct, then the argument of section 5 is fallacious.

This rebuttal will not work because of an important disanalogy between the cases of proposing marriage and awarding the medal, on the one hand, and the case of worship on the other. It may be that Mrs Brown is worthy of a proposal, yet there are circumstances in which it would be wrong to propose to her. However, these circumstances are contrasted with others in which it would be perfectly all right. The same goes for Seaman Jones's medal: there are *some* circumstances in which awarding it would be proper. But in the case of worship – if the foregoing arguments have been sound – there are *no* circumstances under which anyone should worship God. And if one should *never* worship, then the concept of a fitting object of worship is an empty one.

The above argument will probably not persuade anyone to abandon belief in God – arguments rarely do – and there are certainly many more points which need to be worked out before it can be known whether this argument is even viable. Yet it does raise an issue which is clear enough. Theologians are already accustomed to speaking of theistic belief and commitment as taking the believer 'beyond morality', and I think they are right. The question is whether this should not be regarded as a severe embarrassment.

5 MICHAEL MARTIN: ATHEISM, CHRISTIAN THEISM, AND RAPE[5]

Let us assume for the moment that the Biblical position on rape is clear: God condemns rape. But why? One possibility is that He condemns rape *because* it is wrong. Why is it wrong? It might be supposed that God has various reasons for thinking rape is wrong: it violates the victim's rights, it traumatizes the victim, it undermines the fabric of society, and so on. All of these are bad making properties. However, if these reasons provide objective grounds for God thinking that rape is wrong, they provide objective grounds for others as well. Moreover, these reasons would hold even if God did not exist. For example, rape would still traumatize the victim and rape would still undermine the fabric of society even. Thus, on this assumption, in this case, atheists could provide objective grounds for condemning rape – the same grounds used by God.

Let us suppose now that rape is wrong *because* God condemns it. In this case, God has no reasons for His condemnations. His condemnation *makes* rape wrong and it would not be wrong if God did not condemn it. Indeed, not raping someone would be wrong if God condemned not raping. However, this hardly provides objective grounds for condemning rape: Whether rape is right or wrong would be based on God's arbitrary condemnation. On this interpretation, if atheists can provide no objective grounds for condemning rape, they are no worse off than theists . . .

Theists such as Greg Bahnsen . . . suppose that the above dilemma can be avoided by basing morality on the necessary attributes of God's character rather

---

5. www.infidels.org/library/modern/michael_martin/rape.html

than directly on His condemnation.[6] It may seem that to say that God condemns rape as wrong because His character is necessarily good avoids the dilemma, but this is an illusion. Bahnsen argued that in the *Euthyphro* Plato set up a 'false antithesis':

> truth of the matter is that good is not independent of God. Certain behavior is good because God approves of it, and God approves of it because it is the creaturely expression of His holiness – in other words, it is good. To be good is to be like God, and we can only know what behavior is good if God reveals and approves of it. The important point is that good *is what God approves* and cannot be ascertained independent of Him.[7]

Unfortunately, however, Bahnsen's position is not clear. The quotation suggests *both* that something is good because God approves of it *and* that God approves of it because it is good. But these two positions cannot both be maintained at once. Suppose that 'X because of Y' means 'X is caused by Y'. This would mean that when one says that rape is bad because God disapproved of it one means that God caused rape to be bad by disapproving of it. But if one says that God disapproved of rape because it is bad, this would mean that the badness of rape caused God to disapprove of it. But how can what God caused by disapproving of it have caused God to disapprove of it? If 'X because of Y' means 'Y is the reason for X', a similar position arises. If the reason for rape being bad is God's disapproval of it, how can it be the case that rape being bad is the reason for God's disapproval of rape?

In any case, appealing to God's character only postpones the problem since the dilemma can be reformulated in terms of His character. Is God's character the way it is because it is good or is God's character good simply because it is God's character? Is there an independent standard of good or does God's character set the standard? If God's character is the way it is *because* it is good, then there is an independent standard of goodness by which to evaluate God's character. For example, suppose God condemns rape because of His just and merciful character. His character is just and merciful because mercy and justice are good. Since God is necessarily good, God is just and merciful. According to this independent standard of goodness, being merciful and just is precisely what a good character involves. In this case, even if God did not exist, one could say that a merciful and just character is good. Human beings could use this standard to evaluate people's character and actions based on this character. They could do this whether or not God exists.

Suppose God's character is good simply *because* it is God's character. Then if God's character were cruel and unjust, these attributes would be good. In such a case God might well condone rape since this would be in keeping with His character. But could not one reply that God could not be cruel and unjust since by necessity God must be good? It is true that by necessity God must be good. But

6. See Greg Bahnsen, *Theonomy in Christian Ethics*, Phillipburg, N.J., Presbyterian and Reformed Publishing., 1977.
7. *Ibid.*, p. 284.

unless we have some independent standard of goodness then whatever attributes God has would by definition be good: God's character would define what good is. It would seem that if God could not be cruel and unjust, then God's character must necessarily exemplify some independent standard of goodness. Using this standard one could say that cruelty and injustice are not good whether God exists or not.

This attempt to avoid the dilemma by basing objective morality on God's necessary character has another problem. It assumes that there would not be an objective morality without God. However, this seems to beg the question against an objective atheistic ethics. After all, why would the nonexistence of God adversely affect the goodness of mercy, compassion, and justice? Yet, this is precisely what would happen if being part of God's character created the goodness of mercy, compassion and justice. This point can perhaps be made in another way. One could affirm the objective immorality of rape and deny the existence of God with perfect consistency. There is no contradiction in claiming 'Rape is objectively evil and God does not exist.' . . .

Christians seem to assume that God condemns rape and that His condemnation can be supported from reading the Bible. In addition, they assume that God condemns rape on the same grounds that rape is condemned in contemporary society. However, the Biblical position is complicated and only supports the common view that rape is wrong because it harms the victim to a very limited extent. To be sure, one can find rape condemned in the Bible. However, one can also find passages where God seems to be tacitly approving of rape and other passages where rape is condemned but without regard for the victim's welfare.

First of all, in some passages God seems to tacitly sanction rape. In the Old Testament Moses encourages his men to use captured virgins for their own sexual pleasure, i.e., to rape them. After urging his men to kill the male captives and female captives who are not virgins, he says: 'But all the young girls who have not known man by lying with him, keep alive for yourselves' (Num.31:18). God then explicitly rewards Moses by urging him to distribute the spoils. He does not rebuke Moses or his men (Num. 31: 25–27).

Second, when rape is condemned in the Old Testament the woman's rights and her psychological welfare are ignored.[8] For example: 'If a man meets a virgin who is not betrothed, and seizes her and lies with her, and they are found, then the man who lay with her shall give to the father fifty skelels of silver, and she shall be his wife, and he may not put her away all of his days' (Deut. 22: 28–29). Here the victim of rape is treated as the property of the father. Since the rapist has despoiled the father's property he must pay a bridal fee. The woman apparently has no say in the matter and is forced to marry the person who raped her. Notice also if they are not discovered, no negative judgment is forthcoming. The implicit message seems to be that if you rape an unbetrothed virgin, be sure not to get caught.

---

8. I am indebted in what follows to Gerald Larue, *Sex and the Bible*, Buffalo, N.Y., Prometheus Books, 1983. Ch. 16.

In the case of the rape of a betrothed virgin in a city, the Bible says that both the rapist and victim should be stoned to death: the rapist because he violated his neighbour's wife and the victim because she did not cry for help (Deut. 22: 23–25). Again the assumption is that the rapist dispoiled the property of another man and so must pay with his life. Concern for the welfare of the victim does not seem to matter. Moreover, it is assumed that in all cases a rape victim could cry for help and if she did she would be heard and rescued. Both of these assumptions are very dubious and sensitive to the contextual aspects of rape.

On the other hand, according to the Bible, the situation is completely different if the rape occurs in 'open country.' Here the rapist should be killed, not the victim. The reason given is that if a woman cried for help in open country, she would not be heard. Consequently, she could not be blamed for allowing the rape to occur. No mention is made about the psychological harm to the victim. No condemnation is made of a rapist in open country, let alone in a city, who does not get caught.

The only place I know in the Bible where any sensitivity is shown to the victim of rape is in the story of David's son Amnon, who raped his half sister Tamar and then rejected her. The writer of this story describes her immediate grief in some detail. Her brother Absalom revenged her rape by killing Amnon. As Gerald Larue has described it: 'The death of Amnon put the Israelite justice in balance, so to speak, but the pain experienced by the woman was not considered worthy of further record.'[9]

How, then, can atheists meet the debating manoeuvre that atheists can provide no objective reason for not raping people?

First, atheists can argue that it has never been shown that nonreligious ethics is necessarily subjective. Indeed, it can be pointed out that even famous Christian philosophers have denied that atheistic morality is subjective . . .

Second, using the *Euthyphro* dilemma, on the one hand, they can argue that if theists can provide such reasons, so can they. On the other hand, they can argue that on certain interpretations of Christian ethics, theists cannot provide any objective reasons. If rape is wrong simply because God commands it or simply because rape is bad because it conflicts with God's character and God's character is good simply because it is God's character, the badness of rape is completely arbitrary.

Third, atheists should point out that if theists base the wrongness of rape on Biblical interpretation, they are on shaky grounds. In places the Bible condones rape and where the Bible condemns rape, the reasons for the condemnations are neither adequate nor in keeping with enlightened moral opinion.

6 KAI NIELSEN: MORALS WITHOUT GOD[10]

The claim . . . is that only with a God-centered morality could we get a morality that would be adequate, that would go beyond the relativities and formalisms of a nonreligious ethic. Only a God-centered and perhaps only a Christ-centered

9. *Ibid.*, p. 104.
10. *Ethics Without God*, Amherst, N.Y., Prometheus Books, 1990, pp. 83–86.

morality could meet our deepest and most persistent moral demands. People have certain desires and needs; they experience loneliness and despair; they create certain 'images of excellence'; they seek happiness and love. If the human animal were not like this, if man were not this searching, anxiety-ridden creature with a thirst for happiness and with strong desires and aversions, there would be no good and evil, no morality at all. In short, our moralities are relative to our human natures. And given the human nature that we in fact have, we cannot be satisfied with any purely secular ethic. Nothing 'the world' can give us will finally satisfy us. We thirst for a father who will protect us – who will not let life be just one damn thing after another until we die and rot; we long for a God who can offer us the promise of a blissful everlasting life with him. We need to love and obey such a father. Unless we can convincingly picture to ourselves that we are creatures of such a loving sovereign, our deepest moral hopes will be frustrated.

No purely secular ethic can – or indeed should – offer such a hope, a hope that is perhaps built on an illusion, but still a hope that is worth, the believer will claim, the full risk of faith. Whatever the rationality of such a faith, our very human nature, some Christian moralists maintain, makes us long for such assurances. Without it our lives will be without significance, without moral sense; morality finds its *psychologically realistic foundation* in certain human purposes. And given human beings with their nostalgia for the absolute, human life without God will be devoid of all purpose or at least devoid of everything but trivial purposes. Thus without a belief in God, there could be no humanly satisfying morality. Secular humanism in any of its many varieties is in reality inhuman.

It is true that a secular morality can offer no hope for a blissful immortality or a bodily resurrection to a 'new life,' and it is also true that secular morality does not provide for a protecting, loving father or some over-arching purpose *to* life. But we have to balance this off against the fact that these religious concepts are myths – sources of illusion and self-deception. We human beings are helpless, utterly dependent creatures for years and years. Because of this long period of infancy, there develops in us a deep psychological need for an all protecting father; we thirst for such security, but there is not the slightest reason to think that there is *such* security. Moreover, that people have feelings of dependence does not mean that there is something on which they can depend. That we have such needs most certainly does not give us any reason at all to think that there is such a super-mundane prop for our feelings of dependence.

Furthermore, and more importantly, if there is no such architectonic purpose *to* life, as our religions claim, this does not mean that there is no purpose *in* life – that there is no way of living that is ultimately satisfying and significant. It indeed appears to be true that all small purposes, if pursued too relentlessly and exclusively, leave us with a sense of emptiness. Even Mozart quartets listened to endlessly become boring, but a varied life lived with verve and with a variety of conscious aims can survive the destruction of Valhalla. That there is no purpose *to* life does not imply that there is no purpose *in* life. Human beings may not have a function and if this is so, then, unlike a tape recorder or a pencil and even a kind of homunculus, we do not have a purpose. There is nothing we are made for. But even so, we can and do have purposes in the same sense that we have aims, goals, and things we find worth seeking and admiring. There are indeed things we prize and admire; the achievement of these things and the realization of our aims and desires, including those we are most deeply committed to, give moral significance to our lives. . . . We do not need a God to *give* meaning to our lives by making us for his sovereign purpose and perhaps thereby robbing us of our freedom. We, by our deliberate acts and commitments, can give meaning to our own lives. Here man has that 'dreadful freedom' that makes possible his human dignity; freedom will indeed bring him anxiety, but he will then be the *rider* and not the *ridden* and, by being able to choose, seek out, and sometimes realize those things he most deeply prizes and admires, his life will take on a significance. A life lived without purpose is indeed a most dreadful life – a life in which we might have what the existentialists rather pedantically call the experience of nothingness. But we do not need God or the gods to give purpose to our lives or to give the lie to this claim about nothingness. And we can grow into a fallibilism without a nostalgia for the absolute.

There are believers who would resist some of this and who would respond that these purely human purposes, forged in freedom and anguish, are not sufficient to meet our deepest moral needs. Beyond that, they argue, man needs very much to see himself as a creature with a purpose in a divinely ordered universe. He needs to find some *cosmic* significance for his ideals and commitments; he wants and needs the protection and certainty of having a function. This certainty, as the Grand Inquisitor realized, is even more desirable than his freedom. He wants and needs to live and be guided by the utterly sovereign will of God.

If, after wrestling through the kind of philosophical considerations I have been concerned to set forth, a religious moralist still really wants this and would continue to want it after repeated careful reflection, after all the consequences of his view and the alternatives had been placed vividly before him, after logical confusions had been dispelled, and after he had taken the matter to heart, his secularist interlocutor may find that with him he is finally caught in some ultimate disagreement in attitude. Even this is far from certain, however, for it is not at all clear that there are certain determinate places in such dubious battles where argument and the giving of reasons just must come to an end and we must instead resort to persuasion or some other nonrational methods if we are to resolve our fundamental disagreements . . . But even if we finally do end up in such 'pure disagreements in attitude,' before we get there, there is a good bit that can be said. How could his purposes really be *his* own purposes, if he were a creature made to serve God's sovereign purpose and to live under the sovereign will of God? In such a circumstance would his ends be something he had deliberately chosen or would they simply be something that he could not help realizing? Moreover, is it really incompatible with human dignity to be *made* for something? We should reflect here that we cannot without insulting people ask what they are for. Finally, is it not *infantile* to go on looking for some father, some order, some absolute, that will lift all the burden of *decision* from us. Children follow rules blindly, but do we want to be children all our lives? Is it really *hubris* or arrogance or sin on our part to wish for a life where we make our own decisions, where we follow the rules we do because we see the *point* of them, and where we need not crucify our intellects by believing in some transcendent purpose whose very intelligibility is seriously in question? Perhaps by saying this I am only exhibiting my own *hubris*, my own corruption of soul, but I cannot believe that to ask this question is to exhibit such arrogance.

KEY TEXTS

Adams, Robert. *The Virtue of Faith*, New York, Oxford University Press, 1981.

Helm, Paul. *Divine Commands and Morality*, Oxford, Oxford University Press, 1981.

Kant, Immanuel. *Critique of Practical Reason*, translated and edited by Mary Gregor, with an Introduction by Andrews Reath, Cambridge, Cambridge University Press, 1997.

—— *Groundwork of the Metaphysic of Morals* (1783), translated, with analysis and notes, by H. J. Paton in *The Moral Law*, London, Hutchinson & Co., 1972.

Nielsen, Kai. *Ethics Without God*, Buffalo, N.Y., Prometheus Books, 1973; revised edn, 1990.

Wood, Allen W. *Kant's Moral Religion*, Ithaca and London, Cornell University Press, 1970.

BIBLIOGRAPHY

Adams, Robert. 'Autonomy and Theological Ethics', *Religious Studies*, 15, 1979, pp. 191–194.

—— 'A Modified Divine Command Theory of Ethical Wrongness', in *Divine Commands and Morality*, ed. Paul Helm, Oxford, Oxford University Press, 1981, pp. 83–108.

—— 'Moral Arguments for Theistic Belief', in Adams, *The Virtue of Faith*, New York, Oxford University Press, 1981, pp. 144–163.

Beck, Lewis White. *A Commentary on Kant's Critique of Practical Reason*, Chicago, University of Chicago Press, 1960.

Boyd, Richard. 'How to be a Moral Realist', in *Moral Discourse and Practice*, ed. S. Darwell, A. Gibbard and P. Railton, Oxford, Oxford University Press, 1997, pp. 105–135.

Brink, David. *Moral Realism and the Foundations of Ethics*, Cambridge, Cambridge University Press, 1989.

Burch, Robert. 'Objective Values and the Divine Command Theory of Morality', *New Scholasticism*, 54, 1980, pp. 279–304.

Byrne, Peter. *The Moral Interpretation of Religion*, Edinburgh, Edinburgh University Press, 1998.

Chandler, John. 'Divine Command Theories and the Appeal to Love', *American Philosophical Quarterly*, 22, 1985, pp. 231–239.

—— 'Is the Divine Command Theory Defensible?', *Religious Studies*, 20, 1984, pp. 443–452.

Clark, Stephen. 'God, Good, and Evil', *Proceedings of the Aristotelian Society*, 77, 1977, pp. 247–264.

Descartes, René. *Philosophical Letters*, trans. and ed. Antony Kenny, Minneapolis, University of Minnesota Press, 1981.

Despland, Michel. *Kant on History and Religion*, Montreal and London, McGill-Queen's University Press, 1973.

Devine, Philip. *Relativism, Nihilism and God*, Notre Dame, Ind., University of Notre Dame Press, 1989.

Faber, Paul. 'The *Euthyphro* Objection to Divine Normative Theories: A Response', *Religious Studies*, 21, 1985, pp. 559–572.

Findlay, J. N. *Kant and the Transcendent Object*, Oxford, Clarendon Press, 1981.

Firth, Roderick. 'Ethical Absolutism and the Ideal Observer', in *Readings in Ethical Theory*, ed. Wilfrid Sellars and John Hospers, 2nd edn, Englewood Cliffs, N.J., Prentice-Hall, 1970, pp. 200–221.

Freud, Sigmund. *Civilization and its Discontents* (1930), in *The Penguin Freud Library*, London, Penguin Books, 1985, Vol. 12, pp. 245–340.

Gamwell, Franklin. *The Divine Good: Modern Moral Theory and the Necessity of God*, San Francisco, Harper, 1990.

Gascoigne, Robert. 'God and Objective Moral Values', *Religious Studies*, 21, 1985, pp. 531–549.

Geach, Peter. 'Plato's Euthyphro – An Analysis and Commentary', *Monist*, 50, 1966, pp. 369–382.

Gert, Bernard. *Morality: A New Justification of the Moral Rules*, New York, Oxford University Press, 1988.

Hall, John C. 'Plato: Euthyphro 10a1–11a10', *Philosophical Quarterly*, 18, 1968, pp. 1–11.

Heine, Heinrich. *Religion and Philosophy in Germany*, trans. J. Snodgrass, Boston, Mass., Beacon Press, 1959.

Kant, Immanuel. *Critique of Judgement*, translated with Analytical Indexes by James Creed Meredith, Oxford, Clarendon Press, 1928; reprint 1986.

—— *Critique of Practical Reason*, translated and edited by Mary Gregor, with an Introduction by Andrews Reath, Cambridge, Cambridge University Press, 1997.

—— *Critique of Pure Reason*, trans. Norman Kemp Smith, London, Macmillan, 1929.

—— *Groundwork of the Metaphysic of Morals* (1783), translated, with analysis and notes, by H. J. Paton in *The Moral Law*, London, Hutchinson & Co., 1972.

—— *Lectures on Metaphysics*, Cambridge, Cambridge University Press, 1997.

—— *Religion within the Limits of Reason Alone*, trans. T. M. Greene and H. Hudson, Chicago, 1934.

Ladd, John, ed. *Ethical Relativism*, Belmont, Calif., Wadsworth, 1973.

Leibniz, Gottfried Wilhelm. *Discourse on Metaphysics* (1686), edited and translated with an Introduction, notes and glossary by R. N. D. Martin and Stuart Brown, Manchester and New York, Manchester University Press, 1988.

Lewis, C. S. *Mere Christianity*, London, Collins, 1952; Fontana Books, 1964.

MacKinnon, D. M. 'Kant's Philosophy of Religion', *Philosophy*, 50, 1975, pp. 131–144.

McPherran, Mark. 'Socratic Piety in the "Euthyphro"', *Journal of the History of Philosophy*, 23, 1985, pp. 283–310.

Michalson, Gordon E. *Kant and the Problem of God*, Oxford, Blackwell, 1999.

Moore, G. E. *Principia Ethica*, Cambridge, Cambridge University Press, 1903.

Neufchateau, Andrew of. *Questions on an Ethics of Divine Commands*, edited, translated and with an Introduction by Janine Marie Idziak, Notre Dame, Ind., University of Notre Dame Press, 1997.

Newman, John Henry. *The Grammar of Assent*, edited with a Preface and Introduction by Charles Frederick Harrold, New York and London, Longmans Green & Co., 1870.

Nielsen, Kai. *Ethics Without God*, Buffalo, N.Y., Prometheus Books, 1973; revised edn, 1990.

—— *Why Be Moral?* Buffalo, N.Y., Prometheus Books, 1989.

Nietzsche, Friedrich. *On the Genealogy of Morals* (1887), *Basic Writings of Nietzsche*, translated and edited, with commentaries, by Walter Kaufmann, The Modern Library, New York, Random House, 1968, pp. 440–599.

Oliner, Samuel and Pearl. *The Altruistic Personality: Rescuers of the Jews*, New York, Free Press, 1988.

Outka, Gene and John P. Reeder (eds). *Prospects for a Common Morality*, Princeton, N.J., Princeton University Press, 1993.

Owen, H. P. *The Moral Argument for Christian Theism*, London, George Allen & Unwin, 1965.

Palmer, Michael. *Moral Problems*, Cambridge, Lutterworth Press, 1991.

Plato. *Euthyphro*, in *Plato: The Collected Dialogues*, ed. Edith Hamilton and Huntingdon Cairns, trans. Lane Cooper, Bollingen Series 71, New York, Pantheon Books, 1966, pp. 169–185.

Quinn, Philip. *Divine Commands and Moral Requirements*, Oxford, Clarendon Press, 1978.

Rachels, James. 'God and Human Attitudes', *Religious Studies*, 7, 1971, pp. 325–337. Reprinted in *Divine Commands and Morality*, ed. Paul Helm, Oxford, Oxford University Press, 1981, pp. 34–48.

Railton, Peter. 'Moral Realism', in *Moral Discourse and Practice*, ed. S. Darwell, A. Gibbard and P. Railton, Oxford, Oxford University Press, 1997, pp. 137–163.

Ramsey, Ian T. (ed.). *Christian Ethics and Contemporary Philosophy*, London, SCM Press, 1973.

Rashdall, Hastings. *The Theory of Good and Evil*, 2 vols, Oxford, 1907.

Reardon, Bernard M. G. *Kant as Philosophical Theologian*, London, Macmillan, 1988.

Roberts, T. A. 'Morality and Divine Commands', *Proceedings of the Aristotelian Society*, 68, 1968, pp. 49–62.

Schrader, G. A. 'Kant's Presumed Repudiation of the "Moral Argument" in the Opus Postumum', *Philosophy*, 26, 1951, pp. 228–241.

Sharvy, Richard. 'Euthyphro 9b–11b: Analysis and Definition in Plato and Others', *Noûs*, 6, 1972, pp. 119–137.

Silber, J. R. 'Kant's Conception of the Highest Good as Immanent and Transcendent', *Philosophical Review*, 68, 1959, pp. 469–492.

Sorley, W. R. *Moral Values and the Idea of God*, Cambridge, Cambridge University Press, 1919.

Swinburne, Richard. 'Duty and the Will of God', in *Divine Commands and Morality*, ed. Paul Helm, Oxford, Oxford University Press, 1981, pp. 120–134.

—— *The Existence of God*, Oxford, Clarendon Press, 1979, pp. 175–179.

Taylor, A. E. *Does God Exist?* New York, Macmillan, 1945.

Walsh, W. H. 'Kant's Moral Theology', *Proceedings of the British Academy*, 49, 1963, pp. 263–289.

Webb, Clement C. J. *Kant's Philosophy of Religion*, Oxford, Clarendon Press, 1926.

Wierenga, Edward. 'A Defensible Divine Command Theory', *Noûs*, 17, 1983, pp. 387–407.

Wood, Allen W. *Kant's Moral Religion*, Ithaca and London, Cornell University Press, 1970.

INTRODUCTION

All the arguments examined thus far – whether a priori or a posteriori – have attempted in their various ways to justify the belief that God exists. Whether this justification proceeds from an initial definition of God (the ontological argument), or from an analysis of certain common experiences of the world (the cosmological, design and moral arguments), or indeed from an examination of uncommon experiences (the argument from miracles), the ambition remains to provide *reasons* which lead to the valid conclusion that this belief is true. There is one argument, however, that follows a different path. This is the *pragmatic argument for God's existence*. As its name suggests (from the Greek *pragma*, meaning 'deed' or 'act'), this argument bases its case on the practical consequences of belief. Because there appears to be no valid proof for God, whether conceptual or empirical, the only option left, so the argument runs, is to justify belief on other grounds – on grounds of *expedience* – by indicating what practical advantages accrue from it. Accordingly the pragmatic argument makes an overt appeal to individual self-interest, claiming that there are definite benefits to be gained from belief which are not open to atheism or agnosticism. In the pragmatic argument, therefore, it is not *what* is believed that is considered reasonable – to repeat, there are no reasons which can adjudicate on the matter, one way or the other – but rather *the act of believing*, the benefits of this act making it the rational thing to do. The pragmatic defence of religion is therefore both *voluntaristic*, by requiring of the individual an act of will in a situation of choice, and *prudential*, by establishing that this act of believing is the most profitable act, and so one that all rational persons will wish to perform.

The pragmatic argument is to be found primarily in three places in the history of philosophy. It appears most famously in the *Pensées* of the French philosopher and mathematician Blaise Pascal (1623–1662). Another version, much influenced by Pascal's, is given by Bishop Joseph Butler (1692–1752) in his *The Analogy of Religion* of 1736; and its most elaborate presentation is by the American psychologist William James (1842–1910), most notably in his influential essay 'The Will to Believe' of 1897. In this chapter I shall consider only Pascal and James.

Expedience the justification of belief

PASCAL'S PRAGMATIC ARGUMENT: THE WAGER

Pascal's pragmatic argument appears in his *Pensées*, a collection of literary fragments unpublished in his lifetime.[1] It is found in the standard Lafuma

---

1. Various extracts were published in 1670 and 1728, but no complete text appeared until 1844. A major revision was undertaken by Louis Lafuma from 1940 to 1944, while hiding from the

edition as *Pensée* No. 418, under the general heading *Infini-rien* (Infinity-nothing), and appears in the novel guise of a game of chance, better known as *Pascal's Wager* (SOURCE 1: PP. 326–328).[2]

⇐

Born in Clermont-Ferrand, France, Pascal quickly established himself as a mathematical prodigy, publishing in 1639 his essay on conic sections, and in 1642 inventing the first mechanical calculator, which was his main claim to fame during his lifetime. In 1648 his famous experiments with the barometer established the effects of atmospheric pressure on liquids, and in 1654, in conjunction with the mathematician Fermat, he set out the mathematical theory of probability. However, in the same year, on 23 November, he underwent a profound religious conversion – the 'night of fire' – and entered the Jansenist monastery at Port-Royal, although not taking holy orders. He never published under his own name again and thereafter wrote only to assist the Jansenists in their struggle against the Jesuits. The two works for which he is chiefly remembered date from the Port-Royal years. *Les Provinciales*, written pseudonymously, was a defence of the Jansenist Antoine Arnauld, and became an immediate success. The posthumously published *Pensées* (1670) is a set of deeply felt meditations and is Pascal's most important philosophical work. His concern to demonstrate the reasonableness of faith culminates in his famous 'Wager' argument.

Blaise Pascal: death mask (1623–1662)

From the outset it is important not to isolate the Wager from Pascal's own theological perspective. Not only does Pascal, as a devout Catholic, assume that God exists, but he also believes that religion carries with it certain rewards and punishments: in crude terms, theists go to heaven and atheists go to hell. As we shall see shortly, this theological assumption is decisive for the Wager: it allows Pascal to describe the *pay-offs* that accrue to believers and unbelievers. More than that, he characterizes human beings in the traditional symbolism of the Fall: as being separated from the grace of God, and, what is worse, as being indifferent to their predicament, as is evidenced by the fact that they indulge instead in all kinds of trivial amusements or *divertissements* (card playing, dancing, duelling, and so on). Nor is philosophy of any use in this regard. As the traditional theistic arguments have shown, while we can accept the *possibility* of an absolute being, we cannot *demonstrate* this being's existence or non-existence.[3] Men and women are therefore inclined to lapse into an

Pascal's theological presuppositions

Nazis in the manuscript room of the Bibliothèque Nationale in Paris; and it is his subsequent edition (Paris, 1963) which is translated, in the edition used here, by A. J. Krailsheimer, London and New York, Penguin Books, 1966. A useful collection of Pascal's other writings is provided in *Pascal: Selections*, ed. Richard H. Popkin, London and New York, Macmillan, 1989.

2. The argument is not, however, unique to Pascal: the earliest version is proposed by the Islamic philosopher al-Ghazali. For other variants, see John K. Ryan, 'The Wager in Pascal and Others', in the important collection of essays *Gambling on God: Essays on Pascal's Wager*, ed. Jeff Jordan, Lanham, Md., Rowman & Littlefield, 1994, pp. 11–19.

apathetic state, a 'repos dans l'ignorance', in which, being convinced that there is no ultimate solution to their situation, they expend no effort on the search for one.

The Wager is to be understood within the context of this theological scheme, and is designed by Pascal to reactivate man's search for God by appealing not *to the truth of God* but to the self-interest that is best served by *believing in God*; by showing indeed that the religious quest, the *recherche de Dieu*, will not only provide ultimate truth and happiness but also, on a more immediate and baser level, secure greater pleasures than any ordinary *divertissement* could possibly provide. As one author has succinctly put it, the Wager will demonstrate that '*conversion* can outdo *diversion*'.[4]

Wagering on whether God exists or not

Pascal's argument begins by presenting human beings with an inescapable decision: one must decide either that God does exist or that he does not. All of us are therefore forced to bet on one or the other and abstention is impossible: even not acting as if there is a God – not praying, for example, or not giving thanks to God – is held to be, for all practical purposes, equivalent to acting as if there is no God.[5] Since therefore neither proof nor empirical evidence can determine what choice to make, practical considerations must decide the issue:

> since a choice must be made, let us see which offers you the least interest. You have two things to lose: the true and the good; and two things to stake: your reason and your will, your knowledge and your happiness; and your nature has two things to avoid: error and wretchedness. Since you must necessarily choose, your reason is no more affronted by choosing one rather than the other. That is one point cleared up. But your happiness? Let us weigh up the gain and the loss involved in calling heads that God exists. Let us assess the two cases: if you win you win everything, if you lose you lose nothing.[6]

Betting in the God-game is, as in any game of chance, dependent on calculating where the *dominating bet lies*, that is, on where lies the greatest pay-off, given the odds being offered. In the gamble on God, the issue seems fairly clear-cut. For here, while the odds for and against God existing are equal, the pay-off is much greater on one side than the other. If you bet on God existing, and God does not exist, nothing is lost. If you bet on God not existing, and God does not exist, nothing is lost. But if you bet on God not existing, and

---

3. 'The metaphysical proofs for the existence of God', writes Pascal, 'are so remote from human reasoning and so involved that they make little impact, and, even if they did help some people, it would only be for the moment during which they watched the demonstration, because an hour later they would be afraid they had made a mistake.' p. 86 (No.190).

4. J. H. Broome, *Pascal*, London, Edward Arnold, 1965, p. 163.

5. A view held by many other theists. See Peter Geach, 'The Moral Law and the Law of God', in *Divine Commands and Morality*, ed. Paul Helm, Oxford, Oxford University Press, 1980: 'Now for those who believe in an Almighty God, a man's every act is an act either of obeying or of ignoring or of defying that God' (p. 173).

6. *Pensées*, pp. 150–151.

God does exist, everything is lost, i.e., you have lost your chance of everlasting happiness and punishment awaits. The pragmatic thing to do is therefore to bet on God because this bet has the singular return of salvation and not damnation. Accordingly the wager 'God exists' dominates the wager 'God does not exist'. The chart represents Pascal's reasoning at this point.

	Odds	God exists	God does not exist
Bet on God	Even	Happiness (heaven)	No gain or loss
Bet against God	Even	Unhappiness (hell)	No gain or loss

SUMMARY:
PASCAL'S WAGER

Pensées, title page, first edition

It is important to note the fundamental asymmetry of the two wagers. The gambler on God can expect to experience not just the happiness of heaven: he will presumably also experience the satisfaction of being right but not the experience of being wrong. The gambler against God, on the other hand, quite apart from being denied the happiness of heaven, cannot experience the satisfaction of being right but will presumably experience the dissatisfaction of being wrong. So, as Thomas Morris has neatly put it, 'we can say that for atheism there is a final no-satisfaction guarantee, whereas for theism, there is a final no-dissatisfaction guarantee'.[7]

The next phase of Pascal's argument is introduced when he enters the reasonable objection, admittedly in such an oblique fashion that it is easy to miss, that the prudential bet for God is not as dominant as one might think because something is, after all, *lost* when one wagers for God: one loses the earthly life of pleasure which is incompatible with a life of piety. By the same token, of course, one can also say that betting against God has its own *gain* or pay-off: one can lead an unbridled life untroubled by religious restraints.

Is the wager on God the best bet?

7. 'Wagering and the Evidence', in *Gambling on God: Essays on Pascal's Wager*, ed. Jeff Jordan, Lanham, Md., Rowman & Littlefield, 1994, p. 55.

In this respect, then, the result of betting on God when God does not exist, because it requires relinquishing certain earthly happinesses, is *worse* than the result of betting against God when God does not exist, because here no abstention from a life of pleasure is necessary. Perhaps, then, as Pascal remarks, 'I am wagering too much.'

> Let us see: since there is an equal chance of gain and loss, if you stood to win only two lives for one you could still wager, but supposing you stood to win three? . . . it would be unwise of you, once you are obliged to play, not to risk your life in order to win three lives at a game in which there is an equal chance of losing and winning. But there is an eternity of life and happiness. That being so, even though there were an infinite number of chances, of which only one were in your favour, you would still be right to wager one in order to win two; and you would be acting wrongly, being obliged to play, in refusing to stake one life against three in a game, where out of an infinite number of chances there is one in your favour, if there were an infinity of infinitely happy life to be won. But here there is an infinity of infinitely happy life to be won, one chance of winning against a finite number of chances of losing, and what you are staking is finite. That leaves no choice; wherever there is infinity, and where there are not infinite chances of losing against that of winning, there is no room for hesitation, you must give everything.[8]

This is a slightly more complicated argument. Remember that Pascal is responding to the objection that one does, after all, lose something by betting on God's existence: one loses the earthly life of pleasure. Let us first recall that, in any particular game of chance in which the odds are equal, practical reason dictates that we bet according to the greater pay-off: if heads pays twice as much as tails, we bet on heads. Pascal now asks us to imagine a situation in which we have more than one finite existence to stake. Again, the same rule applies: given the equal chance of winning or losing, sense requires that we should bet to maximal effect. Thus if tails involves the loss of one life, and heads the gain of three lives, one again bets on heads. As we can see, in this particular life-game the gain and loss *are always finite*. But this is not the case when one gambles on God: here, while the cost may remain finite (one life), the pay-off *is infinite* (i.e., a life not merely of infinite happiness but of infinite duration). In this calculation, therefore, the essential asymmetry of the gamble again becomes apparent: everything related to our finite existence, including the pleasures that we may derive from it, pales into insignificance beside the 'infinitely happy life to be won'. This argument, concludes Pascal, 'carries infinite weight, when the stakes are finite in a game where there are even chances of winning and losing and an infinite prize to be won'.[9]

The Wager's infinite pay-off

---

8. *Pensées*, p. 151.
9. *Ibid.*, p. 152.

EXERCISE 6.1

Which of the following best expresses Pascal's Wager?

I believe in God because . . .

My employer believes in God.

My upbringing was religious.

My ambition is to become a clergyman.

I shall be rewarded by God if I do.

I shall be punished by God if I don't.

I shall miss out on the pleasures of heaven if I don't.

I want eternal life.

I'm not an atheist.

I enjoy religious services.

I want to lead a moral life (and good people are usually religious people).

Pascal's Wager has shown that agnosticism and atheism are not prudentially rational. But this is not the end of his argument. One last problem remains. This concerns the plight of the unbeliever when faced with the inexorable logic of the Wager. The atheist admits that, as a piece of reasoning, it is hard to fault. But how can intellectual assent move him to a position of personal commitment? In other words, however convincing the Wager may be, he has yet to be convinced that there is anything real behind the gamble. He therefore asks if it is possible, as it were, to turn the cards over and to see if there is actually anything on the reverse. This is, of course, precisely what Pascal's argument has been seeking to achieve, namely, to bring the unbeliever to the point where the search for God becomes an active demand. Pascal replies that the cards will be turned over if one examines the scriptures. But this answer is clearly unsatisfactory to the unbeliever: even though he may thereby be induced to gamble, this is not the same as having true belief. 'I am', he says, 'so made that I cannot believe.'[10] Accordingly Pascal offers the following solution:

> Concentrate then not on convincing yourself by multiplying proofs of God's existence but by diminishing your passions. You want to find faith and you do not know the road. You want to be cured of unbelief and you ask for the remedy: learn from those who were once bound like you and who now *wager all they have*.[11]

If the unbeliever cannot therefore see the truth by examining scripture, he can at least gain immediate and first-hand experience of the quality of the

---

10. *Ibid.*
11. *Ibid* (my italics).

Pascal's advice: to live as if one believed

religious life. He should, accordingly, start 'going through the motions', and do what others have done before him, for example, take holy water, have masses said, and so on. As Pascal says in a famous passage: 'That will make you believe quite naturally, and will make you more docile.'[12] This advice is not as cynical as appears. Pascal is well aware that the Wager, even if indicating what is pragmatically the best option, cannot bring the individual to belief. For that to happen, the habitual emotional and intellectual obstacles to religion must be overcome. This can be best achieved by drawing the person concerned into a form of life in which genuine belief can be directly encountered, into an environment in which a different and more exalted mode of human conduct can be realized. To gamble on God is not merely, therefore, in terms of rational self-interest, the practical thing to do; it also brings one, as it were, to *the fore-court of belief*. To live *as if* one believed, and to experience daily the fruits of belief – honesty, humility, gratitude, good works and sincere friendship – will, it is to be hoped, move the individual in the long run to a more active desire to participate in and enjoy the rich rewards that only the religious life can offer. The Wager cannot of itself create genuine belief; but it can be, and Pascal prays that it will be, the first step towards it.

> I tell you that you will gain even in this life, and that at every step you take along this road you will see that your gain is so certain and your risk so negligible that in the end you will realize that you have wagered on something certain and infinite for which you have paid nothing.[13]

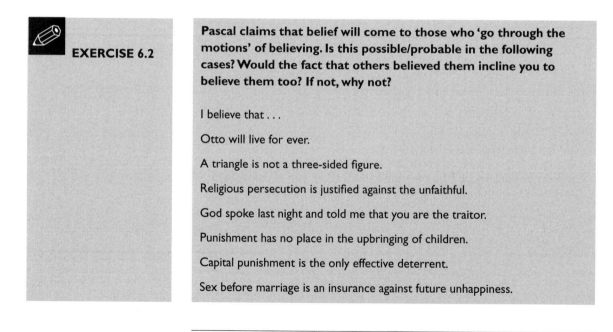

EXERCISE 6.2

Pascal claims that belief will come to those who 'go through the motions' of believing. Is this possible/probable in the following cases? Would the fact that others believed them incline you to believe them too? If not, why not?

I believe that . . .

Otto will live for ever.

A triangle is not a three-sided figure.

Religious persecution is justified against the unfaithful.

God spoke last night and told me that you are the traitor.

Punishment has no place in the upbringing of children.

Capital punishment is the only effective deterrent.

Sex before marriage is an insurance against future unhappiness.

---

12. 'Naturellement même, cela vous fera croire et vous abêtira', *ibid.*, p. 153.
13. *Ibid.*

The only god is the Devil.

Communists are evil.

Mr Micawber is the Messiah.

EXERCISE 6.2
continued

CRITICISMS OF PASCAL'S WAGER

'There are many things that can be said about Pascal's wager, all of them bad', writes George H. Smith,[14] an opinion echoed by the philosopher G. E. Moore, who had 'nothing to say of it except that it seems to me absolutely wicked'.[15] These remarks are not untypical of the way in which Pascal has been treated. Others, however, have been much less dismissive. For them, Pascal's argument is not just theologically revolutionary but positively protean: his theory of gambling inaugurating decision theory and, in the Wager, setting the first infinitistic decision problem.[16] We should note to begin with that Pascal's argument falls neatly into two parts: there is (1) the Wager itself, in which Pascal explains why the gamble on God is the best pragmatic bet; and there is (2) Pascal's advice as to how genuine religious faith is to be obtained.

THE WAGER

The most common and indeed persuasive objection is that Pascal has set the limits of his Wager far too narrowly – as one of his early critics, Denis Diderot, pointed out, 'an Imam could reason just as well'.[17] This remark introduces us to what has become known as the 'many-gods' or 'many-claimants' objection, which argues that the choice Pascal offers us is not as clear-cut as he suggests. For though this is presented as a choice between 'Either God exists or God does not exist', we are in reality being asked to decide between 'Either the *Christian* God exists or there is no God'. Pascal, that is to say, has failed to include other alternatives in the gamble on God – perhaps unsurprisingly, given his own Catholic presuppositions – each of which can lay claim to an infinite gain and each of which can therefore be recommended as a pragmatic alternative: not just the theism of Catholic Christianity but that of Judaism, Islam and many other faiths besides, including, we might add, those sub-divisions within Christianity which regard many aspects of Catholic teaching as objectionable

The 'many-gods' objection

14. George H. Smith, *Atheism: The Case against God*, Amherst, N.Y., Prometheus Books, 1989, p. 183.
15. Quoted by Paul Levy, *Moore*, London, Weidenfeld & Nicolson, p. 214.
16. For further applications of the Wager, see Jordan, *op. cit.*
17. *Pensées Philosophiques*, LIX, ed. J. Assézat, Paris, 1875–77, Vol. I, p. 167. Other advocates of the many-gods objection are Richard Gale, *On the Nature and Existence of God*, New York, Cambridge University Press, 1991, pp. 349–351; Michael Martin, *Atheism: A Philosophical Justification*, Philadelphia, Temple University Press, 1990, pp. 232–234; and James Cargile, 'Pascal's Wager', in *Contemporary Philosophy of Religion*, ed. Steven M. Cahn and David Shatz, New York and Oxford, Oxford University Press, 1982, pp. 229–236.

but which nevertheless brandish the reward of everlasting felicity – for example, the Protestant churches, Quakers, Mormons, Seventh-day Adventists, and so on. In this way the force of the original Wager is largely dissipated. The calculation of individual self-interest within the straightforward *pour ou contre* situation now gives way to a calculation of much greater complexity, in which some account will have to be taken of the different probabilities to be assigned to different theistic beliefs offering the same pay-off (infinite salvation).

Indeed, to extend this argument, it can be said that the calculation required here lies not within a *finite* range of particular beliefs but within an *infinite* range, because of the many religious systems that are logically possible. This point can be made by referring to one of Pascal's earlier remarks: 'I see a number of religions in conflict, and therefore all are false, except one. Each of them wishes to be believed on its own authority and threatens unbelievers.'[18] Quite apart from the faulty logic of supposing that a set of contrary beliefs must include one that is true – for, after all, it is equally possible that all may be false – it is not difficult to see how the suggested conflict between mutually threatening religions can be extended *ad infinitum* to the point where no odds can be given, particularly when, as Pascal acknowledges, God is a transcendent absolute, 'infinitely beyond our comprehension',[19] and so presumably providing no criterion by which any one religion can be validated. Accordingly any form of life that religion (A) commends is or may be condemned by another religion (B); and any form of life that B commends is or may be condemned by another religion (C), and so on. Thus for every religion requiring one course of action, and threatening all others, there is another actual or possible religion threatening that course of action and rewarding all others.[20] It is, of course, logically *possible* that a particular bet (A) that a particular god exists is the correct bet (i.e., that it is this religion, and no other, that brings the pay-off of infinite happiness); but the calculation of the *probability* that A is the correct bet becomes practically impossible when the options available are themselves infinite (i.e., when there is an infinite number of logically possible religions). From this we can see that wagering on the Christian God ceases to have the overwhelming advantage that would commend it to practical self-interest, and that it cannot accordingly be recommended as the dominant bet.

The many-gods objection has laid bare the theological presuppositions of the Wager; but these are apparent elsewhere, not least in what Pascal says the

---

18. *Pensées*, p. 88.
19. *Ibid.*, p. 150.
20. Cf. Antony Flew, 'Is Pascal's Wager the Only Safe Bet?', *Rationalist Annual*, 76, 1960, pp. 21–25: the Wager 'assumes that the tally of possible mutually exclusive, Hell-threatening, systems is finite. On a parochial and unimaginative review this might seem to be true. For the number of such systems which have in fact been elaborated and which have found adherents on this planet must though considerable be considerably less than astronomical. But such a review is parochial, in that it takes in the facts of only one planet; and unimaginative, in that it fails to consider logically possible systems as well as those which have actually been elaborated and believed. There is no limit to the number of logically possible and mutually exclusive alternative systems' (p. 24).

hapless gambler can expect if he bets incorrectly: believing and not believing in God results in the respective gain and loss of eternal happiness. This basic asymmetry means that it makes no practical sense to forgo a life of infinite and heavenly bliss for the sake of a life of finite and earthly pleasure. It is, in other words, precisely because Pascal dangles before the gambler the very real prospect of either damnation or salvation that the gambler appreciates the seriousness of his (unavoidable) position and bets, if he is prudent, as Pascal directs. To do anything else is irrational (SOURCE 2: PP. 328–329).

⇐

There are two important objections to introduce at this point. These have to do with the kind of retributive action God will allegedly take against those who conduct their lives as if he did not exist. In the first place, if God is as Pascal describes him – i.e., revengeful – then, following the Wager, any possibility of his existing, however slight, will pragmatically outweigh any chance of his not existing and so make it prudent to bet on his existence. So much we have seen. However, if God is not as Pascal describes him and the divine punishment to be expected is less severe, then the issue becomes less clear-cut; and indeed if we believe that God is all-forgiving – as many do – and so will not punish even those who deny him, this reduces the rationale of the Wager still further, to the point indeed where gambling against God may be considered pragmatically the better wager (i.e., the finite pleasures on earth may still be enjoyed with the expectation of infinite pleasures to come). This conclusion only serves to show how the infinite expected value attached to Pascal's God quickly dissolves when applied to other logically possible gods, and how the Wager, as Pascal construes it, functions only by a crucial narrowing of how we are to conceive of God. To argue, as Nicholas Rescher does, that the Wager 'is addressed only to . . . the person who is committed to the Christian *idea* of God but hesitates about believing in him' is question-begging: it omits as '*real* possibilities' concepts of God that cannot be excluded a priori[21] (SOURCE 3: PP. 329–330).

The problem of a forgiving God

⇐

Do you consider the following beliefs possible/probable? To what extent, if any, do they undermine Pascal's Wager?

I believe that . . .

a God exists who rewards honest disbelief.

a God exists who punishes those who do not believe in him.

a God exists who punishes those who believe in him for mercenary reasons.

a God exists who punishes no one.

EXERCISE 6.3

---

21. See Nicholas Rescher, *Pascal's Wager: A Study of Practical Reasoning in Philosophical Theology*, Notre Dame, Ind., University of Notre Dame Press, 1985, p. 98. For a sustained critique of Rescher's position, see Graham Oppy, 'On Rescher on Pascal's Wager', *International Journal for Philosophy of Religion*, 30, 1990, pp. 159–168.

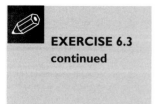

EXERCISE 6.3
continued

a God exists who punishes everyone.

a God exists, and his name is 'Allah'.

a God exists, but no after-life.

an after-life exists, but no God.

an evil demon exists.

many gods exist.

The morality of choice

The second objection is an extension of the first and has to do with the *morality* of the choice before us. Many believe that Pascalian wagering, although perhaps prudent, is morally reprehensible, and this because unbelief should only be punished, if at all, when the person concerned can be rightly *blamed* for it: when it is the culpable result of self-deception or of a deliberate and perverse refusal to do justice to the evidence. 'What is needed', writes Terence Penelhum,

> is that men should see the signs of God, and recognize them as signs of God, and yet still divide themselves into the believers and unbelievers. But this means that the unbelievers refuse to accept the revelations of God for what they are – there is no capacity to believe, only refusal to believe.[22]

This is, I think, a valid point: it underscores the fact that the God of the Wager, should he exist, rewards and punishes according to *actions* rather than *motives* (SOURCE 4: PP. 330–332). Pascal has himself suggested that a person cannot be blamed for rejecting on rational grounds the so-called 'proofs' for God. That being the case, it is difficult to see why atheists or agnostics should be blamed for rejecting the pragmatic argument on rational grounds as well – they might, for example, point to the weaknesses already indicated by the 'many-gods' objection. Even though we may consider their decisions imprudent, we should concede that, if they are rationally convinced after having weighed all the available evidence that there is no God, it is immoral to condemn them for not allowing their self-interests to prejudice their own intellectual integrity, and for not therefore becoming complicit in a system of belief that they rationally disown. Otherwise the believer is not unlike a politician pursuing a policy about which he has strong misgivings solely for the sake of promotion. Penelhum concludes:

> If it is true that men can hear and not be convinced, then unbelief does not necessarily equal self-deception. But then unbelief does not necessarily merit exclusion from salvation. If it does not, then Pascal's

---

22. Penelhum, *Religion and Rationality: An Introduction to the Philosophy of Religion*, New York, Random House, 1971, p. 217.

Wager argument, which presupposes that it does, is morally unworthy of acceptance.[23]

This moral objection has exposed what many take to be the essentially mercenary character of wagering on God. This raises the question of whether theism is the only belief that the pragmatist, even on Pascalian terms, should be advised to adopt. For if, following Penelhum, we agree that *moral unbelief* – that is, unbelief honestly upheld – does not necessarily merit damnation, we might also agree that *immoral belief* – that is, one fuelled by self-interest and deliberately disavowing or suppressing all contrary evidence – does not necessarily merit salvation; that the belief that there is a God, even if correct, when upheld for fundamentally immoral reasons is not one that a moral God is required to reward. This places before us the perhaps surprising option that here too honesty is the best policy, and that a wager against God may turn out to be prudentially the best bet, offering a gain that might be denied to self-serving theists.

> Another possibility is that there might be a god who looked with more favour on honest doubters or atheists who, in Hume's words, proportioned their belief to the evidence, than on mercenary manipulators of their own understanding. Indeed, this would follow from the ascription to God of moral goodness in any sense that we can understand. The sort of God required for Pascal's first alternative is modelled upon a monarch both stupid enough and vain enough to be pleased with self-interested flattery.[24]

Summarizing, then, we can say that belief motivated by greed may be morally more reprehensible than dispassionate unbelief, and that, for all we know, it may not reap the promised reward, particularly given the possibility that (a) an all-forgiving God exists who punishes nobody or (b) a revengeful God exists who punishes those who believe for selfish motives. But there is something else besides. Implicit within this criticism is also the more general view that self-interest inclines us to discard or ignore evidence that we might otherwise acknowledge. In other words, any prudential incentive for believing something tends to obscure our moral obligation not to believe it on insufficient evidence, and so inculcates in us and in others degrees of self-deception which

Is wagering on God mercenary?

---

23. *Ibid.*, p. 218.
24. J. L. Mackie, *The Miracle of Theism*, Oxford, Clarendon Press, 1982, p. 203. There are other, more extreme, versions of the same objection. Walter Kaufmann, for example, imagines a god who punishes only those who act religiously in order to please him and who rewards those indifferent to religion: a god who, as Kaufmann expresses it, would 'out-Luther Luther'. *Critique of Religion and Philosophy*, Princeton, N.J., Princeton University Press, 1978, p. 171. Michael Martin goes even further. He imagines a 'perverse master' who 'punishes with infinite torment after death anyone who believes in God or any other supernatural being (including himself) and rewards with infinite bliss after death anyone who believes in no supernatural being'. *Op. cit.*, p. 231.

will in the long run prove detrimental to society as a whole, making us credulous where we should be, as far as is possible, critically rational. If human cognitive faculties are God-given, then it is difficult to see why their corruption should be rewarded by their creator.[25]

EXERCISE 6.5

In what respects do the following contain moral objections to Pascal?

1 Gambling is wrong; therefore gambling on God is wrong.

2 Religious persecution is justified if it brings the unfaithful to belief.

3 It was not for her to name the murderer: God knows the truth and will punish him later.

4 Because you are an atheist, the good works that you perform have no value for God.

5 Always turn the other cheek, no matter how badly you are treated.

6 Better to be a Flapper than a Protestant. Flappers believe that only Flappers get to heaven, but Protestants believe that other faiths, including Flappers, can get there. So Flapperism is the better bet: nothing is lost if you don't believe it, but everything is gained if you do.

THE LIFE OF FAITH

Unsuccessful criticisms of Pascal

Criticisms of the second phase of Pascal's argument have been much less successful. This is because they have tended to concentrate on what is in fact a misinterpretation of his position, namely, the view that religious belief, quite apart from being prudentially the most rational option, is something that can be acquired simply by *an act of will*. But this is not what Pascal says; indeed, as an objection, he would agree with it. What he does say, however, is something rather different. What he says is that, if we accept the logic of the Wager, but still find it impossible to believe, then we should start living *as if* we believed. By this means the habits of faith will take hold, and place us in a position to appreciate the rich rewards that the religious life has to offer. In other words, living the life of belief, even though we cannot decide to believe, will make it probable that in the long run we shall believe.

Here Pascal has carefully distinguished the means *to* faith from the life *of* faith. That is, it is only after the priority of the Wager has been clearly

---

25. Perhaps the most famous exponent of this line of argument is W. K. Clifford, in his famous essay 'The Ethics of Belief': 'If I let myself believe anything on insufficient evidence, there may be no great harm done by the mere belief; it may be true after all, or I may never have occasion to exhibit it in outward acts. But I cannot help doing this great wrong to Man, that I make myself credulous. The danger to society is not merely that it should believe wrong things, though that is great enough; but that it should become credulous, and lose the habit of testing things and inquiring into them; for then it must sink back into savagery.' *The Ethics of Belief Debate*, ed. Gerald D. McCarthy, Atlanta, Scholars Press, 1986, p. 23.

established – thus making us aware that this is no ordinary gamble but one with potentially catastrophic consequences, involving the loss of our salvation – that Pascal recommends that we live in a certain way; but living this life is not faith itself but only a possible, and by no means foolproof, method of acquiring it: it is, in this sense, contingent upon our acceptance (a) that the Wager is unavoidable and of ultimate significance, and (b) that wagering prudentially (i.e., placing the bet on God) does *not* mean that faith will automatically follow. Faith, after all, is a free gift of God's grace and not, on his part, the compulsory repayment of a debt.

Pascal's remarks about the capacity of human beings to choose to believe – that belief can arise from an initial desire to believe – have undoubted psychological merit. So, too, has his claim that religious belief is somehow *infectious*, and that accordingly human beings, when placed in close proximity to it, will often come to believe in things they would not otherwise have accepted. After all, men and women frequently place themselves or are placed in situations where their beliefs will be *formed* and *reinforced* by close association with others of the same belief. In this sense, there can be and often is a strong *causal connection* between what one believes and the desire to conform to the particular beliefs of the society in which one finds oneself, as is indicated in the extent to which children will so often duplicate the political opinions of their parents. Other features of this connection are of interest. Very often what one person inherits from another is a *factual belief* that something has been or is the case: here what they share is a common belief precisely because they both have the empirical evidence to support and defend it (for example, that Winston Churchill was Prime Minister at a particular moment in British history). But this is not always the case. For not only is it quite possible that what one person believes is not believed by the person who caused it (for example, a doctor, in order to prevent further distress to a terminally ill woman, fosters the belief that she will recover), but it is also possible that both share a *non-factual belief*, that is, a belief that both acknowledge has no empirical support but which they hold nonetheless *because both agree that having this belief generates something that is desired*.[26] This, as Pascal has indicated, is the prudential character of religious faith.

This view also carries considerable psychological weight: indeed, it was this aspect of religion which most attracted the attentions of Sigmund Freud.

I shall not examine Freud's theory in detail here, since I have done this elsewhere;[27] but it is worth remarking that Freud, most notably in his *The Future of an Illusion* (1927), gives a quite precise account of the way in which religion attracts adherents by making itself psychologically irresistible: not only does it fulfil certain desires and satisfactions, such as the need to subdue the external forces of nature by the creation of gods and one's own internal aggressions through the code of neighbourliness and the ethics of conscience,

Psychological strength of Pascal's argument

Freud: the advantages and disadvantages of belief

26. See also Bernard Williams, 'Deciding to Believe', in *Problems of the Self*, Cambridge, Cambridge University Press, 1973, pp. 136–151; and Terence Penelhum, *Reason and Religious Faith*, Oxford, Westview Press, 1995, pp. 39–62.
27. See my *Freud and Jung on Religion*, London, Routledge, 1997, pp. 35–41.

Sigmund Freud
(1856–1939)

Generally regarded as the founder of psychoanalysis, Freud studied medicine initially in Vienna and then in Paris under Jean-Martin Charcot, who first introduced him to the relationship between hysterical paralysis and hypnosis. Freud's first major publication, *Studies in Hysteria* (1895), jointly written with his friend Josef Breuer, classically states that neurotic disorder is due to the repression of the traumatic past events of early childhood. This is the central hypothesis of Freudian psychology, developed in *The Interpretation of Dreams* (1900), arguably Freud's greatest book, and in *Three Essays on Sexuality* (1905), in which he further claims that infantile trauma is sexual (or libidinal) in character – more specifically, that the repressed impulse is 'oedipal' in form: the individual desires to replace the father in the sexual life of the mother. Without question the most notorious aspect of his work, this so-called Oedipus complex dominates Freud's later writings on religion: *Totom and Taboo* (1913), *The Future of an Illusion* (1927), *Civilization and its Discontents* (1930) and *Moses and Monotheism* (1939). In them Freud makes clear that religion is an infantile obsessional neurosis, obstructing the individual's development towards full and responsible maturity. Accordingly, personal and social progress will be better fostered by an 'irreligious education'.

but these desires are themselves so potent that the believer is prepared to subvert his intellect to obtain them, to submit himself to believe things because others believe them, and to accept as true things that he would otherwise regard as fictions.[28] Thus religious faith is characterized as a psychological (and neurotic) disposition so powerful that the need to act *as if* X is true obviates any evidential requirement to know whether X *is* true. The belief in life after death is a case in point. Despite all evidence to the contrary, this belief persists because of the conjunction of two opposing attitudes: of man's narcissistic inability to conceive of his own mortality and his desire to make his own helplessness before death more tolerable.

The question remains, of course, whether the advantages of faith are as Pascal describes them: so obvious and so peculiar to religion that rational people, whatever their initial misgivings, will be prepared to subvert their own intelligence and accept what they would otherwise find unacceptable in order to acquire them. Must we conclude, then, that the virtues of fidelity, humility, true friendship, and so on are distinct benefits not to be found in other, non-theistic, forms of life? For if these benefits are not peculiar to religion but may be acquired elsewhere, they become much less persuasive as pragmatic reasons for adopting a belief. Pascal will reply, of course, that the pleasures offered by religion are distinct in one respect: they alone are coupled with the prospect of infinite and not transitory felicity. This, after all, is why the gambler is urged to bet in one direction rather than another: the calculated utility of belief in

---

28. *The Future of an Illusion*, in Freud, *Civilization, Society and Religion*, London, Penguin Books, 1991, pp. 206–211.

God is greater than the calculated utility of non-belief. This conclusion, however, prompts another question, namely, whether the belief in infinite happiness can also be viewed as a *negative* value, and disbelief as a *positive* value, thus weighting the Wager in favour of agnosticism or atheism.

And this is precisely what Freud does in the closing pages of *The Future of an Illusion*. The fear is that, if religion is unmasked as a neurotic disorder, men and women will no longer feel constrained to obey the precepts of morality, will act asocially and aggressively towards their neighbours, and will be deprived of the consoling comforts of a father-based religion. Freud's reply is uncompromising. Admittedly, the absence of religion can often make life more difficult; but its advantages still outweigh its disadvantages. That morality is now revealed as a human construct, designed to serve the best interests of society and not an external imposition designed to rule us, will make us better disposed towards acting morally. Nor will we any longer have to suffer from the schizophrenic and intellectually corrupting division between what we believe and what is rational to believe. And the fact that there is no other world will throw people back on their own resources and so encourage them to channel their energies into the improvement of their own condition.

> They will have to admit to themselves the full extent of their helplessness and their insignificance in the machinery of the universe; they can no longer be the centre of creation, no longer the object of tender care on the part of a beneficent Providence. They will be in the same position as a child who has left the parental house where he was so warm and comfortable. But surely infantilism is destined to be surmounted. Men cannot remain children for ever; they must in the end go out into 'hostile life'. We must call this '*education to reality*'.[29]

Construed in these terms, Pascal's Wager may drive in the opposite direction to the one intended: that it can be utilized as an argument for unbelief. Here we should remember the original terms of the bet: that there are better pragmatic reasons for believing that a God does exist, even when he may or may not exist, than for believing that he does not exist, even when he may or may not exist. This reasoning now has to be revised. For not only is it possible to conceive of a God who does not reward belief and punish unbelief in the manner prescribed by Pascal, thereby making it uncertain whether any advantage will necessarily accrue to the gambler on God; it is also at least possible to conceive of distinct benefits accruing to the gambler against God – amongst which we may number self-reliance, intellectual rectitude, and a greater concern for human social and moral welfare. Thus it is possible to deny God's existence without fear of subsequent disadvantage and to specify the positive benefits that result from so doing.

The Wager as an argument for unbelief

29. *Ibid.*, p. 233.

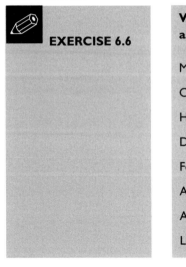

EXERCISE 6.6

Which of the following advantages or disadvantages do you think are more likely to accrue from belief and unbelief?

Moral courage	Independence of mind
Concern for others	Self-sacrifice
Honesty	Concern to obey the law
Distinguishing right from wrong	Revolutionary zeal
Fear of death	Serenity in adversity
A sense of purpose	Self-fulfilment
Aesthetic sensibility	Respect for facts
Loving unconditionally	Gullibility

JAMES' PRAGMATIC ARGUMENT: THE WILL TO BELIEVE

⇒ The clearest statement of James' pragmatic case for God is to be found in his famous essay of 1896, 'The Will to Believe' (**SOURCE 5: PP. 332–338**). This argument is, in many respects, very different from Pascal's, and these should be noted from the outset. In the first place, it is present-looking rather than future-looking: the advantages of theistic belief are taken for the most part to be advantages primarily accruing to the believer here and now, and not, as Pascal has it, primarily those gained in a life after death, assuming of course that God exists.[30] For that reason, we find in James no extended calculation of where, when one wagers on God, the dominating bet lies: of whether, given their respective probabilities, the expected utility of a finite life is more or less than an infinite one. James is well aware, too, of the mercenary character of Pascal's argument – 'such a mechanical calculation would lack the inner soul of faith's reality'[31] – and of the fairly obvious objection that it is an argument which could apply to other religions as well.

James and Pascal contrasted

There are, however, equally clear similarities between the two arguments. Even if James is less overt than Pascal in his calculation of prudential choice, deciding whether God exists or not remains an inescapable decision of ultimate significance: if I do not believe, I 'forfeit my sole chance in life of getting upon the winning side'.[32] Nor will the so-called rational demonstrations of God's existence help us in this regard. In a lecture called 'Philosophy' in

---

30. I say 'for the most part' because there are passages which are very wager-like. See pp. 309–310 below. The final page of the essay 'The Will to Believe' contains a lengthy quotation from Fitzjames Stephen, which is distinctly Pascalian in tone.

31. *The Will to Believe and Other Essays in Popular Philosophy*, New York, Dover Publications, 1956, p. 6.

32. *Ibid.*, p. 27.

A distinguished American psychologist, James grew up in a highly intellectual family: his father was a Swedenborgian theologian, and his brother, Henry, became a famous novelist. After first studying art and geology, James received a degree in medicine from Harvard, subsequently teaching there for thirty-five years. His *Principles of Psychology* (1890) is a monumental work covering the full range of psychological phenomena known at the time. By this time, however, his personal interests were becoming more philosophical in nature, and, influenced by the earlier work of C. S. Peirce (1839–1914) he gradually formulated a pragmatic theory of truth by which the truth of a concept is determined by what empirical difference its being true would make. This theory, set out most fully in his later *Pragmatism* (1907), had immediate implications for James' religious views, most notably in two works: in his famous essay 'The Will to Believe' (1897), in which he claimed that religious belief, though an individual process, can find evidential support in its practical consequences; and in his *The Varieties of Religious Experience* (1907), in which James explored the relationships between religious experience and 'abnormal' psychology.

William James
(1842–1910)

his *Varieties of Religious Experience* (1902), James reviews all the classical proofs and, like Pascal before him, is unimpressed by their empty rhetoric: 'I will not weary you by pursuing these metaphysical determinations farther' is a typically dismissive remark. Such speculations, he says, may be all well and good as theories confirming or reinforcing a *prior* belief; but as explanations of the reality of belief itself, of the concrete feelings and experiences of believers themselves, they are completely useless, worthless inventions of the scholarly mind. From the point of view of *practical religion*, then, these 'metaphysical monsters', even though faultlessly deduced, are to be discarded. If one is looking for an explanation and justification of faith, of *why* people believe and why they have a *right* to believe, one must therefore look elsewhere.

Still more significant for James' own argument is his defence of Pascal's account of how one might acquire belief: of how, if one lives the life of faith, faith may come. At first blush, the suggestion that a person can somehow induce belief through a singular effort of will seems not just 'silly' but even 'vile', not least because there appears to be no discrimination between beliefs, no separation between those for which there is and is not any empirical support, and so no check upon the worst excesses of wishful thinking. Here James cites the celebrated remark of the distinguished Victorian mathematician and philosopher W. K. Clifford: that 'It is wrong always, everywhere, and for every one, to believe anything upon insufficient evidence.'[33] Anything less will be corruptive of both individual and society. James quotes again: 'It is sinful because it is stolen in defiance of our duty to mankind. That duty is to guard

Clifford: evidence required for belief

---

33. *Ibid.*, p. 8. See above, n. 25.

ourselves from such beliefs as from a pestilence which may shortly master our own body and then spread to the rest of the town.'[34]

In many ways James' argument begins with his rejection of Clifford's position. Clifford's view is that *all legitimate beliefs are evidentially justifiable*, and that, where no corroborating evidence is forthcoming, *that belief must be discarded*. What we have here is a *normative principle* – that having evidence is a *necessary* condition of a legitimate belief – and that adopting this principle has *moral implications*: that where a belief contravenes the normative principle, we have a moral duty to reject that belief. For James, however, this argument is thoroughly misguided. For, as he will seek to show, there are some cases in which a person is *morally justified in believing something on insufficient evidence*. This type of belief is what James means by an *overbelief*, that is, a belief going beyond the evidence. Admittedly the circumstances in which these so-called 'overbeliefs' may legitimately occur are severely circumscribed, but they include, as we shall see, cases of religious faith.

What is an 'overbelief'?

At this point James introduces another distinction to make his own position clearer. Clifford is an example of what James calls a 'tough-minded' philosopher: empiricist, materialistic and sceptical.[35] Thinkers of this type worship *facts* and so reject the whole notion of a world beyond our finite experience: they accordingly reject the notion of overbeliefs and so are fundamentally irreligious. There are other philosophers, however, who are 'tender-minded', and who believe that there are vital truths which go beyond anything that science has to tell us: they accordingly embrace the notion of overbeliefs and so are less willing to dismiss the religious hypothesis. The notion of an 'overbelief' is, in this respect, a concept that only a 'tender-minded' philosopher could employ. That the evidence for an overbelief is inadequate does not mean, therefore, that this belief is untrue and so has nothing important to say: it merely means that the determination of its truth is not evidential and is to be sought elsewhere. As will become clear, James seeks to mediate between the 'tough' and 'tender-minded' positions. He does not renounce empiricism in order to safeguard religion – where there are facts, belief cannot remain oblivious of them – and indeed himself employs a form of verificational method to establish religious truth.

Let me now give a more detailed example of an overbelief. Suppose my son, Max, is caught in a burning building and his rescue requires me to jump fifteen feet. Since I am not known for my athletic prowess, the evidence that I shall be able to carry the distance is far from sufficient. Yet nevertheless my belief that I can make the jump may actually contribute to my achieving it. This being the case, I am not only allowed to believe on insufficient evidence but have an actual moral duty to believe if it achieves my goal.

The charge that is often made against James at this point – that he is somehow claiming that something is true if it is believed to be true – is unfounded. James placed his theory firmly within the empirical tradition, and

---

34. *Ibid.*

35. *Pragmatism* (1907), with an Introduction by A. J. Ayer, Cambridge, Mass., Harvard University Press, 1975, pp. 13–14.

in that respect agreed that we cannot change our experiences simply by willing them otherwise. Thus, in the example just given, the belief that I can jump fifteen feet to rescue Max may help me if I can already manage thirteen, but not if I am one-legged and can barely manage three.

> Can our will either help or hinder our intellect in its perceptions of truth? Can we, by just willing it, believe that Abraham Lincoln's existence is a myth, and that the portraits of him in McClure's Magazine are all of some one else? Can we, by any effort of our will, or by any strength of wish that it were true, believe ourselves well and about when we are roaring with rheumatism in bed, or feel certain that the sum of the two one-dollar bills in our pocket must be a hundred dollars? We can say any of these things, but we are absolutely impotent to believe them; and of just such things is the whole fabric of the truths that we do believe in made up – matters of fact, immediate or remote, as Hume said, and relations between ideas, which are either there or not there for us if we see them so, and which if not there cannot be put there by any action of our own.[36]

It is interesting to note in this quotation how James upholds the familiar distinction between truths a priori (analytic) and truths a posteriori (synthetic). This is indeed an underlying assumption on his part, which helps to explain why any belief may be legitimately discarded if neither logically consistent nor consistent with the available facts of our sense-experiences. Here he remains 'tough-minded'. But as A. J. Ayer has perceptively noted, the reason why James does not employ this distinction more prominently is not that he thinks it 'incorrect' but that, in the context of our total system of beliefs, he considers it relatively 'uninformative'.[37] So when the belief depends on facts that are not directly ascertainable, as was the case with the overbelief just cited, other criteria need to apply and a more 'tender-minded' approach is called for. Thus my belief that I could jump the distance was, despite the evidence, *justified* because (1) I *desired* to rescue Max and because (2) having this particular belief *would help to bring his rescue about*. This may be expressed more generally: a belief is legitimate for the individual if having it has practical consequences, i.e., if it enables that person to achieve a goal. This leads us to James' *pragmatic definition of truth*: that an idea is true 'so long as to believe it is profitable to our lives';[38] that '"the true" . . . is only the expedient in the way of our thinking'.[39]

---

36. *Ibid.*, pp. 4–5. James makes the same point many times elsewhere. For a short summary, see his essay 'The Meaning of the Word Truth' in *The Meaning of Truth* (1909), with an Introduction by A. J. Ayer, Cambridge, Mass., Harvard University Press, 1975, pp. 283–285.
37. Ayer, *The Origins of Pragmatism*, London, Macmillan, 1968, p. 199.
38. 'What Pragmatism Means' in *Pragmatism,* p. 42.
39. 'Pragmatism's Conception of Truth', *ibid.*, p. 106.

EXERCISE 6.7

Using James' distinction between the 'tough-minded' and the 'tender-minded', which of the two approaches do you think is the more appropriate to establish whether the following beliefs are true or not?

I believe . . .

that she is a true friend: she paid his hospital expenses.

that she is true to her husband: she never had a lover.

that this music is a true expression of the composer's feelings.

that he loves her, despite his infidelities.

that nothing comes without effort.

that I am not the same man now that I once was.

that Democrats are better people than Republicans.

that life after death is a fiction: when I die I rot.

that arithmetic propositions are devoid of factual content.

that I have been unfairly treated.

The pragmatic test of religious truth

Let us now apply James' pragmatic definition of truth to the question of religious belief. Like Pascal before him, James does not think that religion possesses or is capable of possessing any conclusive theoretic or empirical support – so much at least has been established by the failure of the traditional arguments for God's existence, both a priori and a posteriori. This fact, however, has hardly deterred people from believing: men and women still claim not only that certain religious claims are true but that believing them to be true has distinct beneficial consequences. We may conclude, therefore, that religious belief is an overbelief: that it is held in the full knowledge that the evidence for it is insufficient and that it depends on a conviction that is non-intellectual in character but which nevertheless stimulates the believer to act in a certain way. A religious belief, in other words, may be held to be true if the believer is convinced that it has practical and beneficial consequences for him or her. This, then, is *the pragmatic test of religious truth*. In James' famous words, 'if the hypothesis of God *works* satisfactorily in the widest sense of the word, it is true'.[40]

This theory of belief, as we shall now see, incorporates two interlocking arguments, each covering different situations in which a belief is an overbelief, i.e., when it is a belief that may be justified on pragmatic, rather than evidential, grounds. The first concerns the subjective factor, which is a necessary component of religious belief as an overbelief, and covers those situations in

40. *Ibid.*, p. 143 (my italics).

which the individual is faced with an unavoidable, but intellectually undecidable, choice. This we may call the *right-to-believe argument*. The second concerns the equally necessary practical factor inherent within religious belief as an overbelief, and covers those situations in which the belief is validated by its own practical consequences. This we may call the *will-to-believe* argument. Let us now examine each in turn.

THE RIGHT-TO-BELIEVE ARGUMENT: RELIGIOUS BELIEF AS A 'GENUINE OPTION'

The right-to-believe argument begins by isolating those quite specific occasions when a person is faced with a decision which cannot be decided on either theoretical or empirical grounds. James' argument runs thus:

> The thesis I defend is, briefly stated, this: *Our passional nature not only lawfully may, but must, decide between propositions, whenever it is a genuine option that cannot by its nature be decided on intellectual grounds; for to say, under such circumstances, 'Do not decide, but leave the question open', is itself a passional decision, – just like deciding yes or no, – and is attended with the same risk of losing the truth.*[41]

The cases we are dealing with are therefore of a quite specific type: they deal with decisions reached on a 'non-intellectual' basis, in which the individual is faced with a 'genuine option'. What is a genuine option? This, James explains, involves a choice between two hypotheses that is living (and not dead), momentous (and not trivial), and forced (and not avoidable). Taking each in turn, by a 'living' option James has in mind a choice in which the alternatives are genuine belief-options, such as 'Be an agnostic or be a Christian'. This contrasts with a 'dead' option, such as 'Be a theosophist or be a Jain', in which the choice is unlikely to be confronted or to be of much interest. A 'momentous' option is one in which the decision reached will have significant consequences, involving perhaps a unique opportunity that will not come again – 'Either come with me to Africa or not' would involve a decision of this type, whereas 'Either finish that book today or not' would be comparatively trivial since the opportunity to do so will in all probability be repeated. And finally, a 'forced' option is one which cannot be avoided, like 'Your money or your life'. This contrasts with the 'Either take your umbrella or not', which is a choice that can be avoided altogether by staying indoors.

What is a 'genuine option'?

The following example may help to illustrate what a 'genuine option' involves. Suppose that Rachel is deciding whether to marry Hal, despite the fact that her friends have warned her that he has a reputation as a notorious womanizer. Rachel knows of his past but still believes that he will make a good husband. In this case her belief is an overbelief since her decision to marry him

---

41. *The Will to Believe*, p. 11.

has no evidential support – indeed, in this case the evidence pulls in another direction, suggesting that he will be unfaithful. But she decides to marry Hal nonetheless. Her decision thus involves a 'genuine option': it is *living* because both options – whether to marry him or not – are genuine alternatives; it is *momentous* because it is clearly a decision that will affect her life; and it is *forced* because it is unavoidable, because from a practical viewpoint indecision is tantamount to a decision not to marry him.

EXERCISE 6.7

Which of the following decisions are 'living', 'momentous' and 'forced'?

Shall I go to France or Germany or not?

Shall I pay my rent or not?

Shall I train to be a doctor or not?

Shall I tell the truth or not?

Shall I perform this experiment or not?

Shall I love him or not?

Shall I take this drug or not?

Shall I become a Sikh or not?

Shall I believe that Napoleon was Emperor or not?

Shall I believe that bachelors are unmarried or not?

Shall I believe that Mr Sheppe is a bachelor or not?

Shall I believe that I am a man or not?

Now that we have clarified James' terminology, we can present his right-to-believe argument as follows:

SUMMARY: JAMES' RIGHT-TO-BELIEVE ARGUMENT

1 A genuine option is living, momentous and forced, and cannot be decided on rational grounds alone.

2 When a person is faced with a genuine option he or she must therefore decide according to his or her passional nature.

3 The religious option is a genuine option.

Therefore:

4 The religious option is one that is living, momentous and forced, and can only be decided according to a person's passional nature.

This argument turns on James' description (3) of the religious option as a 'genuine option'. This description is appropriate because belief fulfils the necessary two-fold criteria already established. The first criterion is that when an individual is faced with the decision whether to believe in God or not, he or she must decide on 'passional' grounds alone, *religious belief being undecidable on any other purely evidential grounds*. James has been much criticized for saying this, not least by Bertrand Russell. Russell claimed that it gave religion a licence to think what it pleased, irrespective of what may in fact be the case.[42] But much of this criticism is misplaced, and one has some sympathy for James when he calls it a 'slander' against his own definition of truth.[43] For he is not saying, as Russell seems to think, that, when we have evidence against a belief, the belief may override the evidence, since James agrees that this would be irrational, immoral, and contrary to his own empirical standpoint. What he is saying, however, is that Russell's own definition of truth is too limited (or too 'tough-minded) – that not all beliefs can be validated by their objective reference – and that a more 'tender-minded' approach is required when dealing with the religious belief that God exists, for which there is and can be no validating proof or evidence. In this restricted case, then, when we cannot decide on these terms alone whether this particular belief is true or false, it is neither irrational nor immoral to believe according to our passions. Thus, within these stated conditions, religion legitimately functions as a 'genuine option', establishing thereby a right to believe as our subjective will or 'passional nature' may direct.

The second criterion which establishes religious belief as a 'genuine option' is that *a religious decision is living, momentous and forced*. By saying that it is a *living* option, James claims to avoid Pascal's error of supposing that the calculated adoption of a belief, even though it be a dead option ('believing in masses and holy water') will induce genuine belief – as he says, 'the option offered to the will by Pascal is not a living option'.[44] James also claims in this way to avoid the 'many-Gods' objection, in which a bet may be placed on a belief which is of no special interest to the believer or simply redundant. By calling the religious option a 'living' option, James is making clear, then, that his argument only applies to those for whom the question whether there is a God or not is a live issue, and who are therefore faced with the decision whether to believe or not. This decision is also *momentous* and *forced*:

> we see, first, that religion offers itself as a *momentous* option. We are supposed to gain, even now, by our belief, and to lose by our non-belief, a certain vital good. Secondly, religion is a *forced* option, so far as that good goes. We cannot escape the issue by remaining sceptical and waiting for more light, because, although we do avoid error in that way *if religion*

The religious option as a genuine option

---

42. See Russell, 'William James's Conception of Truth', *Philosophical Essays*, London, George Allen & Unwin, 1910; revised edition, 1966, pp. 112–130.
43. 'Two English Critics', *The Meaning of Truth*, p. 313.
44. *Ibid.*, p. 6.

be untrue, we lose the good, *if it be true*, just as certainly as if we positively chose to disbelieve.[45]

James' Wager

This is the nearest James gets to a Pascalian-type wager. If an individual accepts that the religious option is a 'living' option, then he must also accept that whether he believes that God exists or not will have unavoidable practical consequences: that such are the potential gains and losses involved here that his decision will be necessarily 'momentous' in character, be he theist or atheist, and 'forced' because unavoidable. What, then, are these gains and losses? James describes them in terms of the gain or loss of 'truth' and the gain or loss of a 'certain vital good'. The believer, we are told, cannot avoid risking 'error' because he has already admitted that his belief in God depends on evidence that is 'insufficient'. But he is prepared to take this risk nonetheless because he may thereby gain not just a 'truth' – that his belief is, after all, a true belief because God does in fact exist – but also a 'good', which, if his belief be true, will include eternal life and other blessings. The atheist's decision is equally momentous and forced. He too risks error because the evidence remains insufficient, and by his decision he may also gain a truth – that his belief is a true belief because God does not in fact exist – but lose the possibility of obtaining the 'vital good' of eternal life.

Nor can the momentous and forced character of the religious option be dissipated by a retreat into agnosticism since the consequences for the religious sceptic are equally dramatic and unavoidable. Admittedly he has avoided error because he has made no decision on the evidence; but refusing to decide is a decision nonetheless, and carries with it a high price: he has lost both the chance of believing something that is true (whether God exists or not) and, like the atheist, any chance of the benefits that accrue from belief. Thus even agnosticism entails a momentous and forced decision: it is momentous because it involves the loss of a possible gain; and it is forced because, in this context, to hesitate is to make a decision as passional and inescapable as that required when acting on insufficient evidence.

EXERCISE 6.8

Construct a Jamesian version of Pascal's Wager, taking note of the

Gains and losses of theism

Gains and losses of atheism

Gains and losses of agnosticism.

Which for you is the better bet?

This concludes the first part of James' argument. By establishing that religious belief involves a 'genuine option', James has marked out what he

---

45. *Ibid.*, p. 26.

considers to be the legitimate area in which our 'passional nature' may intrude on the question of whether God exists or not, this being the only option left to us in the absence of any rational investigation which could decide the issue one way or the other. But it is worth repeating: if this argument confirms a *right to believe on passional grounds in the religious situation*, it does *not* confirm the same right in the overwhelming majority of other situations, in which the subjective factor is rightly excluded, i.e., when an option can be decided through rational investigation of the facts, when a more 'tough-minded' approach is called for. James' argument, then, is highly restricted in its scope. A further restriction is imposed by *the nature of the decision by which the right to believe is exercised*: that this right is disposed only when the individual faces a decision that is 'living', 'momentous' and 'forced'. When these elements combine, as they do in religious belief, they designate an option which can only be decided by our passional nature and which carries with it an irreducible risk, requiring the courage of decision.

> Faith means belief in something concerning which doubt is still theoretically possible; and as the test of belief is willingness to act, one may say that faith is the readiness to act in a cause the prosperous issue of which is not certified to us in advance. It is in fact the same moral quality which we call courage in practical affairs.[46]

THE WILL-TO-BELIEVE ARGUMENT: RELIGIOUS BELIEF AS A SELF-VERIFYING GENUINE OPTION

In his first argument – the right-to-believe argument – James has claimed that religious belief as an overbelief, although incapable of being established on theoretical or empirical grounds, presents us nevertheless with an unavoidable decision of risk within a carefully circumscribed area of action. In his second argument – the will-to-believe argument – he next claims that we are entitled to employ pragmatic reasons to help us make up our minds whether to believe or not, there being in effect no other reasons left to us capable of justifying our position. The pragmatic test here is *that an overbelief may be validated as being true by its own practical consequences*. I have already given an example of the kind of thing James has in mind here (Max's rescue) where the belief in the future existence of a fact may itself contribute to produce that fact, or as James expresses it, 'where faith creates its own verification'.[47] He cites many examples drawn from the 'immense class' of cases in which faith in a fact can help create that fact. An individual's belief in his or her own success often contributes to his or her being successful. A woman may fall in love with a man because the man insists that she does, after all, love him. Social organisms, like a government, an army or an athletic team, function through a shared faith

---

46. 'The Sentiment of Rationality', *The Will to Believe*, p. 90.
47. *Ibid.*, p. 97.

that each of their members will do his or her duty.[48] Even a question like whether life is worth living may be answered affirmatively because of the individual's prior belief that living is worth while, where indeed faith beforehand in an uncertified result is *the only thing that makes the result come true*.[49] This helps us to understand more precisely what James means when he says that a belief can *verify* itself. The verification cannot, in cases such as these, consist in whether the claim being made corresponds to the facts that objectively obtain, since we are dealing here with overbeliefs, and thus with beliefs held in the absence of such facts. The verification of an overbelief rather occurs when those consequences of having a belief are realized by having that belief, so that in this particular instance the future fact is conditioned by my present 'will to believe' in its eventual occurrence:

> there is a certain class of truths of whose reality belief is a factor as well as a confessor; and that as regards this class of truths faith is not only licit and pertinent, but essential and indispensable. The truths cannot become true till our faith has made them so.[50]

Manuscript page from James' 'The Will to Believe'

---

48. 'The Will to Believe', *ibid.*, p. 24.
49. 'Is Life Worth Living?', *ibid.*, p. 59.
50. 'The Sentiment of Rationality', *ibid.*, p. 96.

This is unquestionably the most important, original and confusing aspect of James' theory. Let us therefore retrace our steps. Pascal's Wager, we remember, attempted to show that believing in God is the most reasonable thing to do because it is the most pragmatic thing to do, bringing unique advantages. James now extends this argument in one crucial particular: when we say that believing in God is the pragmatic thing to do we confer truth upon that belief because *what is expedient is true*. How does James arrive at this somewhat startling conclusion?

The first thing to stress again is that, for James the 'tough-minded' empiricist, a proposition is true when it is verified. Thus James would have no objection to saying that the statement 'It is raining' is a true statement because confirmed in experience (a posteriori). Within the context of belief, I can legitimately claim on these grounds that my belief that it is raining is a *true belief*, confirmed by an empirical fact. As we have seen, however, this method of verification cannot apply to an overbelief, there being no facts by which this special kind of belief can be corroborated. Are we to say, then, that no over-belief is verifiable and that accordingly we can never say of an overbelief that it is true? This James denies. For there is another criterion of truth that we may employ here, namely, *that a proposition is true when it makes a verifiable and concrete difference in the experience of the individual*. Thus a person may correctly claim that he has an overbelief and that this overbelief is true when having it has made an appreciable difference to his life, i.e., when it has had a practical and verifiable effect upon him, when there have been discernible consequences, when it has somehow 'worked' for him.

The crucial point to realize here is the form taken by the verification of an overbelief. According to the 'tender-minded' approach, verification does not consist in the correspondence with a present or past reality but with a *future reality*, the specific experience of which occurs only because the proposition is believed. In this sense, an overbelief may be called 'true' only when its *prediction* is verified, when the experience it says will happen does happen. We may express this differently by saying that, when we are dealing with an overbelief, verification is subsequent to the belief, that it *evolves*, that an overbelief is not known to be true until it becomes true.

> This thesis is what I have to defend. The truth of an idea is not a stagnant property inherent in it. Truth *happens* to an idea. It *becomes* true, is *made* true by events. Its verity *is* in fact an event, a process: the process namely of its verifying itself, its veri-*fication*. Its validity is the process of its valid-*ation*.[51]

An overbelief is therefore true if there occurs, as a consequence of having it, a definite and real difference within the life of the believer, if its being true has a 'cash-value in experiential terms'.[52] Let us return to Rachel and her marriage

How an overbelief verifies itself

---

51. 'Pragmatism's Conception of Truth', *Pragmatism*, p. 97.
52. *Ibid.*

problems by way of example. Rachel has now married Hal and from the beginning she has the overbelief that 'My marriage will be happy'. Whether this belief is a true belief can only be determined after a series of experiences have been completed, when Rachel is in a position *retrospectively to confirm* that this initial belief has made all the difference to her subsequent life with her husband, that her belief that her marriage *will* be happy has in some sense *made* it happy. In this respect, the prediction of the belief has been shown to be true because it has the requisite 'cash-value': the belief was true about Rachel – i.e., it expressed her genuine desire to be happy with her husband – and having this belief itself contributed to making her belief come true – i.e., that she actually was happy. Rachel can therefore say of her belief ('My marriage will be happy') that it was a *true belief* because it has been verified within her experience, because it 'worked' for her, because it both expressed and served a practical need on her part. That Rachel's belief had practical consequences for Rachel is thus the pragmatic justification for her saying that her belief is true.

By the same token it follows that a religious belief may be deemed a true belief if it is verifiable in the quite specific, and severely restricted, way that Rachel's belief was verifiable: if, that is, it does in fact express a particular desire that is actually held, and if it too possesses a 'cash-value' within the life of the believer, i.e., if having a religious belief does indeed have certain practical consequences which would otherwise not obtain. To assess this argument we need therefore to know two things: (1) what a religious belief affirms; and (2) what practical difference affirming this belief makes in the life of the believer, so that we can say of it that it has 'worked' for the individual concerned.

The content of belief

James' view of the content of religious belief is, as one might expect, dependent on his own particular ideas of God. These, as Bixler has indicated, are many and various:[53] God conceived as 'power', as 'comforter', as 'historically active', as 'responsive', and many others besides – all of these, as James readily admits, being highly speculative in form. However, for the purposes of the argument at hand, there are three ideas of God which are pre-eminent: (1) the idea of God as good; (2) the idea that God, being good, desires that his creation be good; and (3) the idea of God as personal, as a 'Thou' and not an 'It'.

The idea that God is good requires that God's motives, ends, intentions and character be good. This is not to suggest, of course, that this belief, being an overbelief, can be objectively demonstrated and that accordingly the postulate of God is *necessary* to give validity to any ethical claim. In 'The Moral Philosopher and the Moral Life' James makes a plea for ethical tolerance and is careful to say that 'there can be no final truth in ethics'.[54] That said, at the descriptive level, as a description of an *attitude*, the distinguishing feature of religious belief may be characterized as follows: *that there exists a being who is the absolute ground of moral value.*

53. Julius Bixler, *Religion in the Philosophy of William James*, Boston, Mass., Marshall Jones Company, 1926, pp. 123ff.
54. *The Will to Believe*, p. 184.

The next question is: Is this belief a true belief? Or rather: Is this belief verifiable in the sense previously described, that we can say that it has worked (has 'cash-value') for those individuals who believe it? This we can do because the practical difference that is brought into reality by the belief that God is good is a *commitment to lead a life that is good, so that the believer may by his actions contribute to God's plan that the world be good*. This conclusion rests in part on James' view that the salvation of the world is not a certainty guaranteed by an omnipotent and all-good deity; and that consequently human beings can become God's partners in the attempt to make goodness the more probable outcome. So James claims that to 'co-operate with his creation by the best and rightest response seems all he wants of us. In such co-operation with his purposes . . . must lie the real meaning of our destiny.'[55]

On pragmatic grounds, therefore, the hypothesis of God is true because it has made a palpable difference to how the believer lives: it has required of him that he adopt an *active moral life*, which is the *creation of his belief* in so far as his belief has stipulated that by acting morally, and not otherwise, he will contribute to God's plan for the moral perfection of the world. This belief *has become true* because it has *in reality* placed the believer under a moral obligation to act in a certain moral way, in a way that would not have existed without his prior belief that *his moral life makes a difference to the life of God*, that is, to whether or not God will realize his moral purpose for his own creation.

What, then, is the form of life that the believer is obliged to adopt? In his *The Varieties of Religious Experience* (1902) James describes the religious individual as being inspired by the most profound principles and impulses, these being amongst others: rejection of one's baser nature, asceticism, charity and brotherly love, fortitude and patience, purity of life, temperance, self-sacrifice and love for one's neighbour.[56] The saint, for example, 'abounds in impulses to help . . . turns his back upon no duty, however thankless', and is immune to those 'petty personal pretensions which so obstruct our ordinary social intercourse'.[57]

It can be argued, of course, that this form of life need not arise from a religious belief at all and that other secular philosophies have required similar moral behaviour – the non-religious interpretation of Kant's categorical imperative providing the most obvious examples.[58] James claims, however, that the religious demand is quite distinctive, having a force that is both uniquely personal and authoritative. This arises from the fact that the religious imperative

The moral life of the believer

---

55. 'Reflex Action and Theism', *ibid.*, p. 141.
56. *The Varieties of Religious Experience*, London and New York, Longmans, Green & Co., 1941, pp. 259–325. James is aware that these 'fruits of religion' are, however, 'like all human products, liable to corruption by excess' (*ibid.*, p. 339). Thus for every saintly virtue there is a pathological form: 'fanaticism or theopathic absorption, self-torment, prudery, scrupulosity, gullibility, and morbid inability to meet the world. By the very intensity of his fidelity to the paltry ideals with which an inferior intellect may inspire him, a saint can be even more objectionable and damnable than a superficial carnal man would be in the same situation' (*ibid.*, p. 370).
57. *Ibid.*, pp. 369–370.
58. See above, pp. 237–241.

issues from a being who is no abstract cipher but a living 'Thou'. 'The universe is no longer a mere *It* to us, but a *Thou*, if we are religious; and any relation that may be possible from person to person might be possible here.'[59] It is, in other words, the dynamics of person-to-person commitment that heightens the moral commitment required in religious belief, and generates in the faithful a 'moral strenuousness' that would be lacking otherwise. While therefore a moral system is possible without God, the lack of a personal dimension would not make it optimally compelling and would make it fall 'short of its maximal stimulating power'.[60]

> The capacity of the strenuous mood lies so deep down among our natural human possibilities that even if there were no metaphysical or traditional grounds for believing in a God, men would postulate one simply as a pretext for living hard, and getting out of the game of existence its keenest possibilities of zest. . . . Every sort of energy and endurance, of courage and capacity for handling life's evils is set free in those who have religious faith. For this reason the strenuous type of character will on the battle-field of human history always outwear the easy-going type, and religion will drive irreligion to the wall.[61]

This completes the James' will-to-believe argument.[62] Its structure is as follows:

SUMMARY: JAMES' WILL-TO-BELIEVE ARGUMENT	1 An overbelief is true if it makes a verifiable difference to the life of the believer which would not otherwise obtain (i.e., its truth is subject to the subsequent verification of its practical effect upon the believer). 2 Religious belief does make a verifiable difference to the life of the believer which would not otherwise obtain (i.e., its truth is subsequently verified by its practical moral effect upon the believer). 3 Therefore religious belief is true.

---

59. *The Will to Believe*, p. 27.
60. 'The Moral Philosopher and the Moral Life', *ibid.*, p. 212.
61. *Ibid.*, p. 213.
62. In fact, not quite: there is another phase to the argument, where James deals with the empirical (and so verifiable) consequences of prayer and our knowledge of God through the subconscious mind. Even scholars sympathetic to James find his conclusions here unsatisfactory, and for that reason I have excluded them. For a useful summary, see Ellen Kappy Suckiel, *Heaven's Champion: William James's Philosophy of Religion*, Notre Dame, Ind., University of Notre Dame Press, 1996, pp. 113–131.

SUMMARY OF JAMES' THEORY OF BELIEF

I said at the beginning of our discussion that James' theory of belief contains two elements, one subjective and 'passional', the other objective and pragmatic. Let us now see how these two interlock. The first marks out the area in which belief may legitimately exercise its *right to believe*. This right holds exclusively to decisions which are 'genuine options' (i.e., those that are living, momentous and forced), and in which the choice to be made cannot be reached on the basis of empirical evidence – there being in fact no empirical evidence that could apply in these cases. This does not mean, however, that we are dealing here with a choice that has no truth-content. For in the second phase of James' theory we find that belief may legitimately exercise its *will to believe*, that is, verify itself according to the practical consequences that accrue to the believer (i.e., that having this belief has in reality wrought a moral change). Thus we find that the lack of empirical support in the first phase of James' theory is more than compensated for in its second phase, although again in the highly restricted sense that here *the cause is validated by its effects*. A proposition of religious faith is therefore true if it describes what it has itself initiated, if the act of belief brings into actual reality the future practical experience that it anticipates. The will to believe thereby carries with it the means by which the act of faith is guaranteed as true: *by his willing it to be true the man of faith makes it true for him*. This allows him to confirm retrospectively that his belief is true because it has achieved its purpose by 'working' for him.

> The two phases of James' argument

CRITICISMS OF WILLIAM JAMES

As we have seen, James contends that among the beliefs that an individual might adopt some will be verifiable and some will not. Overbeliefs fall into the second category, and as such place a premium on the act of belief and what that act entails – namely, that it be a genuine option, living, momentous and forced – and rather less on the content of that belief, this being strictly speaking impervious to any kind of empirical test that might possibly convince the individual that he or she was wrong to believe it. In many of the cases that James cites, there need be no fundamental objection to this idea (for example, Rachel's belief that 'My marriage will be happy'). The question remains, however, whether this format is appropriate in the case of religious belief. C. B. Martin, in his own analysis of religious experience, has argued that, while one can certainly treat one's experiences as incorrigible, the price of doing so is to empty them of any 'existential claim': that the only thing that I can be certain of is that I have had an experience, not that I have experienced anything 'other' or 'beyond' it.[63] It is worth stressing this point. If no causal relation can be established between an objective reality and my particular sensations, then it would appear that the only thing I am left with is my sensations, a result

---

63. *Religious Belief*, Ithaca, N.Y., Cornell University Press, 1959, pp. 65–88.

which makes it hard to see how these sensations can provide any warrant for any truth-claims whatsoever, except, of course, the fairly trivial claim that I have had these sensations. Many critics, often of very diverse philosophical temper, have suggested that herein lies James' major weakness: that by deliberately depriving the act of belief of any 'intellectual' grounding, to use his term, he has denuded it of any intellectual, let alone theistic, content. James may have established the believer's right to believe, but he is much less clear about *what* is believed other than it *is* believed. For A. J. Ayer this concentration on act rather than content strips James' 'religious hypothesis of all pretension to give any sort of explanation of the world',[64] a view repeated by James' contemporaries A. O. Lovejoy and B. H. Bode, the last-named calling James' theory 'solipsistic'.[65] Not surprisingly, more sympathetic commentators, like Ellen Suckiel, have objected to these interpretations on the grounds that they ignore the other, second strand of James' argument, where he is concerned to verify religious claims.[66] Thus she takes John Hick to task for saying that 'the basic weakness of James's position is that it constitutes an unrestricted license for wishful thinking'.[67] Clearly Suckiel is right to say that James' argument is not 'unrestricted', the restriction being, as we have seen many times, that James' theory only applies to genuine options that cannot be decided by rational investigation, and which therefore require the pragmatic test of truth (which Hick surprisingly ignores in his account). The question is not, then, whether there are no restrictions, but whether the restrictions James imposes are sufficient to save his argument.

Let us look first at James' initial description of religious belief as a 'live' option. A live option is one which appeals to us as being true, and so excludes beliefs which simply make no relevant personal connection. So, while belief in the Mahdi, to give one of James' examples, may be dead to me, it may well be alive to an Arab. Whether a belief is or is not a *living truth* is decided, then, by whether or not it is *perceived* as a truth; and the only way we can know whether it has been so perceived is by knowing that someone *acts* upon his or her perception.

The objection to this is predictable enough: if evidence cannot impinge upon a belief's claim to truth, then anything at all may be believed. I have already mentioned Hick's criticism, which, on the face of it, seems entirely justified. If no evidence is sufficient to overrule an overbelief, then it would appear that the believer may entertain any idea which, if not logically impossible, may be highly implausible. Provided, therefore, that my 'passional

---

64. *Op. cit.*, p. 223.
65. See Arthur O. Lovejoy, *The Thirteen Pragmatisms and Other Essays*, Westport, Conn., Greenwood Press, 1983; and B. H. Bode, '"Pure Experience" and the External World', *Journal of Philosophy, Psychology and Scientific Methods*, 2(5), March 1905, p. 130.
66. *The Pragmatic Philosophy of William James*, Notre Dame, Ind., University of Notre Dame Press, 1982, pp. 124–125.
67. John Hick, *The Philosophy of Religion*, Englewood Cliffs, N.J., Prentice-Hall, 1973, p. 56. A criticism also voiced by Walter Kaufmann in his *Critique of Religion and Philosophy*, New York, Doubleday, Anchor Books, 1961: 'James' essay on "The Will to Believe" is an unwitting compendium of common fallacies and a manual of self-deception' (p. 119).

nature' engages, say, with the claim that 'Sarah of Boston (schoolteacher) is the reincarnation of Joan of Arc', this proposition becomes a 'live' option for me, one upon which I must act (even not acting being an act). This possibility, so the criticism runs, reveals that James' limitation of the 'right to believe' to an area unencumbered by rational investigation is hardly restrictive, and that it gives to the believer a fairly extensive 'right to roam' into any area legitimated by the strength of his or her own feelings.

This criticism, as it stands, is not convincing and is based on a mis-interpretation of James. For it is not the case that religious belief is devoid of verifiable or falsifiable content; and this is so because it is not the case that, once defined, an overbelief should for ever remain an overbelief since other-wise we would have to suppose that an overbelief can never 'die', not even when there is ample empirical evidence against it.

A misinterpretation of James

To clarify this point, let us first examine the way in which an overbelief may be *falsified*. According to James, the pragmatic grounds for believing 'X is true' only *follow* if there are no evidential reasons for believing that 'X is false'. So if, to continue the example given above, I found that there were good reasons for supposing that 'Sarah of Boston was not the reincarnation of Joan of Arc', that belief would have to be jettisoned *as* an overbelief, however much my passional nature might wish to engage with it. More generally, then, it is not *necessary* that the evidence for an overbelief should *remain* insufficient; and for this reason it is a permanent possibility of any 'living' option that it can convert into a 'dead' option. Contrary to the criticism just mentioned, James does not therefore advocate the right of belief to ignore disconfirming evidence and to believe what it will.

It is not, however, difficult to see how this misinterpretation arises. James is extremely imprecise as to how exactly an overbelief is constrained by the 'insufficiency' of its evidence. His meaning here is undoubtedly coloured by his understandable dissatisfaction with the classic proofs for God's existence, from which he drew the not unsurprising conclusion that religious belief cannot be established by metaphysical argument. His reasoning is as follows. By the law of excluded middle, belief in God will be either true or false, so that in this logical sense religion contains the possibility of error. But where the error lies we cannot in fact determine, as the history of the proofs indicates. So Darwin's conclusion that natural selection is inimical to the idea of benevolent design does not prevent others from saying that natural selection is the process through which God works, and Hume's evidential arguments against miracles do not make it irrational to maintain that they occur. We thus arrive at a kind of *intellectual impasse*; and it is primarily this consequence which makes it appropriate to say that the religious option is intellectually undecidable.

But this is not the only or even the most important reason for saying that overbeliefs are evidentially insufficient. Much more significantly, any attempt to establish religious belief on a foundation of objective knowledge is contrary to religion's true nature because the most important characteristic of faith is its passionate exercise of the *will to believe*, a will that can only be activated in a situation of *risk*, where indeed the acceptance of possible error requires the disposition of our 'passional interest' to overcome it. To this extent, then, *knowing* rather than *believing* that God exists would reduce faith's requirement to act with passionate conviction. Indeed, it is precisely because the man of faith sees the cost of error to be so momentous – the loss of the infinite happiness to be won – that he is prepared to sacrifice everything to avoid it and so to give himself 'the sole chance in life of getting upon the winning side, – that chance depending, of course, on my willingness to run the risk of acting as if my passional need of taking the world religiously might be prophetic and right'.[68] Doubt, in this respect, becomes an essential component of faith's conviction.

In one sense, therefore, James would agree with Clifford's 'tough-minded' method: where there *is* evidence that a belief is false, that belief must be rejected. Where he disagrees with him is in supposing that *unevidenced belief must also be rejected*. For where an issue is genuinely unresolved, scepticism is equivalent to denial and by denial the sceptic forfeits the chance of a positive gain – not unlike the 'general informing his soldiers that it is better to keep out of battle forever than to risk a single wound'.[69] Clifford's requirement, in other words, obviates the need for risk in faith and so excludes the one element by which the rewards of faith may be measured: that is, the degree of passional conviction which the believer must bring to bear in order to secure these benefits.

James admits, therefore, that an overbelief may be falsified; he also, and much more clearly, admits that an overbelief may be *verified*. But here more telling objections may be entered. James is referring here to the ability of faith to *verify itself*. This, we recall, is not the verification of the belief's factual content but rather the verification of that belief's *effects*, by which the believer may retrospectively confirm that his belief is true because of the undoubted and actual difference that it has brought about in the way he *acts*. The kind of action that James has in mind here is more exactly a *moral act*, so that what he is actually saying is that 'X is true' for George if in George 'X is true' produces a particular moral effect which would not have occurred otherwise; that having this belief has required George to act in a certain moral way. Similarly, the pragmatic test of the truth of a religious belief consists in the 'cash-value' of the moral difference initiated by the belief in the individual. Whether the propositions 'God exists' or 'God is good' or 'God is a Thou' are true is determined, therefore, by whether the subjective act of believing them brings results that may be retrospectively confirmed as objectively beneficial.

There are, I suggest, five principal objections to this argument, and they are as follows:

1. My first objection need not be developed here since I have dealt with it in some detail in the previous chapter.[70] It is that James' argument depends on a covert form of the moral argument, whereby he wishes to establish a link between acting morally and the belief in God's existence. His argument does

The risks of faith

Five objections to James' theory

---

68. 'The Will to Believe', p. 27.
69. *Ibid.*, p. 19.
70. See above, pp. 259–260.

not proceed from the presumption that there are objective moral values, and that a god is required to create them – ethical objectivism is specifically rejected by James – but rather from the presumption that moral values may be pragmatically evaluated: that if belief A fosters an action B that may be taken as pragmatically beneficial, then the belief A may be held to be true. Or rather: if the belief that 'God is good and desires that his creation be good' does foster behaviour that makes the world a better place, then the belief may be retrospectively confirmed as true. There are, however, two fatal objections to this view. The first is, as we have mentioned before, that there is no reason to suppose that people are any less moral, or any less committed to acting morally, if they do not believe in God than if they do. If there is evidence to suggest that this is incorrect, then James should present it. The second objection is that a moral benefit need not confer truth upon a belief because, after all, the same benefit may be achievable even when the belief is *known to be false* and not merely evidentially uncertain. Hume, we recall, suggests as much when, in his critique of miracles, he refers to the religious enthusiast, 'who may know his narrative to be false, and yet persevere in it, with the best intentions in the world, for the sake of promoting so holy a cause'.[71] This point can be extended. It is quite possible that someone may be privately convinced that a belief in hell is untrue but publicly proclaim it because it produces desirable moral results. So it is not true that only our true ideas are morally useful because this would suppose that our false ideas are never morally useful, which is untrue.

A form of moral argument

2. This prompts my second objection. Just as it is possible that a false idea may produce a morally desirable effect, so a true idea may produce a morally undesirable effect; or, to put the matter in Jamesian terms, religious belief may not have the requisite cash-value when compared with unbelief. We should here recall the earlier criticism levelled against Pascal.[72] While it may be true, for the purposes of argument, that theists are noted for the moral virtues of fidelity, humility and true friendship, it could also be said that atheists are noted for others – for example, self-reliance, intellectual rectitude, social concern – and that these qualities are better suited to survival in our modern competitive world. Michael Martin is in no doubt where the advantage lies:

True ideas may have undesirable effects

> From what we know of religious belief and its relation to education, health care, social class, economic level, and the like, the best guess is that the child from the theistic family is more likely to be ill, to have less education, and to end up in some unsatisfying job than the child from a family of nonbelievers. Insofar as health and happiness and a satisfying job are correlated (which seems likely), the child from the nonreligious family is likely to be happier than the child from the religious family as an adult.[73]

---

71. See above, p. 181.
72. See above, pp. 300–301.
73. Martin, *op. cit.*, p. 243.

Be that as it may, the point is, I think, established: if religious ideas may not be useful, and if what is useful need not be true, then clearly James' pragmatic test fails as the sole criterion for determining whether something is true or not.

EXERCISE 6.9

What criticisms of James does the following dialogue contain? What application do they have to his theory of religion?

'I believed my marriage was happy until I discovered he'd been lying to me.'

'You're better off without him anyway. Men are all the same: he'll only do it again.'

'But why did he have to tell me? I was happy not knowing.'

'Perhaps he had a guilty conscience and needed to tell you the truth?'

'But I didn't want the truth. Couldn't he have just pretended that it wasn't true?'

'So you wanted him to deceive you about his deception? Surely, you wouldn't want to live a lie?'

'Tell that to my children.'

'Well, they may be unhappy now. But in the long run I'm sure they'll be better and stronger people because of it.'

'You're "sure" but you don't "know"'.

'It's a gamble, I admit.'

An evolutionary concept of truth

3. My third objection has to do with James' *evolutionary* concept of truth. The famous line runs: 'An idea is "true" *so long* as to believe it is profitable to our lives.'[74] This suggests, according to G. E. Moore, that for James truth is *mutable*, and that 'the truth of an idea may come and go, as its utility comes and goes'.[75] Again, it is not difficult to imagine a situation in which this might occur. Under the rubric that 'only what is profitable is true', any religious assertion that 'works' (i.e., effects a life-change) will be deemed true. So if, at time T1, an individual experiences a transformation through accepting that 'God exists', that proposition is a true proposition; but if, at time T2, this transformation has not occurred, then that proposition has ceased to be true. Equally, if two people are considering the same proposition at the same time, and one experiences a life-change and the other does not, that assertion – that 'God exists' – becomes simultaneously true and untrue. The upshot of this somewhat confusing state of affairs is that whatever action may follow from the belief in God, this action will be appropriate for me but not necessarily for

74. See above, p. 305 (my italics).
75. 'William James' "Pragmatism"', *Philosophical Studies*, London, Routledge & Kegan Paul, 1922, p. 128.

anybody else. Indeed, any other result would offend the principle that truth is determined by *my* estimate of its profitability, that it has *worked for me* (SOURCE 6: PP. 338–340).

4. The ethical difficulties implicit within this position become apparent when we remember that the life-change being referred to is fundamentally *moral in character.* James commends a theory of moral obligation which, if it is to mirror his theory of truth, must be consequentialist and so always provisional: that what is deemed to be good must fall under the same rubric of expediency, that it will be considered good *only so long as* it is profitable. Because of the alleged impossibility of any metaphysical theory of ethics, the criterion of moral action is not, then, that 'X is good because God deems X to be good' but rather 'The consequences of believing "X is good because God deems X to be good" are good'. What this distinction exposes is that what counts as religious conduct has to be judged by another evaluative criterion – the criterion of expediency – such that it makes sense to ask: 'God wills it, but is it profitable?' But profitable to whom?

G. E. Moore (1873–1958)

No resolution of moral conflict

It is usual at this point to regard James' ethical position as basically utilitarian: that in advancing God's plan for the world individual self-interest should be subordinated in favour of the greater good, and that we estimate the greater good in terms of the public welfare. Utilitarian ethics is, however, notoriously unreliable in two important ways, both of which are directly relevant to James' argument at this juncture. The first is that it is impossible to know when the consequences of an action have been exhausted and that what may be considered a beneficial result now may not be so later. It follows, therefore, that what a believer may consider religious conduct now he may subsequently repudiate, it being contingent, as it were, on its profit-margin. The second is that the utilitarian calculation often leads to courses of action which conflict with what we more usually think we ought to do. The well-worn example here is that, on utilitarian terms, the execution of an innocent man may be justified by its deterrent effect and so conflict with generally accepted notions of justice. So even if we agree that 'God wills X' and that 'X is profitable', the dilemma yet remains: 'Ought I to do X?'

This question, however, is hardly resolved by James, *since it is only when an action is profitable that we can verify that God has willed it.* What happens, therefore, in a situation of moral conflict, where my need to do X may conflict with another's need to do Y? If the answer is that I ought to apply the criterion of profitability, then this hardly helps since the advice will be identical in both cases – that each of us will have acted in a religious way if our moral behaviour was created by our prior religious belief, and if this behaviour has been subsequently shown to be profitable. This, I need hardly say, renders James' use of the term 'religious' quite meaningless in distinguishing one action from another, and so quite irrelevant to the promotion of any particular way of life. We may agree with James that we should disown the belief that a successful harvest requires the sacrifice of a new-born child; but what he fails to see is that the process by which such out-moded beliefs die is the self-same process by which other, equally repugnant beliefs may be easily resurrected.

The 'many-gods' objection

5. One upshot of this – and my fifth objection – is that James, although well aware of the 'many-Gods' objection levelled against Pascal, hardly avoids it himself.[76] It is not merely that every major religion becomes an option (provided it 'works') but that every sectarian interest within every religion becomes an option (provided it 'works'). Indeed, any religion, however bizarre or repellent, can be reactivated by the believer's passional response and so elevated to the status of a 'real possibility', no matter how few or how many accept it. What therefore counts as a real possibility becomes, in effect, an *instance of a subjective disposition*, such that where the disposition changes, so does the possibility. James' critics are accordingly right to complain that he leaves the content of belief quite undetermined and so is quite unable to answer the question of whether what is believed is true or morally decent. The only truth at this point is the truth of the *act*, and religious belief has become no more than the expression of a particular attitude, where believing something to be true can carry no cognitive estimate of whether what is believed is true or whether what is held to be true leads to actions that are morally justified.

CONCLUDING REMARKS

James' 'tender-minded' assumption that empirical considerations cannot be the only determinants of religious belief is certainly correct. I agree, then, that where there is insufficient evidence to decide whether theism is true or not, the right to believe that there is a God is legitimate, particularly when it is additionally held that the exercise of this right brings certain benefits, such as a more 'strenuous' determination to lead a moral life and thereby a possible increase in the sum of human happiness. I also agree with James that the expediency of this belief may itself be verifiable, i.e., that under certain conditions it may be possible to confirm scientifically that having a particular religious belief has indeed brought the desired individual and social change: that, for example, the philanthropic reforms of Mrs Fry, Wilberforce and Shaftesbury were inspired directly by such convictions.

Failure of James' argument

Where James' theory breaks down is in supposing that the profitability of an overbelief confers truth upon it. In other words, while we can correctly say 'It is true that X believes that Y is true' or 'It is true that X has benefited from

---

76. See above, pp. 293–294.

believing that Y is true', it is not the case that either proposition, although verifiable, establishes that Y *is* true, or, to put the matter another way, that the propositions 'It is true that X believes that Y is false' or 'It is true that X benefited from believing that Y is false' are not equally tenable on Jamesian terms. Because therefore the pragmatic theory stipulates that the truth-content of a belief is governed by its practical and moral consequences – i.e., by the *acts* which it initiates – these consequences may equally flow from the belief that religion is untrue and so legitimate atheism as the more appropriate 'genuine option': that believing that there is no 'infinite happiness to be won' may be even more morally and socially efficacious, as we remember Freud supposed.

In the final analysis, then, the weak link in James' argument is the assumption that the truth of a belief is determined and established by its practical consequences. Now, it may certainly be the case that this is the correct explanation of why some people hold theistic views: that their belief is entirely pragmatic. But unfortunately for James pragmatic considerations often lead us in directions opposite to those intended, so that the same considerations may be employed to justify atheism: that this belief is also true by virtue of its 'cash-value'. Indeed, so concerned is James to liberate religious belief from the 'tough-minded' restrictions of evidential certainty that he fails to notice that his 'tender-minded' alternative also licenses belief's denial, and that, if there is any force in his argument, it works both ways. But in the end there is no mileage in an argument which can be employed to deny what it is seeking to justify.

QUESTIONS

1 Consider the following statement in the light of Pascal's Wager:

When I am told that I must believe this, and at the same time call this being by the names which express and affirm the highest human morality, I say in plain terms that I will not. Whatever power such a being may have over me, there is one thing which he shall not do: he shall not compel me to worship him. I will call no being good, who is not what I mean when I apply that epithet to my fellow creatures; and if such a being can sentence me to hell for not so calling him, to hell I will go.[77]

2 In what respects, if any, does the Wager on infinite happiness after death encourage finite unhappiness before it?

3 What assumptions about the nature of God are contained in Pascal's Wager? Are these assumptions sufficient to discredit it?

4 'No religious belief should be justified by mercenary means.' Discuss.

5 Construct a wager in which belief in the non-existence of God is the better bet. How would Pascal reply?

77. John Stuart Mill, *An Examination of Sir William Hamilton's Philosophy*, Boston, Mass., Spencer, 1865, p. 131.

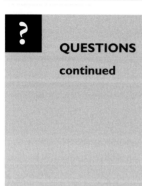

6 Clarify what James means by 'work' in his theory of belief. Thereafter enumerate beliefs that, though true, do not work, and those that, though working, are not true.

7 What ethical problems are posed by James' religious theory?

8 To what extent is James' theory of religion dependent on his theory of truth?

9 Critically evaluate James' claim that religious belief can verify itself.

10 'On James' theory, one can believe anything.' Discuss.

SOURCES: THE PRAGMATIC ARGUMENT

1 PASCAL: THE WAGER[1]

Let us now speak according to our natural lights.

If there is a God, he is infinitely beyond our comprehension, since, being indivisible and without limits, he bears no relation to us. We are therefore incapable of knowing either what he is or whether he is. That being so, who would dare to attempt an answer to the question? Certainly not we, who bear no relation to him.

Who then will condemn Christians for being unable to give rational grounds for their belief, professing as they do a religion for which they cannot give rational grounds? They declare that it is a folly, *stultitiam*, in expounding it to the world, and then you complain that they do not prove it. If they did prove it they would not be keeping their word. It is by being without proof that they show they are not without sense. 'Yes, but although that excuses those who offer their religion as such, and absolves them from the criticism of producing it without rational grounds, it does not absolve those who accept it.' Let us then examine this point, and let us say: 'Either God is or he is not.' But to which view shall we be inclined? Reason cannot decide this question. Infinite chaos separates us. At the far end of this infinite distance a coin is being spun which will come down heads or tails. How will you wager? Reason cannot make you choose either, reason cannot prove either wrong.

Do not then condemn as wrong those who have made a choice, for you know nothing about it. 'No, but I will condemn them not for having made this particular choice, but any choice, for, although the one who calls heads and the other one tails are equally at fault, the fact is that they are both at fault: the right thing is not to wager at all.'

1. Blaise Pascal, *Pensées*, translated with an Introduction by A. J. Krailsheimer, Harmondsworth, Penguin Books, 1966, pp.150–153.

Yes, but you must wager. There is no choice, you are already committed. Which will you choose then? Let us see: since a choice must be made, let us see which offers you the least interest. You have two things to lose: the true and the good; and two things to stake: your reason and your will, your knowledge and your happiness; and your nature has two things to avoid: error and wretchedness. Since you must necessarily choose, your reason is no more affronted by choosing one rather than the other. That is one point cleared up. But your happiness? Let us weigh up the gain and the loss involved in calling heads that God exists. Let us assess the two cases: if you win you win everything, if you lose you lose nothing. Do not hesitate then; wager that he does exist. 'That is wonderful. Yes, I must wager, but perhaps I am wagering too much.' Let us see: since there is an equal chance of gain and loss, if you stood to win only two lives for one you could still wager, but supposing you stood to win three?

You would have to play (since you must necessarily play) and it would be unwise of you, once you are obliged to play, not to risk your life in order to win three lives at a game in which there is an equal chance of losing and winning. But there is an eternity of life and happiness. That being so, even though there were an infinite number of chances, of which only one were in your favour, you would still be right to wager one in order to win two; and you would be acting wrongly, being obliged to play, in refusing to stake one life against three in a game, where out of an infinite number of chances there is one in your favour, if there were an infinity of infinitely happy life to be won. But here there is an infinity of infinitely happy life to be won, one chance of winning against a finite number of chances of losing, and what you are staking is finite. That leaves no choice; wherever there is infinity, and where there are not infinite chances of losing against that of winning, there is no room for hesitation, you must give everything. And thus, since you are obliged to play, you must be renouncing reason if you hoard your life rather than risk it for an infinite gain, just as likely to occur as a loss amounting to nothing.

For it is no good saying that it is uncertain whether you will win, that it is certain that you are taking a risk, and that the infinite distance between the certainty of what you are risking and the uncertainty of what you may gain makes the finite good you are certainly risking equal to the infinite good that you are not certain to gain. This is not the case. Every gambler takes a certain risk for an uncertain gain, and yet he is taking a certain finite risk for an uncertain finite gain without sinning against reason. Here there is no infinite distance between the certain risk and the uncertain gain: that is not true. There is, indeed, an infinite distance between the certainty of winning and the certainty of losing, but the proportion between the uncertainty of winning and the certainty of what is being risked is in proportion to the chances of winning or losing. And hence if there are as many chances on one side as on the other you are playing for even odds. And in that case the certainty of what you are risking is equal to the uncertainty of what you may win; it is by no means infinitely distant from it. Thus our argument carries infinite weight, when the stakes are finite in a game where there are even chances of winning and losing and an infinite prize to be won.

This is conclusive and if men are capable of any truth this is it.

'I confess, I admit it, but is there really no way of seeing what the cards are?' – 'Yes. Scripture and the rest, etc.' – 'Yes, but my hands are tied and my lips are sealed; I am being forced to wager and I am not free; I am being held fast and I am so made that I cannot believe. What do you want me to do then?' – 'That is true, but at least get it into your head that, if you are unable to believe, it is because of your passions, since reason impels you to believe and yet you cannot do so. Concentrate then not on convincing yourself by multiplying proofs of God's existence but by diminishing your passions. You want to find faith and you do not know the road. You want to be cured of unbelief and you ask for the remedy: learn from those who were once bound like you and who now wager all they have. These are people who know the road you wish to follow, who have been cured of the affliction of which you wish to be cured: follow the way by which they began. They behaved just as if they did believe, taking holy water, having masses said, and so on. That will make you believe quite naturally, and will make you more docile.' – 'But that is what I am afraid of.' – 'But why? What have you to lose? But to show you that this is the way, the fact is that this diminishes the passions which are your great obstacles . . .'

End of this address.

'Now what harm will come to you from choosing this course? You will be faithful', honest, humble, grateful, full of good works, a sincere, true friend . . . . It is true you will not enjoy noxious pleasures, glory and good living, but will you not have others?

'I tell you that you will gain even in this life, and that at every step you take along this road you will see that your gain is so certain and your risk so negligible that in the end you will realize that you have wagered on something certain and infinite for which you have paid nothing.'

'How these words fill me with rapture and delight! –'

'If my words please you and seem cogent, you must know that they come from a man who went down upon his knees before and after to pray this infinite and indivisible being, to whom he submits his own, that he might bring your being also to submit to him for your own good and for his glory: and that strength might thus be reconciled with lowliness.'

2 GRACELY: THE DEVIL'S OFFER[2]

Suppose Ms C dies and goes to hell, or to a place that seems like hell. The devil approaches and offers to play a game of chance. If she wins, she can go to heaven. If she loses, she will stay in hell forever; there is no second chance to play the game. If Ms C plays today, she has a ½ chance of winning. Tomorrow the probability will be ⅔. Then ¾, ⅘, ⅚, etc., with no end to the series. Thus every passing day increases her chances of winning. At what point should she play the game?

The answer is not obvious: after any given number of days spent waiting, it will still be possible to improve her chances by waiting yet another day. And any increase in the probability of winning a game with infinite stakes has an infinite utility. For example, if she waits a year, her probability of winning the game would

2. Edward Gracely, 'Playing Games with Eternity: The Devil's Offer', *Analysis*, 58, June 1988, p. 113.

be approximately .997268; if she waits one more day, the probability would increase to .997275, a difference of only .000007. Yet, even .000007 multiplied by infinity is infinite.

On the other hand, it seems reasonable to suppose the cost of delaying for a day to be finite – a day's more suffering in hell. So the infinite expected benefit from a delay will always exceed the cost.

This logic might suggest that Ms C should wait forever, but clearly such a strategy would be self-defeating: why should she stay forever in a place in order to increase her chances of leaving it? So the question remains: What should Ms C do?

3 STICH: RECOMBINANT DNA AND PASCALIAN WAGERING[3]

In the argument I want to examine the particular moral judgment being defended is that there should be a total ban on recombinant DNA research. The argument begins with the observation that even in so-called low-risk recombinant DNA experiments there is at least a possibility of catastrophic consequences. We are, after all, dealing with a relatively new and unexplored technology. Thus it is at least possible that a bacterial culture whose genetic makeup has been altered in the course of a recombinant DNA experiment may exhibit completely unexpected pathogenic characteristics. Indeed, it is not impossible that we could find ourselves confronted with a killer strain of, say, *E. coli* and, worse, a strain against which humans can marshal no natural defense. Now if this is possible – if we cannot say with assurance that the probability of it happening is zero – then, the argument continues, all recombinant DNA research should be halted. For the negative utility of the imagined catastrophe is so enormous, resulting as it would in the destruction of our society and perhaps even of our species, that no work which could possibly lead to this result would be worth the risk.

The argument just sketched, which might be called the 'doomsday scenario' argument, begins with a premise which no informed person would be inclined to deny. It is indeed *possible* that even a low-risk recombinant DNA experiment might lead to totally catastrophic results. No ironclad guarantee can be offered that this will not happen. And while the probability of such an unanticipated catastrophe is surely not large, there is no serious argument that the probability is zero. Still, I think the argument is a sophistry. To go from the undeniable premise that recombinant DNA research might possibly result in unthinkable catastrophe to the conclusion that such research should be banned requires a moral principle stating that *all* endeavors that might possibly result in such a catastrophe should be prohibited. Once the principle has been stated, it is hard to believe that anyone would take it at all seriously. For the principle entails that, along with recombinant DNA research, almost all scientific research and many other commonplace activities having little to do with science should be prohibited. It is, after all, at

---

3. Stephen P. Stich, 'The Recombinant DNA Debate', *Philosophy and Public Affairs*, 7, 1978, pp. 187–191

least logically possible that the next new compound synthesized in an ongoing chemical research program will turn out to be an uncontainable carcinogen many orders of magnitude more dangerous than aerosol plutonium. And, to vary the example, there is a non-zero probability that experiments in artificial pollination will produce a weed that will, a decade from now, ruin the world's food grain harvest.[4]

I cannot resist noting that the principle invoked in the doomsday scenario argument is not new. Pascal used an entirely parallel argument to show that it is in our own best interests to believe in God. For though the probability of God's existence may be very low, if He none the less should happen to exist, the disutility that would accrue to the disbeliever would be catastrophic – an eternity in hell. But, as introductory philosophy students should all know, Pascal's argument only looks persuasive if we take our options to be just two: Christianity or atheism. A third possibility is belief in a jealous non-Christian God who will see to our damnation if and only if we are Christians. The probability of such a deity existing is again very small, but non-zero. So Pascal's argument is of no help in deciding whether or not to accept Christianity. For we may be damned if we do and damned if we don't.

I mention Pascal's difficulty because there is a direct parallel in the doomsday scenario argument against recombinant DNA research. Just as there is a non-zero probability that unforeseen consequences of recombinant DNA research will lead to disaster, so there is a non-zero probability that unforeseen consequences of *failing* to pursue the research will lead to disaster. There may, for example, come a time when, because of natural or man-induced climatic change, the capacity to alter quickly the genetic constitution of agricultural plants will be necessary to forestall catastrophic famine. And if we fail to pursue recombinant DNA research now, our lack of knowledge in the future may have consequences as dire as any foreseen in the doomsday scenario argument.

4 PENELHUM: CRITICISM OF PASCAL'S WAGER[5]

The divine plan as Pascal conceives it involves eternal happiness for some and eternal misery (or at least the loss of eternal bliss) for others. This is the divine purpose that the believer must approve and call good and that the man who wagers properly will make himself approve and call good. And at least a necessary condition of inheriting eternal bliss and not suffering its loss is belief. Now it seems immoral to condemn someone to loss of eternal bliss for any offense, but it

---

4. Unfortunately, the doomsday scenario argument is *not* a straw man conjured only by those who would refute it. Consider, for example, the remarks of Anthony Mazzocchi, spokesman for the Oil, Chemical and Atomic Workers International Union, reported in *Science News*, 19 March, 1977, p.181: 'When scientists argue over safe or unsafe, we ought to be very prudent. . . If critics are correct and the Andromeda scenario has *even the smallest possibility* of occurring, we must assume that it will occur on the basis of our experience' (*emphasis* added).
5. Terence Penelhum, *Religion and Rationality: An Introduction to the Philosophy of Religion*, New York, Random House, 1971, pp. 216–218.

particularly seems immoral to condemn him for not believing something. This, however, is clearly implied in Pascal's argument. And it is, of course, scriptural. The charge can only be rebutted if it can be shown that men who do not believe can rightly be blamed for not believing. If this cannot be shown, then we have a valid moral objection to the Wager argument. For the recommendation of the argument would then be to induce in oneself a state of mind in which one will come to approve a cosmic policy that is immoral – and this would be an immoral recommendation. It would have prudence behind it; but although prudence should be followed if it does not clash with morality, it should not be followed if it does. The question remaining, then, is: Can men rightly be blamed for not believing in God? This would be possible only if believing in God is something that they are free to do or not to do. How can this condition be satisfied? Only if the signs of God's existence are clear but not compelling. Hence there cannot be conclusive and overwhelming proofs, but there must be proofs strong enough to convince those willing to be convinced. God must reveal himself and yet hide himself. All this Pascal says.

It is easy to generate a paradox from the idea that the world points to the presence of a God who hides himself: If he has hidden himself, it could be said, it cannot be that everything points to his presence. But this is too simple, and our own analysis suggests it could easily be false. What is needed is that men should see the signs of God, and *recognize* them as signs of God, and yet *still* divide themselves into the believers and the unbelievers. But this means that the unbelievers refuse to accept the revelations of God for what they are – there is no incapacity to believe, only refusal to believe. The unbeliever, in believer's language, is one who will not admit what he really knows to be true. All men, then, really know that God exists but some hide it from themselves and will not admit it. The atheist, to recall John Baillie again, denies with the top of his mind what he knows with the bottom of his heart. Unbelief, then, comes to be self-deception, the state in which wickedness and foolishness merge and create doubt between them.

Is this conclusion true? Let us restrict it to those who have heard the message of Christian theism, since the position regarding the others is, on the matter of eternal rewards, unclear. Is it true that all those who have heard of God really know that he exists? Put neutrally, is it true that all men who have heard the claim that there is a God have really been to some degree convinced of its truth? Here the division of standards between the believer and the unbeliever cannot be allowed to infect the question. It is not good enough to say, 'Well, to the eye of faith this or that action of men is a clear sign that they are convinced God exists, but to other eyes it is not a sign of this.' This will not do here because we are looking for a sort of conviction that it is blameworthy to smother, and we surely only have this when we can detect the presence of the conviction in another without appealing to it in ourselves. If we look empirically at the matter to see whether it seems likely that this is true, it seems obvious that as a generalization it is false. That self-deception is a pervasive vice is obvious; that is why so much of Pascal still rings true. That men hide their mortality and guilt from themselves is also obvious. That in doing so they are also hiding from themselves a conviction that the Christian way of coping with them is the right one is not obvious. The fact that there are widespread neuroses in our time and that Christianity might be the answer to them does not show that these neuroses are due to the fact that men have refused Christianity, although they have heard of it. Our own day and age shows more clearly than the age of Pascal possibly could that men can, in a clear sense, hear of God and yet be totally untouched in their convictions by what they hear – even though they may recognize their spiritual maladies when the twentieth-century priests, the social scientists, speak about them. This is what it means to live in a secular age.

If it is true that men can hear and not be convinced, then belief does not necessarily equal self-deception. But then unbelief does not necessarily merit exclusion from salvation. If it does not, then Pascal's Wager argument, which presupposes that it does, is morally unworthy of acceptance. Perhaps, of course, it is not a necessary feature of Christian doctrine to insist that unbelief entails exclusion from salvation. But in that case again, Pascal's Wager ceases to have any point.

5 JAMES: THE WILL TO BELIEVE[6]

Let us give the name of *hypothesis* to anything that may be proposed to our belief; and just as the electricians speak of live and dead wires, let us speak of any hypothesis as either *live* or *dead*. A live hypothesis is one which appeals as a real possibility to him to whom it is proposed. If I ask you to believe in the Mahdi, the notion makes no electric connection with your nature, – it refuses to scintillate with any credibility at all. As an hypothesis it is completely dead.. To an Arab, however (even if he be not one of the Mahdi's followers), the hypothesis is among the mind's possibilities: it is alive. This shows that deadness and liveness in an hypothesis are not intrinsic properties, but relations to the individual thinker. They are measured by his willingness to act. The maximum of liveness in an hypothesis means willingness to act irrevocably. Practically, that means belief; but there is some believing tendency wherever there is willingness to act at all.

Next, let us call the decision between two hypotheses an *option*. Options may be of several kinds. They may be – 1, *living* or *dead*; 2, *forced* or *avoidable*; 3, *momentous* or *trivial*; and for our purposes we may call an option a *genuine* option when it is of the forced, living, and momentous kind.

1. A living option is one in which both hypotheses are live ones. If I say to you: 'Be a theosophist or be a Mohammedan,' it is probably a dead option, because for you neither hypothesis is likely to be alive. But if I say: 'Be an agnostic or be a Christian,' it is otherwise: trained as you are, each hypothesis makes some appeal, however small, to your belief.

2. Next, if I say to you: 'Choose between going out with your umbrella or without it,' I do not offer you a genuine option, for it is not forced. You can easily avoid it by not going out at all. Similarly, if I say, 'Either call my theory true or call it false,' your opinion is avoidable. You may remain indifferent to me, neither loving nor hating, and you may decline to offer any judgment as to my theory. But

---

6. William James, 'The Will to Believe' (1896) in *The Will to Believe and Other Essays in Popular Philosophy*, New York, Dover Publications, 1956, pp. 1–31.

if I say, 'Either accept this truth or go without it,' I put on you a forced option, for there is no standing place outside of the alternative. Every dilemma based on a complete logical disjunction, with no possibility of not choosing, is an option of this forced kind.

3. Finally, if I were Dr. Nansen and proposed to you to join my North Pole expedition, your option would be momentous; for this would probably be your only similar opportunity, and your choice now would either exclude you from the North Pole sort of immortality altogether or put at least the chance of it into your hands. He who refuses to embrace a unique opportunity loses the prize as surely as if he tried and failed. *Per contra*, the option is trivial when the opportunity is not unique, when the stake is insignificant, or when the decision is reversible if it later prove unwise. A chemist finds an hypothesis live enough to spend a year in its verification: he believes in it to that extent. But if his experiments prove inconclusive either way, he is quit for his loss of time, no vital harm being done . . .

It is only our already dead hypotheses that our willing nature is unable to bring to life again. But what has made them dead for us is for the most part a previous action of our willing nature of an antagonistic kind. When I say 'willing nature,' I do not mean only such deliberate volitions as may have set up habits of belief that we cannot now escape from, – I mean all such factors of belief as fear and hope, prejudice and passion, imitation and partisanship, the circumpressure of our caste and set. As a matter of fact we find ourselves believing, we hardly know how or why. . . . Our reason is quite satisfied, in nine hundred and ninety-nine cases out of every thousand of us, if it can find a few arguments that will do to recite in case our credulity is criticised by some one else. Our faith is faith in some one else's faith, and in the greatest matters this is most the case. Our belief in truth itself, for instance, that there is a truth, and that our minds and it are made for each other, – what is it but a passionate affirmation of desire, in which our social system backs it up? We want to have a truth; we want to believe that our experiments and studies and discussions must put us in a continually better and better position towards it; and on this line we agree to fight out our thinking lives. But if a pyrrhonistic sceptic asks us *how we know* all this, can our logic find a reply? No! certainly it cannot. It is just one volition against another, – willing to go in for life upon a trust or assumption which he, for his part, does not care to make . . . .

Evidently, then, our non-intellectual nature does influence our convictions. There are passional tendencies and volitions which run before and others which come after belief, and it is only the latter that are too late for the fair; and they are not too late when the previous passional work has been already in their own direction. Pascal's argument, instead of being powerless, then seems a regular clincher, and is the last stroke needed to make our faith in masses and holy water complete. The state of things is evidently far from simple; and pure insight and logic, whatever they might do ideally, are not the only things that really do produce our creeds.

Our next duty, having recognized this mixed-up state of affairs, is to ask whether it be simply reprehensible and pathological, or whether, on the contrary, we must treat it as a normal element in making up our minds. The thesis I defend is, briefly stated, thus: *Our passional nature not only lawfully may, but must decide an option between propositions, whenever it is a genuine option that cannot by its nature be decided on intellectual grounds; for to say, under such circumstances, 'Do not decide, but leave the question open,' is itself a passional decision, – just like deciding yes or no, – and is attended with the same risk of losing the truth.* The thesis thus abstractly expressed will, I trust, soon become quite clear . . .

One more point, small but important, and our preliminaries are done. There are two ways of looking at our duty in the matter of opinion, – ways entirely different, and yet ways about whose difference the theory of knowledge seems hitherto to have shown very little concern. *We must know the truth*; and *we must avoid error*, – these are our first and great commandments as would-be knowers; but they are not two ways of stating an identical commandment, they are two separable laws. Although it may indeed happen that when we believe the truth *A*, we escape as an incidental consequence from believing the falsehood *B*, it hardly ever happens that by merely disbelieving *B* we necessarily believe *A*. We may in escaping *B* fall into believing other falsehoods, *C* or *D*, just as bad as *B*; or we may escape *B* by not believing anything at all, not even *A*.

Believe truth! Shun error! – these, we see, are two materially different laws; and by choosing between them we may end by coloring differently our whole intellectual life. We may regard the chase for truth as paramount, and the avoidance of error as secondary; or we may, on the other hand, treat the avoidance of error as more imperative, and let truth take its chance. Clifford . . . exhorts us to the latter course. Believe nothing, he tells us, keep your mind in suspense forever, rather than by closing it on insufficient evidence incur the awful risk of believing lies. You, on the other hand, may think that the risk of being in error is a very small matter when compared with the blessings of real knowledge, and be ready to be duped many times in your investigation rather than postpone indefinitely the chance of guessing true. I myself find it impossible to go with Clifford. We must remember that these feelings of our duty about either truth or error are in any case only expressions of our passional life. Biologically considered, our minds are as ready to grind our falsehood as veracity, and he who says, 'Better go without belief forever than believe a lie!' merely shows his own preponderant private horror of becoming a dupe. He may be critical of many of his desires and fears, but this fear he slavishly obeys. He cannot imagine any one questioning its binding force. For my own part, I have also a horror of being duped; but I cannot believe that worse things than being duped may happen to a man in this world: so Clifford's exhortation has to my ears a thoroughly fantastic sound. It is like a general informing his soldiers that it is better to keep out of battle forever than to risk a single wound. Not so are victories either over enemies or over nature gained. Our errors are surely not such awfully solemn things. In a world where we are so certain to incur them in spite of all our caution, a certain lightness of heart seems healthier than this excessive nervousness on their behalf. At any rate, it seems the fittest thing for the empiricist philosopher.

And now, after all this introduction, let us go straight at our question. I have said, and now repeat it, that not only as a matter of fact do we find our passional nature influencing us in our opinions, but that there are some options between opinions in which this influence must be regarded both as an inevitable and as a lawful determinant of our choice.

I fear here that some of you my hearers will begin to scent danger, and lend an inhospitable ear. Two first steps of passion you have indeed had to admit as necessary, – we must think so as to avoid dupery, and we must think so as to gain truth; but the surest path to those ideal consummations, you will probably consider, is from now onwards to take no further passional step.

Well, of course, I agree as far as the facts will allow. Wherever the option between losing truth and gaining it is not momentous, we can throw the chance of *gaining truth* away, and at any rate save ourselves from any chance of *believing falsehood*, by not making up our minds at all till objective evidence has come. In scientific questions, this is almost always the case; and even in human affairs in general, the need of acting is seldom so urgent that a false belief to act on is better than no belief at all. . . . The questions here are always trivial options, the hypotheses are hardly living (at any rate not living for us spectators), the choice between believing truth or falsehood is seldom forced. The attitude of sceptical balance is therefore the absolutely wise one if we would escape mistakes.

I speak, of course, here of the purely judging mind. For purposes of discovery such indifference is to be less highly recommended, and science would be far less advanced than she is if the passionate desires of individuals to get their own faiths confirmed had been kept out of the game. . . . On the other hand, if you want an absolute duffer in an investigation, you must, after all, take the man who has no interest whatever in its results: he is the warranted incapable, the positive fool. The most useful investigator, because the most sensitive observer, is always he whose eager interest in one side of the question is balanced by an equally keen nervousness lest he become deceived. . . . Let us agree, however, that wherever there is no forced option, the dispassionately judicial intellect with no pet hypothesis, saving us, as it does, from dupery at any rate, ought to be our ideal.

The question next arises: Are there not somewhere forced options in our speculative questions, and can we (as men who may be interested at least as much in positively gaining truth as in merely escaping dupery) always wait with impunity till the coercive evidence shall have arrived? It seems *a priori* improbable that the truth should be so nicely adjusted to our needs and powers as that. In the great boarding-house of nature, the cakes and the butter and the syrup seldom come out so even and leave the plates so clean. Indeed, we should view them with scientific suspicion if they did.

Moral questions immediately present themselves as questions whose solution cannot wait for sensible proof. A moral question is a question not of what sensibly exists, but of what is good, or would be good if it did exist. Science can tell us what exists; but to compare the *worths*, both of what exists and of what does not exist, we must consult not science, but what Pascal calls our heart. Science herself consults her heart when she lays it down that the infinite ascertainment of fact and correction of false belief are the supreme goods for man . . . .

Turn now from these wide questions of good to a certain class of questions of fact, questions concerning personal relations, states of mind between one man and another. *Do you like me or not?* – for example. Whether you do or not depends, in countless instances, on whether I meet you half-way, am willing to assume that you must like me, and show you trust and expectation. The previous faith on my part in your liking's existence is in such cases what makes your liking come . . . How many women's hearts are vanquished by the mere sanguine insistence of some man that they *must* love him! he will not consent to the hypothesis that they cannot. The desire for a certain kind of truth here brings about that special truth's existence; and so it is in innumerable cases of other sorts. Who gains promotions, boons, appointments, but the man in whose life they are seen to play the part of live hypotheses, who discounts them, sacrifices other things for their sake before they have come, and takes risks for them in advance? His faith acts on the powers above him as a claim, and creates its own verification . . .

There are, then, cases where a fact cannot come at all unless a preliminary faith exists in its coming. *And where faith in a fact can help create the fact*, that would be an insane logic which should say that faith running ahead of scientific evidence is the 'lowest kind of immorality' into which a thinking being can fall. Yet such is the logic by which our scientific absolutists pretend to regulate our lives!

In truths dependent on our personal action, then, faith based on desire is certainly a lawful and possibly an indispensable thing.

But now, it will be said, these are all childish human cases, and have nothing to do with great cosmical matters, like the question of religious faith. Let us then pass on to that. Religions differ so much in their accidents that in discussing the religious question we must make it very generic and broad. What then do we now mean by the religious hypothesis? Science says things are; morality says some things are better than other things; and religion says essentially two things.

First, she says that the best things are the more eternal things, the overlapping things, the things in the universe that throw the last stone, so to speak, and say the final word. 'Perfection is eternal,' – this phrase of Charles Secrétan seems a good way of putting this first affirmation of religion, an affirmation which obviously cannot yet be verified scientifically at all.

The second affirmation of religion is that we are better off even now if we believe her first affirmation to be true.

Now, let us consider what the logical elements of this situation are *in case the religious hypothesis in both its branches be really true.* (Of course, we must admit that possibility at the outset. If we are to discuss the question at all, it must involve a living option. If for any of you religion be a hypothesis that cannot, by any living possibility be true, then you need go no farther. I speak of the 'saving remnant' alone.) So proceeding, we see, first, that religion offers itself as a *momentous* option. We are supposed to gain, even now, by our belief, and to lose by our non-belief, a certain vital good. Secondly, religion is a *forced* option, so far as that good goes. We cannot escape the issue by remaining sceptical and waiting for more light, because, although we do avoid error in that way *if religion be untrue*, we lose the good, *if it be true*, just as certainly as if we positively chose to disbelieve. It is as if a man should hesitate indefinitely to ask a certain woman to marry him because he was not perfectly sure that she would prove an angel after he brought her home. Would he not cut himself off from that particular angel-possibility as decisively as if he went and married some one else? Scepticism, then, is not avoidance of option; it is option of a certain particular kind of risk. *Better risk loss of truth than chance of error*, – that is your faith-vetoer's exact position. He is actively playing his stake as much as the believer is; he is backing the field against the religious hypothesis, just as the believer is backing the religious hypothesis against the field. To preach scepticism to us as a duty until 'sufficient evidence' for religion be found, is tantamount therefore to telling us, when in presence of the religious hypothesis, that to yield to our fear of its being error is wiser and better than to yield to our hope that it may be true. It is not intellect against all passions, then; it is only intellect with one passion laying down its law. And by what, forsooth, is the supreme wisdom of this passion warranted? Dupery for dupery, what proof is there that dupery through hope is so much worse than dupery through fear? I, for one, can see no proof; and I simply refuse obedience to the scientist's command to imitate his kind of opinion, in a case where my own stake is important enough to give me the right to choose my own form of risk. If religion be true and the evidence for it still insufficient, I do not wish, by putting my extinguisher upon my nature (which feels to me as if it had after all some business in this matter), to forfeit my sole chance in life of getting upon the winning side, – that chance depending, of course, on my willingness to run the risk of acting as if my passional need of taking the world religiously might be prophetic and right.

All this is on the supposition that it really may be prophetic and right, and that, even to us who are discussing the matter, religion is a live hypothesis which may be true. Now, to most of us religion comes in a still further way that makes a veto on our active faith even more illogical. The more perfect and more eternal aspect of the universe is represented in our religions as having personal form. The universe is no longer a mere *It* to us, but a *Thou*, if we are religious; and any relation that may be possible from person to person might be possible here. For instance, although in one sense we are passive portions of the universe, in another we show a curious autonomy, as if we were small active centres on our own account. We feel, too, as if the appeal of religion to us were made to our own active good-will, as if evidence might be forever withheld from us unless we met the hypothesis half-way. To take a trivial illustration: just as a man who in a company of gentlemen made no advances, asked a warrant for every concession, and believed no one's word without proof, would cut himself off by such churlishness from all the social rewards that a more trusting spirit would earn, – so here, one who should shut himself up in snarling logicality and try to make the gods exhort his recognition willy-nilly, or not get it at all, might cut himself off forever from his only opportunity of making the gods' acquaintance. This feeling, forced on us we know not whence, that by obstinately believing that there are gods (although not to do so would be so easy both for our logic and our life) we are doing the universe the deepest service we can, seems part of the living essence of the religious hypothesis. If the hypothesis *were* true in all its parts, including this one, then pure intellectualism, with its veto on our making willing advances, would be an absurdity; and some participation of our sympathetic nature would be logically required. I, therefore, for one, cannot see my way to accepting the agnostic rules for truth-seeking, or wilfully agree to keep my willing nature out of the game. I cannot do so for this plain reason, that *a rule of thinking which would absolutely prevent me from acknowledging certain kinds of truth if those kinds of truth were really there, would be an irrational rule.* That for me is the long and short of the formal logic of the situation, no matter what the kinds of truth might materially be.

I confess I do not see how this logic can be escaped. But sad experience makes me fear that some of you may still shrink from radically saying with me, *in abstracto*, that we have the right to believe at our own risk any hypothesis that is live enough to tempt our will. I suspect, however, that if this is not so, it is because you have got away from the abstract logical point of view altogether, and are thinking (perhaps without realizing it) of some particular religious hypothesis which for you is dead. The freedom to 'believe what you will' you apply to the case of some patent superstition; and the faith you think of is the faith defined by the schoolboy when he said, 'Faith is when you believe something that you know ain't true.' I can only repeat that this is misapprehension. *In concreto*, the freedom to believe can only cover living options which the intellect of the individual cannot by itself resolve; and living options never seem absurdities to him who has them to consider. When I look at the religious question as it really puts itself to concrete men, and when I think of all the possibilities which both practically and theoretically it involves, then this command that we shall put a stopper on our heart, instincts, and courage, and *wait* – acting of course meanwhile more or less as if religion were *not* true – till doomsday, or till such time as our intellect and senses working together may have raked in evidence enough, – this command, I say, seems to me the queerest idol ever manufactured in the philosophic cave. Were we scholastic absolutists, there might be more excuse. If we had an infallible intellect with its objective certitudes, we might feel ourselves disloyal to such a perfect organ of knowledge in not trusting to it exclusively, in not waiting for its releasing word. But if we are empiricists, if we believe that no bell in us tolls to let us know for certain when truth is in our grasp, then it seems a piece of idle fantasticality to preach so solemnly our duty of waiting for the bell. Indeed we *may* wait if we will, – I hope you do not think that I am denying that, – but if we do so, we do so at our peril as much as if we believed. In either case we act, taking our life in our hands. No one of us ought to issue vetoes to the other, nor should we bandy words of abuse. We ought, on the contrary, delicately and profoundly to respect one another's mental freedom: then only shall we bring about the intellectual republic; then only shall we have that spirit of inner tolerance without which all our outer tolerance is soulless, and which is empiricism's glory; then only shall we live and let live, in speculative as well as in practical things.

6 MOORE: JAMES' PRAGMATISM[7]

I think he (James) certainly means to suggest that we not only make our true beliefs, but also that we *make them true*. At least as much as this is certainly naturally suggested by his words. No one would persistently say that we make *our truths*, unless he meant, at least, not merely that we make our true beliefs, but also that we make them true – unless he meant not merely that the existence of our true beliefs, but also that their *truth*, depended upon human conditions. This, it seems to me, is one consequence which Professor James means us to draw from the

7. G. E. Moore, *Philosophical Studies*, London, Routledge & Kegan Paul, 1922, pp. 140–143.

commonplace that the *existence* of our true beliefs depends on human conditions. But does this consequence, in fact, follow from that commonplace? From the fact that we make our true beliefs, does it follow that we *make them true?*

In one sense, undoubtedly, even this does follow. If we say (as we may say) that no belief can be true, unless it exists, then it follows that, in a sense, the truth of a belief must always depend upon any conditions upon which its existence depends. If, therefore, the occurrence of a belief depends upon human conditions, so, too, must its truth. If the belief had never existed, it would never have been true; and therefore its truth must, in a sense, depend on human conditions in exactly the same degree in which its existence depends upon them. This is obvious. But is this all that is meant? Is this all that would be suggested to us by telling us that we make our beliefs true?

It is easy to see that it is not. I may have the belief that it will rain to-morrow. And I may have 'made' myself have this belief. It may be the case that I should not have had it, but for peculiarities in my past experiences, in my interests and my volitions. It may be the case that I should not have had it, but for a deliberate attempt to consider the question whether it will rain or not. This may easily happen. And certainly this particular belief of mine would not have been true, unless it existed. Its truth, therefore, depends, in a sense, upon any conditions upon which its existence depends. And this belief may be true. It will be true, if it does rain to-morrow. But, in spite of all these reasons, would anyone think of saying that, in case it is true, I had *made* it true? Would anyone say that I had a hand in making it true, if and only if I had a hand in *making the rain fall*. In every case in which we believe in the existence of anything, past or future, we should say that we had helped to make the belief true, if and only if we had helped to cause the existence of the fact which, in that belief, we believed did exist or would exist. Surely this is plain. I may believe that the sun will rise to-morrow. And I may have had a hand in 'making' this belief; certainly it often depends for its existence upon what has been previously in my mind. And if the sun does rise, my belief will have been true. I have, therefore, had a hand in making a true belief. But would anyone say that, therefore, I had a hand in *making this belief true?* Certainly no one would. No one would say that anything had contributed to make this belief true, except those conditions (whatever they may be) which contributed to making the sun actually rise.

It is plain, then, that by 'making a belief true,' we mean something quite different from what Professor James means by 'making' that belief. Conditions which have a hand in making a given true belief, may (it appears) have no hand at all in making it true; and conditions which have a hand in making it true may have no hand at all in making it. Certainly this is how we use the words. We should never say that we had made a belief true, merely because we had made the belief. But now, which of these two things does Professor James mean? Does he mean *merely* the accepted commonplace that we make our true beliefs, in the sense that almost all of them depend for their existence on what has been previously in some human mind? Or does he mean also that we *make them true* – that their truth also depends on what has been previously in some human mind?

I cannot help thinking that he has the latter, and not only the former in his mind. But, then, what does this involve? If his instances of 'truth-making' are to be anything to the purpose, it should mean that, whenever I have a hand in causing one of my own beliefs, I always have to that extent a hand in making it true. That, therefore, I have a hand in actually making the sun rise, the wind blow, and the rain fall, whenever I cause my beliefs in these things. Nay, more, it should mean that, whenever I 'make' a true belief about the past, I must have had a hand in making this true. And if so, then certainly I must have had a hand in causing the French Revolution, in causing my father's birth, in making Professor James write this book. Certainly he implies that some man or other must have helped in causing almost every event, in which any man ever truly believed. That it was we who made the planets revolve round the sun, who made the Alps rise, and the floor of the Pacific sink – all these things, and others like them, seem to be involved. And it is these consequences which seem to me to justify a doubt whether in fact 'our truths are to an unascertainable extent man-made.' That some of our truths are man-made – indeed, a great many – I fully admit. We certainly do make some of our beliefs true. The Secretary probably had a belief that I should write this paper, and I have made his belief true by writing it. Men certainly have the power to alter the world to a certain extent; and, so far as they do this, they certainly 'make true' any beliefs, which are beliefs in the occurrence of these alterations. But I can see no reason for supposing that they 'make true' *nearly* all those of their beliefs which are true. And certainly the only reason which Professor James seems to give for believing this – namely, that the *existence* of almost all their beliefs depends on them – seems to be no reason for it at all. For unquestionably a man does not 'make true' nearly every belief whose *existence* depends on him; and if so, the question which of their beliefs and how many, men do 'make true' must be settled by quite other considerations.

KEY TEXTS

James, William. *Pragmatism* (1907) and *The Meaning of Truth* (1909), with an Introduction by A. J. Ayer, Cambridge, Mass., Harvard University Press, 1975.
—— *The Will to Believe and Other Essays in Popular Philosophy* (1897) and *Human Immortality* (1898), New York, Dover Publications, Inc., 1956.
Jordan, Jeff (ed.). *Gambling on God: Essays on Pascal's Wager*, Lanham, Md., Rowman & Littlefield, 1994.
Pascal, B. *Pensées*, ed. and trans. A. J. Krailsheimer, London and New York, Penguin Books, 1966.
Suckiel, Ellen Kappy. *Heaven's Champion: William James's Philosophy of Religion*, Notre Dame, Ind., University of Notre Dame Press, 1996.

BIBLIOGRAPHY

PASCAL

Armour, Leslie. *'Infini-Rien': Pascal's Wager and the Human Paradox*, Carbondale and Edwardsville, Ill., Southern Illinois University Press, 1993.

Broome, J. H. *Pascal*, London, Edward Arnold, 1965.

Brown, Geoffrey. 'A Defence of Pascal's Wager', *Religious Studies*, 20, 1984, pp. 465–479.

Cargile, James. 'Pascal's Wager', in *Contemporary Philosophy of Religion*, ed. Steven M. Cahn and David Shatz, New York and Oxford, Oxford University Press, 1982, pp. 229–236.

Clifford, W. K. 'The Ethics of Belief', in *The Ethics of Belief Debate*, ed. Gerald D. McCarthy, Atlanta, Scholars Press, 1986, pp. 19–36.

Davis, Stephen. 'Pascal on Self-Caused Belief', *Religious Studies*, 27, 1991, pp. 27–37.

Diderot, Denis. *Pensées Philosophiques*, LIX, ed. J. Assézat, Paris, 1875–1877, Vol. I.

Flew, Antony. 'Is Pascal's Wager the Only Safe Bet?', *Rationalist Annual*, 76, 1960, pp. 21–25.

Freud, Sigmund. *The Future of an Illusion*, in Freud, *Civilization, Society and Religion*, London, Penguin Books, 1991, pp. 181–241.

Gale, Richard. *On the Nature and Existence of God*, New York, Cambridge University Press, 1991.

Geach, Peter. 'The Moral Law and the Law of God', in *Divine Commands and Morality*, ed. Paul Helm, Oxford, Oxford University Press, 1980.

Gracely, Edward J. 'Playing Games with Eternity: The Devil's Offer', *Analysis*, 58, June 1988, p. 113.

Jordan, Jeff (ed.). *Gambling on God: Essays on Pascal's Wager*, Lanham, Md., Rowman & Littlefield, 1994.

Kaufmann, Walter. *Critique of Religion and Philosophy*, Princeton, N.J., Princeton University Press, 1978.

Landsberg, P. T. 'Gambling on God', *Mind*, 80, 1971, pp. 100–104.

Levy, Paul. *Moore*, London, Weidenfeld & Nicolson, p. 214.

Lycan, William (with George Schlesinger). 'You Bet Your Life: Pascal's Wager Defended', in *Reason and Responsibility*, ed. J. Feinberg, 8th edn, Belmont, Calif., Wadsworth, 1993, pp. 100–108.

Mackie, J. L. *The Miracle of Theism*, Oxford, Clarendon Press, 1982.

Martin, Michael. *Atheism: A Philosophical Justification*, Philadelphia, Temple University Press, 1990.

—— 'Pascal's Wager as an Argument for Not Believing in God', *Religious Studies*, 19, 1983, pp. 57–64.

Morris, Thomas. 'Pascalian Wagering', *Canadian Journal of Philosophy*, 16 (3), 1986, pp. 437–454.

—— 'Wagering and the Evidence', *Gambling on God: Essays on Pascal's Wager*, ed. Jeff Jordan, Lanham, Md., Rowman & Littlefield, 1994, pp. 47–60.

Mougin, Gregory (with Elliot Sober). 'Betting against Pascal's Wager', *Nûs*, 28 (3), 1994, pp. 382–395.

Nicholl, L. R. 'Pascal's Wager: The Bet is Off', *Philosophy and Phenomenological Research*, 39, 1978–1979, pp. 274–280.

Oppy, Graham. 'On Rescher on Pascal's Wager', *International Journal for Philosophy of Religion*, 30, 1990, pp. 159–168.

Palmer, Michael. *Freud and Jung on Religion*, Routledge, 1997.

Pascal, B. *Pascal: Selections*, ed. Richard H. Popkin, London and New York, Macmillan, 1989.

—— *Pensées*, ed. and trans. A. J. Krailsheimer, London and New York, Penguin Books, 1966.

Penelhum, Terence. *God and Skepticism*, Dordrecht, Boston, Mass. and Lancaster, D. Reidel Publishing Company, 1983, pp. 62–87.

—— *Reason and Religious Faith*, Oxford, Westview Press, 1995, pp. 39–107.

—— *Religion and Rationality: An Introduction to the Philosophy of Religion*, New York, Random House, 1971.

Rescher, Nicholas. *Pascal's Wager: A Study of Practical Reasoning in Philosophical Theology*, Notre Dame, Ind., University of Notre Dame Press, 1985.

Ryan, John K. 'The Wager in Pascal and Others', in *Gambling on God: Essays on Pascal's Wager*, ed. Jeff Jordan, Lanham, Md., Rowman & Littlefield, 1994, pp. 11–19.

Smith, George H. *Atheism: The Case against God*, Amherst, N.Y., Prometheus Books, 1989.

Sobel, Jordan H. 'Pascalian Wagers', *Synthese*, 108, 1996, pp. 11–61.

Stitch, Stephen P. 'The Recombinant DNA Debate', *Philosophy and Public Affairs*, 7, 1978, pp. 187–205.

Swinburne, Richard G. 'The Christian Wager', *Religious Studies*, 4, 1969, pp. 217–228.

Turner, Merle B. 'Deciding for God – The Bayesian Support of Pascal's Wager', *Philosophy and Phenomenological Research*, 29, 1968–1969, pp. 84–90.

Williams, Bernard. 'Deciding to Believe', in *Problems of the Self*, Cambridge, Cambridge University Press, 1973, pp. 136–151.

JAMES

Ayer, A. J. *The Origins of Pragmatism*, London, Macmillan, 1968, pp. 183–336.

Bixler, Julius. *Religion in the Philosophy of William James*, Boston, Mass., Marshall Jones Company, 1926.

Davis, S. T. 'Wishful Thinking and the "Will to Believe"', *Transactions of the C. S. Peirce Society*, 8, 1972, pp. 231–245.

Dooley, P. K. 'The Nature of Belief: The Proper Context for James' "Will to Believe"', *Transactions of the C. S. Peirce Society*, 8, 1972, pp. 141–151.

Fontinell, Eugene. *Self, God and Immortality: A Jamesian Investigation*, Philadelphia, Temple University Press, 1986.

Ford, Marcus. *William James' Philosophy*, Amherst, University of Massachusetts Press, 1982.

Henle, Paul. 'Introduction on William James', *Classic American Philosophers*, ed. Max H. Fisch, New York, Appleton-Century-Crofts, 1951, pp. 115–127.

Hick, John. *The Philosophy of Religion*, Englewood Cliffs, N.J., Prentice-Hall, 1973.

James, William. *Pragmatism* (1907) and *The Meaning of Truth* (1909), with an Introduction by A. J. Ayer, Cambridge, Mass., Harvard University Press, 1975.

—— *The Varieties of Religious Experience* (1902), London and New York, Longmans, Green & Co., 1941.

—— *The Will to Believe and Other Essays in Popular Philosophy* (1897) and *Human Immortality* (1898), New York, Dover Publications, Inc., 1956.

Jones, Peter. 'William James', in *American Philosophy*, ed. Marcus G. Singer, Cambridge, Cambridge University Press, pp. 43–68.

Kauber, P. (with P. H. Hare). 'The Right and Duty to Will to Believe', *Canadian Journal of Philosophy*, 4, 1974, pp. 327–343.

Kaufmann, Walter. *Critique of Religion and Philosophy*, New York, Doubleday, Anchor Books, 1961, pp. 129–132.

Kennedy, Gail. 'Pragmatism, Pragmaticism, and the Will to Believe – a Reconsideration', *Journal of Philosophy*, 55 (14), July 1958, pp. 578–588.

Leuba, James H. 'Professor William James' Interpretation of Religious Experience', *International Journal of Ethics*, 14, April 1904, pp. 322–339.

Levinson, Henry. *The Religious Investigations of William James*, Chapel Hill, University of North Carolina Press, 1981.

Lovejoy, Arthur O. 'The Thirteen Pragmatisms', *The Thirteen Pragmatisms and Other Essays*, Westport, Conn., Greenwood Press, 1983, pp. 1–29.

Martin, C. B. *Religious Belief*, Ithaca, N.Y., Cornell University Press, pp. 65–88.

Meyers, Robert G. 'Meaning and Metaphysics in James', *Philosophy and Phenomenological Research*, 31 (3), March 1971, pp. 369–380.

Miller, Dickinson. 'James' Doctrine of "The Right to Believe"', *Philosophical Review*, 51, 1942, pp. 541–558.

—— '"The Will to Believe" and the Duty to Doubt', *International Journal of Ethics*, 9, 1898–1899, pp. 169–195.

Moore, G. E. 'William James' "Pragmatism"', *Philosophical Studies*, London, Routledge & Kegan Paul, 1922, pp. 97–146.

Muyskens, J. L. 'James' Defence of a Believing Attitude in Religion', *Transactions of the C. S. Peirce Society*, 10, 1974, pp. 44–53.

Myers, Gerald E. *William James*, New Haven, Yale University Press, 1986.

Perkins, Moreland. 'Notes on the Pragmatic Theory of Truth', *Journal of Philosophy*, 49 (18), August 1952, pp. 573–587.

Perry, Ralph Barton. *The Thought and Character of William James*, 2 vols, Boston, Mass., Little, Brown, 1935.

Russell, Bertrand. 'William James's Conception of Truth', *Philosophical Essays*, London, George Allen & Unwin, 1910; revised edn, 1966, pp. 112–130.

Seigfried, Charlene. *William James's Radical Reconstruction of Philosophy*, Albany, State University of New York Press, 1990.

Singer, M. G. 'The Pragmatic Use of Language and the Will to Believe', *American Philosophical Quarterly*, 8, 1971, pp. 24–34.

Suckiel, Ellen Kappy. *Heaven's Champion: William James's Philosophy of Religion*, Notre Dame, Ind., University of Notre Dame Press, 1996.

—— *The Pragmatic Philosophy of William James*, Notre Dame, Ind., University of Notre Dame Press, 1982.

Wernham, James. *James's Will-to-Believe Doctrine*, Kingston and Montreal, McGill-Queen's University Press, 1987.

ACKNOWLEDGEMENTS: ILLUSTRATIONS

We are indebted to the people and archives below for permission to reproduce photographs or original illustrative material. Every effort has been made to trace copyright-holders, but in a few cases this has not been possible. Any omissions brought to our attention will be remedied in future editions.

St Anselm, from the 'Our Lady of Bec' icon, courtesy of Cathedral Enterprises Limited, Canterbury

René Descartes, Mary Evans Picture Library

Immanuel Kant, 1791 Staatsbibliothek, Berlin

Bertrand Russell, The Bertrand Russell Peace Foundation

John Hick, John Hick

Karl Barth and typescript page from his Introduction to Anselm, Dr Hans-Anton Drewes and the Karl Barth-Archiv

St Thomas Aquinas, portrait in the Louvre Museum, Paris, courtesy of AKG archive

Aristotle, Mary Evans Picture Library

F. C. Copleston, British Province, Archives for the Society of Jesus

David Hume, AKG archive for the portrait

William Paley, courtesy of The Abbey, Carlisle

Manuscript page from Hume's *Dialogues Concerning Natural History*, Natural Library of Scotland

Epicurus, Mary Evans Picture Library

Charles Darwin, English Heritage for the Down House portrait

HMS *Beagle*, The Natural History Museum, London

Sir Charles Lyell, AKG archive

Thomas Malthus, AKG archive

Frederick Temple, Archbishop of Canterbury, National Portrait Gallery, London

Bishop Joseph Butler, the Dean and Chapter Library, the College, Durham

Antony Flew, Antony Flew

Richard Swinburne, Richard Swinburne

Paul Tillich, Jane Reed and Harvard Divinity School

C. S. Lewis, Walter Stoneman, 1995, National Portrait Gallery, London

Plato, AKG archive

Kant Ms of the *Opus Postumum*, State Library of Berlin

John Henry Newman, AKG archive

Blaise Pascal, death mask courtesy Newnham College, Cambridge

Title page of *Pensées*, Bibliothèque Nationale de France

Sigmund Freud, AKG archive

William James, Pach Brothers Studio portrait, National Portrait Gallery, Smithsonian Institution, Washington

MS p. 62 of 'The Will to Believe' (shelf mark MS Am 1092.5), Ms Bay James and the Houghton Library of the Harvard College Library

G. E. Moore, Timothy Moore

ACKNOWLEDGEMENTS: SOURCES

The following publishers and individuals have kindly given copyright permission for extracts from their publications to be reproduced. Every effort has been made to trace copyright-holders of sourced material for permission to reproduce. This has not been possible in all cases, but any omissions brought to our attention will be remedied in future editions.

Open Court Publishing Co., a division of Carus Publishing, La Salle, Illinois, for 'The Ontological Argument', in *St Anselm's Basic Writings*, trans. S. N. Deane, 1962, pp. 53–55, 316–317.

International Thomson Publishing Services Limited, Andover, for René Descartes, 'The Supremely Perfect Being', translated and edited by Elizabeth Anscombe and Peter Geach, Nelson's University Paperbacks, 1975, pp. 103–105 and G. E. Moore, *Philosophical Studies*, 1922, Routledge & Kegan Paul, pp. 140–143.

Oxford University Press for David Hume, *Enquiry Concerning Human Understanding*, edited by L. A. Selby-Brigge, revised by P. H. Nidditch, 3rd edn, 1975, pp. 26–31, 110–120, 121–122, 124–125, 130–131; also for J. R. Findlay, 'Can God's Existence be Disproved?' in *Mind*, 1948; also (Awaiting) Clarendon Press for Richard Swinburne, *Faith and Reason*, 1981, pp. 185–189.

Macmillan Publishers, Hampshire, for Immanuel Kant, 'The Impossibility of an Ontological Proof', in *Critique of Pure Reason*, trans. Norman Kemp Smith, 1929, pp. 502–506.

T. & T. Clark Ltd, Edinburgh, for John Hicks, 'Necessary Being', in *Scottish Journal of Theology*, December 1961.

Oneworld Publications, Oxford, for Keith Ward, *God, Chance and Necessity*, 1996, pp. 86–95.

The C. S. Lewis Company, Hampshire, for C. S. Lewis, *Miracles*, copyright C. S. Lewis Pte. Ltd. 1947, 1960, pp. 106–111.

Penguin UK for Blaise Pascal, *Pensées*, trans. A. J. Krailsheimer (Penguin Classics 1966), copyright A. J. Krailsheimer 1966, pp. 150–153.

Edward Graceley, MCP Hahnemann School of Medicine, Philadelphia, for 'Playing Games with Eternity: The Devil's Offer', *Analysis*, 48, June 1988, p. 113.

Dover Publications, New York, for William James, 'The Will to Believe' in *The Will to Believe and Other Essays*, 1956, pp. 1–31.

The Monist, La Salle, Illinois, copyright 1970, for D. and M. Haight, 'An Ontological Argument for the Devil', *The Monist*, 54(2), pp. 218–220.

Hume Studies, for Dorothy Coleman, 'Hume, Miracles and Lotteries', *Hume Studies*, 14, 1988, pp. 334–340.

Princeton University Press for Stephen P. Stich, 'The Recombinant DNA Debate', *Philosophy and Public Affairs*, 7, 1978, pp. 187–191.

Internet Infidels, Inc. for 'Atheism, Christian Atheism and Rape' at www.Infidels.org/library.modern/michael martin/rape.html

Blackwell Publishers, for Robert Hambourger, 'Belief in Miracles and Hume's Essay', *Noûs*, 14, pp. 590–592, 599.

Weidenfeld & Nicolson, for Richard Dawkins, *River Out of Eden: A Darwinian View of Life*, pp. 96–98, 102–106, 120–122, 131–133.

Prentice Hall, Inc., for R. Taylor, Metaphysics, 2nd edn, © 1965, pp. 91–97.

The American Humanist Association, publisher of *The Humanist*, for Antony Flew, 'Parapsychology Revisited: Laws, Miracles, and Repeatability', *The Humanist* May/June, 1976, pp. 28–30. ISSN: 0 018–7399.

ROUTLEDGE ENCYCLOPEDIA OF
PHILOSOPHY ONLINE AND THE
QUESTION OF GOD

CHAPTER 1
THE ONTOLOGICAL ARGUMENT

[see GOD, ARGUMENTS FOR THE EXISTENCE OF
SECTION 2: ONTOL.ARG.S]

COMMENTARY

Introduction: a priori and a posteriori arguments
[see: A PRIORI, A POSTERIORI]

Anselm's argument: stage 1

Anselm's argument: stage 2
[see ANSELM AT CANTERBURY]

Descartes' ontological argument
The two stages of the argument: a summary
[see DESCARTES, RENE]

Kant's criticism of the ontological argument (first stage)

Kant's criticism of the ontological argument (second stage)
[see KANT, IMMANUEL]

The ontological argument revisited: Findlay and Malcolm
[see section in (1) 'NECESSARY BEING'; see section in 'GOD, ARG.S FOR
EXISTENCE at (2).

Karl Barth: a theological interpretation
[see BARTH, KARL]

Conclusion

SOURCES

Anselm: The Ontological argument
[see ANSELM entry]

Haight: An ontological argument for the Devil
[no entry]

Descartes: The supremely perfect being
[see DESCARTES]

Kant: The impossibility of an ontological proof
[see KANT]

Findlay: Disproof of God's existence
[see 'NECESSARY BEING']

Malcolm: Anselm's second ontological proof
[see GOD, ARGS FOR EXISTENCE OF]

Hick: Necessary being
[many references to other Hick texts]

CHAPTER 2
THE COSMOLOGICAL ARGUMENT

[see GOD, ARG.S FOR EX. AT SECTION 1: COSMOL.ARG.S]

Introduction: the argument as an a posteriori proof

St Thomas Aquinas: the arguments from motion and cause
[see AQUINAS, THOMAS]

A problem of interpretation: temporal or ontological cause?
St Thomas aquinas: the argument from contingency
[as above]

Criticism (1): the principle of sufficient reason

Criticism (2): the argument from causality

Criticism (3): the concept of necessary being

SOURCES

Aquinas: The five proofs of God's existence
[as above]

Taylor: The principle of sufficient reason

Hume: Objections to the cosmological argument

Hume: The relation of cause and effect
[see HUME, DAVID]

Kant: The impossibility of a cosmological proof
[see KANT]

CHAPTER 3
THE ARGUMENT FROM DESIGN

[see: GOD, ARG.S FOR EX. OF]

COMMENTARY

Introduction

The argument stated (1)

The argument (2): induction and analogy

The argument (3): its analogical form

Hume's critique of the design argument
[see HUME, DAVID]

Darwin's critique of the design argument

Post-Darwinian theories of design
[see DARWIN, CHARLES ROBERT]

The anthropic teleological argument

Swinburne's design argument
[various references]

Conclusion

SOURCES

Paley: The watch and the watchmaker
[References in GOD.ARGS.AND RELIGION, HISTORY OF, PHIL OF]

Hume: The existence of God
[see above]

Darwin: The existence of a personal God
[see above]

Dawkins: God's utility function
[see EVOLUTION, THEORY OF]

Ward: Darwin's gloomy view
[no entry]

CHAPTER 4
THE ARGUMENT FROM MIRACLES

[see GOD, ARG.S FOR EX. OF and MIRACLES]

COMMENTARY

Introduction

David Hume: 'Of Miracles'
[see HUME, DAVID]

Extending Hume's argument: (1) McKinnon and (2) Flew
[see MIRACLES, HUME, MIRACLES, SANCTIFICATION, etc.]

Criticism of Hume (1): laws of nature

Criticism of Hume (2): historical evidence for miracles: Flew and Swinburne

Criticism of Hume (3): evidence of God's activity

Criticism of Hume (4): the contingency definition of miracles ((1) Holland and (2) Tillich) [(1) see MIRACLES and (2) see TILLICH, PAUL]

Conclusion

SOURCES

Hume: 'Of Miracles'
[see HUME, DAVID]

Hambourger: The principle of relative likelihood
[see CONTEXTUALISM, EPISTEMOLOGICAL]

Coleman: Miracles and lotteries
[see RATIONAL CHOICE THEORY]

Flew: Miracles and repeatability
[see HUME, MIRACLES, SANCTIFICATION, etc.]

Swinburne: Evidence of miracles
[see PREVIOUS]

Diamond: Miracles and scientific autonomy
[no entry]

CHAPTER 5
THE MORAL ARGUMENT

[see GOD, ARG.S FOR EX. OF]

COMMENTARY

Introduction: objective and relative moral values

The moral argument outlined

The Euthyphro dilemma
[see PLATO: RELIGION AND MORALITY]

Kant's moral argument (1): autonomy and categorical duty

Kant's moral argument (2): God as the postulate of moral action
[see KANT]

Criticisms of Kant's moral argument

Post-Kantian moral arguments: divine command theory

Conclusion: absolute moral laws without God

SOURCES

Plato: The Euthyphro dilemma
[see PLATO]

Lewis: The Law of Nature

Kant: The existence of God as a postulate of pure practical reason
[see KANT]

Rachels: God and autonomy

Martin: Atheism, Christian theism, and rape
[see THEISM]

Nielsen: Morals without God

CHAPTER 6
THE PRAGMATIC ARGUMENT

COMMENTARY

Introduction

Pascal's pragmatic argument: the Wager

Criticisms of Pascal's Wager
[see PASCAL, BLAISE]

James' pragmatic argument: the will to believe

Summary of James' theory of belief
[see JAMES, WILLIAM]

Criticisms of William James

Concluding remarks

SOURCES

Pascal: The Wager
[see PASCAL]

Gracely: The Devil's offer

Stich: Recombinant DNA and Pascalian wagering
[see RATIONAL, BELIEF, etc.]

Penelhum: Criticism of Pascal's Wager
[see HUME, NECESSARY BEING, etc.]

James: The will to believe
[see JAMES]

Moore: James' pragmatism

INDEX OF NAMES

(References are to Commentary entries only)

INDEX OF SUBJECTS

Freud and Jung on Religion
1997, 256pp. Hb: 0–415–14746–8: £47.50; pb: 0–415–14747–6: £14.99

Reviews of *Freud and Jung on Religion*
'This book should become required reading for all theologians, especially those concerned with the theory and practice of pastoral care, because it offers a readable and insightful account of two of the most important and influential theories of religion by Freud and Jung. . . . A superb piece of work. Other theological writers would do well to aim at such clarity and quality.'
                                                        – *Religion and Theology*

'Palmer's work is certainly one of the best introductory texts to date on Freud and Jung's work on religion.'
                                        – *Journal of Contemporary Religion*

'The complex relationship between Freud and Jung and particularly their eventual disagreement over religion are delineated in Michael Palmer's valuable study. . . . Palmer's analysis sharpens the debate over the contribution to our understanding of Freud and Jung on religion and, if for no other reason, deserves to be read, discussed and debated further.'
                    – *Bulletin of the British Association for the Study of Religion*

'Palmer focuses on the psychologies of religion put forward by Freud and Jung and manages two considerable feats. The first is that of marshalling Freud's thought in such a way that its roots in his life and its continuities as well as discontinuities are all understandable. The second feat is the greater: that of presenting Jung's thought clearly and coherently. . . . Having attempted to introduce Freud and Jung to undergraduate and postgraduate students of the psychology of religion for the past eighteen years, I welcome Michael Palmer's book as a valuable resource for the future, both for clarifying my own thinking and for leading students to a firm grasp of the ideas discussed by these two key figures.'
                                            – *Scottish Journal of Religious Studies*

Philosophy of Religion: A Introduction with Readings, Stuart Brown Open University, UK, 2000, 184pp. Hb: 0–415–21237–5: £40; pb: 0–415–21238–3: £12.99

Philosophy of Religion: A Contemporary Introduction, Keith E. Yandell, University of Wisconsin at Madison, US 1998, 424pp. Hb:0–415–13212–4: £40; pb: 0–415–13214–2: £12.99

Routledge Encyclopedia of Philosophy, edited by Edward Craig, Churchill College, Cambridge, UK 1998, 8680pp. Package: 10-volume boxed set (print) and 1 CD-ROM with a licence for up to 10 simultaneous users within your campus. 0–415–16917–8: £2,495 (+VAT)

1998, 8,672pp. Print format: 0–415–07310–3: 10-volume boxed set: £2,150

Electronic format: 0–415–16916–X; CD-ROM (with a licence for up to 10 simultaneous users within your campus: £2,150 (+VAT)